LORD HERVEY

Eighteenth–Century Courtier

D0075427

Lord Hervey as Vice-Chamberlain

LORD HERVEY

Eighteenth-Century Courtier

ROBERT HALSBAND

1974
Oxford University Press
New York and Oxford

Oxford University Press, Ely House, London W. 1

GLASGOW NEW YORK TORONTO MELBOURNE WELLINGTON
CAPE TOWN IBADAN NAIROBI DAR ES SALAAM LUSAKA ADDIS ABABA
DELHI BOMBAY CALCUTTA MADRAS KARACHI LAHORE DACCA
KUALA LUMPUR SINGAPORE HONG KONG TOKYO

Dedicated to the memory of

my wife

RUTH ALICE N. HALSBAND

Preface

'THIS world consists of men, women, and Herveys', a remark by his friend Lady Mary Wortley Montagu, indicates Lord Hervey's uniqueness, his complex and enigmatic character.* His name appears so frequently in political and literary histories of eighteenth-century England that it is surprising to find he has never been the subject of a full-length study, although large biographies have been devoted to his wife and to his third son, the eccentric Earl of Bristol and Bishop of Derry. Political and literary historians and the ordinary reader have had very little available to satisfy their curiosity about him: his memoirs of George II's reign, in which he wrote of himself only obliquely and for a span of less than eight years; the biographical sketches by John Wilson Croker (in 1848) and by Romney Sedgwick (in 1931) in their editions of the memoirs; a pair of chapters in the superficial family history by D. A. Ponsonby; and an amateurish selection of his letters over a twelve-year period, edited by Lord Ilchester.

I have subtitled this biography *Eighteenth-Century Courtier* because Hervey held the appointment of Vice-Chamberlain to the King's Household for ten years, a decade that was the most consequential and eventful period of his life. His residence at court and intimacy with the Royal Family, while enhancing his usefulness to Sir Robert Walpole, the Prime Minister, also allowed him to witness the peculiar family predicament of the second Hanoverian monarch and to write the memoirs that are so brilliant both as human drama and as dynastic history.

I have not confined the biography to his life at court, but have set down as fully as the evidence allows the story of his life from the year of his birth in 1696 (even his existence *in utero* is documented) to his death as a broken, bitter man in 1743; and I have

---

* A variant of the phrase by Horace Walpole is more limited and more provocative—that there were three sexes: men, women, and Herveys.

(Notes are placed at the back of the volume; when directly relevant to the text they are set at the foot of the page.)

investigated his family relationships and marriage as well as his homosexual passion for two friends, Stephen Fox (later Lord Ilchester) and Francesco Algarotti, the versatile writer and cosmopolite. New materials, particularly in the Hervey Manuscripts and Holland House Manuscripts, have enabled me to discuss his private life more frankly than would have been possible or permissible in an earlier day

In treating his political career I have concentrated not on the general history of his time but rather on those issues that involved him personally, either in his Parliamentary career or in his political pamphlets—which are so excellent that even Horace Walpole, who detested him, praised them very highly. In treating his literary career I have tried to elucidate his satiric controversies, particularly with Alexander Pope, against whom he wrote some wretched verse and prose pamphlets. He played still another literary role as a *persona* in other writers' satires, most strikingly as the contemptible Sporus in Pope's *Epistle to Dr. Arbuthnot*. That character-portrait, unmatched in all of English poetry for its virulence and rancour, has given Hervey his most substantial reputation. He was also depicted by Henry Fielding as Miss Fanny in *Shamela* and Beau Didapper in *Joseph Andrews*. As a result of this portraiture, especially from the pens of such literary masters, Hervey's satiric *persona* has been accepted as the likeness of the man himself. To many readers Sporus is not a satiric creation but Lord Hervey himself. Yet obviously his historical portrait should be derived not from literary caricature, however vivid, striking, and memorable, but rather from the documented account of his life and career.

In trying to recreate the life of a man dead for more than two hundred years one can only hope that enough materials have survived the accidents of time and the solicitude of descendants to tell the full story. Fortunately, a mass of materials has remained, especially Hervey's own letters (most of them unpublished) and his father's diary and letter-books. In his own memoirs of George II's reign, after narrating an episode in great detail, he wrote: 'If I am thought to be too particular in relating little circumstances of this kind, all I can say for myself is, that I have no guide to guess at what will please other people in reading these papers but what I find pleases myself best in works of the like nature.' This detailed biography can perhaps be justified in the same manner. In addition, what better way is there to depict a man whose life is so little known? The reader may be surprised by the abundant amount of dialogue that is spoken by the characters, especially by Hervey himself. Not a syllable is borrowed or invented; it is all the actual speech that he set down, for he had a remarkably sensitive ear and skilful pen. And his private letters, so keenly tempered to his correspondents, are in effect a form of conversation—witty, vivacious, life-like. All these words were once carried on living breath from one person to another, or transmitted in Hervey's large, upright script to be read by sympathetic eyes. His biography should at least replace the monstrous satiric character with a human being.

Contents

List of Plates

LORD HERVEY

Eighteenth-Century Courtier

PROLOGUE: 1740

Lord Keeper of the Privy Seal

JOHN, LORD HERVEY OF ICKWORTH, heir to his father's earldom of Bristol and member of the House of Lords, stood in solemn dignity before the Privy Council on 1 May 1740. He was richly dressed for the occasion, in a suit of opulent brown cloth trimmed with gold braid and adorned with gold buttons. The long, flaring coat, which reached below his knee-breeches, lent weight to his slender frame but made him seem shorter than he was. His dark eyes, wide open in an expression of candour, were set in a thin pale face framed by a full-bottomed powdered wig and a high white collar with lace. Even now, at the age of forty-four, he was remarkably youthful-looking and delicately handsome.

He listened attentively as the oath was read to him: 'You shall as far forth as Your Cunning and Discretion sufficeth truly, justly and evenly, Execute and Exercise the Office of Keeper of the King's Privy Seal. . . . So help You God and by the Contents of this Book.' Cunning and discretion Hervey had in plenty; the ritual phrase, a remnant of medieval verbal pageantry, fitted him well. For his badge of office he had already received from the King's own hand the privy seal, a silver medallion slightly more than three and a half inches in diameter, to be used to seal the King's documents with red wax. Its Latin inscription saluted George II as King of Great Britain, France, and Ireland; the quarterings on the coat of arms, however, added Hanover—still an important attachment for the second monarch of the Hanoverian dynasty in England.

The Lord Keeper had custody of the seal only for his term of office, but he could keep the rich purse (valued at £21) given to him as protection for the seal. Aside from its trappings, the office brought him £3,000 a year in salary and diet-allowance as well as 'all other Fees, Profits, and Advantages therunto belonging'; and he was assigned five clerks and an office-keeper to perform the drudgery of the office. (A year later Hervey secured the reversion of a clerkship for his eleven-year-old son Frederick, which would automatically appoint him to the first vacancy; a deputy could then be hired to perform the duties.)

The post of Lord Privy Seal was one of great distinction. Previous Keepers of the Privy Seal under George II had been such powerful peers as the Duke of Devonshire and the Earl of Godolphin (son-in-law of the great Duke of Marlborough). Not only was the appointment a great achievement for Hervey personally but for both his mother's and father's families as well. His maternal grandfather and his paternal grand-uncle had both held court posts under Charles II but none of his forbears on either side of the family had reached such an eminence as this.

A week before the ceremony of taking oath of office, Hervey's father, Lord Bristol, enjoying his peaceful old age at Ickworth (his seat in Suffolk), had made an entry in his diary. 'Wednesday, the king deliver'd the Privy-seal to my son the Lord Hervey, with many gracious expressions of acknowledging his past services etc.' In spite of his love for his son and pride on his appointment, Bristol could not feel much enthusiasm, for as a recalcitrant country Whig he had always opposed Walpole and disapproved of his son's loyalty and service to him. At first Bristol grudgingly admitted that although the Privy Seal was an honourable office, Hervey had certainly earned it by his 'close & slavish attendance' for more than ten years as Vice-Chamberlain to the King (an office Bristol regarded as below the merits of his abilities) and by his successful support of Walpole's measures. He followed this by warning Hervey that as Walpole's second-in-command he would be burdened with the Minister's inevitable failure; and he returned to that theme by quoting Sir Walter Raleigh's advice to his son, cautioning him to discontinue a friendship with an overgrown greatness that would either crush him if it fell or 'grow insolently weary of support' and spurn him if it stood long.

They would not have long to wait before one of these possibilities came to pass.

I

Family and Education

1696–1714

THE HERVEY FAMILY had been settled in Suffolk since the fifteenth century, when a Bedfordshire gentleman named Thomas Hervey married Jane Drury, sole heiress of Ickworth Park, and moved to that manor, three miles from Bury St. Edmunds. To this day it remains the seat of the family, though in keeping with the times its great house, built by one of Lord Hervey's sons, is now owned by the National Trust.

John Hervey, father of the courtier and memoirist, was born in Bury in 1665, the elder son of Sir Thomas Hervey, knight. Since Sir Thomas's elder brother (John Hervey) was childless, he and his newly-born son were heirs in turn to the family seat at Ickworth. The boy attended the Bury Grammar School, of which his father was a governor, a school so excellent that pupils came to it from counties beyond Suffolk. He seriously applied himself to his studies. When he later accused himself of 'fatal idleness' at school he was only teasing his old schoolmaster. He also studied hard at Clare Hall, Cambridge, where he matriculated but did not take a degree. (Cambridge awarded him an LL.D. in 1705.) He was sufficiently grounded in Latin to contribute some verse to the collection published by the University in 1685 to lament the death of Charles II and to welcome to the throne James II.

Hervey's uncle, who died in 1679, had been an M.P. and Treasurer of the Household to Charles II's Queen; and his grandfather Sir Humphrey May had been Vice-Chamberlain of the Household to Charles I. Their family prosperity depended to some extent on their appointment to court posts. Being courtiers, it might be said, was their profession. That, along with marriages to rich heiresses, was the way the family rose and prospered. When not at court they lived in their snug, secure world of the squirearchy; and they grazed their flocks, ploughed their rich fields, and collected their rents. They found no appointments open to them at the court of William and Mary, particularly since William of Orange seemed to favour his own countrymen. But since he had no heir to succeed him and Princess Anne would come to the throne, the Hervey family could afford to be patient before trying to resume their ambitious career at court.

Young Hervey grew to be a very handsome man, robust in body and stature, and of a fair complexion. The disfiguring wig that he wore could not conceal the steadfast eyes and the stubborn, out-thrust lower lip and firm jaw. All his life he loved country pursuits, especially horse-racing, and equally detested the noisy, crowded cities of London and Bath. Yet he was far from being a rude country bumpkin. He read widely in historical and theological works, and was able to quote with ease from the Roman poets and prose-writers. An enthusiastic lover of music, he played the flute and violin to the end of his life, and was fond enough of plays and opera to become (in 1704) a charter subscriber, at the cost of one hundred guineas, to John Vanbrugh's new theatre in the Haymarket, in return for which he was entitled to free entry.

He married twice, both times for love and both times to heiresses. When he was twenty-three years old he courted and won as his wife Isabella, only surviving child of Sir Charles Carr, M.P., of Aswarby, who had owned large estates in Lincolnshire, worth between five and six thousand pounds a year. Hervey and his wife occupied a house in Bury, and during the London season—generally the duration of the Parliamentary session—he rented a house in the fashionable parish of St. James's. As a young man his income was ample—almost £2,000 a year, and his marriage was extraordinarily happy. His wife bore a son, Carr, then a daughter, and died at the birth of a second daughter, after having been married only five years. Neither a second wife and family, nor the passing of many years could erase from Hervey's mind his great love for Isabella; and at his own death, more than half a century later, he directed that all her letters to him, along with other mementoes, should be placed in his coffin.

A year later, when his father—his 'best and dearest Friend'—died, Hervey inherited his estates and the post of High Steward of Bury St. Edmunds. Only a few months previously, in March 1694, he had been elected to Parliament in a by-election to fill the unexpired term of the deceased member for Bury. As a constituency Bury's franchise was restricted to the town corporation of thirty-seven members, and since they had regularly returned Hervey's father, they continued to demonstrate their loyalty by electing him. As expected, he took his seat on the Whig side of the House.

A man of his uxorious temperament could not remain without a wife for long. The year after his wife's death he began to court Elizabeth Felton, of a Suffolk landed family, a suitable wife for the young squire. Her father, Thomas Felton, M.P., of Playford Hall, was soon to succeed to a baronetcy, and had (like Hervey's uncle) found his path to prosperity at Charles II's court; he had been Groom of the Bedchamber to the King and Comptroller of the Queen's Household. Her mother, long since deceased, had been daughter and heir of the third Earl of Suffolk. Elizabeth was eighteen years old at the time, a high-spirited, sharp-tongued girl, very willing to fall in love with the handsome young widower. He courted her with appropriate sentiment, sending some of his own love-poetry to his 'bright Armida', and she responded in the same vein to her 'charming Suffolk swain'. This was merely preliminary and ornamental; the essential business of the courtship followed.

Hervey first applied to the girl's uncle, the Revd. Dr. Henry Felton, with a letter that he copied and endorsed: 'My dear father having living & dying desird me to marry again, there being but one son by my first ever-dear wife.' A short time later he submitted his formal marriage proposal to his future father-in-law, and then successfully negotiated the financial terms of Elizabeth's dowry and his settlement. His desire for Elizabeth, even if stimulated by filial obedience and sustained by legal safeguards, came from his heart. 'My ever-new Delight' was how he addressed her. They were married by Dr. Felton on the evening of 25 July 1695 in the church at Boxted, some nine miles from Bury. A few days later he brought his bride to meet the members of the Bury corporation, who greeted them ceremoniously dressed in their robes of office.

Marriage did not lessen his ardour, nor did it restrain him from expressing it. 'My dear dearest life', he writes to his wife, explaining that he 'coud not loose so favourable an opportunity to repeat the old sentence, Dear dear, how I do love you'. Elizabeth Hervey,

on her side, matched him in devotion. Love, family, and fortune
—all were consummated in their marriage.

ii

Having married again for the purpose, among others, of begetting
sons, Hervey had little cause for disappointment. His wife bore
seventeen children in all, of whom eleven—six of them boys—
survived to adulthood. Her first child was saluted even before
birth when (in April 1696) she informed her husband, 'our young
unknown frind is as well as can be, considering his uneasy habi-
tasion'. Expecting to bear a son, she was not disappointed. She lay
in at their house in Jermyn Street, and after what the anxious
father described as 'a painful perillous labour' of almost seventeen
hours she bore a son on 15 October 1696. Ten days later the
infant was christened John (after his father) by Dr. William
Wake, rector of St. James's parish church; and standing as godparents were Sir Thomas Felton, his grandfather, Baptist May, his
father's uncle, and the Duchess of Lauderdale, aged widow of the
politician who had wielded great power under Charles II. (Felton
may have been indebted to her for his favour at Charles's court.)
    From his infancy, Jack—as his doting parents called him—
worried them by his illness, particularly since his half-brother
and half-sisters had such good health. While Hervey was at the
Newmarket races his wife reported that their year-old son 'crys
night and day with his teeth, and sleeps very little, and will eat
nothing but his [wet-nurse's] buby'. He developed a cough so
bad that Dr. Radcliffe, the leading physician of the day, prescribed
the air of Kensington, but was unwilling to let him be moved any
farther from his reach.
    His feeble health made his parents dote on him all the more.
When Hervey had to be at Newmarket he asked his wife not to
let 'pretty Jack forgett his affectionate papa'. Solicitously she
moved into the nursery to be near him at night when he was not
sleeping well. She reported to Hervey that one day their son
called for his 'dear Papa; he cryd and would not be quiet in the
morning till they carried him into your dressing-room, and then
he went directly to your closet door, knocking and calling upon
you to let him in'. Both parents showed great care and affection
for him, but it was his father, evidently, whom he loved the more.

As the family grew more numerous they needed more room, and in 1698 Hervey moved them to a large house in St. James's Square, which his uncle had bought in 1677. At first he rented it from his widowed aunt, who lived in Holland, and at her death two years later he came into full possession of it. He wasted no time before insuring it—for £5,000, a little less than it had cost to build. This large, elegantly designed mansion was a suitable town-house for the prosperous squire and M.P.

Perhaps his expansive mood led him to reflect that although he now owned houses in London and in Bury he lacked a suitable family seat on his ancestral acres at Ickworth, which his aunt's death had released to him. The mansion house there, unoccupied for eighty years, had fallen into ruins; with its roof-tiles gone, the timbers and floors were rotting away. Instead of repairing or rebuilding it Hervey decided to occupy a farmhouse about half a mile away, and he began to enlarge and improve this modest dwelling.

To oversee the alterations he travelled up to Suffolk in the spring of 1702, taking with him Jack and three of his other children. His affection for 'dear Jack' led him to share his bed the first night of their journey, although the restless six-year-old boy disturbed his sleep. At Ickworth he dutifully attended church twice each Sunday, accompanied by his children. He made no secret of who his favourite was, assuring his wife that he regrets their separation so much that 'I'll make ye best of my present resource, dear Jack, your faint resemblance, by kissing him a 1000 times in remembrance of his dear mother'. When the entire family was finally installed at Ickworth in the autumn it consisted of the parents, seven children, and twenty servants. By the following year Hervey had stocked the park and farm with herds of deer, sheep, and cows.

He intended the farmhouse to be their temporary home until he could erect a truly 'noble seat', and in the summer of 1703 he discussed its design with John Vanbrugh, the versatile soldier, playwright, and architect. By then Vanbrugh had designed Castle Howard in Yorkshire for the Earl of Carlisle, and was soon to begin his most ambitious creation, Blenheim Palace, for the Duke of Marlborough. But nothing came of Hervey's ambition to build at this time.

Hervey had another ambition to signalize his rise in the world—

the acquisition of a peerage. Sarah, Duchess of Marlborough, whose husband was in the high tide of his military fame, and who herself was the most intimate friend of the newly crowned Queen Anne, had promised Sir Thomas Felton that when any new peers were created she would use her influence on behalf of his son-in-law. But at the new court, where the Tories were in the ascendant, the Queen had determined to elevate to the peerage four Tories, and they refused at first to accept that honour if a Whig shared it. The indomitable Duchess was not easily put off; she pressed her husband and Lord Godolphin, the Lord Treasurer, to support her request. As she recalled the episode in her memoirs many years later: 'Mr. Hervey had laid aside all hopes of the peerage, and was therefore surprized to the last degree, when a message came to him from the duke of Marlborough, that he must come on such a day by the back stairs [of St. James's Palace], to kiss the Queen's hand for being made a peer.'

Bribery was often the path to a peerage, but the Duchess later insisted that she obtained a title for Hervey only out of generous friendship. His fees for the honour of being made a baron, the lowest rank in the peerage, cost him £150. He chose the title of Baron Hervey of Ickworth, and the motto he put on his coat of arms—'Je n'oublierai jamais'—was apposite, for throughout his life he never forgot his patroness's generosity. On 22 June 1703 he was formally introduced in the House of Lords, and proudly took his place among the peers. Since he had to vacate his seat in the Commons and his eldest son (Carr) was still to young to 'inherit' it, for the time being no Hervey sat in the Lower House.

Prosperity continued to favour their family. In 1708 Hervey's father-in-law, Sir Thomas Felton, won the valuable appointment of Comptroller of the Queen's Household, with emoluments that came to about £1,200 a year (and plate valued at £400). But he held it only a few months. In March 1709 he died, and Lord Hervey, accompanied by Jack, attended the hearse on its slow procession from London into Suffolk. (Lady Hervey stayed in London, probably because she was pregnant; she gave birth to a daughter two months later.) Felton had bequeathed his entire personal estate to Jack, except for the pictures, which went to Lord Hervey.

The court post that Felton held was not so easily passed on.

Lord Hervey strenuously solicited it for himself, but it went instead to another claimant, more agreeable to the Tory Ministry. His disappointment did not wear off easily, and he made no secret of his dissatisfaction. At least the future looked promising, for Queen Anne had no surviving children, and the Act of Succession would bring to the throne a Hanoverian monarch who would favour the Whigs. Lord Hervey fortified his allegiance by ordering from a goldsmith medals of the Princess Sophia of Hanover, her son the Elector, and the Electoral Prince. In the House of Lords he signalized his opposition openly by signing the Protest to the bill censuring the Spanish military campaign waged when the Whigs had been in power, and a year later the Protest to the Tory peace treaty with France.

By this time the Queen had broken with the Marlboroughs, and so the Duchess could not exert any influence on Hervey's behalf. The Duke, however, could still pay 'distinguishing civilities' to Carr Hervey, who visited him in Flanders while on the Grand Tour; and Hervey thanked him with extravagant gratitude. Lady Hervey, who became increasingly hot-tempered as she grew older, did not share his exalted respect for the Duke's family. After having been a slave to the Duke's daughters, she at last plucked up the courage to endure their ridicule no longer. When the Duchess of Montagu (the Duke's second daughter) called her a fool she replied before the whole assembly of ladies that perhaps it was so 'but she was honest and had lain with nobody but her own Lord'. The squabble was talked about everywhere, but had no effect on the political alliance between Hervey and the Marlboroughs.

As the conflict between Whigs and Tories sharpened, Lord Hervey displayed his allegiance more openly. On New Year's Day 1712, just after the Queen had removed Marlborough's army command, Hervey gave a large dinner at his house in St. James's Square to which came Marlborough, Count von Bothmer (the Hanoverian envoy), and all the prominent Whig lords. A week later he again received Marlborough, who was accompanied this time by Prince Eugene of Savoy, the great Imperial general, then on an unsuccessful mission to England to persuade the Government not to make peace with France. But with the Queen in ill health and the Hanoverian succession a certainty, Hervey could afford to be patient.

iii

As a boy Jack Hervey was almost never apart from either or both of his parents. During the summer of 1705, along with two brothers and two sisters, he spent about six weeks with them at Aswarby, the estate Carr Hervey had inherited from his mother. The following summer Jack, then ten years old, was the only one of their children who accompanied them to Aswarby, and from there on a round of visits. With several relations they travelled to Chesterfield, in Derbyshire, spent the night there, and the next day dined at Chatsworth with the old Duke of Devonshire. They then continued north to Doncaster and York, attended services in the Minster on Sunday, visited the Archbishop at his palace on Wednesday, and dined with the Earl of Carlisle on Friday, after which they retraced their route to Aswarby. A fortnight later they returned to Ickworth. For such a young boy these visits introduced him precociously into the world of powerful privilege; and this in turn may explain why aristocratic assurance and prejudices were so integral a part of his character.

His formal education, of course, had not been neglected. It was entrusted to a tutor, a 'Mr. Richar' (perhaps a Huguenot named Richard), who was a stern and conscientious taskmaster, for when the boy accompanied his father to his grandfather's burial in Suffolk, he took along lessons to work on. From an early age he learned French, finding it easy and congenial. A French dancing master was engaged to instruct him, and a French chaplain was employed in the household to read prayers. When his father was at Newmarket (in the spring of 1709) the thirteen-year-old boy sent him a letter in French—entirely written by himself, he boasted to his mother, but it was so well written that his father was suspicious. 'I wish the orthography, as well as the sense of it, were all his own,' he remarked to Lady Hervey, 'knowing the former not to be so correctly attainable at his age.' The boy could write (and speak) French with the same facility he showed in English, and Lord Hervey simply underestimated his ability in languages.

Besides houses in London, Bury St. Edmunds, and Ickworth, Lord Hervey maintained a racing stud at Newmarket, conveniently on the road between London and Bury. He at first rented and then bought a house there, staffing it with servants and

2. Lord Hervey as a Child

stableboys. During the racing season—in April and in October—
Newmarket was thronged with a 'great concourse of the nobility
and gentry'. From his early boyhood Jack accompanied his father
there. In the spring of 1711, when they travelled up from London,
Lord Hervey was able to send his wife a pleasing report of the
journey her 'two Jacks' had taken: 'that I might be able to send
you a particular account of him, [I] venturd to make him my
bedfellow, but was disturbd neither by his coughing nor restless-
ness, having slept soundly the whole night. As to his dyet, he eat
heartily of the beef and butter at Epping, did the same of a fricassee
of chickens at Hockeril, and of his own accord broke into the
paper where the plum-cake lay on this side of [Puckeridge], and
having lookd over the horses we supped on mutton and were in
bed before ten.' It was a hardy regimen for the boy, whose ill
health as an adult forced him to regulate his diet with great care.

At Newmarket he entered fully into all the activities of the
race meeting. He needed money for betting, and since he would
not ask his father for any, his mother (then in London) obligingly
told her husband of it. She also repeated some gossip that she
knew would please him—that at a dinner she had been told by
Lord Dorset that Jack was the chief jockey at Newmarket. He
enjoyed the carefree life there so much that he disobeyed his
father and stayed an extra day after he had been ordered to leave,
and to make matters worse played dice at the chocolate house. The
news sadly vexed his mother, who regarded horse-race betting (like
card-playing for herself) as a socially acceptable form of gambling.

For some reason, perhaps disobedient behaviour such as Jack
had shown at Newmarket, his father determined to send him to
a public school, where he would be subject to stricter discipline.
Westminster was chosen, the famous and venerable school whose
origins go back to the fifteenth century. Along with Jack went
three of his younger brothers (two of them thirteen years old, and
one eleven). They were all admitted to the school in January 1712.
As the eldest of the Hervey boys, and in fact rather mature to be
entering at the age of sixteen, he was entrusted to carry the fees
for payment to the headmaster.

In the final decades of the seventeenth century Westminster
School had prospered under the rule of Dr. Busby, famous for the
severity of his piety and discipline. At the time the Hervey boys
entered, the recently appointed Dr. Robert Freind was headmaster,

a scholar of such great social gifts that the school was increasingly preferred by aristocratic families. At his retirement many years later he was honoured by some verse from Stephen Duck, the thresher poet (who, of course, had never been a pupil at the school):

> Review thy Toils, and see what polish'd Peers
> Honour thy forming Hands, and studious Cares . . .
> Let Hervey's Muse her Tutor's Worth proclaim,
> And Pelham's Royal Trust declare thy Fame.

The curriculum at which the Westminster pupils toiled was predominantly classical—Latin and Greek grammar, a careful reading of the Roman writers: Virgil, Horace, Ovid, Terence, Cicero, and Livy, and exercises in rhetoric. As part of their class-work they were required to analyse the passages they read, to point out oddities of style, figures of speech, antitheses, witticisms, and so on. One product of Hervey's labours is a paraphrase of a Horatian ode, a dialogue between Horace and Lydia. It is his earliest surviving literary composition, proudly endorsed by his father as having been written in 1713.

In later years Hervey protested that his training at Westminster had left no residue of learning:

> . . . all I learn'd from *Doctor Freind* at School,
> By *Gradus, Lexicon,* or Grammar-Rule;
> Of Saphic, Lyric, or Iambic Odes,
> Or *Doctor King's* Machinery of Gods,
> Has quite deserted this poor *John-Trot* Head,
> And left plain native *English* in its stead.

But this humorous modesty is easily refuted by his familiarity with Roman literature and by the rhetorical virtuosity of his writing, the result in some degree of the thorough training forced on Westminster scholars. Each year the scholars performed a Latin play before an audience; and during the time Jack Hervey was there two plays were staged: *Ignoramus* by George Ruggles, a comedy ridiculing lawyers and their profession, and the classical *Phormio* by Terence. Perhaps—for the cast lists do not survive— Jack, who in later life showed a great interest in the theatre, played in these productions.

The Hervey boys did not have to endure the rigours of living within the school, where pupils rose at five in the morning to make their beds and sweep up. With a servant to look after them, they boarded in a large house owned by Dr. Freind adjoining the school. About eighty boys, sons of the nobility and gentry, lodged there with a dame in charge, probably assisted by a young usher.

'Public Schools are the Nurseries of all Vice and Immorality', says Parson Adams, voicing the opinion of Henry Fielding (who had attended Eton). And William Cowper, a pupil at Westminster some years after Hervey, denounced it in scathing terms:

> Would you your son should be a sot or dunce,
> Lascivious, headstrong; or all these at once . . . ?
> There shall he learn, ere sixteen winters old,
> That authors are most useful pawn'd or sold;
> That pedantry is all that schools impart,
> But taverns teach the knowledge of the heart. . . .

This is no doubt the exaggeration of a sensitive and disturbed poet; the more measured opinion of Edward Gibbon, who spent two years at the school, was that there a 'boy of spirit may acquire a prævious and practical experience of the World'. Whether or not Jack Hervey cultivated vice along with learning while at Westminster, at least he was not isolated from the practical world that lay beyond its Gothic buildings.

iv

During school holidays Jack was free to travel with his parents or to stay at Ickworth with their numerous family. In the spring, only a few months after he had entered Westminster, he spent a week at Ickworth before accompanying his father to Newmarket. They travelled with the Duke of Bolton and his son, Lord Harry Poulett, recently returned from Lisbon, where he had been in the suite of the English ambassador. As a gentleman-rider at Newmarket Jack was beaten in one race, and became so dejected that he refused to wait for the next race but went home. He had better luck another time when he rode a Hervey horse named Ickworth, and won the Queen's plate.

In a less hectic mood the sixteen-year-old boy, while passing the long summer vacation at Ickworth in 1712, sent a rapturous letter to his father (then in Lincolnshire) extolling the pleasures of country life and retirement. Lord Hervey approved of such mature wisdom in the boy, though he reminded him in return that his sentiments had been expressed by Cicero, Horace, Virgil, and the Delphic oracle—as Jack no doubt already knew—and that he had omitted two country felicities from his list: a chaste wife and agreeable books.

At the end of July, he joined his father to begin their round of country visits together. When they reached Lord Wharton's seat (Winchendon) in Buckinghamshire they stayed three nights. The bright, attentive schoolboy, besides admiring the famous racing-stable there, undoubtedly listened eagerly to the political talk that went round the dinner-table of the Whig magnate. At the end of August Jack and his father reached Bath in time for the season at that popular spa in the west country, where they were joined by Lady Hervey. After a month's visit they travelled by way of London to Newmarket for the season there.

In the spring holiday of the following year (1713) Jack again expected to accompany his father to the races. Before leaving London they had been cajoled by Lady Hervey into pledging that he would not ride his colt Union, evidently a difficult animal to control. As they approached the town he could not hide his deep disappointment at his mother's injunction. He was so disturbed, in fact, that during the night his father heard him talk in his sleep: 'Pray, lett me ride him,—& after that—I will, I will; you shant refuse me.' And during his waking hours he tried to persuade his father to let him ride the colt. 'His working brain coynd & urgd a hundred Jesuitisms in order to evade your request to me at parting', Hervey tells his wife, but he kept his word; 'no part of his persuasion (which did not want for rhetorick neither) could ever shake ye firm resolves I had taken to gratify your (give me leave to call it) weakness for this once, since it tends to nothing but effeminacy, the very worst of education; his age, strength & stature is now at such a crisis that you must determine to be content to see him live a shrimp or risque something to inable him to commence man. I'm of council for ye latter.' The conflict between his over-solicitous mother and his hearty father stands out as a shaping influence on the personality of the boy. Shrimp or man?—he was to be something of both.

The outcome of the race justified his father's indignation, for Union won the match, beating the Duke of Rutland's colt to win the purse of £500. Union had 'made so fine a figure on ye flatt', Hervey pointedly tells his wife, 'that Jack woud have become him much better than ye rider your injunction forcd me to substitute in his place. Could you imagine ye mortification it provd to us both . . .'. The boy's judgement could sometimes be better than his father's, for in another race one of their horses won the Queen's plate because Jack, having carefully observed the previous heats, countermanded his father's orders, and instructed the jockey not to give the horse his head until the last mile. He showed great acuteness beyond the track, for he was a very careful book-keeper in calculating the precise accounts of bets and stakes. He was 'so inamourd with ye pleasures of this place,' his father remarks, 'that he has no spiritts (comparatively) any where else.' His work as a schoolboy, plodding through Latin exercises, must have seemed very tame compared to the thrill of galloping over the flat at Newmarket, with the pounding thud of hooves under him, and of seeing (out of the corner of his eye) the admiring crowd of spectators.

It was a triumphal conclusion for Lord Hervey's activity as a horse-breeder and racer, for a few months later he decided to dispose of his stable. It occurred to him to present several of his horses to the Elector of Hanover, and he asked his son Carr, then in Hanover at the completion of his Grand Tour, to inquire at the Electoral court whether such a gift would be acceptable. If it were he planned to send Jack along to accompany the horses to Germany, and the boy could thus ingratiate himself with England's future king. But to his disappointment the Elector politely declined the gift. Fearful that the refusal might have been a mark of unfriendliness, Lord Hervey hastily asked Carr to convey to the Elector his profound respect and loyalty, and to remind him that he had been 'a most constant, zealous promoter of every measure that originally introducd or could since any way strengthen ye security of their succession; wheron everything that's precious to a free, Protestant poeple entirely depends'. It was not the first time, nor the last, that Hervey tried to ingratiate himself with George I.

And so instead of an exciting journey to Hanover, Jack had to content himself with the customary visit to Ickworth, and then to Bath with his parents for the season in August. He had by now completed his schooling at Westminster, where he had been for one and a half years, and was ready to be entered at the University.

V

Accompanied by his mother and father Jack Hervey travelled
down to Cambridge from Ickworth on 19 November 1713 to be
entered at Clare Hall, the college where his father and his half-
brother had matriculated. On arrival a candidate was customarily
examined for his academic fitness; and the next day John Hervey,
having been found fit, was formally admitted (in the middle of
Michaelmas term).

Compared to the rural beauty of Ickworth Park and the splendid
urbanity of St. James's Square, Cambridge was a depressing
town, so abominably dirty that after a shower or winter-thaw its
narrow streets were deeply mired, and vehicles could pass each
other only with difficulty. The buildings in many parts of the
town were small and low; an English traveller thought they
looked more like huts for pygmies than homes for men. At least
the University buildings were handsome and spaciously set out.
Clare was particularly striking because of its fine, new buildings.
Its hall, wrote Mr. Spectator (Richard Steele), used to be the
ugliest in the town, and was now the neatest.

In intellectual discipline and training the University had
stagnated to a notorious degree. The few courses of lectures were
so sparsely attended that the professors could just as well have
spoken to bare walls. As to the college tutors: in the opinion of the
finicky Thomas Gray, some twenty years later, they were all
'sleepy, drunken, dull, illiterate things'. But in attending Clare,
Hervey was more fortunate than most undergraduates. Its principal tutor was Richard Laughton—by reputation 'the famous
pupil-monger'—and he had helped give the college its excellent
reputation. He was very agreeable to visitors, spoke French
notably well, and was proud of the college library, which though
not large had many good books. Laughton's fame had made
Clare Hall fashionable; and a Fellow of the neighbouring Trinity
College had to admit that 'a confluence of nobility and gentry'
had been drawn to one of the 'least colleges' not only by the
virtue of one man but by the society of his aristocratic pupils.

As senior proctor of the University Laughton was noted for his
strict discipline and his severity in enforcing the statutes. Hervey's
father insisted that he obey Laughton, and sternly reproved him
when he failed to. Laughton had forbidden him to associate with

a Mr. Finch. 'Example is so infectious', Lord Hervey lectured him, 'that our first and chiefest care should be to find out & frequent men of ye most sober & virtuous conversation, since we insensibly fall into ye imitation of ye manners of ye company we consort with, and gradually become ye very men whose images at first frighted us.' There were two Mr. Finches at Cambridge then, sons of Lord Nottingham; which of them aroused Laughton's disapproval and Hervey's friendship is not known.

In addition to Laughton, another tutor was charged with supervising Hervey—Thomas Seaton, a clergyman and a Fellow of Clare since 1704. He had been irresolute in accepting the position as tutor, and then suddenly relinquished it (in July 1714) without prior notice. Lord Hervey berated him in an angry letter for his 'abrupt departure from my service, joyned to the small significa- tion (it seems) you have been of to my son, either in his studies or other attendance on him'. Laughton evidently could not find any Fellow at Clare suitable or willing to replace Seaton, and so a Fellow of Trinity Hall, William Herring by name, was chosen for the position.

In being under Laughton's supervision Hervey profited in other ways. Laughton was a staunch champion of the philosopher and theologian William Whiston, who regarded him as his 'Bosom Friend'. (Whiston had been expelled from Cambridge in 1710 for his heretical opinions and writings.) Laughton was also a firm advocate of Newtonian physics, which was only then replacing Cartesianism at the University, and he was a friend of Richard Bentley, the great classical scholar. In his later years Hervey flaunted unorthodox religious opinions and an interest in the new science; he had laid the groundwork at Clare.

His course of study, however, was predominantly classical; and if it was like the curriculum drawn up (in 1707) by a Fellow of Clare, he read the Roman poets and prose writers daily, and each week wrote Latin themes and verses and translated passages from Greek and Latin. Besides his classical studies he had to be prepared to face his tutor in a wide range of studies, including philosophy, history, Parliamentary pleadings and speeches, logic, algebra, and geometry. The nimbleness of mind and wide range of knowledge he displayed in his later years had, like his free- thinking, been developed to some extent at the University.

All these virtues of intellect could be abused. The future Lord

Chesterfield, who was a contemporary of Hervey's at Cambridge (Trinity Hall), later accused himself of being an 'absolute pedant': when he talked his best, he quoted Horace; when he wanted to be facetious, he quoted Martial; and when he wanted to sound a fine gentleman, he talked Ovid. Besides these dubious advantages, Chesterfield blamed the pedants of that 'illiberal seminary' for encouraging in him 'a sauciness of literature, a turn to satire and contempt, and a strong tendency to argumentation and contradiction'. These characteristics could have been applied by Hervey to himself in later years.

And if the undergraduate wanted some relaxation from a studious regimen, Cambridge offered varied distractions. Coffeehouses, particularly one called the Grecian, were popular with both undergraduates and Fellows, who usually flocked there after chapel, and spent hours talking or reading the newspapers sent up from London. Besides the coffee-houses, which were forbidden to undergraduates unless they had their tutors' permission, there were taverns and ale-houses, forbidden to them altogether. In nearby Sturbridge, the fair at the end of the summer drew its patronage from the University, though any undergraduate who attended without written permission from his tutor was subject to a fine. 'From Sciences we solemnly repair/ To Ropes, and Fiddles, and a bounding Fair' sang Laurence Eusden (in 1714), a future Poet Laureate; and his verse also celebrated the 'Sunday-Nymphs' seen on the lawns of Clare Hall. With his turn for satire Hervey later sketched the career of a rich country squire's son at Cambridge: 'he went vigorously through a Course of Academical Learning; drank with his Tutor, lay with his Laundress, run in Debt to his Tailor, bilkt the Proctor, broke the Chapel Windows, and then took a Degree of *Master of Arts*.' How much of this was autobiographical? Only the learning and the degree (in 1715) can definitely be ascribed to Hervey.

The University was no haven from the political turbulence in the summer of 1714 that became more intense as Queen Anne's health became more precarious and Jacobite hopes more desperate. Although the succession to the throne had been legally formulated to pass to the Elector of Hanover, the Jacobite wing of the Tories hoped to bring over the Pretender, who was biding his time in France. Of the two universities Oxford tended to be Tory in its sympathies, with a fringe of Jacobite extremists, whereas

Cambridge was—in the phrase of a disapproving undergraduate
—'a sad whiggish place'.

As soon as news of the Queen's death reached Cambridge on
1 August, the Elector was proclaimed. (The undergraduates were
then enjoying their long summer vacation.) Two days later a
stately procession of college heads and doctors from all the University faculties saluted their new monarch by walking solemnly
to the market cross. The University also observed the death of
Queen Anne and the accession of George I with the customary
collection of poems written by its Fellows and undergraduates.
No English verse marred the dignity of its Latin, Greek and
Hebrew. The contribution of John Hervey to this collection was
eighteen lines of Latin verse entitled 'Ad Regem'. In his first published writing he thus expressed allegiance to the Hanoverian line.

2

An Indefinite Future

1714–19

AT THE BEGINNING OF SEPTEMBER 1714 Lord Hervey returned to London with his family to await the King's arrival; and on the 18th he proudly put a notation in his diary: 'King George & ye Prince of Wales arrivd at Greenwich about 6 in ye evening: where I had ye honour to kiss both their hands.' He was present when they arrived at St. James's Palace two days later, at the 'most magnificent entry that ever was seen'. But his proudest moment came a month later at the Coronation, 'at which solemnity I walked in ye procession as Earle of Bristol'. He had given considerable thought to the choice of a title. At his request his friend Vanbrugh, who was Clarenceux king of arms, had sent him a list of eleven extinct titles to choose from. He chose Bristol—a city without any connection to his family—probably because the last holder of that title, dead since 1698, had been a Tory; and the new Lord Bristol could flatter the King that a Tory had been replaced by a loyal Whig.

Rewards would accrue not only to himself but to his family. His eldest son, Carr, assumed the courtesy title of Lord Hervey. During the final months of his Grand Tour, Carr had been elected M.P. for the family-controlled seat of Bury St. Edmunds; and in Hanover he had become acquainted with the Electoral heir, soon to become Prince of Wales. Within a week of the Prince's arrival in England Carr sent him an obsequious letter (in French) asking for a post at his court. He soon became Groom of the Bedchamber, an appointment that could be held only by sons of earls. Lord Bristol was further honoured (on 1 November) when the King supped at his house. The Hanoverian reign opened very auspiciously for the Hervey family.

No doubt a court appointment for Jack Hervey would have been sought by his father had he not still been at the University.

Lord Bristol took a serious view of his son's education, for he had 'a more than ordinary passion to see him perfectly accomplishd, and thereby first among mankind too'. When Jack paid a visit to Ickworth the following spring (1715) Lord Bristol hoped it would not interfere with his intended public exercises (apparently a University disputation) or cause him to lose any time from his studies.

After Caroline, Princess of Wales, arrived in October to join her husband, the scramble for court appointments became more intense. Since the King had no queen-consort with him—his wife having been imprisoned many years earlier for alleged adultery—all the appointments open to ladies were to the Princess of Wales's court. Lady Bristol was determined to win a place there. Since her marriage twenty years before, her character had hardened: life in court circles had turned her into a sharp-tongued gossip and a fanatical card-player who loved the whirl of London social life. Now she bent every effort to win a place that would keep her there, with the added *douceurs* of Royal friendships and an annual stipend paid quarterly. She attended the Coronation with the Lord Chancellor's wife, Lady Cowper, who then wrote in her diary that Lady Bristol 'had still a greater Mind to be a Lady of the Bedchamber than I had'. Four days later the appointment went to Lady Cowper.

As Lady Bristol saw others favoured while she was being passed over, she became frantic. When the Italian-born wife of the Duke of Shrewsbury was appointed a Lady of the Bedchamber (on 14 November) she became so indignant that, to the annoyance of the Princess of Wales, she publicly threatened to have an objection raised in the House of Commons that the Duchess should be forbidden the post because she was a foreigner. Actually the Duchess had been naturalized since 1706; and the Princess, who disliked her, had been bullied by the King into accepting her. (Her husband was the King's Groom of the Stole, Keeper of the Privy Purse, and Lord Chamberlain.) On another occasion Lady Bristol engaged in an elaborate intrigue in her attempt to be appointed Mistress of the Robes, and again she failed.

She did not give up easily; besides, the vacancies were only gradually being filled. In March 1715, when she bore a daughter, she tactfully chose as baptismal names Louisa Caroline Isabelle in honour of the infant's godparents: the King, the Princess of Wales, and the Marchioness of Dorchester, whose husband was soon to be created Duke of Kingston and appointed Lord Privy Seal. While her husband remained at Ickworth she urged Carr to solicit a post for him, but without success because—in Bristol's opinion —the King thought him sufficiently rewarded. He consoled himself in the country with the company of his 'cargoe of children'. Still she urged him to come to London, this time to help her win a place at Court.

To further her efforts, Lady Bristol cultivated the friendship of the King's German favourites. She went to the opera with Madame von der Schulenburg, one of the King's mistresses, and supped with Madame Kielmansegge, his other one. Another German lady at Court, not so important as the Royal mistresses, was the Countess of Bückeburg, Lady-in-Waiting to the Princess of Wales. The Countess, who was a very stout woman, once displayed her arrogance and conceitedness by telling Lady Cowper that English women did not look like women of quality because they held their heads down and always looked a fright, whereas the foreign ladies held up their heads and held out their breasts to make themselves look more stately and noble. To which Lady Deloraine (whose husband was a Gentleman of the Bedchamber to the Prince of Wales) replied, 'We show our Quality by our Birth and Titles, Madam, and not by sticking out our Bosoms'. Lady Bristol cultivated this assertive German lady by presenting her portrait to her; and Lord Bristol dutifully paid the bills for both the picture and its frame.

Yet in spite of his eagerness to win appointments for himself and his family, Bristol deliberately offended the King and the Ministry when the Septennial Bill, so important to the Hanoverian Whigs, was introduced in Parliament in April 1716. Under the Triennial Act, then in effect, a new election would take place in 1718, and the Ministry were fearful that the King's unpopularity might bring a Tory majority in the House of Commons. Besides, the Whigs wished to be spared the crushing expense of frequent elections. Under a Septennial Act the House of Commons then sitting would perpetuate itself until 1722. While the bill was being formulated Lady Bristol urged her husband, then at Newmarket, to hasten to London since it might be introduced in the House of Lords, probably on Wednesday, 11 April. He replied (on the 9th) that he could not 'possibly beleive that a Bill which so nearly concerns the priviledges of all the people shoud be first meddled with by the Peers'; and he would not return to London until 'the monster's first appearance' in the Upper House. On Tuesday the 10th the bill had its first reading in the Lords. The King, when he saw Lady Bristol that day, pointedly asked her whether her husband was in town, and she replied—with more tact than truth—that she expected him the next day.

He actually returned before the bill had its second reading, on the 14th, when the Princess of Wales herself attended the session because she considered it so important. The bill was returned to committee, and a Protest entered in the Journals of the House, signed by twenty-four Lords, Bristol among them, giving their reasons for opposing it. The Protest was ineffectual, of course, and the bill was passed by a vote of 69 to 36, and then in the Commons by 264 to 121, after which it quickly received the Royal Assent. Bristol had opposed the bill so conspicuously that the Princess of Wales on meeting Lady Bristol sharply remarked to her that since her husband had left the court to join the Tories he should leave them forever. To which Lady Bristol replied, 'If your Highness calls voting for the ancient laws and liberties of England a leaving the Court you may depend on it he has left the Court for ever'. It was a bold answer (and a prophetic one as well). When the Princess next saw Lord Bristol at a Drawing-Room she publicly insulted him.

Why did Bristol so conspicuously offend the Ministry and court from which he expected so much patronage to flow to his family? Lady Bristol's reply to the Princess of Wales suggests that he did it out of deep conviction rather than political partisanship, for in effect the Septennial Act strengthened the House of Commons, emancipating it from dependence on the Crown and the House of Lords. With his deep-seated conservatism Lord Bristol did not want to see the balance of power disturbed; and whether or not his point of view was justified, the fact that he clung to it is a tribute to his integrity.

ii

Even in his cloistered university life Jack Hervey could feel the political reverberations of the new dynasty. On the night of George I's birthday (28 May 1715) some students rioted, and on that of the Pretender, two weeks later, Jacobite undergraduates broke windows and cried, 'No Hanover'. A year later rioters attacked Clare Hall, where the scholars were 'miserably insulted for their loyalty to the Government'. But by then Hervey was no longer there, having left in Christmas 1715. Perhaps taking advantage of the privilege (given to peers' sons) of exemption from examinations, he took the degree of M.A. permitted after six terms, though he actually stayed for seven.

Then, having rejoined his family, he resumed his customary routine. During the next two months he passed most of his time in his father's company—a week at Newmarket, a few days at Epsom, a visit to their family at Ickworth, and then to London, where they witnessed the Parliamentary agitation over the Septennial Act. Though he was now a young man of twenty, his education was not yet completed; his father's diary entry for 4 June 1716 records its final stage: 'Munday, dear Jack sett out from London towards Paris, in order to his farther travels; wherin I beseech God Almighty to protect & perfect him ye man I wish to see him.' At the last moment the indulgent father had pressed on him ten guineas 'for his pocket'.

He was accompanied by a tutor, Daniel Jouneau, a Huguenot reared in England since infancy, who had attended Oxford and had been trained as a physician. (His father, a clergyman, had been the future Lord Chesterfield's tutor.) Thirty-one years old at this time, Jouneau was thoroughly experienced as a guide, having been in charge of two English boys who were educated on the Continent. He was thus qualified to look after Jack Hervey.

Since Elizabethan days the Grand Tour had been an important part of the education of young men of aristocratic or wealthy families. It generally consumed three years, allowing them to travel, study, and see the sights mainly in France and Italy and then, homeward bound, in the German States and the Low Countries. They sometimes, if very wealthy, travelled with elaborate entourages—shortly before Hervey left, the eighteen-year-old Marquess of Wharton also sailed for the Continent, on an allowance of £1,000 a year, accompanied by six ordinary footmen, a running footman, a valet-de-chambre, two sets of coach horses, and a tutor; but most of the Grand Tourists were, like Hervey, guided and taught by a single 'bear-leader'. Cautious parents usually preferred that, instead of staying in Paris with its many temptations, the young man settle in a provincial town where the air and the moral atmosphere were purer and where, in the absence of compatriots, he could concentrate on studying the language as well as horsemanship, duelling, and dancing. But Lord Bristol allowed his son to proceed directly to Paris.

In his first view of the French capital Hervey was probably struck, as so many travelling English were, by its contrast with London—streets neatly paved with stone and regularly lighted at night, and handsome houses made of stone and beautified with gardens. A good part of his time must have been spent visiting churches and palaces to see the paintings and sculpture on view. The gardens of the four royal palaces were open to the public (except to mechanics and liveried servants); that of the Tuileries, designed by Le Nôtre, with its magnificent trees, was particularly popular. On summer evenings it was thronged with polite society, who walked about in the cool air, especially during the season that Hervey was in Paris, for the city suffered from extraordinary hot weather and drought.

If he wished to observe a side of Paris life where mechanics and servants were not excluded he could visit the Fair of St. Lawrence, in progress each year from July until the end of September. It was one of the sights foreigners were taken to—much better arranged than London's St. Bartholomew's Fair, with shops set out in neat rows and well lighted. Hervey had been commissioned by his mother to buy a mantua and petticoat—elaborate and rich outer garments for formal occasions; and he was able to send them through one of her friends in time for her to wear to the Prince of Wales's birthnight ball.

As he sauntered through the spacious *allées* of the palace gardens he would have noticed the clothes and cosmetics worn by the French of quality. The women he observed were fantastically absurd in their dress and monstrously unnatural in their cosmetics. From cheeks to chin their faces were overlaid with shining red varnish that glistened as though aflame. A few years later the nineteen-year-old Lord Boyle, also on the Grand Tour, thought that the women troweled themselves with red; he also noticed that the Frenchmen, 'Animals called Beaux' and reeking of perfume, 'paint themselves white, and look paler than poor *Banquo*'. If Hervey later used white make-up, as satirists charged, it was *à la mode* in Paris; and he preferred to look like a pale Frenchified beau rather than a red-faced English hearty.

As the son of an English peer he had an entrée into the court circles in Paris, and was introduced no doubt by the English ambassador, Lord Stair, who had been appointed the previous year. Although Stair was busy keeping track of Jacobite intrigue and helping to negotiate the terms of the Triple Alliance (between the English, French, and Dutch, signed the following January), he would not have neglected his normal duty of receiving a peer's son on the Grand Tour. Hervey's fluency in speaking French was a great advantage, for people at court had no interest or patience in conversing with anybody who was not a master of their language.

While France was ruled by the Regent, nephew of Louis XIV, the chief figure at court was the six-year-old Louis XV. He did not appear in public as frequently as customary because of the great heat and the prevalence of smallpox during these months, but he could occasionally be met walking in the garden of the Tuileries; and on the eve of the Feast of Saint Louis, when a great concert was given there, he supped on the palace terrace and was greeted by an immense crowd below with cries of 'Vive le Roi'. It was one of the handsomest celebrations that one could witness. Hervey could also have attended the great reception given by the Duc d'Antin in honour of the Duchesse de Berry: first a magnificent supper, then a comedy in the Italian manner played in the brilliantly lighted garden, with the best singers and dancers from the opera performing during the entr'actes, and finally a great display of fire-works.

Apart from the numerous Royal family—who included Louis XIV's bastards and the peers, treated by Saint-Simon with such concern and passion—Hervey may have met in court circles a fellow Briton, John Law. This Scotsman, whom the Regent had allowed to establish a bank only a few months earlier, was the financial wizard then beginning his phenomenal career with the Mississippi Scheme (that collapsed in 1720). He was considered by the snobbish Saint-Simon to be not quite a gentleman, but he was an ingratiating man, tall and handsome, and a great favourite with the ladies. There were in Paris other Britons, many of them Scottish, whom Hervey would carefully have avoided—Jacobites who had fled there after their abortive invasion the previous year.

Lord Bolingbroke, their attainted leader, had been dismissed by the Pretender that spring, and in August was living in Paris, absolutely despised wherever he went.

One man in Paris whom Hervey definitely met was the Abbé Jean Terrasson, a noted *philosophe* and savant, a member of the Académie des Sciences and ultimately one of the Forty Immortals of the French Academy. A man of great intellectual virtuosity, he became involved in the controversy about the ancients and moderns that flared up anew after he published (in 1715) a book on the *Iliad*; and in the years ahead he was to publish books on finance, the East India company, philosophy and religion, a translation of Diodorus Siculus, and his *chef-d'œuvre*, a philosophical romance set in ancient Egypt. Hervey could easily cultivate his friendship, for abbés and men of learning were readily accessible to foreigners. The Abbé Terrasson, who was later appointed to the chair of Greek and Latin philosophy at the Collège de France, had a reputation for exceptional patience in guiding his students outside as well as within the classroom.

When Hervey boasted to his father of his worthy friend he mentioned that the Abbé was about to publish a new work (a supplement to his book on the *Iliad*). Lord Bristol, who already knew of him, held him in high esteem: 'Midas-like every thing must become gold that he thinks fitt to handle.' The fond father was even more pleased to know the extent of the Abbé's friendship toward his son: 'I am glad to hear of his intended voyage hither, & am yet better pleasd to find a man of his exquisite taste should value your conversation enough to make him deferr his journey till your return, a compliment you may be justly proud of, & one I could feel a thrô satisfaction in, were it not attended with ye allay of keeping him longer from us.' Lord Bristol knew how to deliver a compliment gracefully, but the Abbé, who was perhaps exhibiting an unusual degree of *délicatesse*, never visited England.

Lord Bristol had received his son's letter from Paris not through the post, which he considered unreliable, but by the hand of Anne Oldfield, a leading actress of the day (in both comedy and tragedy). 'Mrs. Oldfield has made your Mama a visitt,' he told Hervey, '& was wellcome to us both, because she brought me a letter from you, which entertaind us better than she with all her witt & ridicule on France could do; your simile of the Invalides was worth her whole conversation.' Although a stage performer, Mrs. Oldfield had earned her social credentials by being mistress first to Arthur Mainwaring, Whig politician and journalist, and after his death to Colonel Charles Churchill, illegitimate nephew of Marlborough; and it was probably through him that Hervey's letter had been sent. Besides his clever simile for the Hôtel des Invalides (the immense hospital built by Louis XIV for old and disabled soldiers), the precocious young Hervey had explained to his father that the French gave greater encouragement to the arts and sciences than the English did; but Bristol patriotically insisted that their attainment in the arts was only mediocre because they had no geniuses, though he graciously conceded that because they were so particularly kind and courteous to his son he was willing to think of them as favourably as they did of themselves.

Although he had already spent several months in Paris, Hervey still showed no inclination to leave. Lord Bristol then reminded him of the lesson to be gained from Fénelon's *Télémaque*, in which the young Prince stayed at each place only as long as was necessary to exercise his virtue and acquire experience. Since Hervey's prudence and principles have served for the former purpose and his 'industrious curiosity' for the latter, Bristol concludes, he should leave Paris. Hervey may have sighed as a traveller, but he obeyed as a son.

iii

The Grand Tourist in Paris customarily took a southward route to the provincial cities of the Midi, and from there into Italy, the Mecca of his cultural pilgrimage. But Hervey's father directed him to another route altogether—one that would take him to the source of privilege and patronage.

George I had returned to his beloved Hanover at the end of July for his first visit since he had reluctantly departed almost two years before. He spent the summer in agreeable pursuits—drinking the waters at Pyrmont, shooting partridges at Herrenhausen (his summer palace surrounded by magnificent gardens), and hunting game from his lodge at Göhre. His entourage included a secretary of state, and other advisers for his official business, and for his pleasure Madame von der Schulenburg, who had been given the title of Duchess of Munster (in the Irish peerage), and Madame Kielmansegge. He could in addition enjoy the company of the younger and prettier Countess von Platen, his Hanoverian mistress, who had preferred to remain at home when her master left to accept the English crown.

Since it was reported that the King would return to England at the beginning of November 1716, Hervey's father urged him to hasten to Hanover by the most direct route—through Austrian Flanders and Holland. Eager to reach Hanover as soon as he could, Hervey arrived at Brussels after its gates had been shut for the night, and was forced to find lodging in a miserable inn at a nearby village. His father, after hearing of his misadventure, read him a moral lesson: that his sorry experience might teach him to arrive at fortified places before their gates were shut and to relish 'with a better gusto than formerly' the good beds and food provided for him at home.

When he reached Hanover he saw a town that, compared to Paris or London, seemed very provincial indeed. As the seat of the Electoral family it was populous enough, and like other German principalities, it mimicked the Versailles of the Sun King. The Electoral Palace was actually a castle on the banks of a river near the town wall, a large and spacious building built around several square courts. The King, in a very affable mood, dined and supped constantly in public, and his company of actors played every night in the palace theatre. He seemed to be so happy at home in Hanover, a visiting Englishman remarked to his friends, that he believed the King had forgotten the accident that happened to him and his family on 1 August 1714. Soon after Hervey arrived he was presented to the King. Eager to assert his independence he did not take his tutor (Jouneau) with him at the presentation, a breach of etiquette for which his father later reproved him. The monarch whom he confronted was a pleasant-looking, good-natured, elderly gentleman. Far from scintillating, he was so sober and stolid that in the opinion of some, had he been in private life he would have been called an honest blockhead. He knew no English, and was past the age of trying to learn it, but young Hervey could easily speak to him in French.

Among the other English visitors in Hanover at that time, one of the most conspicuous was Lady Mary Wortley Montagu, who was accompanying her husband to his new post as ambassador to

Turkey. Still a young woman (of twenty-seven) she was gaining a reputation as a wit and *bel esprit*. Until the previous year, when an almost fatal attack of smallpox had ruined her looks, she had been a pretty, dark-eyed woman. Now, with her eyelashes gone and her skin pitted (though covered with cosmetics) she could no longer depend on her beauty to attract admirers; instead, taking advantage of her husband's diplomatic appointment and her own abundant cleverness and vivacity, she shone in court circles wherever they went. The rivalry between the English and Germans at court in England was sharper here, for the Hanoverian ladies resented the fact that since Lady Mary's arrival the King had taken little notice of them, not even of Madame Kielmansegge; the English rejoiced that he preferred one of them to his own countrywomen. Hervey must certainly have known Lady Mary in London, where they frequented the court circle, particularly since she was a friend of his mother, whom she later favoured with virtuoso letters from Turkey. Since the English clung together at Hanover, Hervey could witness and enjoy his countrywoman's social success.

What was Lord Bristol's purpose in directing his son to Hanover? Not to win any patronage from the King: that could be attempted more easily and at more leisure in London. When the Elector had gone to London accompanied by the Prince of Wales, he had left behind his young grandson, Prince Frederick, as his representative, with a full court retinue to sustain his dignity. The princeling, nine years old when Hervey met him, was an agreeable-looking boy, with the light blond hair of his mother. He was surprisingly quick and polite in conversation, and seemed to have an abundance of wit and good sense far beyond his years.

Hervey had been sent to Hanover simply to ingratiate himself with the Prince. As his father put it: 'when you see and are sure ye foundation in Prince Frederick's favour . . . is laid as indelibly as you know I woud have it, and I know you are capable of con-triveing, you may think of returning homewards.' As the heir presumptive the Prince would control future patronage rich beyond the dreams of the most avaricious place-hunter, yet even as a child he was a source of patronage. His mother, in England with the Prince of Wales, was fully aware of this, for at this time, when she was pleased with Lord Rochester's six-year-old son, she told the child he should be Groom of the Stole to her son when he came over to England. But it was many years before Prince Frederick was permitted to join his family, not until his grand-father's death in 1727 put him next in succession to the throne. His later friendship with Hervey, complex and curious as it was, thus had its beginnings at the Electoral court.

Lord Bristol was remarkably optimistic in his expectations that the King would reward his family. Although he had been neglec-ted since receiving his earldom, he hoped that some small tokens of beneficent royal favour might fall on his son whatever the reason they had been kept from him. (It is odd that he overlooked the simple explanation for his disfavour: his opposition to the Sept-ennial Bill.) Through Lady Bristol he suggested that the King should promise Hervey the first guidon's post—as junior officer in a troop of cavalry—or a company in the guards that came vacant. Lady Bristol, on her side, when promised some influence by a lady at court—probably one of the King's mistresses—generously asked that it be used on her son's behalf.

Since Hervey's main objective in Hanover had been accom-plished and the King was about to return to England, he naturally assumed that he could continue his Grand Tour, begun only six months before, and travel to Italy. But, as his father regretfully announced, his 'Mama's tears & fears are both so very predominant whenever Italy is but mentiond, that rather than put my self into ye uneasy scituation of standing answerable for all accidents that may happen in such an expedition, I am forcd not only to sacri-fice my own judgment but your improvement to her foolish fondness.' Again, as with his riding in the Newmarket race, his mother's foolish anxiety interfered with his own fond wishes. He was therefore instructed to return to England with the King and his party. And so, smarting from the disappointment of having to cross the English Channel instead of the Italian Alps, he was reunited with his family. In the diary entry for Saturday, 19 January 1717, his father did not forget his recent errand: 'ye King arrived at London from Hannover. My son Jack came over with his Majesty from thence.'

iv

When Jack Hervey returned to London his parents and brothers and sisters were at Ickworth. So eager was he to see them that he rode up to Hockerill the next day to meet them on their way to London; and they all then returned to St. James's Square.

Although he would not come of age until his twenty-first birthday in October, his father put him on an allowance of £200 a year in February, and paid such expenses as those for his fencing lessons, which he continued to take. His father, he later remarked, had an 'ungiving temper', but Bristol's frequent generosity to him showed that he could overcome it. In March his father paid him almost £1,000 due to him as heir to his grandfather Felton's estate, and a week later conveyed some properties to him. Since he still lived at home he had ample spending money. But because of his reckless gambling at cards (basset) he piled up a debt of fifty guineas to one Jack Bannister. Lord Bristol agreed to pay it on condition that he make a 'most solemn promise' that as long as he lived he would never again punt at basset—that is, would not put up any stakes against the bank. He could thus continue to play that popular game, though more cautiously.

During the summer he was removed from such temptations when he accompanied his parents on their customary visits to Ickworth and Aswarby. After returning to Suffolk they were visited by Sir Samuel Garth, the physician, wit, and poet, who had been an undergraduate in Cambridge at the same time as Lord Bristol. A zealous Whig, generally regarded as one of the best-natured men in the world, he was a welcome visitor. He stayed first at the Bristol house in Bury, and from there was taken out to Ickworth, which he admired so much that he promised to celebrate it in a poem if he ever wrote any more verse. (Two years before he had thus honoured the Duke of Newcastle's estate, Claremont.) Before he left, he accompanied the family to the fair at Bury, where his cheerful company made it seem full of wit and gallantry.

Even in his country retirement Lord Bristol could not forget his family concerns, which extended beyond the careers of his first two sons. His family had by now grown to five sons (besides Carr and Jack) and five daughters. Thomas, aged eighteen, was enrolled at Christ Church, Oxford, in April 1717; and William, his brother born the same year, began his naval career that summer on a man-of-war bound for the West Indies and Mexico. After Thomas was joined at Oxford by his brother Henry, who was two years younger, Lord Bristol lectured them on their poor

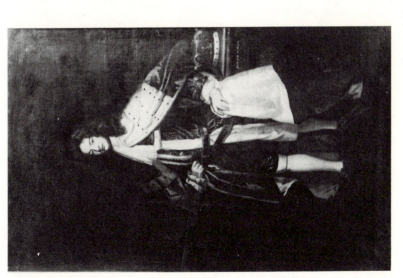

3. Earl and Countess of Bristol

work there, and tried to incite them to diligence by asking Carr
to threaten Henry that unless he had 'a good stock of learning' he
would never recommend him to an appointment at court. The
family took for granted that their future prosperity lay there.

Exactly how they could advance themselves at court was now
complicated by the quarrel in the Royal Family. Even before
coming to England the King had been on poor terms with his
son, and he had further antagonized him when he left to visit
Hanover, for instead of appointing him as his Regent he merely
named him Guardian of the Realm and Lieutenant, grandiloquent
titles with carefully circumscribed power. The King on his side
had been irritated by reports reaching him in Hanover that his
son was winning noticeable popularity with his English subjects.
Decorum was still observed, however, and on his return to
England the King had been met at Blackheath by his son, whom
he received with open arms and took into his own coach to ride
to St. James's Palace. The division between father and son was
paralleled in the political scene, when a schism among the Whigs
resulted from the King's dismissal of Lord Townshend in April
1717. Walpole, his brother-in-law, immediately resigned (with
others) to form an Opposition that centred on the Prince of
Wales. By June it was reported in a newspaper that the Prince,
who with his family still lived at St. James's Palace and at
Hampton Court, was looking for a house.

But the open rupture between the two courts came in November, after the Princess gave birth to a son. At the infant's christening
the Duke of Newcastle stood godfather at the desire of the King
but against that of the Prince of Wales, who voiced his displeasure
with some harsh words. Misunderstanding him, the nervous and
fidgety Newcastle told the King that his life had been threatened.
The King was indignant; he put his son under house arrest,
and a few days later expelled him from the palace.

The Royal quarrel was the scandal of Europe. The King's
secretary informed all the foreign courts so that in London
the ambassadors as well as the King's Ministers and members of
his household were forbidden to visit his son. In January 1718 the
Prince moved into Leicester House, and in May took over Richmond Lodge as his summer residence. Before the quarrel the King
had been content to live modestly and retiringly, mainly in the
company of his familiar Hanoverian attendants. By contrast the

court of his son and Caroline, Princess of Wales—a flaxen-haired German beauty of ample figure—had seemed the centre of wit and gaiety. Although the Prince was very conscious of his rank, a proud, unbending man, his clever wife, whom the King called 'cette diablesse madame la princesse', favoured English attendants, spoke the language easily, and piqued herself on intellectual interests. She enjoyed the informal company of witty, learned, and fashionable men and women. After the breach the King livened up his court by keeping a public table for dining, and by holding regular Drawing-Rooms and frequent balls. In contrast the Prince of Wales's court now seemed only second-rate.

Which of the rival courts would the Herveys frequent? They preferred to lend their loyalty to that of the Prince; he had rewarded them most recently with Carr's appointment. Like others who shared their allegiance they could not have over-looked the simple fact that the King was fifty-eight years old, and that his heir was in excellent health. Their loyalty was soon rewarded. At the beginning of 1718, four of the Princess's Ladies of the Bedchamber resigned, presumably because of the breach between the courts. Although the King considered asking Parliament for the right to control the Prince's household, that privilege, granted by letters patent, was inalienable. Lady Bristol, who had begun her campaign for the post more than three years before, was finally appointed to one of the vacant places, as her husband noted with great satisfaction in his diary under the date of 31 March 1718. Her salary was £500 a year, and she was to serve the Princess in close attendance at court for a period of up to a month at a time when she was 'in waiting'. Beyond the prestige and salary, her proximity to the future Queen Consort held out rich potential rewards, and so in spite of recurring spells of ill health she clung to her post, enduring its arduous duties and close confinement until it was terminated by the Queen's death twenty years later.

Although she and her husband continually complained to each other of their cruel separation, Lady Bristol loved the bustle and intrigue that surrounded the Royal Family as much as her husband loved the rural peace of Ickworth. When separated they exchanged letters as though they were still young lovers. He called her his Goddess and himself her idolizer, her 'insatiable lover and faithfulest of frinds'. His sentiment could sink to bathos: 'The poor mare you sent back with her shoulder out of its place,' he assured her, 'could not feel half ye pain I did in parting with thee.'

Still, he was far from resenting the cause of his painful separation—the Prince of Wales's favour. He sent him a horse as a gift, which (Lady Bristol reported) charmed His Highness. From Ickworth Park he sent seven fawns (one died *en route*) which pleased the Prince so much that he fed them with his own hand, and displayed them to the Princess and her attendants. Lord Bristol had even reserved his favourite racehorse Union for Prince Frederick, though the princeling remained in Hanover.

Now that Lady Bristol had won a court appointment her husband could not enjoy her company during the leisurely summers at Ickworth. After they arrived there (on 8 July), accompanied by Jack, she could stay only eleven days before returning to London to prepare for her duties at Richmond. Sir John Vanbrugh was then at Ickworth, having been invited again by Bristol to choose a site for a new mansion. His earlier plan to rebuild Ickworth Hall in 1703 had come to nought; now he seemed to be in earnest. The materials were already there—wood, brick, and stone, salvaged from the ruined old house. But the new mansion was never built. Visitors later noticed the heaps of building stone that remained in view. One of them in 1731 admired the park as the finest by far that he had ever seen, with large trees (worth £25,000) 'all truly magnificent and agreeable'; but he was astonished that such a large family could live in the small, tenant's house. Exactly why Lord Bristol never built his mansion is not known; perhaps, as gossip reported, he had suffered an unlucky run at gambling. Still, he was in an optimistic mood as he said farewell on the same day to Vanbrugh, who presented him with some architectural plans, to his wife, who was about to return to court, and to Jack, who accompanied her and who might profit in one way or another by being with her.

For Lady Bristol it was a 'dismal journey' although Jack did all he could to divert her. A week later, suffering from terrible rheumatism, she took to her bed. During her illness Jack, who was sharing Carr's lodgings in Richmond, sat by her at breakfast, and both brothers dined and supped with her. While writing to her husband she dropped her pen, too faint to finish the letter, and Jack took it up to tell his father that the doctor had spent the

night at her bedside, and that both the Prince and Princess had
been very kind to her. Mrs. Howard, Woman of the Bedchamber to the Princess, had even offered to sit up with her all
night.

A week later, by which time Lady Bristol had recovered, she
was joined by her husband and one of their daughters. Because
of her poor health the family changed their routine of staying at
Ickworth and Aswarby for the summer; instead, accompanied by
Jack, they set out for Bath (on 6 August) in the hope that the
waters would relieve her rheumatism. They stayed there for
more than two months, enjoying the varied social life of the
fashionable spa.

v

The following winter, while the King and the Prince of Wales
remained unreconciled, their breach was widened by the Peerage
Bill, which was brought in by the Ministry in February 1719.
Its object was to prevent the Prince, when he came to the throne
as George II, from creating any new peers to enable him to fill the
House of Lords with a majority who could outvote the supporters
of Sunderland's administration. Lord Bristol, who supported the
Prince, took great interest in the debates on the bill, attending
eleven of the twelve sittings in the House of Lords until, in mid-
April, it was put off to the next session. (It was then passed by the
Lords but decisively defeated in the House of Commons, where,
predictably, Carr Hervey voted against it.) Then the King, after
having again refused to appoint his son Regent in his absence, sailed
off to his beloved Hanover.

The Hervey family went to their own customary summer
retirement for the season, Hervey accompanying his parents
(in mid-June) to 'sweet Ickworth', as Lord Bristol habitually
called it. Lady Bristol could remain only a fortnight before
returning to her court duties at Richmond. To cheer his father's
spirits after she left, Hervey exploited his literary talent with
a 'ludicrous composition of his own' (his father writes) 'supposd
to be an amourous epistle from Clack to Squire on their separation'. (Squire was a woman servant at Ickworth whose gallant
was named Roger Clackstone; and their separation was evidently
a satirical parallel to that of the Bristols.) It was an excellent

composition, in Lord Bristol's opinion, and he offered to send it to his wife if mirth were scarce at Court. In reply she asked for it, thinking it to be verse, and Bristol sent it, pointing out that it was 'in prose but nevertheless entertaining'. By now Hervey had shown an alarming zest for writing verse. This worried his father, who feared that his constant rhyming would stand in the way of his advancement in the world.

His health, which had been robust during his adolescence, now worried his parents. He suffered from eye-trouble, and for a while wore a silk patch over one eye. What he called a 'humour' (watering) afflicted him if he caught cold, rode in the dust, or indulged in too much reading or writing by candlelight. In later years, after he had run 'the gauntlet through the hands of all the famous oculists, doctors, and surgeons in England' he discovered a simple cure in an eye-water sold by an old woman in Brentford; and henceforth he used it to prevent his eye disorder.

His quiet summer at Ickworth was occasionally enlivened by visits to nearby towns in Suffolk. In August he accompanied his parents on a three-day visit to Ipswich, where they attended a public assembly of almost two hundred gentlemen and ladies, passing the afternoon in conversation, gallantry, news-mongering, and card-playing. He then returned to London with his mother at the end of the summer. Lord Bristol—writing 'From forsaken Ickworth'—lamented that he was doubly deserted because Jack had announced his resolution of not returning for the rest of the year. He preferred to stay with his mother at Richmond and in London for the sake of what Bristol called the 'pompous elegant pleasures of a Court'.

His future career—he was already twenty-three years old—still needed to be settled. What would it be? The Parliamentary seat for Bury, traditionally occupied by a Hervey, was already filled by Carr. A suggestion came from the Prince of Wales, who pointed out to Lady Bristol that by the death of an M.P. in Aldborough (Suffolk) that seat was now vacant, and that Lord Bristol and his kinsman Sir Thomas Hanmer should try to have Jack elected. (Hanmer, M.P. for the county of Suffolk and a leading Tory, had joined the Opposition centred in the Prince of Wales.) Speed was essential, Lady Bristol was warned, because a rival candidate had already gone down to Aldborough to electioneer, and Lord Strafford was putting forward a candidate of his own. A few days later she informed Bristol that their friend Richard Hill, retired statesman and diplomatist and a close friend of Hanmer's, had promised to write 'to lett him know how agreable it woud be to our Court to gitt Jack chose at Alborough'.

But Bristol tried to discourage the plan. The attempt would result in a loss of time and money, he pointed out realistically, unless Jack could 'resolve to take more proper pains for himself, not only to make interest to gett into Parliament but to make a more significant figure when he is in it than ye perpetual pursuit of poetry will enable him to do'. Yet he wanted to please his wife: 'since your heart is so sett upon it, I will try what Sir Thomas Hanmer can do for him.' In applying to Hanmer he confessed that his wife had 'nothing nearer her heart than to see her son Jack in Parliament'. In the meantime the Prince of Wales continually asked Lady Bristol if anything was being done to forward her son's election.

Lord Bristol now felt that the time had come to speak out plainly. Unless Jack was willing to leave London and go to Aldborough to make himself known there—the election was six weeks away—he would be defeated; 'he must be told there are but two waies of succeeding in making an interest, the one by down right bribery, (which I hope no child of mine will ever practise,) the other by his infusing into ye electors an oppinion of his ability and integrity.' Perhaps he ought to lay aside all thought of getting into Parliament, Bristol continued, 'till he can push his pretensions in ye upper house'. He evidently thought that Jack would be more successful winning a peerage in the future than an election at this time.

At least Bristol's plain speaking brought an unequivocal reply from his wife on Jack's behalf as well as her own: 'we both agree to give you no farther trouble about Alborough, for niether his purs nor (I hope) his principles will agree with it.' Satisfied as he was by their decision, Bristol could not resist sermonizing: Jack, whose eyes were again troubling him, had run counter to sense and common experience in preferring to live in London rather than Ickworth, where he could live gratis; and he ought to think of all this if he ever intended to incur the expense of standing for Parliament.

3

Husband, Lord, and M.P.

1720–5

ALTHOUGH HERVEY HAD FAILED to persuade his father (and himself) that he should stand for Parliament he had succeeded on another road to advancement, and that was his social success at court. He was lent a room at Richmond by Charles Selwyn, a Gentleman-Usher to the Princess of Wales, and whenever he wished he was permitted to borrow one of the Prince's coaches through the kindness of Lord Lumley, Master of the Horse. He was so admired at Richmond, his proud mother reported, that he was not permitted to return to London until the court moved there. When Richard Hill, who lived at Richmond, invited him to dine with the Speaker of the House of Commons (Sir Spencer Compton) and a large company he had to decline because he had already accepted an invitation from Mrs. Howard.

Henrietta Howard, who served as the Prince of Wales's mistress as well as the Princess's Woman of the Bedchamber, was the centre of the English circle at the Princess's court, where the English rather than Germans were favoured. She was noted for her discretion and gentility, and even pretended that the Prince's friendship for her (which, in fact, was a liaison of convenience rather than passion) was merely platonic. In contrast to her, the Princess was also attended by six Maids of Honour, who were young, pretty, and often giddy. In some naughty verse entitled *The Court Ballad*, Alexander Pope had paid equivocal tribute to their virtue—the Maids were presumed to be virgins—and sincere appreciation of their gaiety and high spirits.

The most conspicuous of these maids was Mary Lepell, a strikingly pretty girl, with a graceful petite figure and a bright alert face. She was the daughter of a Danish gentleman who had come to England as Groom of the Bedchamber to the consort of the future Queen Anne. He had then, after marrying Mary Brooke, a moderately rich Suffolk heiress, become naturalized as a British subject; and after entering the military service he rose to the rank of brigadier-general. Their daughter, born in 1700, was educated more thoroughly than most girls of her social class. She had read very widely, and although she understood Latin perfectly well, she wisely concealed it. Having passed all her life at courts, she had acquired all the manners of easy good breeding and politeness.

Molly Lepell, as she was called, had been appointed Maid of Honour at the remarkably early age of fifteen, a post more than honorary since it paid £200 a year. She evidently charmed everyone at court, where she bore the nickname of *Schatz* (treasure), a sign that the German contingent thought well of her too. The playwright Nicholas Rowe, who was twice her age, claimed to be in love with her, as everybody was, and composed some graceful verse about her irresistible charm:

> I counted o'er the long, long score
>   Of laughing Cloe's lovers;
> Which, sad to see! besides poor me,
>   Full forty-nine discovers.
> But Cupid cries, 'Her nimble eyes
>   Will quickly end your sorrow:
> Fifty a day, for that's her play,
>   She kills—you'll die tomorrow.'

If all this was mere persiflage, in a gracefully witty vein, Mary Lepell had been involved in a more serious kind of courtship in the spring of 1716 with Colonel Adolphus Oughton, former A.D.C. to Marlborough. He was regarded as 'the Compleatest Courtier of this time', and after the death of his rich wife two years earlier he was in litigation in an attempt to secure her wealth. His friends doubted that in his next 'amorous Campain' he would succeed so richly. But nothing came of his courtship of Mary Lepell, perhaps because she had no great fortune. That disadvantage did not, however, discourage another suitor.

Hervey must have known her at court, certainly after his mother had been appointed there. But their first recorded meeting was on 28 October 1719, when he and his mother dined at Lady Grizel Baillie's house. The others at table that afternoon were

Lady Grizel's daughter Griselda Murray, who lived with her parents, and Mary Lepell. After dinner the four ladies went off to Drury Lane, where Anne Oldfield was playing in *The Chances* (the play by Fletcher, altered by the Duke of Buckingham). Soon after, the friendship between the handsome Jack Hervey and the pretty Molly Lepell became the subject of comment. John Gay, welcoming Pope back from his Homeric labours early in 1720, shows the poet being greeted by his friends:

> Now Hervey, fair of face, I mark full well,
> With thee, youth's youngest daughter, sweet Lepell.

By this time Pope had known Molly Lepell for several years. His brilliance as a poet—he had already published the *Essay on Criticism*, *The Rape of the Lock*, and the *Iliad* translation—had given him an entrée into the circle of wits and courtiers at St. James's. The handicaps he suffered for his Roman Catholic religion, his poor health, and his crippled, stunted frame were overlooked because of his sensitive and ingratiating personality. At Hampton Court he romped with the Maids of Honour, of whom Miss Lepell seemed to be his favourite. He had walked alone with her in the garden one moonlit night for three or four hours. When she fell ill in March 1720, and hoped that country air would speed her recovery, she stayed at his house in Twickenham; and he attended her out of 'true friendship'. Not all her friends at Court had known of her illness. 'Pray give my service to Miss Lepell', one of them wrote to Mrs. Howard at the end of April, 'and tell her I am glad I did not hear of her illness until it was over. I believe it would have saved Mr. Harvey a great deal of pain if he could have been as ignorant of it.' It would have been difficult for Jack Hervey to be ignorant of it, for—as their friends did not yet know—Molly Lepell was his wife.

ii

On 21 April 1720 Lord Bristol recorded in his diary that his 'dear & hopeful son Mr. John Hervey was marryed to Mrs. Mary Le Pell'. With characteristic warmth and courtesy he assured his 'dear daughter' that he was thoroughly pleased to be able to call her by that endearing name. 'My son has shewn ye nicest skill in choosing you,' he assured her, 'since in you alone he could securely promise himself not only every quality essential to his own happiness, but has also made a wise provision to intaile good sense & virtue (its constant concomitant) on our (now) flourishing family'. He reinforced his benevolent sentiments with an invitation to the couple to make their home with him.

Although he approved of the marriage at the time it took place, Lord Bristol later (1733) declared that one of the 'greatest griefs' of his life was that Jack had married a woman who lacked a considerable fortune as dowry. He firmly believed that all his sons should marry 'worthy, wealthy' women, as had been his own practice. With all 'those advantages of person, wit & beauty' that Hervey possessed, Bristol thought, he should have made a match with a great heiress instead of one so modestly endowed. (Two years earlier a newspaper had mistakenly announced his imminent marriage to a daughter of the Duke of Rutland; such a match would have pleased Lord Bristol.) Mary Lepell did, in fact, have a dowry, though a small one, and Hervey refused to make use of it, perhaps because it was entailed on their children.

Hervey himself could not have been unaware that his marriage was financially imprudent. Why, then, had he married Mary Lepell? His general philosophy of matrimony was that a man must choose whether to marry for power and grandeur, or for beauty and an agreeable person—that is, for convenience or for love. His own choice proves that he married Mary Lepell simply because he loved her.

For six months they kept their marriage a secret; as late as August their friends still called Mrs. Hervey by her maiden name. Why the match was kept a secret can only be surmised. It was sanctioned by both families; and although decorum demanded that a Maid of Honour ask permission of her Royal Mistress before marrying, the Princess of Wales would have no reason for withholding it. But then Mary Lepell would have had to resign her court appointment, which she had held for five years. By waiting until October to announce her marriage and her resignation she was paid for two additional quarters. Presumably she could not live openly with her husband during those months, and so she remained with the other Maids of Honour at court when on duty or with her mother in their house on Great Marlborough Street.

The marriage of Lord Bristol's eldest son and heir was a graver matter. Still a bachelor at twenty-nine, Carr had promised his

father that if a bride could be found wealthy enough to build
a mansion at Ickworth and to increase the family estate he would
marry. In February 1720 Bristol had found such an heiress—the
only daughter of a gentleman worth £7,000 a year—only to have
the match rejected by Carr. Bristol did not hide his disappointment, for he feared that unless his family fortune were enriched
by his heir's marriage he would not be able to make suitable
provisions for his numerous younger children.

A further trial of Lord Bristol's patience with his two eldest
sons came from their speculation in South Sea stock. The passing
of the South Sea Act (in April 1720) had started a wave of infla-
tion that soon doubled the value of stock that had sold for £126
at the beginning of the year; and each new subscription was
eagerly bought up as soon as issued. The speculative fever became
universal. That summer Carr sold Aswarby, his estate in Lincolnshire, against his father's advice, and invested the capital in South
Sea stock, boasting to Lady Bristol of the great riches he would
acquire. In August, when the stock and the fever were at their
height, nothing else was talked of at Court. Everybody bought
stock, even Lady Bristol and her daughter Elizabeth. Hervey
planned to borrow five or six thousand pounds (at ten per cent
interest) in order to buy into the next subscription, but his father,
who disapproved of his speculation, bound himself to raise the
money rather than to let him pay such extortionate interest.
Before the last subscription opened (on 22 August), both Carr
and Hervey were greatly in debt. Then the bubble burst, and the
stock plummeted—from a high of £900 to £240 (in October).
The ensuing panic shook the Government to such an extent that
the King hastily returned from Hanover to try to restore calm.

Hervey was able to survive the disaster. By some means, probably by selling out just before the crash, he cleared for himself the
great sum of £20,000; and he promised his father he would keep
it intact and not break into it for any gambling. By the beginning
of October he had gone to Bath to drink the waters and gloat over
his gains. His wife—still regarded by the world as Mary Lepell, a
virgin Maid of Honour—was in Bath at the same time, secure in
the knowledge, her father-in-law thought, that her husband
loved her beyond himself.

A few weeks later, on 25 October, their marriage was announced
in London. They took a small house on Bond Street, which

Hervey later referred to disparagingly as a 'deal-box'. Lord Bristol gave him £315 to buy 'silver plates & dishes when he went to Housekeeping'. The young couple could now live together openly as man and wife. They were such an elegant pair that their union was celebrated by versifiers:

> Bright Venus yet never saw bedded,
>   So perfect a beau and a belle,
> As when Hervey the handsome was wedded,
>   To the beautiful Molly L[epel]l.

iii

During the early years of their marriage the Herveys busily went about together paying calls on their friends. Lady Mary Wortley Montagu, in a dour mood, complained to her sister in Paris of the 'ardent affection that Mrs. Hervey and her dear spouse took to me. They visited me twice or thrice a day, and were perpetually cooing in my rooms.' At first Lady Mary was complaisant but then grew weary of these 'Birds of Paradise' and fled to Twickenham as much to avoid their persecution as to save her own health.

The hoop-skirt worn by a fashionable lady could hide, as it did from the sharp-eyed Lady Mary, one detail of Mrs. Hervey's appearance that she would have mentioned along with the other gossip. For only a few weeks later—on 3 August 1721—Mrs. Hervey gave birth to a son. Although both Lord Bristol and his wife were then in London they did not wait for the christening; five days later Lady Bristol left for Bath, and he, feeling 'so very disconsolate without her', left for Ickworth the next day. The names chosen for the infant were George William, and his godparents were the King, the Princess of Wales, and Lord Bristol. (The breach between the two courts had been healed the previous year when the King and his stubborn son were reconciled.) As customary, the King and the Princess would be represented by proxies; and Hervey urged his father to be there in person. But encouraged by his wife, Bristol refused to make the journey back to London, and begged to be excused. Rather grandly, he thought a proxy should be as acceptable for himself as the Lord and Lady of the Bedchamber were for the Royal sponsors.

Although not present at the christening of his first grandchild, who was his heir presumptive, Lord Bristol asked Hervey to reward the nurses with ten guineas, which he later repaid; and he undertook to pay all the expenses of the boy's education—for schools, tutoring, and travel abroad. Lady Bristol was attentive, though from afar. Worried by reports that London was 'very sickly' she urged Hervey to move to Ickworth with his family; he sent word, however, that since his wife was recovering her health very slowly they could not think of a journey as yet. They could make shorter journeys, for after sending their child to Ickworth with a nurse, they went off to visit William Pulteney, who had rented Ashley Park, Lord Shannon's house at Walton-on-Thames.

Pulteney, twelve years older than Hervey, was already a political figure with an impressive past and a promising future. A graduate of Westminster School, Christ Church (Oxford), and the Grand Tour, he had been elected to Parliament when he was only twenty-one, and remained a conspicuously steadfast Whig during the Tory ascendency of Queen Anne's later years. He was still, at this time, politically allied with Robert Walpole. His enemies accused him of avarice, a fault not lessened by his enormous wealth (his London property alone brought him £10,000 a year); and he had become even richer by his marriage to a great heiress, in 1714, who was besides a great beauty. At the time of his visit Hervey was charmed by the 'lively ready wit' of Pulteney, whom he regarded as a man of parts, and by Mrs. Pulteney's beauty and informality.

By the middle of September, his wife having recovered all her strength, Hervey prepared to journey to Ickworth with her. Although they were 'so mad and unadvisd' as to plan to travel there in one day they were prevented 'by the greater prudence' of Lord Bristol. They arrived on the 20th to find their son flourishing. Bristol could boast that 'Little George is so well and thriven since he came, that that epithet will not long suite him'.

The health of the male infant Hervey was all the more precious as that of his uncle Carr became poorer. While the family were in London (in January 1722), enjoying the social season, Carr remained at Ickworth recovering from a severe illness. In letters signed 'Your most affectionate Brother', Hervey tried to amuse him with witty gossip. The London physicians had not had much luck lately, he remarks in one letter; the old Duke of Bolton had 'made his Exit in a most extraordinary manner . . . he dy'd of an Ulcer in his Bowels occasion'd by a dose of Cantharides which he took in order to metamorphose threescore into five & twenty for the Use of Mrs. —'. (The Duke—described by Hearne the antiquary as 'a most lewd, vicious Man'—actually died of pleurisy.) His death had inspired two ribald epitaphs that Hervey copied out for his brother's amusement.

> Lett this be say'd to his Praise,
>   Tho Fate from the World has tore him;
> He dy'd in endeavouring to raise
>   A Friend that lay dead before him.

The other was briefer:

> Beneath this Stone his Grace's Body lyes,
> Tis now a Prey to Worms it was to Flys.

He also sent along some verse that he said was claimed by Lady Mary Wortley Montagu, and that he found as incomprehensible as herself. He could easily pick up the ephemeral verse that circulated in manuscript in the court and social circles he frequented, where making verse (Lady Mary said) was almost as common as taking snuff.

Although neither Hervey nor his wife held any appointment at court they continued to frequent it, especially when Lady Bristol was serving her period of waiting. At the beginning of June, when she was at Richmond, Hervey urged her to dine at Mrs. Pulteney's, where he was a familiar guest. By the end of the month Lady Bristol was re-united with her doting husband at Ickworth. Her cynical friends in London had their doubts as to the sincerity of her connubial devotion. Lady Mary, for example, observed that she had left off card-playing and grown 'Young, blooming, Coquette and Galante'; and to make up for time mis-spent she was credited with having two lovers—'the greatest compliment in Nature to her own Lord, since tis plain that when she will be false to him, she is forc'd to take 2 men in his stead, and that no one Mortal has merit enough to make up for him.' Lord Bristol would not have felt flattered—or amused.

Since Lord Bristol's spacious house in St. James's Square was unoccupied, Hervey and his wife moved into it. He enjoyed London too much to rusticate himself at Ickworth, though he protested to his mother that he was not staying in town because of its pleasures, only two of which he could name: one of them the assemblies given by M. Fabrice, the King's confidential secretary, and the other the excursions on the river: 'to doe the fish justice,' he continues, 'I swear I think the Thames better inhabited than its Shores. Those that love an angle or nett may find very pretty Company amongst the water-Brutes but there's no tast can be gratify'd amongst the Land-ones.' He promised his mother to leave London on 8 July, the day after he finished some 'little busyness' he had there.

At Ickworth he and his wife went on excursions with Lord and Lady Bristol—to Ipswich and afterwards to see Lady Bristol's estates in that neighbourhood. Then, after a fortnight, when Lady Bristol had to leave for Richmond to go into waiting, he tried to cheer his disconsolate father by showing (in his father's opinion) 'all the treasures of his compositions in verse and prose . . . both most ingenious'.

Because of his delicate health he worried his father by his carelessness, driving in an open chaise and without an overcoat when a cold easterly wind was blowing. He ran a high fever that at first subsided, and then he became so seriously ill that he was confined to his room for all of September, attended by the doctor at least once a day. Then, having suddenly 'mended to a miracle', he was put on a regimen of ass's milk and Pyrmont water (from the German spa); and in the mild weather he was able to go out again in the coach or on horseback. His father was touchingly solicitous. One day when Jack wished to drive his wife and son about the park and was already in the coach, his father noticed that he was not wearing a coat, and made him climb down to put one on. It was only another sign of the love and attention that his father lavished on him.

iv

It was a cause of serious concern to Lord Bristol that the Hervey-controlled seat for Bury had been lost by Carr in the election of March 1722. A new opportunity arose in October with the death of Sir Robert Davers, who sat for the county seat. A by-election would soon be held. Everybody at court advised Lady Bristol that Carr should be put forward as a candidate, but Bristol would not hear of it. Had not Carr lost the seat for Bury because of his negligence? Carr himself believed that he would soon be raised to the House of Lords, and strongly advised that Jack Hervey should stand for the county seat; he even promised to go down to assist him in the election. So sanguine was he, in fact, that he even suggested that should his petition challenging the Bury election be upheld and the incumbent ousted, their next brother, Thomas, could have that seat since Jack would have been elected for the county.

This was the second time that Jack had been put forward, and again Lord Bristol patiently and firmly discouraged the suggestion. He was too little known outside of the immediate vicinity of Bury to run for the county seat; his health, especially since his recent illness, was too delicate to allow him to go about drinking with country gentlemen and shifting his lodgings often; and (finally) he lacked the necessary qualification of owning land worth £600 a year, and Bristol could not arrange this in so short a time. As in her earlier campaign Lady Bristol failed to persuade her husband. Carr's petition to unseat the Member for Bury for bribery and corruption, filed in the House of Commons on 25 October, was defeated; and on the 31st the county elected Sir William Barker as M.P. No member of the Hervey family now sat in the House.

In the meantime Hervey and his wife enjoyed the healthful Suffolk air and his father's company. Lord Bristol told his wife (on 10 October) that Hervey said nothing of when he and his wife would leave Ickworth. That was odd, she replied, for they had written to Alexander Pope to expect them on the 13th; and she added tartly: 'I have not had the honour to hear from either since I left them.' They finally left, on 18 October, accompanied by Lord Bristol.

Self-interest was the reason that Bristol left his beloved Ickworth for loathsome London, for Lady Bristol and Carr had passed on reports that the Ministry planned to make overtures to him; as Lady Bristol phrased it, 'you seem to be at present the mistress they intend to pursue'. He coyly assured her that he would withstand all allurements unless they came from true lovers of the country. Lady Bristol had prudently marshalled other reasons why he should come to London—to demonstrate his zeal for the Protestant succession and to assist Carr's petition on the Bury election.

Soon after he reached London, Lord Bristol was received in private audience by the King on 26 October 1722, when he assured

His Majesty (in French) that he would demonstrate sincere fidelity all his life. 'Particularly in the present juncture', a phrase he used, indicates what had impelled his declaration—the Jacobite conspiracy for restoring the Stuarts to the English throne. Its central figure, Bishop Atterbury, had been arrested in August, and other suspects were later rounded up. In the trial of one of them in the House of Lords, Bristol spoke (on 23 January 1723), but the articles of impeachment against Atterbury himself, sent from the House of Commons, did not reach the Lords until 9 April. Impatient to return to Ickworth, Bristol departed a few days later, taking all his children with him, while Lady Bristol went to Bath. She urged him to return to attend the House of Lords, where Atterbury was to plead his case on 6 May, but he refused with the modest excuse that the 'Publick cannot want the attendance of such a cypher as I am'. His vote was not necessary, after all; Atterbury was found guilty by a large majority, and deprived of his offices and exiled for ever. In Bristol's absence Hervey served him as political correspondent, sending reports that Bristol praised 'as full as clear yet succinct an account of the B[ishop]'s tryal, together with the passages in the other House relating to the Papists Bill, as, had I been present, I could not have understood them better'. This would prove to be valuable experience for Hervey's own Parliamentary career—when, if ever, he would have one.

Leaving London as he did, Bristol also missed by only a few days the birth of his second grandchild, a girl, who was born on 15 April. She was an exceptionally pretty infant, with very dark eyes and a dimple. At first she was ill, but soon Hervey was able to make his father easy with news that 'the black-eyed girl' was again well.

The arrangements for the infant's christening caused a tiff between the parents and Lady Bristol, who was predisposed to quarrel with them. During the child's illness she had offered some advice to Jack, 'but wether that any more then any other from me will be taken I cannot tell', she complained to her husband. She was to be a godmother to the child, and since she would be in Bath when the christening took place in London she had to choose a proxy; yet, she pointed out, she had not been told who the other godparents would be or what name the child would be given. The parents had suggested Lepell, the mother's family name, to which Lady Bristol had irritably replied that in that case the Lepell grandmother should stand instead of herself. Finally, with Lord Bristol attempting to soothe his wife's hurt feelings, the christening took place; the godfather was William Pulteney, and the godmothers were Lady Bristol, represented by a proxy, and Mrs. Hervey's grandmother.

Poor Lord Bristol tried to be fair to both parties in the dispute, quoting to his wife the maxim that 'quarrels would seldom last long, were there not some small faults on both sides'. Aside from family amity, he pointed out, the breach was a disadvantage to Lady Bristol at court since it would prevent her from receiving valuable advice on questions of etiquette that Mrs. Hervey knew from her experience as a Maid of Honour.

One specific point of etiquette that Lady Bristol needed to know concerned her son Felton, aged twelve at the time, who had been appointed page to the Princess of Wales. He had been ill of smallpox in February; and since his face had not completely healed by May, shortly before he was to go into waiting, was he fit to appear before the Princess? Apparently he was, and so he took up the appointment. After several months, however, he incurred the displeasure of his Royal Mistress—because he had been spoiled by those around her—and this put him into such a deep melancholy that he had to resign. (Lord Bristol's other sons were less troublesome and more easily settled—Henry in the army and William in the navy.)

Jack Hervey and his wife continued to attend court, and they were always welcome. In June they accompanied the Prince and Princess of Wales to Richmond. A month later they visited the Pulteneys at Ashley Park, and then travelled into Oxfordshire to pass the remainder of the summer at Lord Cadogan's seat there. In the garden near the house stood a gilt statue of a nymph; and to amuse the company Hervey improvised some verse that he entitled 'The Statue Speaks to my Lord', neat and witty couplets that drew a parallel between a fashionable London belle and the glittering nymph, and concludes with advice to my Lord:

> Gild her but well, you may with ease
> Carry her naked where you please.

Toward the end of the summer Hervey suffered a recurrent attack of his stomach disorder. He consulted Dr. Arbuthnot, who advised him to take the Bath waters. He then asked his father whether to go to Ickworth or Bath. Lord Bristol, believing that Bath would benefit him more, suggested to Lady Bristol that she invite Hervey and his wife to lodge in the same house where she lived so that they would not need to maintain their own table, but in spite of her invitation Hervey preferred to lodge at Ickworth and share his father's table. He could enjoy his father's company only for a short time, for Bristol hastened to Bath—'that Bedlam', he called it—rather than endure his wife's absence any longer.

Carr, his eldest son, was also in Bath at that time, struggling to recover his health. He had been a great disappointment to his father because of his refusal to marry and his rashness in selling Aswarby to invest in the ruinous South Sea Bubble. He was, in Lady Bristol's judgement, 'utterly ruind both in reputation and fortune'. Ten days after his father had left Bath, Carr died (on 14 November 1723). His courtesy title, along with his right to inherit the earldom of Bristol, passed to John Hervey.

v

The new Lord Hervey soon saw his future brightened by a proposal of his father's. One of the Parliamentary seats for Bury St. Edmunds was held by James Reynolds, a sergeant-at-law. Since at this time there was a vacant place on the King's Bench, Lord Bristol proposed to Reynolds that he would do all he could to help him procure the judgeship (which would then promote him into the House of Lords) if Reynolds would help elect Lord Hervey to the House of Commons in his place. Ordinarily Bristol assumed a very virtuous posture in such matters. When his son William asked him to procure a better rank than a naval lieutenancy, he refused; neither his honour nor conscience would ever allow him to trade in them for himself or for others, even one 'so near or dear' as one of his sons. He was willing to make an exception for the sake of his dearest son and heir. Far from being reluctant or discouraged the third time that he was teased with the possibility of becoming an M.P., Hervey was hopeful. But the affair moved very slowly, and for the time being Reynolds remained without a place on the bench and Hervey without a seat in the Commons.

Lord Hervey's health was still cause for anxiety, and in the off-season quiet of the spring he had gone to Bath to recover his strength. Some doggerel verse written by Lady Mary in April 1724 contains the gossip that 'Lady Hervey [is] with child, and her Husband is dying'. While he was still away Lady Hervey gave birth to a son, their second, on 19 May; and a month later, by which time the father was again in London, the child was christened Augustus John. This time there was no complication in the choice of godparents, who were the Prince of Wales, Lord Godolphin, and Hervey's favourite sister Elizabeth, who a fortnight earlier had been married to Bussy Mansel, a Welsh M.P. and politician.

Perhaps because of his increasing family Hervey asked his father for an additional annuity, but his father patiently replied (in July) that his own income had fallen by £1,000 a year, that he bore the expense of educating many children, including Hervey's, and that if he sold off any more land he would not be able to retain the dignity of his earldom. (Lord Hervey could not be impervious to the last reason.) Bristol suggested, instead, that he economize by living without expense at Ickworth with his family and servants. Hervey evidently did not even have a coach of his own at this time; when he and Lady Hervey went off to visit Lord Berkeley they borrowed Lord Bristol's. After completing that visit Hervey left his wife behind in London and accompanied his parents with some of their family to 'sweet Ickworth'. After his visit there, he was joined by Lady Hervey for a sojourn at Bath.

On his previous visits to that spa during its season Hervey had accompanied his father, who had no doubt supervised his activities; now that he was his own master, and accompanied by his wife, he could enjoy its life more freely. If a visitor arrived with a set of horses—a sign of affluence or prominence—bells were rung and the Master of Ceremonies, who at this time was the famous Beau Nash, called on him. Once installed in his lodgings the visitor went out for an early morning bath in the mineral waters, between six and nine o'clock, then to the Pump Room to drink the waters, listen to the band, and watch the bathers who had arisen late. Unless he ordered a public breakfast in the Assembly Rooms to entertain his fashionable friends, he would take his morning meal with other men at a coffee house or in his lodgings with his wife. A daily service was held in the Abbey at noon; it is unlikely that

4. Lord and Lady Hervey, 1723

Hervey attended it. The dinner hour was from two to three, after which he might return to the Pump Room or, if the weather was fine, walk about in order to look and be looked at. Tea was taken in the Assembly Rooms. The evening, if he wanted to enjoy all of its activities, could be filled with visiting, gambling, dancing at the ball (held every Tuesday and Friday), or attending the theatre. With this strenuous social regimen only the most robust of invalids could survive a convalescence there.

It was, of course, a great gossip-centre; and word reached Lady Bristol, who was in waiting at Richmond, that Hervey was in perfect health and had grown fat, and that he and his wife entertained extravagantly. This did not restrain him from participating in the gallantry that flourished there. For Lady Bristol heard that 'he is much taken up in pursuit of the same lady he began with in the spring, who they say is there in great beauty'. He was too busy, Lady Bristol comments sarcastically, 'for so unfashionable a thing as duty and affection to parents'. Lady Hervey was also in disfavour; Lady Bristol tells her husband that the young couple would probably visit Ickworth because London as well as their pockets would be empty. She varied her sarcasm a few days later; they would not stay at Ickworth long because in London the opera and Parliament would open together. How can her animosity be explained, this transformation of Lady Bristol from a doting, over-protective mother to a sarcastic, disapproving observer? The change took place after Hervey's marriage, and it must have been unreasoning jealousy on her part when she realized that in spite of the devotion and love she had lavished on her favourite son, she had been displaced by his young, pretty wife.

Lord Bristol, concerned at her increasing hostility sent her what he called a gentle 'sermon' advising her 'to forget and forgive every thing you think your son has been wrong towards you in'; and she in turn promised to control her 'sallys of human frailty', though she hoped at the same time Bristol would enforce what is due from children, 'for those to whom much is forgiven, of them shall much be required'.

Perhaps her heart softened a little at the news a few days later from her husband that Jack 'lay a dying with the cholick from 2 a clock yesterday morning till near noon', until a huge dose of laudanum and a glyster made him more comfortable. His illness prevented him from going to Bury St. Edmunds to entertain the corporation on the Prince of Wales's birthday (30 October); instead he went three weeks later. He and his father still coveted the Parliamentary seat held by Reynolds.

As his mother's contempt for him grew she found new fuel to feed it. He and his family left Ickworth with Lord Bristol (on 1 December) to return to London. Knowing that the coach could not hold all of them Lady Bristol was out of humour that her husband would even think of leaving behind their two daughters (Ann and Barbara, 17 and 15 at the time), whom she wanted in London. If Bristol chose to prefer his son's two children to her own, she firmly protested, 'it will shock me so that I shall hate the sight of them'. What could Bristol do? He effected a compromise: as his coach travelled up to London it was crowded with (besides himself) Lord and Lady Hervey, both their children, and only the elder of his daughters.

Lady Bristol could not have been placated. Her hostility toward her daughter-in-law was a conspicuous titbit of scandal among their friends. They quarrelled in public in February 1725, Lady Mary gossiped, and 'in such a polite manner that they have given one another all the Titles so liberally bestow'd amongst the Ladys at Billingsgate'. Lady Hervey, who had better control of her temper, found that 'vast civility, much coolness, and great distance' were not only 'the best preservatives, but the only acquirers' of her mother-in-law's good graces.

Lord Bristol's loyalty to his son had greater scope the following spring. More than a year had passed since he had opened negotiations with Sergeant Reynolds, M.P. for Bury St. Edmunds. When Reynolds's appointment to the bench was imminent in March 1725, Bristol energetically set about to prepare the way for his son. He sold some of his property in Lincolnshire to buy land in Suffolk for the requisite land-income. He wrote from London to the chief magistrate of Bury to convene his friends to declare Lord Hervey's candidacy, promising that as soon as Reynolds's warrant was signed he and his son would come to Bury; and he promised to pay all the expenses. He also wrote to the Revd. Robert Butts, who held the living at Ickworth church, asking him to rally their friends and win over their adversaries. In return he promised that Butts would be appointed one of the King's Chaplains by the Lord Chamberlain, the Duke of Grafton, who was a neighbour at Euston. (Butts was appointed three years later.)

When Bristol's coach left London bound for Ickworth and the nearby election at Bury, his wife would at least have approved of its list of passengers: Hervey, who after all had to go, was accompanied by neither wife nor children but by three sisters and a brother-in-law. Lady Hervey had preferred to stay in London, where she made the 'Top Figure in Town', Lady Mary reported, going twice a week to the Drawing Room and twice to the opera 'for the Entertainment of the Public'.

At Bury, Lord Bristol found that his friends were so faithful that he was likely to meet little if any opposition. The actual election, on 2 April, he described most vividly and feelingly to his wife:

My son was yesterday chosen Burgess for Bury in the most honourable manner, as his father and good grandfather had always been before him, having had the votes of every member of that substantial Corporation, to which choice the Town gave their universal approbation by lining every street and window between my house (from whence he was attended by all the gentlemen and clergy of Bury and its neighbourhood) and the Guild-hall, crying as we passd along with musick, drums and morrice dancers before us, 'A Hervey, a Hervey, long live & flourish that noble and honest family, etc.'

It was an auspicious opening for the public career of John, Lord Hervey, M.P.

4

Political and Romantic Attachments

1725–7

AFTER SPENDING AN AFTERNOON in Bury visiting and thanking the gentlemen who, true to the old tradition, had elected a Hervey, the new M.P. and his father returned to London. Since Parliament was then in session he could take his seat immediately, on the Whig side of the House. The most important measure before them was a petition filed on behalf of Lord Bolingbroke, who, having spent ten years abroad after his impeachment and attainder, had already been partially pardoned; he now petitioned for the restoration of his estates and his seat in the House of Lords. The King finally agreed to restore his estates, but not his seat, and Walpole reluctantly concurred; but several of the King's officers objected to his lenity. One of them, to show how complimentary his opposition was, declared that 'he loved the King better than he [the King] loved himself; and hated his Enemies more than he did'. The bill was passed by a large majority, and sent to the Upper House. Lord Bristol, who regarded himself as a true Whig, spoke against it with great force, and afterwards was one of the five lords who signed a violent protest against its passage on 25 May. His zeal for the Hanoverian line was matched by his hatred of Jacobites; Hervey felt, and presumably voted, the same way.

After Parliament rose at the end of May, Hervey and his wife travelled to Bath, somewhat earlier than the customary autumn season when the resort was crowded with fashionable folk. He had only recently read and been converted by a book temptingly called *Health and Long Life* written by Dr. George Cheyne, the learned and accomplished physician who lived in Bath; he found it so reasonable and so conformable to his own observations that he resolved to put himself entirely under Dr. Cheyne's care. He was advised to take the waters for six weeks and not to eat meat, and at the end of that time to go on a milk diet for two months. This regimen put an end to his dreadful attacks of colic, and he was forever grateful to the physician whom he called his Æsculapius.

Social activities and recreation, such an essential part of the cure at Bath, were not excluded. Hervey attended a Saturday breakfast where more than eighty guests ate and gossiped, and he played cards every night. Lady Hervey tried to amuse their friends at court by sending Mrs. Howard chatty letters. In one she describes the elderly military hero, Lord Peterborough, who wore his riding boots all day because, it was said, he had brought no shoes with him. 'It is a comical sight', she continues, 'to see him with his blue ribbon and star, and a cabbage under each arm, or a chicken in his hand, which, after he himself has purchased at market, he carries home for his dinner.' Mrs. Howard could not fail to be interested since she and Peterborough were then engaged in a romantic liaison carried on purely by letters.

Hervey and his wife stayed at Bath until the middle of July, when they returned to London, and from there paid short visits to friends—to the Prince and Princess of Wales at Richmond, and to Mrs. Howard at Marble Hill, her newly built villa in Twicken-ham. At the end of the month, after Hervey had made a brief visit to Ickworth, he was joined by his wife and four-year-old son for a visit to Pulteney at his 'very agreeable' house at Walton-on-Thames. One of his fellow guests was Dr. Arbuthnot, so that if he needed to, he could consult him about his health.

In London itself Hervey found amusing things to do, even during the summer doldrums, while the King was in Hanover and the Prince of Wales at Richmond. He attended Bartholomew Fair, which opened at Smithfield at the end of August for three days, and was frequented by persons of all classes. One could see goods set out for sale, freak shows, quack doctors, corn-cutters, tooth-drawers. The group of friends who accompanied him in-cluded Pulteney, the beautiful and spirited Duchess of Queens-berry, and the Prince of Wales with a contingent from Richmond. He told his mother about his excursion: 'as I happen to have so singular a Tast as not to be fond of rost Pigg, gilt Ginger-Bread, & having my Pocket pickt, I can't brag of having been extreamly entertain'd there.' He was sure she would agree.

His relations with his mother, which had been tense and unpleasant, had now entered a benign phase (of short duration). When he tried to amuse her by telling about his round of visits he apologized (with elaborate wit) for the dullness of his letter by protesting that he writes to her 'not as a Lady of the Bed-chamber but as a Mother, since I make my Applications entirely to your good-nature, a Quality I should no more expect to find in a Courtier than I should to fail of it in a Parent'. Lady Bristol was even, at this time, a fond grandparent, for she invited him to send his two eldest children to live with her. Grateful to her for her generosity he declined the invitation.

Since Lady Hervey was again pregnant, their 'deal-box' on Bond Street was too small for their increasing family. He had set his heart on a better house. By October he found one, on Great Burlington Street, just north of Lord Burlington's grand mansion in Piccadilly. It was a modest-sized town house, three storeys high, with dormer windows in the roof, and on each floor three rooms, two of them large, with front and back stairways taking up the rest of the space.* He was able to buy the lease from Sir William Stapleton for £3,600.

How could he raise so large a sum of money? The old Duchess of Marlborough, in later years (when she hated him), wrote that because the King used to talk to Lady Hervey so conspicuously the young couple thought up an extraordinary scheme: Lady Hervey went to the Drawing-Room every night and attracted the King's attention in such a 'vehement manner' that it became the diversion of the town; whereupon the Ministry and the Duchess of Kendal (formerly Madame von der Schulenburg) became alarmed, and gave her £4,000 on condition that she desist. However improbable this sounds, there is some evidence to support it. When their friend Stephen Fox bought the house five years later he paid £4,000 not to Hervey but to Lady Hervey—which suggests that she had originally paid the purchase price. And there is Lady Mary Wortley Montagu's remark (in August 1725) that 'Lady Hervey is more Delightfull than ever, and such a Politician that if people were not blind to Merit she would govern the Nation'. If this were true then Lady Hervey was reversing the usual fate of ladies at court—by being rewarded for guarding her virtue.

* It still stands today, with a fourth storey added, as No. 31 Old Burlington Street.

But another source of Hervey's purchase money, if not so bizarre, is more plausible. The day after he moved he informed his mother on 16 October that he had been at great expense to put himself into a 'creditable House' and was therefore obliged to call in all his 'desperate Debts' including what she owed him for his winnings at cards; besides, he continues, 'what assistance afterwards you intend me as a Volunteer I shall be very thankfull for, & would take it as a great Favour'. In other words, he raised the sum needed to buy the house by scraping together whatever money was owed to him, asking donations from his parents, and perhaps drawing on his own capital.

The following winter (by which time they were well settled in their new house) Lady Hervey was still being gossiped about for vainly paying court to the King. Lady Mary, after pointing to Mrs. Murray's affair with a duke, continued: 'Her Freind Lady Hervey by aiming too high has falln very low, and is reduc'd to trying to persuade folks she has an Intrigue, and gets no body to beleive her, the man in Question taking a great deal of pains to clear him selfe of the scandal.' When (many years later) Horace Walpole read this comment he made it more explicit: that the King had 'made love to her, but she certainly did not yield'— a rather puzzling comment since she is described by Lady Mary as the aggressor.

That her coquetry was aimed at the King is echoed in a witty ballad written in secret by Pulteney and Chesterfield, and sent to her in the name of a begging poet. Although she was pleased to be complimented as the 'beautiful Molly La—l' wedded to 'Hervey the handsome', she wrote to the poet, not knowing he was bogus, to ask him to change two *double entendres* in the ballad. Instead the authors changed them to single *entendres*—probably these:

> Or were I the King of Great Britain,
>   To chuse a Minister well,
> And support the Throne that I sit on,
>   I'd have under me Molly La—l.

and the other:

> Heaven keep our good King from rising,
>   But that rising who's fitter to quell,
> Than some lady with beauty surprising,
>   And who should that be but La—l.

She was evidently not displeased with the coarse compliments in the ballad, but only with having been taken in by its authors.

In the *beau monde* where Lady Hervey moved she was so prominent as a beauty that gallants who shared the universal passion for 'love of fame' pretended to have enjoyed her favours. The poet Edward Young, who frequented that world, cites her in his satires:

> And *Hervey*'s eyes, unmercifully keen,
> Have murder'd fops, by whom she ne'er was seen.

In the opinion of Charles Hanbury Williams, who knew the Herveys, she was incapable of love; her 'total, real indifference to mankind has hindered her ever having a lover'. But this is too worldly, too Chesterfieldian, an explanation for her not taking a lover. Instead, it proves her consistency of character; since she had married Hervey for love she remained faithful to him. A flirtation with the King, particularly if innocent, can be regarded as a tribute to her husband's ambition.

ii

During the summer of 1726 Hervey altered his customary routine. After leaving Lady Hervey and their children at Ickworth, he accompanied his father and sister Ann up to London, collected Lady Bristol at Richmond (where she had just completed her month's waiting), and set off on a series of visits. They dined with the old Duchess of Marlborough at St. Albans, called in at Lord Halifax's house near Northampton, stopped to look at Althorp, Lord Sunderland's seat, on their way to Lichfield, where Lord Griffin, a relation of Lady Bristol's, took them to see some estates whose ownership they shared. Then by way of Stafford they travelled into North Wales to visit Sir Thomas Hanmer at Bettisfield Park. Lord Bristol was very fond of his old kinsman, though Hervey thought him boring, a 'sensible, impracticable, honest, formal, disagreeable man'. He had recently taken as his second wife a very young woman, who was very far from sharing his sober temperament, as she proved by her later scandalous career when she eloped with Tom Hervey.

After their quiet visit of ten days, the Bristol family set out for Bath, going by way of Worcester and Gloucester, and arrived at the spa near the end of August. Hervey, who was joined there by his wife, stayed for three months, an unusually long visit for him. In a reversal of their usual roles his father fell seriously ill, with Dr. Cheyne acting as his physician, while Hervey's health flourished. As one of his festive activities he gave a private ball for Lady Walsingham, the King's illegitimate daughter (by the Duchess of Kendal), for which his father paid the bill. It was no political disadvantage to entertain a lady with such strategic connections.

In Bath Hervey, with the leisure to indulge in his literary pastime, was probably inspired to write a long, ambitious poem. It told of the personal tragedy suffered by Sophia Howe, who had been a Maid of Honour at the same time as Molly Lepell. She had fallen in love with Anthony Lowther, an M.P.; and when he tried to end their affair she left her lodgings in Richmond dressed in men's clothes and rode to his house in Pall Mall to look for him, but he eluded her by slipping out the back door. The shock and disappointment drove her out of her senses, and she was put under restraint by her mother and friends. Although this had occurred in 1720, her death in April 1726 must have stimulated Hervey's sympathetic imagination.

He chose to tell her sad tale as an epistle in the style of Ovid's *Amores*, where legendary heroines lament their tragic love affairs. In Hervey's poem, *Monimia to Philocles*, the heroine tells her lover—who surely must have known—how he betrayed her after she loved him unwisely and too well, and how she has been scorned by her friends and abandoned by him. The monologue unwinds slowly and turgidly; in its conclusion, with the faltering accents of pathetic tragedy, Monimia asks and exclaims:

> Why then this care?—'tis weak—'tis vain—farewell—
> At that last word what agonies I feel!
> I faint—I die—remember I was true—
> 'Tis all I ask—eternally—adieu!—

Like so much of the verse written by wits and courtiers Hervey's elegiac poem was circulated in manuscript among his friends. Lady Mary, who herself liked to compose pathetic monologues, transcribed it into one of her notebooks as being by Hervey. It somehow fell into the hands of a printer, as such manuscripts often did, and he issued it in a pamphlet with a Dublin imprint, dated 1726. Since it was anonymous Hervey could not profit by the applause, if any, that it might win. But to his friends and enemies at court it announced his emergence as a poet. Lady Mary too had a taste for versifying. It could be a dangerous pastime, as they were to discover in the future.

iii

While at Bath in the autumn of 1726 Hervey unexpectedly began a friendship that was to have important consequences for him. Henry Fox, his new friend, was the younger son of the late Sir Stephen Fox, who by his service to Charles II had earned universal esteem and an enormous fortune. After attending Eton, Oxford, and Lincoln's Inn, Henry had settled at Redlinch, his family estate in Somerset. He was a robust young man of twenty-one, fond of country sports as well as of gambling and wenching; both of these he could pursue at Bath, which was only twenty miles from Redlinch. His constant good humour and seeming frankness made him a welcome social companion.

By the time Fox left Bath on 22 November to return to Redlinch, Hervey was his warm, effusive friend, writing to him the next day in the elaborately witty style of French preciosity. 'Tho the Loss of You & the want of a certain resource I used to have in very Spirits have made me very unfit for writing,' he says, 'Yet the pleasure[s] of conversing with you are so fresh upon my remembrance that I can't help doing the thing that seems most like repeating them.' After more in the same vein he continues, 'I insist on being told what you doe from Morning to Night in the Country, & . . . I would now & then be glad to be told what you think. I have an unbounded Curiosity with regard to those I love, but your Reservedness I fear will make it live upon as slender Dyet as a patient of Dr. Cheyne's. I should be glad to have your pen goe halves with your Gun, & by my good will would never have you shoot of a post-Day.' His greatest satisfaction in reflecting on their brief acquaintance, he concludes, is to think it 'an earnest of a long future Friendship'.

When Fox replied, a week later, Hervey had already returned to London, and although busy he took the time to send a long reply. His thoughts were divided between his friend and his friend's losses at Bath, he tells him; 'I shall renew my attack when you come to town, for the pleasure of being loved by one so amiable is one I can't part with, without some struggle. In the meantime I shall ply you frequently with Letters to keep a place in Your Remembrance tho' I lose ground in your Heart, an Exchange nothing could induce me to make but the fear of losing You all.' Then, in contrast to this romantic strain, Hervey abruptly becomes earthy and ribald: he is sending some tobacco, an Italian grammar, a couple of French novels; and, in order that Fox's amusements should not become serious in their consequences either to himself or to a lady he had mentioned, he was also sending 'a dozen preservatives from Claps & impediments to procreation, which at the rate of two doses a week I have computed will be physick enough for You whilst you Stay in the Country; & as these evacuations may be of use to Your Constitution when thus sparingly repeated, so I solve my Conscience by telling my self I have only acted the part of a wise physician & not perform'd the Office of a pimp'. With this mixture of elegant persiflage and coarse masculine jocularity Hervey tried to woo the rather hearty young man whom he had so warmly taken up.

After a fortnight's impatient waiting for a reply from Fox he complains of his disappointment: 'knowing Your Eyes to be the only Inlets into your Heart, I could never expect (whatever I might desire) to hold any place in the one, after being removed near a Month from the other'. He tries to exert all his intellectual charm, quoting La Rochefoucauld, and tartly concluding: 'A Letter antedated or a complaint of the remissness of the post is too stale a Deceit to pass, so that if you would have it succeed some other must be thought of.' His reproaches were so successful that they stimulated Fox to send a letter quoting La Bruyère, which Hervey then matched with his own favourite La Rochefoucauld. Intellect and wit were beginning to dominate sentiment in Hervey's epistolary flirtation.

Along with a new friend at Bath Hervey had acquired a revival of good health and high spirits; and these he was able to take back to London. The event that engaged everybody's attention there was the spectacular case of Mary Toft of Godalming, who claimed—and was believed by many—to have given birth to a succession of rabbits. Nathaniel St. André, Surgeon and Anatomist to the King, was so convinced of this strange phenomenon that he published a report of it. Physicians, scientists, and great numbers of the nobility and fashionable society journeyed down to Guildford, where Mrs. Toft had been taken, to see the miracle.

On 29 November she was brought to London for a more careful examination by surgeons; and a steady stream of the curious also wanted to see for themselves. Hervey was among them.

'I was last Night to see her with Dr. Arbuthnot, who is convinced of the Truth of what St. André relates,' he wrote to Fox on 3 December 1726; 'every Creature in town, both Men & Women, have been to see & feel her; the perpetual emotions, noises, & rumblings in her Belly are something prodigious: all the eminent physicians, Surgeons, and Man-midwifes in London are there Day & Night to watch her next production.' The Prince of Wales's secretary, Samuel Molyneux, whose main scientific interest was astronomy, swore to Hervey that he himself had taken one part of a rabbit out of her body when she was in labour. 'In short,' Hervey concludes, 'the whole philosophical World is divided into two partys . . . & between the downright affirmations of the one hand for the reality of the fact, & the philosophical proofs of the impossibility of it on the other, no body knows which they are to believe, their Eyes or their Ears.' A thoroughgoing sceptic, Hervey refused to commit himself. He did not have to wait long to learn the truth; four days after his visit Mrs. Toft confessed that it had all been a hoax. Hervey could congratulate himself that unlike the genial Dr. Arbuthnot he had not been taken in.

He had been urging Fox to come to London, and at the beginning of January 1727 Fox set a date but then had to postpone it because of Stephen, his elder brother. Hervey's reply is fraught with ironic implications: 'I hate your Brother without knowing him, (which perhaps is the only way one can hate him) for postponing another Week a pleasure I have waited for so long, & expected with so much impatience.' The spate of letters then ceased: Henry Fox had finally come up to London, where he and Hervey could resume in person their burgeoning friendship.

iv

Only a few days after the Hervey family were settled in their new house Lady Hervey gave birth to a daughter, her fourth child. She was christened Mary; and her godparents were Mrs. Lepell, the dowager Duchess of Marlborough, and Sir Robert Walpole. Hervey's choice of the Prime Minister neatly balanced his choice of Pulteney as godfather for his previous daughter. Socially he could be friendly to both men, but ahead of him lay the choice of whom he would support in the House of Commons. For, as he could have observed at the opening of Parliament in January 1726, Pulteney's conflict with Walpole had sharpened into open opposition. Its main cause, in Hervey's opinion, was Pulteney's great desire for the appointment of Secretary of State; Walpole had given it to the Duke of Newcastle instead. Considering himself slighted, Pulteney publicly vowed not only revenge, but utter destruction of Walpole. This was the state of affairs when Hervey began his career as a young M.P. During this initial period he was absolutely ignorant of Parliamentary business, according to Charles Hanbury Williams, and hardly attended the sessions. But he always supported Walpole and the Court party and never Pulteney and the Opposition.

The Opposition had been greatly strengthened by Bolingbroke's return from exile, for even though forbidden to sit in the House of Lords he could contribute his immense abilities as a political writer. This newly formed Opposition differed from what Walpole had contended with in the past: it appealed to the general public (instead of only to the House of Commons) by means of pamphlets and newspapers. The *Craftsman*, first issued on 5 December 1726, contained political essays that insistently and monotonously attacked whatever policies the ministry put forth. It was an immediate success. It had the best writers against the court, in Hervey's opinion, and of these Bolingbroke and Pulteney stood out as leaders.

Within a month of the *Craftsman*'s first appearance, Bolingbroke, wishing more scope for his attack on Walpole, published a sixteen-page anonymous pamphlet entitled *The Occasional Writer, No. I*. He points out, with clever irony, that since political pamphleteers win far greater rewards than savants or poets, he is resolved to become a 'State-Writer', and therefore offers his service to Walpole; and he then continues with his main burden— an attack on the foreign policy of the Minister and his brother, Horatio, who was ambassador to France. He followed this, about a month later, with *The Occasional Writer, No. II*, dated 3 February 1727. Opening in the same ironic vein as his first pamphlet he regrets that the Minister has not accepted his offer to serve; and he continues by again attacking Walpole's foreign policy.

Only about a week later an anonymous reply to this was published by a defender of Walpole; and it was Hervey who wrote it, his first identified political pamphlet. Although he had been a Member of Parliament for almost two years, he had apparently not yet taken any conspicuous part in its debates on the infrequent occasions when he attended. Here, in his first political activity, he was squarely on Walpole's side.

He entitled his attack on Bolingbroke's pamphlet *An Answer to the Occasional Writer No. II*, and immediately unmasks its author as a 'once Rt. Hon. Lord' before continuing:

Your Miscellaneous Letter being in print, and addressed to no Body, I thought any Man had a right to Answer it, and the more inconsiderable the more equal a Correspondent is he to one of your approved Integrity. I am greatly surprized that your Offers of *Service should be treated with Contempt*, for that seems appropriated only to real Merit; so that I cannot but impute this ill Success to the great Modesty and Sincerity with which you acknowledged your self *to have taken upon you the Character of an infamous Libeller*. But surely your Modesty is extended too far, when you say, that you only *take upon your self a Character* which was really given you by the universal Consent of Mankind; and I have still a better Opinion of you, since you fairly confess that in this, as upon most other Occasions, instead of *biting others you have bit your self*.

Hervey, himself anonymous, continues to unmask Bolingbroke as author of the *Occasional Writer*. 'How often has your Friend *Gulliver* lamented', he asks, 'that he could say nothing in *Harry's* [Henry St. John, Lord Bolingbroke] commendation, but what must necessarily be taken in an ironical Sense?' He also reminds Bolingbroke of his devious politics in 1714, when the Tories fell. Except for these personal sarcasms Hervey patiently replies to Bolingbroke's strictures on Walpole's foreign policy—at this time of friendship with France and cautious neutrality toward the Austrian Emperor. As an appendix to his argument Hervey adds a brief reply to the *Occasional Writer, No. I*. His anonymity was evidently successful.

This exchange of pamphlets was conspicuous enough to be mentioned in the House of Commons a few weeks later, when Walpole complained of the malicious libellers of the time. If they were encouraged to persist, he said, a race of men might spring up who would interfere with Parliamentary business; and this was being done out of the greatest personal enmity to him that was perhaps ever known, as in the *Occasional Writer*. Thereupon Pulteney asked to be heard, and adroitly tried to turn Walpole's argument in his own favour: he hoped that nobody in the House had written the *Answer to the Occasional Writer*, which reflected on a man [Bolingbroke] who was only supposed to be the author of the *Occasional Writer*.

Bolingbroke was not silenced by Hervey's *Answer*; instead he issued the *Occasional Writer, No. III*, dated 13 February 1727, as a reply to it, saying that he was convinced that the *Answer* was written by Walpole himself. Bolingbroke's third pamphlet was in turn answered by the anonymous (and unattributed) *Letter to the Occasional Writer on Receipt of his Third*, which the Ministry thought so effective that great numbers were distributed and it was reprinted in the *London Journal*. Having completed his auxiliary campaign Bolingbroke thereafter put all his polemic energies into other pamphlets and *The Craftsman*.

During this session of Parliament in 1727, Hervey, for the first time since his election to it, took part in its business. A Member of Parliament pointed out that the Emperor's Resident in London had presented a Memorial to the King 'couch'd in a very indecent and injurious Stile' and then, far worse, had arranged for it to be translated and published—thus making it an appeal by a foreign power to the people of Great Britain against their Sovereign. Both Ministry and Opposition joined to express their resentment with an Address to the King. On 14 March Hervey was sent from the Commons to the Lords to arrange a conference between both Houses for the purpose of agreeing on the wording of the Address. At the meeting, held in the Painted Chamber, the Address was approved and then presented to the King.

On the Ministry's behalf Hervey also used the brouhaha about the Memorial as the opportunity for a brief satirical pamphlet entitled *The Occasional Writer, No. IV. To His Imperial Majesty*. With a mixture of straightforward argument and light irony he informs the Emperor, the darling of the Opposition, how effectively the Memorial has unified the English in love for their King and gratitude to his Administration.

In taking on the most formidable pamphleteer that the Ministry faced, Hervey had performed a considerable service for them; and the clarity and strength as well as skilful irony of his writing

were qualities that they needed for their side. Hervey no doubt
expected to be rewarded. At some time before the summer of
the following year he was awarded a pension of £1,000 by the
Court. Since his pamphleteering on the Ministry's behalf was the
only service he performed during this interval the pension must
have been his reward as well as his incentive to continue to lend
them his support.

v

'I hate your Brother without knowing him', Hervey had told
Henry Fox; at the end of January 1727, when both brothers came
up to London, he met the object of his hatred. Stephen Fox,
twenty-three years old at the time, was eight years younger than
Hervey. He was delicately made, with a slight, small-boned frame
similar to Hervey's, and a pale, sensitive face. After attending
Eton and Christ Church, Oxford, he had spent two years on the
Grand Tour to the Low Countries, France, and Italy, before
returning to Redlinch. From his father he had inherited estates
worth more than £5,000 a year; and from his mother, a solemn
admonition when she was on her death-bed in 1719: 'Don't be
a Fop, don't be a Rake. Think on your name, Stephen Fox; that
I hope will keep you from being wicked . . .' His mother's
advice suited his own inclinations, for he much preferred country
life and pastimes to London's excitement and temptations. 'He
is such a Country Gentleman', Lady Hervey later remarked, 'that
unless one cou'd be metamorphos'd into a bird or a Hare he will
have nothing to say to one.' He was a sympathetic listener, however, and from the beginning of their friendship Hervey could
easily say enough for both of them—either in person or through
his letters.

Only the previous year (in May) Stephen had been elected to
Parliament in a by-election for Shaftesbury, Dorset, and he now
took his seat among the Tories. During the three months that he
stayed in London—evidently in lodgings in St. James's Street—
he and Hervey established a friendship that continued to flourish
after they parted. For as soon as Parliament rose (at the end of
May) he returned to Redlinch. From there he expressed his regret
that he was not still in London, to which Hervey replied (on
1 June), 'I can't help takeing a malicious pleasure to hear the

5. Stephen Fox

Country affords you so few [pleasures] of any kind, & that your Joys there are at so low an ebb that a sound Horse & a big belly'd pheasant are the only ones you have yet experienced . . . if Your wishes were very strong (since your Horses are so very sound) what hinders the gratification of them?'

Perhaps Hervey is merely indulging in one of the elaborately gallant letters that flowed so easily from his pen. But he reveals himself as more than an epistolary virtuoso in his letters to Stephen. 'For my own Part,' he later confessed to him, 'my Mind never goes naked but in your territorys.'

'I won't tell you,' he continues (in his letter of 1 June), 'how I feel every time I goe through St. James's Street because I don't love writing unintelligibly; & the more faithful the description was, the farther one of your temper & way of thinking would be from comprehending what it meant. I might as well talk to a blind man of Colours, an Atheist of Devotion, or an Eunuch of f——.' And then, teasing Stephen more directly: 'That regret for the Loss of any body one loves & likes is a sort of Sensation you have merit enough to teach, tho' I believe you'll never have merit enough to learn it.' His intent was obviously to encourage Stephen to deny that accusation; and, as can be judged by the rapid progress of their friendship, Stephen was willing both to love and to like.

Since Stephen assured him that his letters stood foremost in his list of pleasures, Hervey tried to amuse him (on 13 June) with a lengthy story of the opera feud between Faustina and Cuzzoni, the reigning prima donnas on the London stage. But he has more important matters to deal with when he asks him about Redlinch, 'whether you have done wishing for me there yet or not, & if You are still enough acquainted with me for me to venture thither without an Introductor. I think of you very often . . .'

Although he regretted the departure from London of what he called the Redlinch coterie he made the most of his deprivation. At the end of May he attended the Prince of Wales's birthday celebration, where he endured 'a great Croud, bad Musick, trite Compliments upon New Garments & Old Faces in the Morning, feasting & drinking all Day, & a Ball with execrable Dancers at Night'. The weather was so warm in June that he joined a party on the river, stayed up until three in the morning, bored by talk about the rival opera singers, and did not go to bed until four o'clock. Although he claimed to be too busy in town to visit Lord Bateman he went to stay three days with Lord Berkeley at Cranford Park in Middlesex. He regarded Berkeley as an honourable man, haughty and tyrannical, in character rough, proud, hard, and obstinate, with some excellent natural parts, but so uncultivated that he was totally ignorant of every branch of knowledge except his profession—the navy. What could he have found worth cultivating in this rugged old sea-dog? As First Lord of the Admiralty and a Lord of the King's Bedchamber, Berkeley was a man of considerable importance and substance; and Hervey's ambition impelled him to move closer to the sources of political power. Lord Berkeley and Stephen Fox attracted two contrasting sides of Hervey's aspirations: the desire to succeed in the public world of politics and court favour and—in view of his abnormally intense friendship with Stephen and Stephen's successor—the hunger to find happiness in the private world of sentiment and love.

5

House of Commons and Travel Abroad

1727–9

AT THE BEGINNING OF THE SUMMER 1727, when George I departed for Hanover, the Court at Richmond settled down to a somnolent recess. That mood was dramatically shattered the afternoon of 14 June when Walpole arrived from Chelsea to inform the Prince of Wales that he was now king; his father had died just before reaching Hanover, as Walpole had been informed by a courier. Walpole then asked for orders, and was curtly told to report to Sir Spencer Compton, the Prince's Treasurer and the Speaker of the House of Commons. He returned to London in a discouraged frame of mind, fearful that his career was over. When he offered to help draft the King's declaration to the Privy Council, Compton—characterized by Hervey as 'a plodding, heavy fellow'—gratefully and innocently agreed. This enabled Walpole to prove how unqualified Compton was to replace him as first minister. The following day all the Members of Parliament who were in town assembled at Westminster to take oaths of allegiance to George II, with Hervey serving as deputy for the Duke of Dorset in administering the oaths. They were to meet again in a fortnight's time.

Lord Bristol wasted little time before soliciting patronage from the new monarch. On 17 June he was received in audience at Leicester House, and after assuring the King that he had always showed an unwavering zeal for the Hanoverian dynasty and that he was not seeking any rewards for himself, he asked only that 'whatever distinction' he deserved might be shown to Lord Hervey, 'whose establishment in your majesty's favour is ye thing in this world I have most at heart, & therefore beg your majesty would on this happy occasion promise some way or other to provide for him; his affection & fidelity I will stand bound for; his abilities I hope will answer for themselves.' What the King promised was later called by Lord Bristol 'solemn promises' from 'a superior order'. With the Ministry still unsettled firm promises could not be made.

During the period immediately after the accession it was generally assumed that Walpole would be dismissed, and that Compton would take over his appointments and power; he was universally courted, while Walpole was shunned by all except Hervey and Charles Churchill, M.P., who (since 1715) remained unswervingly loyal to Walpole during his entire career. Hervey was astutely able to foresee how the wheel of fortune would turn at this delicate juncture, and he exerted his abilities in a remarkably subtle way. He sent an anonymous letter to Walpole in a disguised hand. 'I am one of the many you have obliged,' it begins,

and one of the few that will never forget it. My gratitude for these obligations, and the desire I have to do you service, is the sole occasion of this letter; nor have I so mean an opinion of your understanding, or so good a one of my own, as to imagine that, at this very important crisis, you can want my advice how to act. But though you are too skilful to want counsel, yet the most skilful may want intelligence; and there are certainly schemes on foot to impose upon you.

He then discloses information that had come to his knowledge 'merely by accident and the babbling indiscretion of a fool who wishes you ill,' that, in brief, the King would use Walpole's service in the House of Commons to procure an extraordinarily large grant for his Civil List and would then discard him.

Walpole took advantage of this unexpected information by acting with wisdom and boldness. He confronted the Queen with the letter as evidence of how the world regarded his unsettled situation, and thus forced her and then the King to assure him that they intended to keep him in their service. Ultimately Hervey revealed to Walpole that it was he who had sent the letter, and he thus won an extra measure of gratitude for his loyalty.

He dined at Walpole's house the day before Parliament convened, along with Thomas Winnington, M.P., a great friend of the Fox brothers. (Stephen, who had been in London briefly, had departed before the session opened.) The only important business to be taken up—since writs for a new Parliament would be issued in August—was the settlement of the King's Civil List and the Queen's jointure (if she outlived him). With Walpole's management the House voted larger grants than had ever been made before—£900,000 for the King and £100,000 for the Queen. In Hervey's later judgement: 'To such a pitch of extravagance did these contending parliamentary bidders raise the price of Court favour at this royal auction.' That Walpole could put this through so successfully finally persuaded the King of his usefulness, then and for the future. Yet as a further test between Walpole and Compton, the King asked each of them to write his speech dismissing Parliament, and when he chose Walpole's it was clear to the world who would be his Prime Minister.

As soon as Parliament rose, Hervey and his wife accompanied his father to Ickworth, where they arrived on 20 July. The two men immediately began to campaign in Bury for the forthcoming election. In one day they made no fewer than thirty-five visits, receiving a warm welcome everywhere. In the midst of this bustle Hervey unexpectedly received a summons from Walpole to meet him at Houghton Hall, his almost completed house in Norfolk. He arrived there shortly before 14 August. Although he complained that he should be in Bury looking after his own affairs instead of in Norfolk, forty miles away, he found it all very agreeable and everybody in such good spirits that the days seemed too short. General bonhomie rather than politics engaged them most of the time.

He hurried back to Bury in order to be there for the election on 18 August. Not unexpectedly he was unanimously chosen. His mother, by then at Ickworth, was politic enough to send an account of it to Mrs. Howard: 'I remember the king used sometimes to like to hear how such sort of affairs went; and I flatter myself this will be pleasing to him, since their majesties may be very well assured whatever interest we gain will always be laid out for their service.' She boasts that the other seat for Bury could have been won by Thomas Hervey had Lord Bristol not promised it to her cousin Colonel Thomas Norton, who lived near Bury and was more favoured by Lord Bristol than by her. She was able to console her son Thomas by securing for him an appointment as equerry to the Queen, at £220 a year. She, of course, retained her post as Lady of the Bedchamber. As in the previous reign the Hervey family continued to ascend the ladder of royal patronage.

ii

Whatever pleasurable satisfaction the Hervey family had in their good fortune was tempered that summer by the death of two of Lord Bristol's daughters. Barbara had died at Ickworth just before the Bury election. Elizabeth, who had been married for several years, died in London in September after a long and excruciating illness; it was a terrible blow to Hervey, for (as he phrased it) he loved her 'better than all the rest of our nursery put together'. Her death almost caused his own. Concerned by his intense grief and melancholy his father advised him to submit to God—a submission far easier for Lord Bristol than for his free-thinking son—and to be grateful that his wife and all his hopeful children had been spared. 'I can never make my self so compleatly wretched as to think ye cheif ornament of my family gone,' his father consoled him, 'as long as God vouchsafes to spare your more valuable life.'

Unable to shake off his grief, and in wretched health besides, Hervey sought recovery with his new, sympathetic friend. He paid a visit to Redlinch to stay with Stephen Fox, who (he later wrote) 'loved me too well not to take a part in anything that made me uneasy and do all in his power to alleviate the weight of it'. (Lady Hervey had remained at what he called 'her Hermitage', probably Ickworth). Accompanied by Stephen he moved to Bath, and they remained there two months, revisiting Redlinch during the first week of November.

He evidently did not attend the Coronation in London on 11 October 1727. Lady Mary Wortley Montagu, his comrade-in-wit, sent him a description of it that—if like the one she sent to her sister in Paris—was brilliant and amusing. It was very entertaining, she merrily wrote, 'to Observe the variety of airs that all meant the same thing, the Business of every walker there being to conceal Vanity and gain Admiration . . . In General I could not perceive but the Old were as well pleas'd as the Young, and I (who dread growing Wise more than any thing in the World) was overjoy'd to observe one can never outlive one's Vanity.' Hervey was so delighted with her letter that he read aloud two or three passages to Henrietta, Duchess of Marlborough, eldest daughter of the great Duke, then on a visit to Bath with her lover William Congreve. The Duchess thought it so witty that she guessed Lord Chesterfield had written it.

Although his health and spirits were restored he suffered at this time a profound disappointment, probably that he had not been offered a political or court post by the Ministry. He confessed this to his father, who reassured him that paternal love and trust were unwavering, and that 'should other friends only give you ye pleasure of thinking they are so without finding any fruit from their professions, & should ye solemn promises which have been made by those of a superior order faile me too, yet as long as it shall be in my power to supply the defects of both' then Hervey could always depend on him. Consoled by his father's loyalty he returned to London to face a political future that was still uncertain.

He had been accompanied there by Stephen Fox, who soon left him to return to his country pursuits. In the first letter he sent after him he writes 'Adieu' and then adds: 'If you had felt half the reluctance to pronounce that word that I find in writing it we had been at this moment together in Jerman Street.' His friendship, so quickly growing more fervent, was not one-sided; he recollected what Stephen had once said to him: 'you were so convinced 'twas impossible for you to be happy or even easey when you were from [me] that you had resolved for the future never to be out of my sight whenever it was avoidable.' In fact, Stephen planned to rent a house in London at this time, probably in order to be close to Hervey for longer periods than their brief visits. Hervey was his house-agent. Accompanied by Henry Fox he inspected a small house on Grosvenor Square that rented for £400 a year and was ready to be furnished. It had four good rooms, he reported, which Stephen misunderstood to mean four good rooms on each floor—a reasonable assumption at that high rental. Nothing, however, came of the search at this time.

Hervey still suffered from occasional bouts of ill health. In December 1727 he was so much out of order with giddiness that he stayed at home for two days, hardly able to walk the length of his room. He generally spared Stephen a recital of his illness, or he tried to embellish his account with a witty turn. The surgeon 'Amyand has putt a fresh Costick to my Cheek,' he tells him, 'but the pain I am most impatient under is from the Costick your absence has putt to my Heart.' His social activity flourished as before; he attended a dinner at the French ambassador's and from there went directly to a ball.

With Parliament scheduled to open in January 1728 he had more serious concerns. He spent much of his time with Henry Fox and Winnington, who talked only of politics from morning to night. 'I hear of nothing but Petitions, journals, Treatys, Alliances &c.' he complained to Stephen. The opening of Parliament—with a newly crowned king and a newly elected House of Commons—was more than routine this year. Arthur Onslow was elected Speaker in place of Compton, who had been created Lord Wilmington because Walpole preferred to remove his former rival to the pastures of the Upper House. After the King opened the session (on the 27th) with what Hervey calls 'a sort of hereditary speech' it was Hervey himself who moved the Address of Thanks. Customarily an Address of Thanks was moved and seconded by members of the House selected beforehand by the Administration. They were usually office-holders or members who aspired to office. That Hervey was chosen for this first Parliament of George II was a clear sign of the Ministry's regard for him as well as of his own aspiration for office. Despite some Opposition demurs, which only aroused general indignation, the Address was unanimously passed.

This was Hervey's first speech in Parliament. His style of oratory, some listeners thought, was to speak very slowly, with a gravity and solemnity that seemed ill-suited to his delicate figure. But his father applauded his speech and repeated to him what one of the aldermen of Bury had told him: that everybody who heard his 'maiden essay' had been pleased with it, and that 'nothing was slavish or dependent, nothing unworthy ye patriot himself'. In the months that followed he was appointed to several Parliamentary committees—on roads and churches. The inactivity of his first two years in the House of Commons was giving way to participation; but then illness prevented him from continuing it. At the beginning of March a violent fever confined him to his bed for several days and to his room for several weeks. He was attended by both Dr. Cheyne and Dr. Arbuthnot. Rumour-mongers put him past recovery and on the point of dying; yet in mid-April he was seen riding with Mrs. Oldfield, the actress, in her coach. During his illness Stephen was in London, and never left him but to eat or sleep, and not always for that. In May, before Parliament rose, both of them left London to stay at Redlinch, where Hervey could continue his recuperation.

He was apparently completely recovered in June, when he returned alone to London. His recent visit to Redlinch was warm in his memory as he reminds Stephen of their walks through 'Hervey-Grove'; and he could project his aroused imagination in a sentence so fraught with emotion that it sounds like the text for a Handel aria: 'I hear you in the deadest Silence & see you in the deepest Darkness.' He dined out now more frequently—at Richmond and at Cranford, where the other guests at Lord Berkeley's house were Lady Bolingbroke and Lord Carteret. He had grown a great rake, he boasts to Stephen: 'I sup & sitt up, & in a little time I believe you will hear of my getting drunk, breaking windows, beating the watch, being knock'd down by a Constable, & lying all night in the Round-House.'

'Adieu,' he concludes his spirited letter (of 22 June) to Stephen: 'I continue my resolution of leaving England the 10th of next Month & hope you will find it necessary to be in town longer than you thought before you go.' A few days later he again refers to Stephen's being in London and to his own departure: 'I go the 10th: how long it will be necessary for you to be in town before that you know best.' He could be so casually cryptic because of a fact that emerges in the entry Lord Bristol made in his diary on 12 July: 'Friday, my invaluable son Lord Hervey went on board ye William & Mary yacht with ye Duke & Dutchess of Richmond & Mr. Fox, bound for Ostend, to proceed thence to ye Spaw.'

iii

Why Lord Hervey left England in 1728 may seem to have a simple, clearcut explanation. Two years after his return he drew up a long document entitled 'An Account of My Own Constitution and Illness . . . For the Use of My Children' in which he states that he suffered so frequently from trembling nerves, giddiness, and fainting spells, that he had no time to lose if he wished to live, and he imagined that he could be cured in a warm climate. Yet during the month before his departure he made no mention of ill health; on the contrary he seemed cheerful and animated. Some reason besides ill health must have wafted him beyond the sea. When he resolved to go abroad, he explains (in his 'Account'), Stephen Fox 'with an affection and friendship I am as incapable of forgetting, as any nature but his is incapable of feeling, offered to go with me to any part of the world, and for as long as I pleased'. If this is what he wanted his children to read, he put it rather differently in some verse that he wrote in Italy and addressed to Stephen.

> Thou dearest youth, who taught me first to know
> What pleasures from a real friendship flow,
> When neither int'rest nor design have part,
> But all the warmth is native of the heart.

The journey was opposed by his physicians, he says, and he himself was reluctant, but Stephen forced him 'to explore a warmer sun, And seek a milder shore'.★

It was not considered odd that his wife should remain at home. True, she had young children, but they could have been left at Ickworth under the care of their nurses and doting grandfather. Accompanied on his journey, then, by his affectionate friend, Hervey was in a sense completing the Grand Tour that had been curtailed by his mother's fears when he was a young man. Stephen himself had taken the Grand Tour four years earlier, accompanied by Dr. John Wigan; now he travelled with an intimate friend instead of a bear-leader.

The yacht in which they crossed the Channel belonged to Charles Lennox, second Duke of Richmond. Born in 1701, a grandson of Charles II, he had been privately educated and had travelled for three years before going into the military service. He was at this time A.D.C. to the King and a Lord of the Bed-chamber, and was happily married to a daughter of Lord Cadogan. Hervey had the greatest admiration for him, considering him friendly, benevolent, generous, honourable, and thoroughly noble in his way of acting, talking, and thinking. He was an excellent companion, in constant spirits and very entertaining. But because he was not formally educated at school or university, people underestimated his intellectual attainments. (He was a Fellow of the College of Physicians and of the Royal Society.) Queen Caroline told Hervey, some years later, what she thought of his friend: 'he is so half-witted, so bizarre,'and so grandseigneur,

---

★ His mother's explanation is different: that 'becaus his Father wou'd not allow him any thing to live upon . . ., was the cheif reason for his going abroad, more then his want of health' (letter to Sarah, Duchess of Marlborough, 7 May 1737, Blenheim MS.). Her testimony is suspect because of her bitter hatred of her son when she wrote this.

and so mulish, that he is as troublesome from meaning well and comprehending so ill, as if he meant as ill as he comprehends.' Both Hervey and Stephen found him and his Duchess delightful company, and their friendship continued to flourish long after their excursion to the Continent.

When the yacht anchored at Ostend the whole party travelled to the Spa, a watering place very popular with the English. The usual period of time for a cure was six weeks. Of its various springs Hervey chose one called Poulhon, a balsamic water containing iron salts. It was situated in the town centre, in a fine stone building with an inscription that promised it would 'remove obstructions, dissolve hard swellings, dry up a superfluity of moisture, and strengthen weak limbs, if drunk with proper advice'. During the first three weeks Hervey's health improved to a surprising degree, but then the weather turned so wet and cold that he lost all benefit of the waters. After three more weeks, he became as ill as he had been on arrival. Nothing had been gained.

He then travelled with Stephen to Paris, where they lived quietly. The King, who was now eighteen years old, had been married for three years to the daughter of the King of Poland. Hervey had not yet seen either of the royal pair, he tells his mother (on 30 September), but the Queen was to come from Versailles to Paris 'in great Pomp & devotion to the Church of Nôtre Dame to bribe Heaven with some trumpery, Vow for a Dauphin, & proceede immediately on to Fountainebleau to the King in order to joyn corporal aids to these spiritual means for the completion of her wishes'. His gossip was not invented wit, for the Queen's accouchement of a female child at the end of July had been a great disappointment; and so at the beginning of October after addressing prayers for a son to the Virgin at Notre-Dame and Sainte Geneviève, against the advice of the medical faculty she intended to sleep with the King at Fontainebleau.

As on his earlier travels Hervey had been asked by his mother to purchase something for her, probably cloth from Liège; and since he had failed to, he now promised to find some 'inferior trappings from this Place, where fashions are come to that extravagance that unless they wear their Pettycoats over their Heads as often in publick as they do in private I can't comprehend what they can invent next to make people stare'.

While he enjoyed Paris, Lady Hervey—who pityingly described herself to Mrs. Howard as a 'melancholy wife'—anxiously appealed to Fox to send her a full and frank account of her husband's health (but to keep her request a secret): she wanted to know 'how he looks, if he sleeps well, sweats o'nights, what stomach he has, and a thousand impertinent questions'. The state of Hervey's health was better known to Winnington, who had been kept informed; it was neither better nor worse than when he had left England, and Winnington very much feared such would be the case when he returned from Italy. Behind his scepticism seems to be the notion that health was not the main motive of Hervey's journey southward.

He was now well enough to leave Paris for Italy but had to wait for letters of credit from London. He and Fox then took the overland route through Lyons and the Alpine pass of Mont Cénis, arriving in Turin by 4 November; and after a brief visit to Florence, they continued on to Rome.

iv

At last Hervey found himself in the Eternal City, the place of greatest interest in the Grand Tour. He could regard it as eternal not because it was the seat of the Papacy (which he regarded merely as a source of superstition) but because it was still so visibly the capital of the ancient Roman Empire, whose history and literature he knew so well. He had to postpone exploring it because Stephen had become ill with a very bad chest-cold, and then, when a surgeon was called in to blood him, his arm became infected and turned dark from wrist to shoulder. It was now Hervey's turn to be faithful nurse and attendant as he stayed close to his friend. 'We live as much alone,' he tells his mother, 'as if we were in the Desert of Libia. There are Operas, Musick in the Churches, in the Pope's Chappel, & every night at some assembly in private Houses, but I have not heard a Note since I came, nor so much as seen St. Peter's.' His wife, unaware that Stephen himself was so ill, appealed to him again to look after her husband: 'For God's sake, Sir, continue to use your utmost indeavors to prevail on him to take *the* medicine' (a 'mercurial medicine' prescribed by Dr. Broxholme). Hervey's task as nurse was made more difficult because Stephen's valet had died, so that (as Winnington remarked when he heard of it) 'I am affraid Ste will be obliged to put on his own Breeches.'

The arrival in Rome of two young Englishmen did not escape the notice of the British secret agent who was stationed there (mainly to keep track of the Pretender and his court). The Baron de Stosch, who signed his French dispatches with the very English name of John Walton, reported (on 5 December o.s.) to the Secretary of State in London the recent arrival of 'mylord Harvay et Mr. Fack'. This may explain why the King was able to surprise Lady Bristol at St. James's with the news that her son had arrived at Rome, although neither she nor Lady Hervey had yet received any word from there.

At first Hervey thought that the air of Rome would improve his health but he soon changed his mind. He busily went about consulting the leading physicians but they were unable to diagnose his illness. The wisest among them, reported Stosch, named it *Hypochondria*. Hervey then decided to move south in search of warmer weather, and on 29 December o.s. left for Naples with Stephen, who had by now recovered from his illness.

Although the weather in Naples was reputed to be mild Hervey became ill again, and was confined to his bed with a high fever. Stephen never left him day or night. 'His good sense made his company a constant amusement and his care never a trouble', Hervey later recalled (for his children's benefit). 'His spirits enlivened and comforted but never overcame or oppressed me. He showed an incessant reasonable and tender concern for me, without all the fiddle-faddle impertinence of officious attention, which is often affectation, always teasing, and never useful.' His wretched health varied greatly; sometimes he seemed to be improving, yet he still suffered from fever and dizzy spells, and seldom spent a day without fainting. His bedchamber faced the sea, so that he could at least look out to see the beautiful Bay of Naples.

He blamed his bad health on the severity of the winter. 'And this much I must say of this charming land,' he sarcastically comments, 'this reputed Eden, the garden of the world, that travellers pretend is one perpetual scene of uninterrupted spring, that I never suffered more from cold, or knew a winter of more severe and uncertain weather in England, than I experienced during my three months' habitation in this place.' When he and Stephen left

Naples on 9 April, the spring was so backward that on some trees the leaves had hardly budded, and the Neapolitans walked about wrapped in their warmest clothes.

In Rome again they enjoyed the warmth of approaching summer so much that they were convinced that Hervey could win back his health if he remained in a warm climate. Probably at Stephen's suggestion and expense Hervey had a portrait bust of himself carved by a young French sculptor resident in Rome, Edme Bouchardon, winner of the *Prix de Rome* in 1722. Its technique of suave classical simplicity shows Hervey's face in a contemplative mood; and with short hair and a toga fastened over his left shoulder he looks like a young patrician of ancient Rome. The feverish, swooning invalid seems unrelated to this idealized, calm youth. The signed marble portrait remained in Stephen's possession, while a plaster replica was kept by Hervey.★ By the time they left for Florence, at the beginning of June, Stosch, whose previous dispatches had noted that Hervey was eating meat, and had less fever and fewer fainting spells, finally reported that both travellers were completely recovered from their indispositions.

The warm Florentine summer fortified Hervey's recovery, and he was able to reassure his wife at the end of June with a 'very good account of his health'. Danger came, now, from an unexpected quarter: a violent earthquake that shook the city. When his wife and father knew that he was unhurt, they could congratulate him on his safety as well as his health.

As his spirits livened so did his writing. 'Behold now, beloved!' he put in a postscript to Stephen's letter to Henry, 'This is the fourth Letter I have written unto thee since my departure from Naples, & why I write now I can give no very good reason since the Lord of Redlinch, my Master & Tyrant, has already acquainted you with the particulars of what at present alone employs our thoughts [the earthquake]. I am better every Day, my Spirits revive, & my embonpoint returns.'

During the panic caused by the earthquake, money was so scarce, Hervey informed his wife, that very fine things could be bought cheaply from the Florentines. Lady Hervey passed on the hint to Mrs. Howard: 'if you care to make any use of his *virtù* and

---

★ The original was formerly at Melbury House, the seat of Stephen's descendants; the plaster replica and a marble copy remain at Ickworth. See Plate 6.

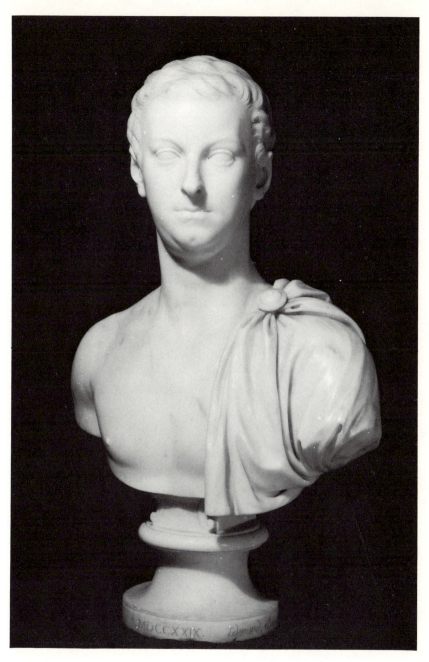

6. Lord Hervey, 1729

their poverty, write your commands to him immediately.' For his own use he had been given £150 by his father with instructions to please himself by purchasing 'some curiosities' on his travels in Italy. Such an opportunity arose when he was shown a set of thirteen large marble statues, mythological figures, carved in 1574 by Pierre de Francheville, a pupil of Giovanni da Bologna. The Duke of Marlborough had almost bought the whole group for Blenheim Palace but squabbled over a few hundred crowns. Since they were still available Hervey offered a large price for four of the figures. Perhaps he intended them as adornment for the garden at Ickworth. But his offer was rejected because the sellers wished to dispose of the whole group *en bloc*. (In 1750 they were bought for the Prince of Wales and sent to England.)

In Florence he felt in such excellent health that he thought it beneficial to have an operation performed on a tumour that grew under his chin, an ugly protuberance that made him uneasy when he moved his head. The treatment was to cut an incision on the surface and to insert a caustic that would eat away the growth. In his impatience to have it done quickly he forced the surgeon to apply an excessive amount of very strong caustic. The pain was so severe that he fainted dead away. He recovered after a few days, and to the end of his life bore a large scar under his chin, clearly visible when he lifted his head.

The surgeon who performed the operation was probably the learned and humane Antonio Cocchi. Hervey had told his mother of his good fortune in meeting at Florence 'one Man . . . who both knows 'tis possible to communicate one's Ideas in other Languages besides Italian, & has a notion of there being inhabited Countrys beyond the Alps: two branches of knowledge that few Gentlemen on this side of them arrive at. He practises Physick . . . I pass a great deal of my time with him & with more pleasure than I have done any other part of it since I left Spa.' He found Cocchi extraordinarily sympathetic, and a strong antidote against the dullness of Florence. He had complained to Lady Mary 'how little Satisfaction a sociable Animal can recieve amongst these People, where Pride makes Access so difficult, & Ceremony & Ignorance make their Acquaintance, when you have attain'd it, so troublesome & so little worth cultivating. Painting, Sculpture, Musick, & Architecture are fine amusements, but where Society is wanting they lose their Merit . . . As to their

Government & their Religion here, one makes one melancholly & t'other makes one laugh.'

He would have found Florence very boring except for the company of Dr. Cocchi. The doctor was (in Horace Walpole's opinion) 'a very free thinker'; and Hervey later recommended him to Henry Fox for this very reason: 'You will like him because he has no Affectation, & he You, because you have no Belief.' Dr. Cocchi was not unique in being intellectually emancipated; other travellers found that all the learned men in Florence were so notoriously atheistic that they admitted it without fear of the Inquisition. Hervey was fortunate to have met a Florentine who was an erudite and skilful surgeon as well as a libertine.

v

In August, as soon as the wound on his neck was healed, Hervey left Florence with Stephen. Stopping first at Pisa, they inspected the Gothic church and famous leaning tower, but had to stay at a vile inn with musty, unaired beds, coarse food, and clouds of gnats. They intended to take ship at Leghorn, but fickle winds and a bad vessel sent them instead back over the plain to Pisa (in a thunderstorm) and then to Lerici. After a night made sleepless because of fleas and bed-bugs they were able to set sail in the clear morning, but storms drove them into the port of Genoa. Hervey now decided to take the tedious, uncomfortable (but at least safe) land route, and they stayed in Genoa for three days before setting out. It was, he thought, the most beautiful city he had seen on his travels. George Jackson, the British consul, looked after them; he entertained them with a dinner of ortolans, and took them on a sightseeing tour. (For a long time Hervey gratefully remembered Jackson's kindness, and when closer to the sources of preferment tried to help him advance in the consular service.)

In Turin, the next city they stopped in, the two travellers met Francis Colman, envoy to Tuscany, on his way there with 'his pretty Wife / Who seems to dread a Florence-Life', Hervey later wrote to his own wife in a long, verse letter. Stephen plied Colman with questions about English news and politics, Hervey continues:

> Whilst to your Love and Merit true,
> My sole enquiry was of you.

They concluded their visit by going to court to meet the King. It was an agreeable prelude to their 'dreadful Journey' across Mont Cénis pass, and they were happy to reach Lyons, where they could rest. On 11 October they departed for Paris.

Unlike their previous visit to the French capital this was filled with activity. Most stimulating to Hervey was his renewed friendship with Voltaire, even then famous for his writings, wit, and courage. Voltaire had fled to England in 1726, and remained there for almost three years. He had been fascinated by the charm and beauty of Lady Hervey and by the graciousness of Hervey, whom he later recalled as one of the most amiable men in England. He had reason to be grateful to Hervey, who had helped enroll subscribers for a new edition of the *Henriade*, published in March 1728, with Lord Bristol, Lady Hervey, and Hervey listed as buying copies. Now that Voltaire had returned to Paris Hervey called on him, and showed him the long verse-letter about Italy that he had sent to Lady Hervey. Voltaire was so impressed that he copied it, and in his *Letters Concerning the English Nation* (first published in London four years later) he paid tribute to this poetical description, part of which he translated and attributed to a young English nobleman who had visited him on returning from Italy.

The British ambassador in Paris was Horatio Walpole, Sir Robert's brother, and undoubtedly it was he who conducted Hervey and Fox to visit the court at Versailles. There they saw the infant Dauphin. They also dined with Cardinal Fleury, the King's former preceptor and now first minister. It was useful preparation for Hervey's re-entry into the world of courts and politics that he had left behind in England more than fifteen months before. He arrived in London on 25 October 1729, in his father's words, 'in perfect health & safety according to my prayers'.

6

'Marks of Distinction'

O N HIS RETURN TO LONDON Hervey stayed for a week in his house on Great Burlington Street with Stephen Fox. (Lady Hervey was probably at Ickworth with their children.) In the languorous summer heat of Florence he had forsworn all worldly ambition:

> I envy not the foremost of the great,
> Not Walpole's self directing Europe's fate.

He wished only to retire to Ickworth, he had reflected in his verse addressed to Stephen:

> From bus'ness and the world's intrusion free,
> With books, with love, with beauty and with thee;
> No farther want, no wish yet unpossess'd
> Cou'd e'er disturb this unambitious breast.

However sincere he thought his pose of retirement, the sharp-witted Lady Mary knew better:

> Returning vigour glow'd in every vein,
> And gay ideas flutter'd in the brain;
> Back he returns to breathe his native air,
> And all his first resolves are melted there!

It would have been difficult for him to keep his 'first resolves', for he unexpectedly found himself in the middle of a political tug-of-war.

During his absence abroad the struggle between Walpole and Pulteney had broken out into open warfare. By this time Walpole, secure in the friendship of the King, enjoyed a 'plenitude of power' as Prime Minister, leader of the House of Commons, party manager, and head of the Treasury (in control of public patronage and secret service money). Pulteney, the leader of the aggressive Opposition, sought recruits to swell his forces. Although Hervey had been a personal friend of Pulteney's he had always attached himself in public and political conduct to Walpole, and was indebted to him for his pension. While he had been abroad, Pulteney—along with Lady Hervey, who detested Walpole—planned to persuade him to give up his pension and abandon the Minister; and to compensate him for his loss they hoped to induce Lord Bristol to settle an annuity on him. The old Duchess of Marlborough, who also hated Walpole fiercely, was then brought in to help persuade Bristol to settle £600 a year on Hervey if he would support the Opposition in the House of Commons. As further persuasion to turn him away from Walpole, he was told that the Minister had tried to make love to Lady Hervey, but he decided to take no notice of it.

When, during his week in London, Hervey met with Pulteney this scheme was broached, but he did not (he confesses) reply 'openly, honestly, and fairly'; he should have told Pulteney that he would not turn on those who for no service had given him the £1,000 pension that had enabled him to go abroad to regain his health. Instead he told Pulteney that his father's 'ungiving temper' and family obligations would make it difficult to arrange a suitable financial settlement. Pulteney then tried to win him over by predicting as a certainty that the Ministry would fall and that a general insurrection would threaten the King, and promised that when he came to power there was nothing Hervey could ask or wish that would not be done for him. As Pulteney outlined the Opposition's plans he worked himself into a passion of 'coarse invective and rambling extravagance', and thus their meeting ended. From that time their friendship began to cool, though only gradually.

Parting from Stephen, who remained in his house, Hervey set out on 2 November for Ickworth, where he was reunited with his family. He promptly performed his nuptial duties with Lady Hervey, for a child was born to them exactly nine months later.

His political future greatly concerned his father, who now assured him of £600 a year if he would join the Opposition. He was forced to say what he should have said earlier: that he intended to resign his pension but would continue to support Walpole and the Ministry because they had so generously given it to him. He reinforced his decision in a lengthy letter to Walpole (dated 5 November), resigning the pension because he wanted to support the Ministry in Parliament without the appearance of being paid to do so. He had accepted the pension in the first place as a token 'of some future mark of his distinction . . . I must entreat the King, whenever he shall think proper, to consider me in some manner which I shall not be ashamed to own'. In effect his letter (as he himself remarked) pleased neither Walpole, who regarded it as a 'gentle preface' to forsaking his service, nor Pulteney, who (when told of it) regarded it as a bond for continuing in that service. His strategy seems clearly prudent: by giving up his pension yet promising to support Walpole he was soliciting an appointment more profitable and dignified. Only his future actions—and future rewards—would show whether Walpole or Pulteney was right.

Soon after his return to London he was able to spend a morning 'tête-à-tête' (his phrase) with Walpole, who had by then received his letter. 'Caresses, fine Words and professions were not spared,' he tells Stephen, 'but you know Ministers promise as Lady Bolingbroke commends, assez volontiers; in short, I was, what perhaps your Opinion of my Vanity will make you think impossible, mightyly flatter'd & not at all pleased.' He remembered their meeting in a different manner in his *Memoirs*: that when Walpole voiced the suspicion that he was defecting from the Court party he assured him that 'he would take the first opportunity on meeting of the Parliament publicly to demonstrate himself as much attached to his interest as ever'. Only there could he prove the sincerity of his intentions.

ii

By the time Hervey returned to London, Stephen had left for Bath, where he planned to join him. 'I *must* see you soon,' he impatiently writes (on 15 November); 'I can't live without You; Choice, tast[e], Habit, prejudice, Inclination, Reason & every thing that either does or ought to influence one's thoughts or one's actions makes mine center in & depend on You. Adieu, le plus aimable & le plus aimé qu'il y est au monde.' His love for Stephen was so penetrating and pervasive that at a dinner and concert given by the Duke of Richmond, when he requested

Bernacchi to sing an aria that they together had heard him sing in Naples, 'Before it was half over, I felt my Heart thump, my Throat swell, & my Eyes fill.' Everything he experienced he had to tell his friend: 'My Mind requires You constantly as my Constitution does the Sun,' he writes only the next day, and then confesses—as he had before—his fear that he loves more than he is loved in return: 'I wish you felt just so to me; we should pass many fewer Hours than I fear we are now like to do, asunder.'

He made the most of his deprivation, energetically going about in London. At a dinner given by Lord Lansdowne he was observed by a lady there as quite recovered, and looking better than she had ever seen him. 'I am grown already quite an English fine Gentleman,' he boasts to Stephen, 'I do a hundred different Things of a Day & like none of them; yawn in the Faces of the Women I talk to; eat & drink with Men I have no friendship for; play despising the Court & live in the Drawing-Room; rail at Quidnuncs & go hawking about for News; throw the faults of my Constitution upon the Climate; flatter aukwardly, railly worse, & in short make none of my Actions conducive to the pleasure or profit either of my-self or any Body else.' He blamed Stephen for his being so indifferent to other people; every one else paled when compared to him.

As December approached, when he would again be with Stephen, he could not hide his impatience. After several postponements he finally left on 9 December to meet him at Bath, where they may have stayed a short time before continuing on to Redlinch. He was in exultantly hearty spirits, the result of good health and bracing air and exercise. 'As to our manner of living here,' he confided to his friend Lady Mary, 'I can't imagine what you mean by talking of Matrimony, Holy Bands, Worldly Fetters, &c.—there is not a female here but Mr. Fox's Sister [Mrs. Digby], & she, you know, was executed six months ago . . . I have always profess'd that if I loved a Man never so well, unless I had hopes of rescuing him from the Hang man, I would never attend him to the Scaffold.' The ambiguity of his remark was piquant not only in its context at the time but in its forecast of the future.

Hervey's friendship for Stephen Fox was so peculiarly intense that the question must be asked and an answer attempted: was he expressing an affectionate camaraderie or a homosexual passion?

It is easy to misread the witty sentiments written in the tradition of French gallantry; and in English court circles such effusively sentimental letters passed between ladies and gentlemen who had long since given up sexual intercourse, and also between persons of the same sex whose tastes were exclusively for persons of the opposite. If such letters are neutral as evidence of sexual involvement, there are some of Horace Walpole's as a young man (written to Lord Lincoln) and of Thomas Gray's in middle age (to Bonstetten, a young Swiss) that hint of an emotion beyond mere friendship. But it would be difficult to cite a series of letters from one man to another that exposes such a profound, unequivocal love as that in Hervey's letters to Stephen.

Could he have felt what a later diarist, writing of George Selwyn's fondness for Lord March and Lord Carlisle, called 'sentimental sodomy'? For Selwyn, a stout, healthy man, who had known women (infrequently) in his youth and who never had an unnatural taste or appetite imputed to him, was attached to these two young men with 'all the extravagance and blindness of passion'. One may wonder, then, whether Hervey's extravagant passion for Stephen was a kind of sentimental sodomy.

Unlike proof of his heterosexual activity (his children), the evidence for his homosexuality is necessarily vague and oblique. One of his letters to Stephen (on 1 June 1727, five months after they met) contains a paragraph that may imply a physical relationship between them. 'You have left some such remembrancers behind you,' he writes, 'that I assure you (if 'tis any satisfaction to you to know it) you are not in the least Danger of being forgotten. The favours I have recieved at Your Honour's *Hands* are of such a Nature that tho' the impression might wear out of my Mind, yet they are written in such lasting characters upon every Limb, that 'tis impossible for me to look on a Leg or an Arm without having my Memory refresh'd. I have some thoughts of exposing the marks of your pollisonerie [lewdness] to move Compassion, as the Beggars that have been Slaves at Jerusalem doe the burnt Crucifix upon their Arms; they have remain'd so long that I begin to think they are equally indelible.'* What else could Hervey have

---

* It has been suggested (by the late Romney Sedgwick) that Hervey refers to bruises suffered while indulging in some innocent horseplay with Stephen. This would be plausible were it not for the fact that during the next six years Hervey's letters to him are simply love letters.

Kensington Aug: 10: 1734

Dear S.r I am extreme full of busyness to Day, having
a long Letter, & two of no small Consequence to write
by order of my great Friend & Patroness; but no
busyness can ever make me neglect what you desire,
or prevent my finding time to do any thing that
you say would give you a moment's Pleasure.
for absent or present I love you most unfeignedly,
& uninterruptedly.

In the first Place I must tell you I have
executed all your's, & my Friend Winnington's
Comissions; I have given the Plan to Bridgman,
sent the Warrant to Nanny, & wrote about the
mole-hill Engine to Ickworth. employ me often in
Things more material when my good fortune will enable me to be of service
to you in such; & in Trifles when it will not.

7. Autograph letter from Lord Hervey to Stephen Fox

meant except that he still bore the marks of love-making? that he is reliving the delicious moments of Stephen's caresses, which were vigorous enough to leave visible (black and blue) marks on his limbs?

Another fragment of evidence that has survived is a letter written about Hervey, a few weeks after his death, by Charles Hanbury Williams, once his friend and latterly his political enemy; he tells Henry Fox, who had also broken their friendship: 'Upon my word Lord Hervey has left Winnington a very *handsome legacy* & I suppose he'll *enter* into possession immediately—I suppose Lord Lincoln won't *push* at him any more. If he does, Hervey will certainly appear *backward* to him. Poor Fitzwilliam!' Cryptic though this is, and only identifiable in part, Williams's underlinings clarify his meaning. Lord Lincoln was famous among his friends for his large penis and for his indefatigable use of it, as both Williams and Horace Walpole gossiped. And the young Earl Fitzwilliam, when he was to be married a year later, was so frightened out of his wits before the wedding that he had a fit, and it was postponed to the following day. Horace gleefully passed this titbit of gossip on to Williams.

Before his infatuation with Stephen, Hervey had apparently not been involved in any such friendship with a man.★ He was at the time thirty-one years old, and six years earlier had married a pretty young woman for love and had begun to father a family. The only gossip about his extra-marital affairs, uttered by his mother at Bath, was his interest in a woman whom he had pursued in London. He was an exceedingly handsome man, of delicate rather than rugged cast, and as he grew older his manner became increasingly effeminate. In his sexual make-up could he have been bisexual—until now predominantly heterosexual but with an incipient tendency that, when he met a stimulating as well as responsive object, flared up to become a love that (before our day) dared not speak its name?

★ In the volume of letters that contains those to Stephen the first twenty-six pages—before the Fox series begins—are torn out, probably by the first Marquess of Bristol, who 'edited' Hervey's *Memoirs* in similar fashion. Possibly these contained a previous, more explicit, romantic correspondence. Besides, the letters to Stephen are in the hands of secretaries who copied them under Hervey's direction. He may thus have excised other explicit statements, and allowed some extravagant ones to remain only because they could be interpreted innocently. See p. 103 below.

iii

When Hervey returned to London for the opening of Parliament
Stephen accompanied him, and remained there during the four
months session. The fact that Stephen was a Tory and voted
against the Administration did not disturb their friendship. After
the King's Speech, on 13 January 1730, which made much of the
recently concluded Treaty of Seville, the Ministry's spokesman
who moved the Address of Thanks did not win Hervey's admiration, as he informed Henry Fox in the country. 'Lord Fitz-
williams's performance was darker, thicker, & heavyer,' he writes,
'than the Fog of this Day, in which I am now writing & yawning,
& vainly wishing for Light. I am sorry when God thought fitt to
send such a Piece of original Obscurity & Chaos into the World
as that Head . . . To say truth I fear his Dullness is contagious, for
tho' the House satt till eleven at night I neither heard one Argument above the Style of a Coffee-House, or one Joke above the
Mirth of an Ale-House.' The Opposition, led by Pulteney,
vigorously attacked the treaty; and in the House of Lords, where
the Address of Thanks was also passed, Bristol signed the Lords'
Protest. Privately Hervey believed the treaty very advantageous
to England, though he evidently did not voice his opinion on the
floor of the House.

The Lords' Protest contained ten detailed objections to the
King's Speech on the advantages of the Treaty of Seville. For
some reason—perhaps in the expectation that the Opposition
might raise the issue in the future—Walpole determined on a
reply to the Protest, and asked Hervey to write it. For Hervey it
was the first opportunity since his return from the Continent to
support the Ministry. Before embarking on his travels he had
supported them with his replies to Bolingbroke's *Occasional
Writer*; and he now confronted the same antagonist.

A printed Paper intitled the L: Protest having lately fallen into my
Hands, [he begins urbanely] I hope it will not be thought too presum-
ing in me to take notice of some Particulars it contains, for as it is to
be concluded that every thing from the Press is design'd for the use of
the Publick, so the Publick, in my opinion, has an undoubted Right to
discuss the Validity & Strength of all Arguments so transmitted to them,
& to examine if the tendency of those Arguments be to inform or mis-
lead.

He intends to disprove these 'plausible & pompous arguments', but he first sarcastically identifies Bolingbroke (though not by name) as the author of the Protest, and wonders why the Lords who refused to let him sit in their senate now accept his opinion. He continues his attack on Bolingbroke before reaching the main section of his essay—a refutation of the ten parts of the Protest, each in turn. In his conclusion he apologizes for any 'unbecoming warmth' caused by his indignation against a man 'who working unseen, like a Mole, is, by his dark underground Operations, incessantly striving to raise Stumbling Blocks in the Paths of the Unwary, & to disturb & ruin whatever Soil he frequents. . . .'; and he concludes with stately Ciceronian cadences to belabour the treacherous, still unnamed Bolingbroke.

When Walpole read Hervey's manuscript draft of the essay he evidently realized that to accuse someone not in the House of Lords of having written their Protest (an official Parliamentary document) might lay the author and printer of such a pamphlet open to prosecution for breach of Parliamentary privilege. He therefore gave the draft to Lord Ilay, who was trained as a lawyer, for his opinion. Ilay, manager of Walpole's Scottish affairs, was (in Hervey's opinion) a mixture of virtues and vices: 'a man of parts, quickness, knowledge, temper, dexterity, and judgement; a man of little truth, little honour, little principle, and no attachment but to his interest'. In revising the essay for publication Ilay's tactic was to pretend that the Lords' Protest was a forgery that had been concocted by fictitious Lords. To begin with he provided a title-page that he headed: 'A Detection of the Author of A late spurious Pamphlet intitled the Lords Protest', and beneath it a six-line quotation from *Paradise Lost* about the Apostate Angel. In the essay itself he struck out several long passages by Hervey and substituted his own to strengthen the pretence that the Lords' Protest was a 'most impudent piece of Forgery & most Satyrical Libel on those Great Persons whose Names are there prostituted to this Author's [Bolingbroke's] vile purpose'. Where Hervey had written 'their L—ships' he substituted 'The Author & his accomplices'; for 'Protesters' he substituted 'Forgerers'; and he inserted 'those who personate' before 'Members of a British Senate'.

It was a clever stunt, but dangerous since the authentic Lords and their Protest were in effect ridiculed; and perhaps for that reason the essay was not published. It remained among Walpole's papers, a sample not only of Hervey's fluent skill as a controversial-ist but of his unpensioned allegiance to the Ministry.

A far more controversial measure was imminent—the bill for continuing 12,000 Hessian troops in British pay for one year longer. The Opposition charged that the troops were not required for England's protection but were solely for Hanover's. 'The Debate on the Hessians . . . has sett every body's expectations agog', Hervey tells Henry Fox. It was this bill, Pulteney had predicted to Hervey, that would raise an insurrection. But when it came to the floor (on 4 February) the inflammatory criticism that Pulteney had uttered privately was only insinuated, and much more gently than most people expected.

This time Hervey was among the Ministerial speakers. His friend Winnington reported to Henry Fox that the long debate on the Hessians 'was only managed by the small artillery, the great guns not firing . . . Lord Hervey spoke for them very well'. His defence was impressive enough to be admired by Lord Egmont, a careful listener, who called it 'a long and studied speech, which did him a great deal of honour, and the more, that he made it seem extemporary, by replying to particular objections and arguments in the course they had been urged, some of which perhaps had never entered his imagination'. The debate, which started at one o'clock, lasted until eight. Appointed teller, Hervey observed Stephen cast his vote with the Opposition of 169 against the Administration's 248. It was a busy day for Hervey, who could not sit down to dinner until eleven; more important, he dined with Walpole. One of the subjects they must have discussed, as the claret went round, was Hervey's future, especially since there could not have been any doubt in the Minister's mind as to where his allegiance lay.

The exact target of the Opposition's next attack was unknown to the Ministry when Sir William Wyndham moved that a day be designated to consider the state of the nation. On the day, 10 February, the Opposition startled the Ministry by accusing them of having permitted the harbour of Dunkirk to be rebuilt and refortified in violation of the Treaty of Utrecht (signed in 1713). As early as April 1728 Walpole had received reports of the rebuilding of Dunkirk harbour, and in November had pointed this out to Cardinal Fleury. Yet in May 1729 the Dutch (through Chesterfield at the Hague) complained that the work was still going on. The Opposition were justified in accusing Walpole's Administration of laxness. The proof was so clearly set forth by testifying witnesses that, as Hervey observed, 'the whole House was in a flame, and the ministry stronger pushed than they had ever been on any occasion before'. Walpole very cleverly stalled for time; before the resolution could be moved, he said, he needed certain documents as well as a report from an English inspector who that very day had left for Dunkirk. He thus gained a fortnight to prepare his own defences, and he made the most of it. One of those pressed into service was Hervey.

Everybody was concerned with politics more than ever before, he tells Henry Fox ten days before the crucial debate was to take place. 'I am upon this occasion just in the same Situation with People who go *randying* & hate Tobacco; they detest smoaking, can't do it, make them-selves sick with trying at it, & live in a Cloud of it every Day of their lives.' But, he then asks (in French), how can it be avoided? His rhetorical question was a modest understatement, for he was busy writing a pamphlet in defence of the Ministry.

Entitled *A Summary Account of the State of Dunkirk, and the Negociations relating thereto*, it was issued anonymously. Its subtitle reflected his actual position as M.P.: 'In A Letter from a Member of Parliament to the Mayor of the Borough for which He Serves.' It is relatively brief (twenty-seven spaciously margined pages), its tone is reasonable, and its arguments clear and simple. To begin with, the author hopes that the Mayor will find his account 'as faithful and impartial in what he relates, as in the Execution of the great Trust you have reposed in him'. He then relates how the harbour was partially repaired by the inhabitants of the town, and how as soon as the English Ministers knew of it they protested to the French court, who promised to intercede, but not to do so publicly until after the Treaty of Seville, then in progress, had been completed. The French King had just then issued an order for the harbour to be reduced to its required condition; and proof of this was offered in an appendix, the order published at Versailles on 27/16 February 1730. On the morning of the 20th, a copy of the order had actually arrived in London, just in time, bringing 'great joy' to Walpole and his brother.

Since the House was to take up the Dunkirk affair on 27 February, Hervey's pamphlet must have been published in the previous week. As a letter from an anonymous M.P. it could be read more sympathetically by the Members in the House, most of whom were not allied to the Opposition but were independents who wished to judge the issue fairly.

Walpole handled the 'state of Dunkirk' debate in masterly fashion. As a result, Hervey observed, 'instead of voting any Censure upon the Administration, as the Malcontents gave and concieved hopes of, an Adress of thanks to his Majesty for his early Care, & Congratulations upon the Success of that Care, was resolved upon by a Majority of 270 to 149'. Without taking any part in the debate, Hervey sat through to the end at four o'clock in the morning. His spirits were so high that he went out to dinner afterwards to celebrate, sat up till six, and rose from his bed at ten in the morning to walk from St. James's to Kensington.

In retrospect and in the privacy of his *Memoirs* Hervey was able to confess what he could not in his pamphlet: that the fortifications had actually been restored to almost their original state by the inhabitants of Dunkirk 'not by the command, yet by the connivance of the Court of France'; and he reflected wittily that 'this Dunkirk storm, that was very near shipwrecking the Administration, entirely blew over, and those who raised it had nothing to comfort them for not having demolished the Walpoles but the glory of bragging that their industry had re-demolished Dunkirk'.

iv

Even before his speech on the Hessian bill Hervey had wondered about the 'Alterations at Court', which it was said would not be made until after the Parliamentary session ended. 'My own affairs are at a full stand,' he tells Henry Fox, 'as well as every other Body's that has any expectation or tenures from the Court.' Having demonstrated his unpensioned loyalty to Walpole on the floor of the House of Commons and (anonymously) in a published pamphlet, he wondered what his reward would be, while assuming that it would come to him after Parliament rose in mid-May. But any M.P. who accepted a government post had to vacate his seat, and then only on a writ issued by the House could he stand in the by-election to regain it. Since Walpole was unwilling to let the seat for Bury lie open through the summer, he bestowed his reward on Hervey at the end of April—the post of Vice-Chamberlain

to the King's Household, and with it membership of the Privy
Council. Newspapers reported it on 30 April, and Hervey took
his oaths on 7 May. He replaced Lord Harrington, who for his
success in negotiating the Treaty of Seville was appointed Secretary of State (in place of Lord Townshend, Walpole's brother-in-
law, who was thus eased into retirement). Hervey duly vacated
his Parliamentary seat, and the House issued a writ for the Bury
election to be held on 16 May.

He travelled up to Suffolk, probably in the company of the
other candidate for Bury, Colonel Thomas Norton, who had also
vacated his seat on being appointed Deputy Governor of Chelsea
Hospital. The election did not go smoothly. A Captain Draper,
who wished to oppose them, could not muster support. In a fit of
insane pique he captured the corporation's band of musicians on
the day of election, and locked them in a room to play for him
instead of the candidates. When a town alderman tried to reason
with him the Captain stabbed him in the shoulder and arm, and
was arrested. In the election itself both candidates were unanimously returned; and after a celebration ball they returned to
London to take up their respective posts.

As Vice-Chamberlain, Hervey performed the duties of the
Lord Chamberlain, who was at that time the Duke of Grafton;
and he was assisted by the Lord Chamberlain's secretary and two
clerks. In practice he or the Lord Chamberlain had to be in
residence all year round to supervise such functions as receptions
for ambassadors and Royal visitors, celebrations of birthdays and
anniversaries, balls, concerts, Drawing-Room receptions (held
twice a week during the London season), and Royal marriages and
funerals. He also had the duty of assigning, repairing, and furnish-
ing lodgings at court. When the court moved, as it frequently did,
between the palaces at St. James's, Kensington, Windsor, Richmond, Hampton Court, and Kew, he had to assign servants,
transportation, and lodgings; and if disputes arose among the
attendants and servants as to their duties or perquisites he had to
arbitrate. He could, of course, deputize his clerks or secretary to
perform the routine tasks.

Hervey's compensation for this responsible and exacting post
was an annual salary of £600 from the Exchequer augmented by
£559 from the Cofferer, more than a thousand pounds in all.
(Four years later the King added £1,000 a year to his salary.) In

addition he had an apartment at St. James's Palace, large enough to shelter his wife and perhaps his children, and living quarters in the other palaces. As visible emblems of his office he wore a gold and jewelled key. With its dignity, emoluments, and perquisites, the appointment measured up to his expectations at this time— a 'mark of distinction' that he would not be 'ashamed to own'. Although he frequently complained of his arduous duties he must have found the post congenial and satisfying or he would not have accepted it to begin with and kept it for ten years; and he resigned it only to accept a higher one.

Did Walpole appoint him Vice-Chamberlain in order to profit by his intimacy with the Queen, as is sometimes said? There is no evidence that before his appointment he enjoyed any special favour with her, though he already knew the Royal Family since he had attended their court for more than ten years. But his appointment put him in frequent and close contact with them; and his access to the King and Queen during what he calls 'their private and leisure hours' deepened his friendship with the Queen and his understanding of the King. And as time passed, the Queen's sympathy and affection for him grew far beyond what she felt for her own son Frederick, Prince of Wales.

While Prince Frederick had been kept in Hanover during his grandfather's reign he had been awarded suitable honours: created Duke of Gloucester and inducted (*in absentia*) into the Order of the Garter and then created Duke of Edinburgh. When his father ascended the throne he could no longer be kept in exile; and in December 1728 he had been brought to England without any fanfare, and a month later invested as Prince of Wales. He made a very favourable impression at court. Lady Bristol thought him 'the most agreeable young man that is possible to imagine, without being the least handsome, his person little but very well made and genteel, a livelyness in his eyes that is undiscribable, and the most obliging address that can be conceivd'. Others remarked on his informality—'frankness and affability in his way very different from his rank, and very engaging'.

When the Prince had arrived in England Hervey was still abroad, but on his return he immediately renewed the friendship he had deliberately cultivated in Hanover twelve years earlier. His new impression of the Prince, as set down in his *Memoirs*, is relatively impartial: 'The Prince's character at his first coming over . . . seemed much more amiable than it was upon his opening himself and being better known. For though there appeared nothing in him to be admired, yet there seemed nothing in him to be hated—neither nothing great nor nothing vicious.' Hervey even makes allowance for the Prince's terrible family relations: 'he had a father that abhorred him, a mother that despised and neglected him, a sister that betrayed him, a brother set up to pique, and a set of servants that neither were of use to him, nor were capable of being of use to him, nor desirous of being so.' Even before his appointment to court Hervey spent time with the Prince; with two others he had accompanied him on a walk from St. James's to Kensington Palace. He was now to be very frequently in the company of the amiable heir to the throne.

From 10 June they were all in residence at Windsor, where Hervey occupied his newly fitted apartment. He was soon faced with his first important ceremony—the Feast of St. George, particularly important that year because the nine-year-old Duke of Cumberland (the future Butcher of Culloden) was to be made a knight of that order. Hervey had to be instructed as to bows, steps, attitudes, since he was to walk, and officiate, as Lord Chamberlain. It was a gruelling ordeal, as he recollected it (for Stephen's amusement and sympathy): 'I was Yesterday from seven a Clock in the Morning till two this Morning, constantly upon my Legs, excepting half an Hour that I was at Dinner, & about an Hour that I lay down in the afternoon, to compensate for which trouble I had the recreation of seeing one sett of performers Bowing till their Backs aked, four Hours in the Morning; another sett eating till they spew'd, & drinking 'till they reel'd at Noon; & a third dancing & sweating till they were ready to drop, at Night.' Clearly his office was no sinecure.

The normal court activities could be as sedate as attending the King and Queen when they dined in public (every Sunday and Thursday) or as energetic as accompanying them on their frequent stag-hunts. To Mrs. Howard, the King's demure mistress, it was a dangerous pastime: 'We hunt with great noise and violence, and have every day a very tolerable chance to have a neck broke.' What Hervey ironically described as his 'present prevailing Amusement' was stag-hunting twice a week 'in the Heat of the Day, an infinite Mob, a Cloud of Dust, & the Ground as hard as

Flint'. But it had delights as well as dangers: 'Lady Burlington was knock'd off her Horse by the Bough of a Tree, Lady Essex thrown into a Bog, & Lady Bell Finch, if it had not been for a precautionary Pair of Breeches, upon the like Occasion had sold the whole Company a Bargain. This is the Gazette of Windsor.'

Occasionally he tried to escape from the prescribed routine. One day, while the Prince was shooting in Richmond Park, he slipped away to call on Lady Mary at Twickenham but she was not at home. He had hoped to entertain himself while the Prince was beating the woods. 'I have been so ty'd by the Leg this Summer at Windsor', was his apology for neglecting her. Court routine was occasionally varied—as when Colley Cibber sent a troupe of comedians from Drury Lane to perform at Windsor— but only rarely. 'What can I tell your Ladyship from hence?' he asks his mother. 'The Circle of our employments moves in such unchangeable Revolutions that you have but to look at your watch any Hour in the four & twenty & tell your-self what we are doing as well as if you were here, *for as it was in the beginning is now & ever shall be, Court without end, Amen*.' Court without end was to be his fate for the next decade.

v

With almost unfailing regularity Hervey complained to Stephen, his most frequent correspondent, that his court duties deprived him of the company of the one person in the world he wanted most to be with. Even when the King was especially gracious and in uncommon good humour he could not, because of that deprivation, be happy. He had a taste of happiness at the end of July— Stephen's company at Windsor for a few hours; but then he had to ride to London (he complained) not with Stephen but with Walpole and Lord Scarborough. If he had only to consider his own pleasure he would never part from him. 'The only time I spend entirely to my Heart's Content when I am from you', he tells him in mid-August, 'is that in which I indulge my-self in writing to You.'

They again managed a brief meeting when Stephen paused at Windsor on his way to Somerset. Hervey had never parted from him with more regret: 'the Tears came into my Eyes a hundred times between Windsor and London, with reflecting we were now to be divided for a longer time than ever we had been asunder before (that I could recollect) since our first acquaintance.' Their friend Charles Hamilton, Lord Abercorn's son, accompanied Stephen to Redlinch. 'How I envy Mr. Hamilton to be sure of waking to You every Morning,' he confesses, 'to have You for the first object for his Eyes every time they open & the last every time they close.'

When Stephen tried to console him he protested:

What are the Royal pleasures you talk of, my dear dear Ste., which are not given equally to every Subject? Do the trappings of Royalty make the amusements of the country more agreable? Are the Chaises easyer or our Boats safer for being gilt? Is the Air sweeter for a Court, or the Walks pleasanter for being bounded with Centinels? What Entertainment does Windsor afford that can not be found at Redlinch? But transpose that Question & I should quickly answer, the greatest Joy I ever did or can know.

He then makes the startling proposal that instead of seeing each other on visits they should have a 'common home'—a difficult goal to attain, he admits, but not impossible if pursued with sufficient determination. Until that could be arranged they continued to visit each other. 'You talk of my going to You in November,' he reminds Stephen at the end of August, 'but say nothing of coming here in September. Is it possible for You to pass a Day without thinking of it? I can't.'

He was in London in time for his wife's lying-in on 1 August, when she 'was deliver'd of a thumping Boy', as he informed their friend Lady Murray; 'she suffer'd a good deal, but not more than I think every Woman deserves at the Hands of a poor Mortal that she throws involuntaryly into an existance where it has so few Chances to be happy & so many to be miserable.' The boy was his third son (and fifth child), and in choosing a namesake he was able to compliment the Prince of Wales. Frederick's baptism, entered in the register of St. James's Church, took place at Hervey's house in Great Burlington Street, the godfathers being the Prince and the Duke of Richmond, and the godmother Henrietta, Duchess of Marlborough. Instead of sending a proxy the Prince did them the honour of attending himself.

It was a harrowing day for the father. He had arisen at five in the morning to dash up to Windsor to wait on the King, and then back to London immediately after dinner to receive the Prince at his house, where a supper was laid out after the baptism. He could not get to bed again until past two in the morning—half-killed with fatigue, he tells Stephen, but the evening had gone off much better 'than things of ⟨that⟩ Form generally do. Every Body was gay, easy, & seem'd pleased; but particularly the Prince & Duchess of Marlborough, who are so taken with one another that I am not sure it will not end in a Flirtation.' (The Duchess's long-standing lover, William Congreve, had died the year before.)

As the summer drew to an end court activities at Windsor did not let up. 'I have been hunting all this morning with the King', Hervey tells Stephen, 'in the worst Country, the worst Wether, and with the worst Dogs that ever poor Sportsmen were curs'd with.' He was so tired when he returned to his apartment that he went to bed immediately, dined upon chocolate, but then had to go out to walk with the King.

An unexpected consequence of his being at Windsor was that the Dowager Duchess of Marlborough, who lived at the Old Lodge in Windsor Park, invited him to dinner. He thought it odd that she should be so friendly, since their political loyalties were so opposed, but she persisted. He was soon able to send his mother more startling news:

The first thing that presented it-self yesterday at the Rendezvous for the Stag-hunting was her Grace of Marlborough, flying in an easterly Wind & an open Chaise, her Hands in Flannel & her Shoulders in Embroidery; & what was in her Heart I know not, but out of her Mouth flow'd nothing but Oyl & Honey. Many Douceurs pass'd between her, the King, the Queen, & Sir Robert [Walpole]; & after what has happen'd I don't think it at all impossible but the next News I send you may be that she has danced all night at Court of the Birth-Day.

He was surprised to find their friendship budding anew in what he thought was the very depth of its winter. Perhaps she again hoped to persuade him to abandon Walpole and join Pulteney in the Opposition.

He had been looking forward so hungrily to Stephen's visit in September that he blamed himself for his dissatisfaction: 'I have made it impossible for me to live without You.' Yet he still tried to see himself objectively. 'I have often thought', he confides in him, 'if any very idle Body had Curiosity enough to intercept

& examine my Letters, they would certainly conclude they came rather from a Mistress than a Friend; but it must be people that were unacquainted with You who made that Conclusion; otherwise they might know that Reason would make one as fond of your Society as passion could make one of any other Body's.' (The sceptic may wonder whether this assertion was a defence against prying eyes then or later.) How true this high-minded assertion was can be judged by his next, hurried letter, as he awaited Stephen's arrival, when it was 'as impossible for me to say more as it would be for me ever to tell you, had I time to write volumes, how warmly, how tenderly, how gratefully, how contentedly and unalterably I am Yours. Adieu, mon bien aimable, mon bien aimé,' followed by four lines of love poetry in Italian (probably quoted from an opera).

'Every Body has some Madness in their Composition, & I freely acknowledge you are mine,' he tells Stephen, who was about to leave Redlinch for Windsor; and he concludes: 'Adieu, que je vous aime, que je vous adore: & si vous m'aimé de même venez me le dire.' If this is the expression of a friendship based on Reason, the two men must have passed their time in the most passionate pursuit of that Platonic ideal. They remained together for more than two months.

Hervey had to stay with the court as it moved to Richmond for two weeks, and then to St. James's (on 28 October) in time for the King's birthday celebration on the 30th. A sadder duty for an old friend awaited him. Early that year Anne Oldfield, a friend of his family, had acted the leading part in James Thomson's verse tragedy, *Sophonisba*, for which Hervey had obligingly written an epilogue. On 3 March he had attended the third performance, the author's benefit night, at Drury Lane, but another's epilogue was spoken and by Mrs. Cibber. Mrs. Oldfield became seriously ill in the summer, and died on 23 October. Her corpse, carried to Westminster Abbey to lie in state in the Jerusalem Chamber, was then buried in the Abbey at night 'in great Funeral Pomp and Solemnity'.* Hervey was one of the pall-bearers. He also served as an executor of her will, which divided her

---

* Pope satirized her vanity at her death in his *Epistle to Cobham*, lines 242–7 (*Poems*, III. ii. 36); and Voltaire contrasted her splendid burial with the disgraceful one of Adrienne Lecouvreur, who because she was an actress was denied last rites and burial in consecrated ground (Theodore Besterman, *Voltaire*, 1969, pp. 162–3).

considerable estate between her two sons, both born out of wedlock and fathered by the two men whose mistress she had successively been.

A more agreeable legal transaction awaited him, the answer probably to his rhetorical question to Stephen that summer: 'why should we see one another by Visits, but never have a common home?' Since he now had an apartment in St. James's Palace he could dispose of his house in Great Burlington Street; and Lady Hervey and their children could stay at his apartment or at his father's houses in St. James's Square and Ickworth. He therefore assigned the lease of his house to Stephen Fox (on 14 November), and through Hoare the banker Stephen paid over to Lady Hervey the sum of £4,000. The house, which was not far from the palace, thus became the common home of the two friends.

vi

As the autumn of 1730 drew on, even though Parliament was not to convene for some months, the Opposition press kept up its relentless attack on the Administration. 'Here one is more and more involved with politics every day', Hervey complained (in November) to Dr. Cocchi in Florence. 'I am so bored with Craftsmen, with Pamphlets and all the Gibberish of a free Government that if I did not look upon them as the natural consequences of our Liberty I would be driven to desperation by them, for it is impossible to keep one's self from reading them.' In fact, he did more than read them; he burst out as a pamphleteer himself in an episode that was to have a dramatic denouement.

The *Craftsman* was still the leading Opposition paper, its political essays written mainly by Pulteney and by Bolingbroke. Hervey now took up its challenge by replying. Towards the end of November his *Observations on the Writings of the Craftsman*, a thirty-page pamphlet, was issued by James Roberts, who generally published for the Ministry. Unlike the frequently strident tone and invective of the *Craftsman*'s writers, Hervey pitched his 'observations' in calm and reasonable language. 'I am not ignorant of the unequal Terms,' he begins, 'upon which he enters the Lists in a Paper-War, who draws his Pen on the Defensive Side; those who engage the Malice of Mankind to their Party will generally, I fear, lead more numerous Troops, and find much better

Encouragement than those who sollicit their good Nature or appeal to their Justice.'

As an impartial observer, he then sets himself to examine the design, progress, and effects of the *Craftsman* in its attacks on the King and on Walpole's policies and alleged corruption. One *Craftsman* (14 November) is singled out for having used the convenient but specious device of drawing an historical parallel between Edward IV and his wicked Queen (a prudent way of libelling Queen Caroline), which Hervey asserts is mischievously false. To hammer home his point, he soon followed this pamphlet with another: *Sequel of a pamphlet intitled Observations on the Writings of the Craftsman*; and in this he applied himself specifically to correcting the historical statements put forth by the *Craftsman*'s writers, who drew their material from Paul Rapin's *History of England*.

In the meantime Nicholas Amherst, editor of the *Craftsman*, had published an *Answer to the Observations on the Writings of the Craftsman* (postdated 1731); and although Hervey dismissed it in his *Sequel* as undeserving of a reply, he attacked it in the third of his pamphlets in this sequence: *Farther Observations On the Writings of the Craftsman. Or Short Remarks upon a Late Pamphlet, entituled, An Answer to the Observations on the Writings of the Craftsman*. Again Hervey accuses the *Craftsman* of distorting history to attack the Ministry and, with sarcastic flattery, the King himself. If the Ministry is really guilty of misdeeds, he asks, why must proof be sought in past history and dead monarchs? His conclusion is that the *Craftsman*'s purpose is to make the King 'the proper Object of their Odium and Resentment; so full does this wicked Purpose of theirs stare you in the face, through every Line of this impudent and treasonable Invective'.

Hervey's authorship of the pamphlets was probably suspected by the Opposition writers, for he was attacked by one of them as a 'frothy Author' in a flimsy pamphlet called *Three Pamphlets; Entituled, Observations on the Writings of the Craftsman. The Sequel and farther Observations Examin'd*. It may seem remarkable that in the space of about one month—for he left London on 17 December—Hervey should have published three pamphlets; but he was a facile writer, and his arguments against the *Craftsman* were well rehearsed.

During these weeks he was prevented from writing to Stephen

Fox for the best of possible reasons—they were both in London; and when Stephen did leave, on 4 December, they planned to meet a fortnight later. 'You have been gone out of Town, my dearest Ste. but four days,' he writes impatiently, '& I have sigh'd for it at least four hundred times', after which he constructs a verbal arabesque to exhibit his unchanging, undying love. Until he could join him he sent letters, though in pain from both tooth-ache and heartache. Finally, accompanied by his valet Maran, he left for Salisbury, where Stephen was to meet him with horses or a coach to accompany him to Redlinch.

On his journey he did not forget to write to his friends at court, particularly the Prince of Wales; and the Prince lost no time in replying: 'My Dear Hervey, I reciev'd Sunday evening your Letter from Salisbury, & am mighty sensible that fatigue at one Side, & pleasures, Balls, and fine Ladys at another side did not make you forget Orestes, the warm Orestes, to his Dear Pilades.' After more chatter about dancing and marriage, he sends along a 'foolish Sottish Ballad' and concludes: 'Adieu, my Dear Chicken.* Take care for you burn the ballad or I'll kill you. Frederick P.' Hervey answered promptly, and as promptly had the Prince's reply while he was at Redlinch: 'These two days we have had no remarcable things at Court, except that Mylord Chicken went into Sommerset Shire.' Then, after some political gossip and a satiric sketch of the Duke of Newcastle, the Prince continues: 'I have many little drolerics still to tell you but the time presses, so I end, but being a fraid that this Letter should be opened if I sent it directly to you, so I make a direction to Mr. Fox, as if it was written to You by a Lady, to make you be teazed a little about it. Adieu my Dear, Frederick P.' Only a close, informal friendship between the two men could have elicited such high-spirited, giddy letters from the Prince, who evidently regarded Stephen as a watchfully jealous friend of Hervey's.

Since he remained at Redlinch to the last possible moment (2 January 1731) Hervey had to speed back to London, covering one hundred miles in nine hours, even though he paused at Windsor Lodge; but the Duchess of Marlborough was out, and so he continued on to St. James's without dinner. In London he busied

---

* Hervey thus referred to himself. After a hunt, when one of their party rode through the rain in an open chaise, he writes: 'we Chickens . . . chose the ignoble Safety of a dry Coach with Glasses drawn up' (to Stephen, 9 Sept. 1730, H MS.).

himself, along with his own affairs, with Stephen's, who was to
join him in a fortnight. He hired a footman who could shave; and
he spoke to the upholsterer about furniture that would go into
the house on Great Burlington Street, which he had formerly
lived in with his wife and children and would now share with
Stephen.

vii

Shortly before the Parliamentary session opened, Hervey was
again pressed into service by Walpole; he had already proved
himself to be one of the most effective of the Ministry's writers.
His duty this time was to write only the preface to a pamphlet by
another. 'The enclosed I believe you will like; I do', he tells
Stephen (on 7 January). 'If I could be as sure when I write of
writing only to Your Eyes as I am when I speak of speaking only
to Your Ears I could tell you some things you would be curious
to know, but thinking upon paper is so unsafe that these Subjects
must not be discuss'd till we meet. I have chid the pamphlet Man
& he promises Amendment and punctuality for the future.' What
he enclosed in his letter was probably his own 'Dedication' to
a pamphlet by William Yonge, M.P., about to be published.

*Sedition and Defamation Display'd: In a Letter to the Author of the
Craftsman* was published anonymously by J. Roberts. Its mock-
dedication, also unsigned, is an eight-page piece, elegant and
polished compared with the essay it introduces. Addressing the
patrons of the *Craftsman*, its author begins: 'Gentleman, As I am
a Member of the Community which you are endeavouring to
disturb, a Friend to the Constitution which you are labouring
to overturn, and a faithful Subject to the King whom you daily
insult, you have no Right to expect a Panegyrick from me.' He
then sketches a character-portrait of one of the patrons (Pulteney,
though not by name) as a young gentleman endowed with many
advantages, yet a slave to his passions: irresolute, jealous, vain,
self-centred, 'determined to hold the highest Offices in the State,
or to censure and confound *all* the Measures of the Government,
under any other *Administration*; he at length renounced at once
all former Friendships and Principles, vowing the Destruction of
those who had distinguished him by a peculiar Regard, betraying
private Correspondencies, and endeavouring to distress *that
Prince* and *that Family* to which he owed the highest Obligations.'

The dedicator then turns to the other *Craftsman* patron, Boling-broke, describing him with sharper acerbity as an infamous traitor. The British must decide whether it is worth distressing or embroiling their country for the sake of such men; 'But if no such Persons are in Being, this Dedication is thrown away, and it would be in vain to subscribe myself, Gentlemen, your Humble Servant, &c.' Neither the 'Dedication' in the form of a letter (by Hervey) nor the essay, which is not a letter (by Yonge), gives any hint that they were written by different men.

In the essay (*Sedition and Defamation Display'd*) the author castigates the *Craftsman* and *Fog's Journal*, calling them 'infamous Retailers of Lies, Scandal, Sedition, and Treason', whose Billings-gate language proves they were not written by gentlemen. He gives examples of their exaggerations, fabrications, and outright falsehoods; spurns their hypocritical protestations of patriotism and love of liberty; and finally recommends that since they slander the King and incite the people their authors should be punished. Yonge, who wrote this long attack, had been a suppor-ter of Walpole's since the previous reign. He was a Lord of the Treasury, and later in the year succeeded to his father's baronetcy. In Hervey's private opinion he was 'a ductile courtier and a parliamentary tool' of Walpole's; 'a great liar, but rather a mean than a vicious one . . . good-natured and good humoured, never offensive in company, nobody's friend, nobody's enemy'. It was Walpole, probably, who asked Hervey to write the dedication to Yonge's attack.

Hervey was under a severe strain from his work as well as from some malaise connected with politics which he does not identify except that it made him 'burn all inward' and feel 'really very uneasy'. The day after he wrote to Stephen, while attending the Queen's Drawing-Room and talking to the Prince of Wales, without any warning he suddenly lost consciousness and dropped to the floor as though he had been shot. Three men (including Walpole) carried him into the Queen's bedchamber to revive him, after which he was brought down to his own apartment, and blooded and cupped. By the next morning, when he was given medicine, he was completely recovered. It was probably an epileptic seizure, called by one courtier 'falling sickness'.

Two weeks later, with no apparent after-effects of his seizure, he attended the opening of Parliament (on 21 January 1731). The

King having made his customary opening speech and the House of Commons having moved for an Address of Thanks, Pulteney introduced an amendment that the King be advised not to wage any war in Flanders or upon the Rhine. This was strenuously opposed by speakers for the Ministry, among them Walpole, his brother, Yonge, and Hervey. The amendment was defeated, and the Address passed—a handsome victory for the Administration Whigs. 'Whether the enemy had nothing to say, or were not prepared, I know not,' one of the victors wrote, 'but a more piti-full figure they never made, nor greater joy and triumph ever appeared among our friends.'

On the day before he attacked the Ministry in the House of Commons Pulteney had delivered to Richard Francklin, printer of the *Craftsman* and other Opposition papers, a lengthy discourse in the form of a letter, dated 20 January and signed Caleb D'Anvers (the *nom de plume* of the *Craftsman*'s writer). As one of the 'patrons' who had been chastised in the pamphlet by Yonge, with Hervey's preface, Pulteney now fought back with *A Proper Reply to a Late Scurrilous Libel, Intitled Sedition and Defamation Display'd*. Mistakenly assuming that Hervey had written the entire pamphlet Pulteney launched the first attack on him, one that would provide the basis of his long career as a satiric *persona*.

'*Dear* Sir,' Mr. D'Anvers opens civilly enough, 'I have hitherto declined taking any Notice of those pretty Declamations, with which you have been lately pleased to oblige the Publick; and look'd upon them only as little Flights or Exercitations of a Genius, which had a Mind to try its Strength in Politicks.' He speculates on their authorship—a public-school boy or a boarding-school miss—until he is informed they are the productions of 'pretty Mr. *Fainlove*'. When he promises not to hurt Mr. Fainlove because of what the ladies would say, his informant replies, 'Nay, you know that He is a *Lady* himself; or at least such a nice Composition of the two Sexes, that it is difficult to distinguish which is most prædominant.' Quotations from Horace and Ausonius reinforce his point before he spells it out explicitly: 'But though it would be barbarous to handle such a *delicate Hermophrodite*, such a pretty, little, *Master Miss*, in too rough a Manner; yet you must give me Leave, my Dear, to give you a little, gentle Correction, for your own good.'

Mr. Fainlove has carried the jest too far, Pulteney continues, by fouling his mouth with 'such *paw* Words as *Traytor* and *Villain*. The Dialect of *Billingsgate* is very unbecoming a *Court-Education*, and will destroy all Pretensions to the Character of a *fine Gentleman*, which you have taken so much Pains to acquire, and which you would, I dare say, be almost as loth to lose as your *Place*, or even *another Tooth*.' Here Pulteney could not have been more specific, for only a few weeks before, after suffering pain from a loose tooth, Hervey had been forced to have it pulled.

'You should never talk, my Dear, of *Baseness, Ingratitude* and *Treachery*'—which Hervey had charged Bolingbroke with— 'because People will be apt to call some Things to Mind, which you ought to wish forgotten.' Then, before levelling his attack on Walpole, Pulteney pays tribute to his advocate as a 'Circulator of Tittle-Tattle, a Bearer of Tales, a Teller of Fibs, a station'd Spy'. Yet Pulteney seems genuinely puzzled as to Hervey's exact share in the two parts of the pamphlet: 'And now, *my Dear* . . . whether you compiled, or only dedicated the piece'; whether Walpole contributed to it, or 'whether you discompos'd the Lillies and Roses of your Cheeks by a painful Collection of all those Common-place Reflections' he will continue to address him. He later returns to that question: 'Whether you wrote the Whole of this *abusive Libel*, or not, your *Observations* and *Sequel* deserve this Treatment . . .' Thus Hervey is being punished not only for his possible share in the pamphlet and its dedication but for his authorship of the attacks on the *Craftsman* published a few months earlier.

Hervey's accusation (in the 'Dedication') that Pulteney had been disloyal to Walpole stung Pulteney into turning the accusation against him: that he had 'particular and very great Obligations to a *certain Person* [Pulteney]', who took him into his house as one of his own family and defended his character;

This *former Patron* of yours was, at least, the remote Cause of your obtaining the very *Employment* you now enjoy; and your *present Patron*, as destitute as He is of *Friends*, would have thought you too insignificant an Acquisition to have been purchas'd at so high a Price, if it had not been for the Additional Satisfaction of having purloin'd you from his *next Door Neighbour*.

(Both Walpole and Pulteney lived in Arlington Street.) This is a puzzling accusation: Hervey, although a personal friend of Pulteney's, had never been politically connected with him; his allegiance had always been to Walpole. Perhaps Pulteney is turning the tables. Since Hervey has accused him of ingratitude to *his* patron, then how neat to accuse his accuser of the same sin toward himself! If Pulteney thus lied—a pamphleteer does not write under oath—his lie has been repeated by later satirists and historians.

The most shocking of Pulteney's insults was still to come. In the *Observations on the Writings of the Craftsman* Hervey had argued that despite that paper's accusation of corruption in the Administration no proof had been offered. 'But you seem, *pretty Sir*,' Pulteney now writes, 'to take the Word *Corruption* in a limited Sense and confine it to the *Corrupter*—Give me Leave to illustrate This by a parallel Case—There is a certain, unnatural, reigning Vice (indecent and almost shocking to mention) . . . It is well known that there must be *two Parties* in this Crime; the *Pathick* and the *Agent*; both equally guilty. I need not explain These any farther.' In other words, having called Hervey a hermaphrodite—the eighteenth-century term for homosexual—Pulteney now, by innuendo, accuses him of homosexual practices.

A charge of homosexuality, should it involve the 'abominable crime' of sodomy, was a serious felony, punishable by death. Since Pulteney's accusation was oblique and intended only for ridicule it did not have any legal consequences. But socially its implications were grave, for any friend of a flagrant homosexual could be regarded as guilty by association. The Prince of Wales was one of Hervey's close friends; and Stephen Fox was conspicuously his most intimate friend and most frequent companion. (Yet Stephen was never, either then or later, accused of sharing Hervey's alleged sexual deviation.) If Pulteney's accusation was to some extent true, in that Hervey's passion for Stephen was at least homoerotic, one essential objection to his lampoon remains: in a political fracas he used as a weapon a personal insult completely unrelated to politics. Lord Chesterfield, when he read the pamphlet, thought that Hervey would be 'excessively hurt with it', and that it was 'too personal and scurrilous to do any honour to the supposed authors, so that upon all accounts it had better have been let alone'.

The moment of publication for this pamphlet with its outrageous innuendo was singularly ironic: in Parliament, Hervey had just—with triumph and joy—helped defeat the Opposition led by Pulteney. Soon after he left the House his pamphlet-man put into his hands the newest publication of Francklin's printing shop. As Lady Hervey reported the episode later to an intimate friend, 'When that monstrous paper came out, which I think a very improper reply, my Lord, who reads all papers, saw it, and soon resolved & determined what to do.' What he resolved to do surprised his friends, his enemies, and perhaps himself.

7

The Honourable Miss Vane

1731–2

AFTER HERVEY HAD READ THE PAMPHLET he told Stephen and Henry Fox that he intended to challenge Pulteney to a duel. They 'beg'd him to defer it, not that they wou'd advise him one way or other but that they wou'd have him quite cool before he made any fix'd resolution'. (This, the most authoritative account of Hervey's retaliation, is his wife's full explanation, which she sent only a week later to their friend Lady Murray, then in Bath.) He waited three days; and on the morning of 25 January 1731, he sent Henry Fox to Pulteney with a letter at the end of which he asked him to answer 'some questions, two of which he puts thus: *Did you ever lend me any money?* (because you know that seemed to be hinted at in the paper); *Did you or did you not write the Paper intitled a Proper reply* etc.?' Fox was also to ask Pulteney to name the time and place for them to meet.

To the first question Pulteney replied that he had never lent Hervey anything, and that it was absurd to take one paragraph as hinting at any such thing. As to the other question, before he answered it he wanted to know whether Hervey had written *Sedition and Defamation Display'd*. (The dedication was not mentioned.) Fox was sure that Hervey had not, but since he had no orders to say anything he offered to go back to Hervey for an answer. He was evidently at Pulteney's house in Arlington Street, only a few minutes' walk from Hervey's apartment in St. James's Palace. He soon returned with Hervey's answer: that he 'had not writ it, but that was nothing to the business in hand, & desired his answer to my Lord's question. P——y seem'd shocked when he heard the *Sedition & Difamation* was not his'. Pulteney then said that whether or not he had written *A Proper Reply* did not matter, 'for he was so leagued with people that he must justifie it', and therefore his answer was yes; and he left it to Fox to choose a place and time. Fox named the New Walk in St. James's Park (the northern end, now called Green Park) at four o'clock that afternoon.

That same morning Lady Hervey, who as yet knew nothing of this conversation, observed that Hervey was so cheerful that she thought he would simply write a reply to Pulteney's 'monstrous' attack. He drank his chocolate with her, gave her 'a ridiculous paper of verses' to copy, and then as he left for the House of Commons, said he would dine that afternoon with some members. There he met Henry Fox, and they strolled in the park, as they usually did. In a little while Pulteney and his second, Sir John Rushout, walked out into his garden, which opened to the park. (By an odd coincidence Rushout, an M.P., had recently married Fox's niece, daughter of Lady Northampton.) They came out to meet Hervey and Fox. Although it was a frosty day, with snow covering the ground, the duellists stripped down to their shirts. As they were drawing their swords Hervey told Pulteney that in his pocket he had a paper stating that the duel was at his instigation and asking the King to protect Pulteney from the consequences of killing him if that should happen.

They then crossed swords. Hervey was lightly wounded in the side and nicked in four or five places on his hand, while Pulteney suffered only a cut in his hand. Then (Lady Hervey continues) 'they closed in, which in all probability wou'd have been fatal to one if not both of them but the seconds by consent rushed in upon them and seized their swords, upon which Mr. Pulteney said, "Let us contend no more, my Lord," and embraced him'. (Hervey simply bowed without saying anything, another report adds.) Fox then led Hervey off to Stephen's house, where his wounds were dressed.

In effect, Lady Hervey continues, the duel ended a friendship of twelve years, and even though Mrs. Pulteney had visited her a few days later she refused to return the call. She had since heard that Pulteney was trying as much as possible to suppress the pamphlet, and had forbidden the printer to sell any more copies.

Although much of Lady Hervey's account of the episode is hearsay, it deserves credence because she was closer to two of the principals (her husband and Henry Fox) than any of the others who gossiped about it. In telling her correspondent, Lady Murray, that Hervey did not write *Sedition and Defamation Display'd* (which was true) or its dedication (which was not) she was perhaps being cautious lest her friend, in such a gossip centre as Bath, should reveal what Hervey wished to deny. Since he had not been asked by Pulteney whether he had written the dedication he had not needed to admit being its author.

Hervey's wounds were so slight that Lady Hervey was not even aware of them when she saw him that evening; and only the next morning did he tell her of the duel. Two days later he was well enough to attend the annual meeting of Westminster scholars (which Pulteney also attended), and the following day the Drawing-Room at St. James's, where he could receive his friends' congratulations. His favour at court was considered to be so high that newspapers carried erroneous reports of his elevation to the House of Lords. At St. James's the duel 'made a great noise', Lady Irwin told her father, Lord Carlisle, 'and I fancy upon the whole will turn to Lord Hervey's service, he knowing well how to make a merit of this at Court; and besides, most people had the same opinion of Lord Hervey before Mr. Polteney drew his character with so much wit; but nobody before this adventure thought he had the courage to send a challenge.'

Lord Bristol, however much politics made him sympathize with Pulteney, did not waver in his loyalty to his son, who (he thought) had 'upon the justest provocations sent a challenge to his till then suppos'd friend' for publishing 'so false & odious a character'. Even less partial judges would have agreed with him. In a pamphlet defending Pulteney some years later an anonymous champion writes that both men acquitted themselves with honour:

The Reflections thrown out in Mr. **'s *Proper Reply*, &c. which gave Occasion to the Duel, were intirely personal to the noble Lord, and all dispassionate Readers thought them foreign to the Merits of the Question betwixt them. On the other hand, the noble Lord, by sending the Challenge to Mr. ** . . . was a Deviation from the strict Principles of Decorum; since it was never understood, that a Quarrel, begun with the Pen, should be decided by the Sword.

The fact that Hervey had attempted to settle the quarrel with his sword did not rule out his using a pen. Would he retaliate with a personal attack on Pulteney? Lord Chesterfield, still at this time a member of Walpole's party, thought that since the Opposition press attacked with invective, they 'should be answered in the same manner, and we should not content ourselves with reasoning with enemies that fight with poisoned arrows'. But such was not Ministerial policy, nor Hervey's. A reply, perhaps by Hervey, took the form of a pamphlet: *A Letter to Caleb D'Anvers Esq.*, published soon after its provocation. 'Worthy Sir,' it opens, 'You have been pleased to *divert* the Town lately with a very humerous Performance, called *A Proper Reply, &c.*' Then, after ridiculing Caleb for his puerile humour, the author confronts him with the more serious charge: 'But as you are pleased to intersperse among these trifling Witicisms, several Aspersions as scandalous and malicious as they are false . . . to defame and asperse with your usual Sincerity, Truth and Good-Manners, it is not so proper to be silent.' He does not intend, he states, 'to take any Notice of those Personal Reflections which you have thrown on the Author, or supposed Author, of *Sedition Display'd*; these have been already answer'd in a *proper* Manner'. In other words, the personal insult had been answered by a duel; the pamphlet would now answer the political arguments; and it does so with a light tone and leavening of anecdotes.

At about the same time as this reply was published, William Arnall, another ministerial writer, issued *Observations on a Pamphlet Intitled an Answer* . . . defending the Administration in a straightforward manner. He digresses to criticize Pulteney's tactics, mildly asking, 'Are unmannerly ribald Jests, upon the Loss of a Tooth belonging to one Gentleman, or a Button belonging to another, a national Inquiry?' (The missing button was Horatio Walpole's, whose slovenliness was notorious.)

Neither the duel nor the paper battle surrounding it altered the political picture to any extent except to sharpen the animosity between the two men most directly involved. Earlier periods of Parliamentary warfare had led to more violence; the duel between Hervey and Pulteney was the only celebrated one of its time.

ii

The literary consequences of Hervey's duel were far more enduring than the wounds inflicted. Pulteney's cruel lampoon put into circulation vivid material for satirists from Grub Street to Twickenham, and initiated Hervey's career as an object of satire, a career that would outlast his life. His existence as a person at

A Full and True

ACCOUNT

OF A

Sharp and Bloody DUEL,

Which was fought in St. James's-Park, *on* Tuesday *the* 26th. *of* January, 1730. *Between* William Poltney Esq; *and the* Lord Harvey. Mr. Fox, *and* Mr. Ruffet *were the two Seconds.*

ON *Tuesday* the 26th of *January*, 1730. In St. *James's* Park, their happen'd a Sharp and bloody Duel between Efq; P———y, and the Lord H———y, being a Man a true Lover of his Country, and has always Good him for the welfare of his Fell w Subj.cts, which perhaps did make him not fo well Refpe&ed as could be wifh'd for by all true Englifhmen, who when they have a friend ought to moke much of him, for in thofe miferable times, who find but few many there is anded that would plunder and Pilledge this our flourifhing Nation, nay and i think if the Eyes of Mankind were open they would fee who ftrives to Ruin and undoe teem.

And becaufe that brave and generous Temper'd Man would not put a Bridle upon his Temper, but boldly Speak his Countries Woos, and the bafe Tranfactions of a Great M—— of S——, muft he be Challeng'd to anfwer'd the Threat, becaufe he is not a Bird of the Feather, which makes the Rooks and Crows peck d at him, becaufe it is impoffible that the mpoffible that the Innocent Dove's Feathers fhould be like thofe of Robins, who has deck'd himfelf in Plumes of Gold; which the Generous P——y fcorns to obtain by a vicious or covetous Temper, which he oft nti es publickly declar'd; which cauted many of Robins Neft to make Reflections on this Innocent Gentleman, which cauted a Challenge, there being a Heart burning between the Lord H——y and Efq; P——y.

Which was a Sharp and Bloody Duel, each exerting themfelves in the greateft Paffions that ever Men were in. The Lord H——y receiv'd three flight Wounds, and the Valiant P——y receiv'd a flight Wound on his Wrift.

Sir Wm. R——el who was chofe to be Second to P——y, upon fome ill ufage he drew his Sword, and Challeng'd Mr. F--x, Second to the Lord H——y to anfwer at the Point of Sword, but being afraid to draw his Sword, it put S r Wm. R——t into a great Agony. But feveral of the Nobily happen'd to come by and parted them; but it is hop'd fuch Feuds and Diftactions will end among Noblemen, till Robin is brought to Juftice, which is the Hearty defire of all true Englifhmen, that all Things may be brought to a True Light.

LONDON: Printed for Meffieurs FIGG and SUTTON.

8. The Duel, 1731

court, at home, and in the world at large went on as before, but a new Lord Hervey had been born. Disregarding or ridiculing his brave challenge, satirists lifted from Pulteney's pamphlet the caricature of an effeminate courtier, and the scandalous innuendo of homosexuality, to create a *persona*. Alexander Pope, in turn, was to expand, refine, and polish it to create one of the greatest satirical portraits in English poetry.

In the poems, ballads, lampoons, and caricature prints that followed in the wake of the duel, politics remained the dominant satiric theme. A London printer issued a crude, smudged print of Hervey and Pulteney crossing swords in a park-like setting; and in the foreground, like a Mephistophelian mentor, stands Walpole (the Order of the Garter prominent on his chest) pointing his finger at Hervey as though directing him. Another print, also engraved at this time, puts the same scene inside a windowed room into which peers a burly figure (Walpole again) from whose mouth issue the words, 'Let them cut one another's Throats!' Hervey was clearly depicted as Walpole's minion and victim.

The anonymous author of some verse entitled *The Duel*, inscribed to Pulteney, coupled a charitable view of Hervey with a hopeful forecast:

> A Flight of Temper and unguarded Youth,
> Perhaps seduc'd him from the Paths of Truth:
> Warn'd by th'Event, he may again return,
> Repent his Errors, and his Follies mourn;
> At least his Wounds the Marks of Honour are,
> And all its Marks he, in that Cause, can wear.

But it was not characteristic of political satire to be so benign. From the same publisher (A. Moore) came *An Epistle from Little Captain Brazen, to the Worthy Captain Plume*. Its title continues: 'To which is added, An Answer to the said Epistle. In which The Character of Iago is set forth so as to be understood by the meanest Capacity.' The reader of any capacity could recognize Hervey as little Captain Brazen scolding the admirable Captain Plume (who had beaten him in the duel):

> *Compelled* I was, 'tis true, to yield,
> And leave you Master of the Field;
> You had my Life within your Pow'r,
> Oh! curse, ye Gods, th'unlucky Hour.

In spite of this, Captain Brazen continues, he will defend his friend Walpole, whom he calls the saviour of Europe.

Opposition writers often attacked Walpole by using historical or literary parallels to make their points (and also to evade prosecution for libel or breach of privilege). The duel found a place in the *Authentic Memoirs of Cardinal Wolsey*, a prose pamphlet that accuses Walpole of scheming for the 'young Nobleman' to challenge the Gentleman to a duel only to serve his own ends. Using *Othello* as a literary source, another pamphlet casts Walpole as Iago, Pulteney as Cassio, and Hervey as Roderigo, whom Iago encourages to challenge Cassio to a duel. The Shakespeare play's cast was then borrowed in a derisive pamphlet of doggerel verse whose title reveals its plot: 'The Countess's Speech To her Son Roderigo, upon Her first seeing him, after he was wounded in his late Duel . . .'.

The notoriety of the duel persisted: the following year a ballad opera (never staged) called *The Intriguing Courtier* presents a Lord Whiftler, whose duel is forbidden, much to his cowardly satisfaction. 'If I should be killed,' he reflects, 'the *Muses* will lose their darling Son, and the Ladies break their Hearts.' And even two years later, a pamphleteer, in dissecting John Gay's ballad opera *Achilles*, asked (rhetorically): 'Is not the *Duel* fought between that Hero Ajax and a *Great* Lord, a plain Representation of what lately happened between a *Little* Lord and a *Great* Commoner.' The duel was remembered by another satirist who in a ballad opera that dealt with Walpole's bribery and his defeated Excise Bill calls Hervey by the name of Lord Challenge.

At least one satiric attack, issued soon after the duel, used as its material Pulteney's ridicule of Hervey's effeminate manner. The broadside ballad called simply *The Duel* combined political and personal satire as it sang in mock-heroic accents of the fierce combat between 'a Youth that is *In*, and a Man that is *Out*':

> It matters not how this Quarrel did rise,
> With *Miss* and—with *Master*, and *Master* and *Miss*;
> Or whether a Coward he should not be stil'd,
> Sets his Sword to a *Woman*, and Wit to a *Child*.

But political bias dominated these attacks; anti-Ministerial writers used the duel as a weapon against Walpole.

If Hervey was perturbed by seeing his name and reputation

stigmatized he gave no sign of it. But if he was the author of a ballad published a few weeks after the duel (and ascribed to him on insufficient evidence), he was in excellent humour and spirits. *Journalists Displayed* is a good-natured, rollicking exposure of the Opposition's vociferous patriotism:

> I'll tell you the Way these Complainants to quell,
> *Ribbledum, Scribbledum, Fribbledum, Flash,*
> Give all of them Places, and all will be well,
> *Satyrum, Traytorum, Treasondum, Trash*;
> 'Twill be no more Slavery, Bribery, Knavery,
> Irruptions, Corruptions, and Some-body's Fall,
> But stand up for Royalty! punish Disloyalty!
> Stock it and Pocket the Devil and all.

Although Hervey took no further part in the House of Commons debates that session, theatregoers were reminded of his allegiance (on 22 April 1731) when *The Welsh Opera* by Henry Fielding was put on as an after-piece at the Haymarket, and ran for nine performances. In it the groom named John, in a minor role, faithfully does the bidding of the butler named Robin, a name frequently bestowed on Walpole by Opposition writers. After Parliament rose (at the beginning of May), the groom may have done the butler's bidding. The *Craftsman* of 22 May, reviving the controversy that had led to the duel, defended Pulteney as a true patriot and Bolingbroke as an honourable man. It was answered by *Remarks on the Craftsman's Vindication of His Two Honourable Patrons*, which repeats and elaborates the familiar charges against both Opposition leaders. Its author only glances at the personal attack on Hervey (in *A Proper Reply*) by claiming that although he exposes the political life of the *Craftsman's* patrons as a warning to the public, he scorns to deal with their private lives as they do with those of their opponents.

This pamphlet has generally been attributed to either Hervey or William Arnall. When Lady Hervey read it at Ickworth she was apparently puzzled, and inquired of Stephen Fox 'to know the true Author of the *Remarks*; I'll tell you my reason for it: there is a paragraph in it which is word for word what a gentleman said on reading the Craftsman at our lodgings the night my Lord [Hervey] and you came to town. Don't you remember both the thing and the person? If you do, send me word truly whether you think he had any share in writing it. I don't think 'tis like his stile in common discourse, but this rencontre struck me.' Who was the unnamed gentleman?

Certainly not Hervey, whom Lady Hervey always refers to as 'my Lord'; besides, he was present when the gentleman spoke. Since Hervey himself attributed the authorship to 'Arnold', the gentleman Lady Hervey recalled must have been William Arnall, a lawyer by training, who was Walpole's ablest and most richly rewarded mercenary writer. But Pulteney believed that Walpole was its author; he wrote to his relation Francis Colman (on 12 June) that 'a Pamphlett came out a few days ago supposed to be writ by Sir Rob. Walpole himself wherein I am treated with great acrimony; It is necessary I should reply, and speedily too, so that if I can I must dip my Pen in gall'. He replied with *An Answer to One Part of a Late Infamous Libel* and so indiscreetly—revealing some remarks that Walpole had allegedly spoken about the King—that his name was struck off the list of privy councillors by the King. His opposition to Walpole was now irremediably set.

iii

Hervey spent the first few weeks of the summer with his wife and family at Ickworth before returning to London to rejoin Stephen Fox. Since he wrote to his wife only rarely she asked Stephen to scold him for her, but the scolding was ineffective, and she continued to depend on him: 'I beg . . . you'll be so good to let me know how he looks,' she writes (at the beginning of July), '& what spirits he is in. Is there no hopes of his making us a visit this summer?'—a curious question from a wife to her husband's friend. 'And won't you keep your word with me? I can assure you the Park is in the full perfection of beauty . . . Adieu. For the future I'll omit all ceremony, and cease to subscribe my-self what I shall never cease to be, Your Faithful humble Servant.' How fortunate for Hervey that his wife should share, instead of resent, his fondness for Stephen!

With Stephen in tow he accompanied Walpole to Houghton Hall for a week's visit. It was the first time he had been invited to join a 'Norfolk Congress', the house-party held twice a year by Walpole for his more intimate friends. He found the informality there particularly agreeable. In the house full of guests everybody did what he pleased, paying as little attention to the others as he might to neighbours in London. Dinners were snug little parties of some thirty men 'up to the Chin in Beef, Venison, Geese, Turkeys &c. and generally over the Chin in Claret, Strong Beer & punch'. Politics was not much discussed; instead the conversation, stimulated no doubt by the new magnificent house, dealt with architecture and with planting. On excursions they dined at Raynham Hall, Lord Townshend's house, and even went as far as Lord Lovel's house, Holkham, near the sea, and Sir Andrew Fontaine's at Narford, 'the prettyest Trinket' Hervey had ever seen: 'Lord Burlington could not make a better Ragoust of paintings, Statues, Gilding, & virtù.'

From Norfolk Hervey and Stephen paid their promised visit to Ickworth, travelling in an open chaise through constant rain with the wind full in their teeth, and after staying there only a few days returned to London and Hampton Court. But Stephen, Hervey's 'only true & lasting pleasure', had to leave for his own house in Somerset, and Hervey would not see him for three long months. 'Mon Dieu,' he exclaims in his first letter, 'que Novembre et Redlinch sont loin!'

At Hampton Court, Hervey would at least have his wife's company. She arrived there probably on 13 August, the day that the Lord Steward ordered that she be given three pats of Richmond butter and a quarter of a pint of cream *per diem*. As wife of the Vice-Chamberlain she enjoyed these little perquisites. Hervey had resumed his court routine, riding every morning with the Queen, and on hunting days staying on the side of the chaise in which she followed the hunters. In the Queen's familiar company he could relax. One day, when Walpole in his office as Ranger of Richmond Park received them in his ceremonial dress (which included a sash across his shoulders), Hervey improvised some clever verse to the tune of a French song. In it he predicted that while Walpole wore the cord that way, Pulteney might some day wear another kind of cord (around his neck). First Hervey and the Queen sang it together, and then the whole company took up the tune, and often repeated it throughout the day.

The Queen tried to profit by her growing intimacy with Hervey to win his father over to the court side. But Lord Bristol resisted with courtly firmness, asking his son to say 'all you think due to her Majesty for the great honour she does me in seeming to think me yet worthy of becoming her proselyte after those, from whom I have deserved at least common Christian usage, have treated me more like a renegado than a true believer'. Since his political creed was based on sound orthodox principles, he continues, and since he has practised it with sweet satisfaction in an age full of Whig heresies, he would not change it. (He kept abreast of Opposition politics, buying at this time a seven-volume collected edition of the *Craftsman* in the best paper and binding.) Still concerned at Hervey's illness at Ickworth, he was convinced it had been caused by tea, 'that detestable, fatal liquor', which (he warns) would eventually hasten his passage through death's door; 'and then what must become of your country, wife & children, & our forlorn family?' Paternal love blinded him to the contradiction of thinking that the fate of his country hung on the life of one whose politics were so ruinous to it.

Hervey's attendance at court deepened his friendship not only with the Queen but with the Prince of Wales. He had, at the Prince's request, written to him profusely from Houghton and Ickworth, calling himself in one letter Hephaistion, the name of Alexander the Great's intimate friend. 'I believe your Royal Highness is by this time quite tired of your Norfolk Gazettear,' he gracefully remarked before returning from the country, '& will be as glad as I shall be of my return to Hampton Court tho for different reasons: I shall rejoice in the Hope of having more of You, You in the expectation of having less of me, as You will find it easyer to shutt your Door to my Visits than your Eyes to my Letters.' Of course the Royal door was not shut to him; in fact, when the Prince was taken ill after a Saturday hunt and grew worse the next morning, he sent for Hervey to be fetched from chapel. Feeling better after a blooding he asked all to leave except Hervey, whose conversation soothed him until he fell asleep. When they were not together his image was frequently before Hervey's eyes, for he had presented him with a gold snuff-box bearing his portrait.

His friendship with the Prince, as it grew warmer, did not lessen his devotion to Stephen. At a large dinner-party the Lord Chancellor, mistaking Hervey's neighbour at table, drank to Stephen's health, calling him by name. Thereupon, Hervey later told Stephen, 'without the least affectation, I assure you, I colour'd and felt just as I imagine your favorite & fondest Mistress would have done upon the same Occasion'. As his friendship with the Prince bloomed he reassured Stephen. 'I love you & love you more than I thought I could love any thing,' he writes a week after he had blushed like a mistress. 'I have recieved a Letter from you to day which no body who loved you less could deserve. Adio carissimo.'

But in an unguarded moment, or with a miscalculated confession, he told Stephen that he wished he could love the Prince as well as he loved Stephen. How Stephen reacted can be inferred from Hervey's distraught apology, sent only ten minutes after he had read his reply: 'The Tears you speak of are at this Distance so infectious that I hardly see the Words I write.' He reassures him, in the most abject terms, of his unalterable love. In wishing to love the Prince so well he had 'ly'd egregiously; I am as incapable of wishing to love any Body else so well, as I am of wishing to love You less. God forbid any Mortal should ever have the power over me you have, or that you should ever have less. . . . Adieu, if I was to fill a thousand Reams of paper it would be only aiming in different phrases & still imperfectly to tell you the same thing, & assure you that since I first knew you I have been without repenting & still am & ever shall be undividedly & indisolubly Yours.' Stephen could hardly have hoped for a more reassuring declaration.

The lovers' misunderstanding ended a few days later, when Hervey pronounced an end to it: 'you offended imprudently, I resented it extravagantly; you repented agreably, I forgave you willingly, & the whole has concluded . . . to my satisfaction . . . Absent or present, sleeping or waking, sick or well, in Crouds or alone, You are generally upermost in my Thoughts; the Cause of every uneasyness I suffer at present & the Object of every wish & hope of pleasure I form for the future.' His emotion was so strong it overflowed in a long, philosophical poem he sent to Stephen from Hampton Court, regretting his life spent in the 'glare of courts, and luxury of state', wasting precious hours away from his beloved friend.

In his country retirement Stephen, who was aware that Hervey at court was surrounded by temptation, occasionally displayed a twitch of jealousy toward other possible rivals besides the Prince of Wales. There was at court the Countess of Tankerville, whom Hervey regarded benignly as a 'handsome, good-natured, simple woman'. 'We are to lose Lady Tankerville this Week,' Hervey told Stephen (on 4 September), 'which will be a great Mortification to the whole Court, as well as to her.' When Stephen then accused him of having fallen a victim to her allure, he answered in forthright terms: 'You guess very ill about the Conquest you imagine Lady Tankerville's agreable folie, naiveté charmante & Beauté naturelle made in a certain Heart.' Many had sojourned in his heart, he insists, but few had governed it.

Whenever he could he escaped from court to stay with Stephen. Soon after their parting in the summer (1731) he had begun to plan a brief reunion in Wiltshire, when Stephen would be at Maddington, his small shooting-box 'sacred to sweat and Spaniels' (in Hervey's phrase). They planned to meet at Basing-stoke in October, to spend only the weekend at Maddington. 'The next time I talk to You', he wrote just before his departure, 'it will not be upon paper.' Hence the details of their brief rendezvous cannot be known with the explicit clarity of his conversations on paper. On Sunday, after they parted, he 'fretted & was sick all the way' back to Hampton Court, and there took to his bed for a day and a night to recover from the pain of having left Stephen. He had returned in time to attend a great ball, and still exhausted from his visit and journey he crept away early, leaving the Prince to sup with several ladies, including Lady Hervey.

The Prince could not have enough of his company. He invited him to Kew, where they played at nine-pins all day, and did not dine until five. Such a late dinner, Hervey tells Stephen, was 'à la Redlinch as to the Hours, not a bit so in any other Particulars: You know then how well I was entertain'd'. Afterwards he had to return to Hampton Court on horseback in the dark and cold, with his dinner in his throat, in order to dress and play cards with the King. He could not help comparing the little house on Salisbury Plain in the company of one he loved with Royal palaces and friendships, but ambition and its attendant duties dictated his course.

iv

The arrival in London (on 14 October) of the Duke of Lorraine brought a welcome change in the monotonous court routine. As Francis III, the Duke had succeeded his father two years before.

He was an important pawn on the chessboard of European politics, for he was both a relation of the Austrian Emperor, Charles VI, and the husband-presumptive of Maria Theresa, the Emperor's heiress. While touring the Netherlands he had been told that the English King would welcome a visit from him, and so after obtaining permission from the Emperor he accepted the invitation. Lord Chesterfield, ambassador at The Hague, thought him the most agreeable (*aimable*) prince he had ever met. Although he was travelling incognito, he still moved in a setting of formal ceremony. The Imperial ambassador, at whose London house he stayed, brought him to Hampton Court, where Hervey, as Vice-Chamberlain, awaited him in the Cartoon Gallery to lead him through to the King's private apartment. (From there the Lord Chamberlain led him to the Queen's apartment, and then to the Prince of Wales's.)

Hervey carefully and dispassionately observed him: 'a pretty Figure of a Man,' he reported to Stephen, 'tho low & rather thick, ill made & worse dress'd. He wears his own Hair, has a very handsome Face, like the King of France, but a more sensible, more lively & a more good-natur'd Countenance. He seems very easy & very well-bred. He ran the Gauntlet . . . through a Croud of Starers & whisperers without being disconcerted.' Had he understood English he might have been disconcerted by a play put on in his honour at Hampton Court, by a company from Drury Lane. As related by Hervey:

I thought his not understanding it would be a Misfortune; but I have chang'd my Mind, for if he had I should, as a damn'd proud Englishman, [have] blush'd for two Hours together. The play was the *Recruiting Officer* & one of the Jokes, a Fellow's saying that *the King of England was greater than any Emperor in Christendom.* How disagreably foolish this would have been had the Man for whose Entertainment the Play was given known what they were saying.

Hervey's first favourable impression was strengthened; the more he saw the Duke the more he liked him. 'He is well-bred, with more nicety, more ease & more constant presence of Mind than any Body I ever met with & has the most beautifull, most sweet, & most sensible Countenance I ever beheld.'

The flurry of entertaining also put Hervey in the Prince of Wales's company more often, and their friendship grew closer. When Newcastle gave a great dinner for the Duke and invited forty guests but tactlessly excluded the Prince and Hervey, the Prince indignantly told Hervey of it. When anyone showed their dislike of him by coupling him with the Prince, Hervey reassured him, he would always say (in a line from a French song): 'These affronts are Favors.' To which the Prince immediately replied, 'You take every Occasion to be agreeable & they to be disagreable.' Hervey could tell Stephen of these marks of friendship without fear of jealousy, particularly since he reassured him at the end with: 'Adio, sempre amabile, & sempre amato.'

Impatient to leave for Redlinch after the Birth-night celebration (on 30 October) Hervey sent ahead some Rhine wine, fussed to decide whether to meet Stephen at Hertford Bridge or Basingstoke, and requested a coach for himself and a horse for Maran, his valet. On the day that the Royal Family left St. James's for their country retirement at Richmond, he could depart to stay with the friend he had called (in the letter that preceded him) 'mea vera & sola Voluptas'. During their fortnight together they were confined to the house by incessant rain. Fox's sister, Mrs. Digby, and her husband were there; and they filled their time with eating, drinking wine or tea, playing cards, and chattering and reading. Hervey could never have too much of Stephen's company; they both returned to London on the same day as the Royal Family.

He had the pleasure of Stephen's company for only a few days; and in spite of his 'showing plainer' than words that he wanted him to stay another day, Stephen left unexpectedly. 'Why did you not come to my Lodgings for a Minute after the Opera?' he asked afterwards. 'I did not stay a quarter of an Hour with the Prince; he went immediately to bed & I came home.' (He could not ask Stephen to accompany him because he was uncertain how long the Prince would keep him.) Perhaps Stephen was piqued by Hervey's attendance, yet it was an unavoidable duty.

Hervey now had before him the exhausting round of entertainment that preceded the Duke of Lorraine's departure. A magnificent supper and ball given by Newcastle kept him up so late one night that he felt half dead, and expected to be carried off in a hearse the next night after the Prince of Wales's ball. But at least he enjoyed the Duke's company, who was as great a romp as Stephen or himself. When invited to a masquerade with the Duke, the Prince, and a suite of eighteen, he 'pleaded Chicken,

Head-ach, fear of sitting up &c. and gott off'. Curiosity drove him to it (though not in costume), where, finding everything just as he thought, he felt as superior in all the whirl and confusion as an infant in Abraham's bosom viewing 'the noisy senseless Bustle of a World he was originally design'd to be a Member of, & which he had the Good Luck to slip out of'. He was pleased to see the Duke continue to enjoy the festivities, 'happy as the Night was long, flying about, talking to every Body he met, pleasing & pleas'd'.

The day before leaving, the Duke walked in Kensington Gardens in the morning with the Queen and her suite (including Hervey) until it began to rain. They all returned to St. James's at full gallop in open chaises, wet to the skin and bespattered with mud like stage-coach postilions. On 8 December he boarded his yacht at Greenwich, 'regretting and regretted'. Hervey, who too easily observed the flaws in those he met, could find none in this paragon: he still thought him handsome, cheerful, sensible, well bred, and obliging: 'Never any Body had the good Fortune of pleasing so universally.' The Duke's departure, he told Lord Bateman, had 'put the Town into a universal Mourning; it is the Fashion for the Women to cry'. He was not exaggerating, for he had evidence close at hand. 'The Duke of Lorraine has carr[i]ed the hearts of all our fine ladys away with him,' Lady Strafford wrote (more than two weeks later); 'Lady Harvey has cryed every day since his departure and says she can't injoy anybody's company now that agreeable creature is gon.'

v

While on his visit to Redlinch (in November) Hervey had sent long, strenuously clever letters to the Prince of Wales in order to keep their friendship from slackening. 'If it would not be too bold for Hephestion to pry into the Sanctum Sanctorum of your Employments,' he had written (referring to himself again as Alexander the Great's intimate friend), 'I would ask whether Roxana or Statira is at present in Favour.' He again brought up the titillating subject of the Prince's amatory pursuits when he recounted the trial of a poacher on Stephen's estate, and then asked, 'What Game you poch, Sir, what you hunt, what you catch, or what runs into your Mouth, I don't pretend to guess; if you think fitt to tell me I shall soon be in the way of being inform'd.' If Hervey was in fact the Prince's confidant he had much to be informed of.

For the Prince had begun to poach soon after his arrival in England. One of his earliest catches may have been Lady Abergavenny; the honour of this greatly pleased her husband. The Prince was later rumoured to be keeping a Papist in a private house hired for the purpose, and then an Italian opera singer. He cast a wide net in his flirtations—an apothecary's daughter, the junior Duchess of Marlborough (as observed by Hervey at his son's christening), a farmer's wife at a country dance near Hampton Court (when the indignant farmer rewarded him with a beating). But in the autumn of 1731 he had begun to concentrate his attentions on a young lady who was one of his mother's Maids of Honour.

The Honourable Anne Vane, eldest daughter of Lord Barnard, had held her court appointment since at least 1726, when she was twenty-one. She was related to the staid Countess of Oxford, who (she gratefully acknowledged) was as a mother to her in every way; and her 'violent friendship' for that lady made her conspicuously ridiculous at court. Perhaps she hoped that some of Lady Oxford's blatant respectability would rub off on her. While in Bath for her health (in October 1730) Miss Vane had been so disturbed by reports from court that she was with child that she forced herself to go out in public frequently, against her health and inclination, to disprove the gossip. She had been rumoured as about to marry Lord Harrington, but he apparently had his way without marriage. She then transferred her favour to Hervey (the exact beginning of their liaison is uncertain); and while he at Redlinch had been encouraging the Prince of Wales to tell him who his *inamorata* of the moment was, the Prince could not perhaps tell him for a simple reason—it was Miss Vane herself. She had easily been persuaded to accept the unofficial and as yet unannounced appointment as his mistress.

Could she have been so repulsive as Lord Egmont describes her —a fat and ill-shaped dwarf, with nothing good to recommend her, neither sense nor wit? She was, besides, probably marked by smallpox. The Prince's passion for women was wittily analysed by Horace Walpole:

like the rest of his race, beauty was not a necessary ingredient. Miss [Vane], whom he had debauched without loving, and who had been

9. Frederick, Prince of Wales, 1736

debauched without loving him so well as either Lord Harrington or Lord Hervey, who both pretended to her first favours, had no other charms than of being a Maid of Honour, who was willing to cease to be so upon the first opportunity.

However much others may have disapproved or sneered, the Prince was proud of his battered conquest, and commanded his courtiers to pay their respects by visiting her.

Hervey innocently maintained his precious friendship with the Prince through the autumn (1731), either through spirited letters from Redlinch or in his company, until it took a new, dramatic turn. He fretted for a whole week (in mid-December) before confiding in Stephen: 'that Fool the Prince plagues my Heart out. He is as false too as he [is] silly, & appears every thing he is not by turns, but wise; yet the Mask of common-sense, if he knew how to get it, would disguise him more than any other; he could put on nothing so unnatural, nothing so unlike.' Unfortunately Hervey could not be more explicit, 'for Paper is as great a Blab as a human Creature'. So intense was his indignation that he revealed to his father that he had been deceived and betrayed by a friend whom he really loved—though he worded it so cautiously, in fear of post-office prying, that his father remained uncertain who that friend was.

He could be more explicit with Stephen because they used a cipher for the Prince's name; and on Christmas Day, with feelings far from charitable, he raged again: 'I have almost every Day fresh Instances of the Falsehood as well as the Folly of [the Prince], & since it is impossible to correct the first, wherever it is so natural, I am not very solicitous as you may imagine to rectify the Errors of the Last.' Then, as he continues his tirade, he shifts from the singular to the plural: 'Lett their Folly fall on their own Head, & their Wickedness on their own Pate. They neither know nor suspect that I have detected them, nor ever shall, for the easiest, the most natural & the justest Revenge one can take upon People who imagine they impose upon one, is to let them fancy they do: & instead of being their Dupe, let them make themselves their own.' He has fretted at 'their Conduct' a good deal, he confesses, but for the future is resolved to think and speak of it as little as possible; and he would no more divulge his being vexed, he tells Stephen, 'than you would formerly have done your being clap'd' —a bizarre comparison to make.

It was more than sexual jealousy and humiliation that infuriated him; a political element had entered the new liaison in the person of another man—George Bubb Dodington. A wealthy M.P. controlling several boroughs, a Lord of the Treasury since 1724, and still an adherent of Walpole's, though twice he had hoped to supplant him, Dodington was a man of good parts and a great deal of wit, but so conceited that his overbearing and insolent manner made him universally disliked. He now became the conspicuous companion of Miss Vane and the Prince of Wales. Hervey was convinced that it was Miss Vane who had persuaded the Prince to allow Dodington to attach himself to them, an attachment that would inevitably have political consequences. Hervey thus had double cause for bitterness: he was displaced at the same time as Miss Vane's lover and as the Prince's intimate friend and adviser.

The full story of Hervey's friendship and enmity with the Prince of Wales is probably lost forever. His private memoirs of the court of George II, which he began to write in 1733, contain a frank and full account of his association with the various members of the Royal Family from the King's accession in 1727 to the Queen's death ten years later. When the autograph manuscript and a copy of it passed on to Hervey's grandson, the first Marquess of Bristol, he tore out and destroyed a long section—from May 1730 to the late summer of 1732, the precise period of Hervey's intimacy and quarrel with the Prince of Wales. His motive must have been to protect George III's father as well as his own grandfather. The fact that he allowed other scandalous revelations (Miss Vane as Hervey's mistress, for example) to remain in the copy of the memoirs is evidence that what he read and destroyed for the years 1730 to 1732 he regarded as far too shocking to remain among his family papers in either the autograph or the copy.

vi

At the time their friendship was dissolving Hervey and the Prince of Wales were jointly involved in a comedy at the Theatre Royal in Drury Lane that they had sponsored and perhaps helped to write. Even while *The Modish Couple* was in rehearsal (in December 1731) many 'Persons of Quality' attended; and finally, after a postponement—the prologue calls it 'homely Christmas Fare'—

it opened on 10 January 1732. What the audience saw was a comedy of intrigue set at Hampton Court, where a fashionable, adulterous couple named Lord and Lady Modely attempt to win control of an heiress who outwits them by secretly marrying the man she loves. It is Restoration comedy *réchauffée*, neither better nor worse than other plays on the boards.

But one passage in the play pokes fun at the raucous behaviour of theatre audiences, a dangerous satiric target at a time when they were easily aroused to rioting. Henry Fielding, who wrote the epilogue to the comedy, later recalled that on the first night could be seen 'Critics in Embroidery transplanted from the Boxes to the Pit, whose ancient Inhabitants were exalted to the Galleries, where they played on Catcalls'.* The noisy objections were repeated the next night, and on the third, which was customarily the author's benefit night, the Prince of Wales attended, among what a newspaper called 'one of the finest Assemblies of Persons of Quality that has been seen'. Hervey was probably among them. While the play was in progress two men in the gallery created a disturbance, and were hauled out by soldiers on duty there.

On the fourth night the audience refused to let the play begin, but called for another. Their spokesman told the anxious theatre manager that the soldiers' action the previous night had struck a blow at the liberty of British subjects; and since no other play could be put on at such short notice they were content to collect their admission money and leave. The episode was not purely theatrical. In Egmont's opinion, it was 'beneath the Court to take on them the patronage of this simple play, and risk their authority against the universal judgment of the town'. The audience were probably incited by members of the Opposition, who saw the occasion as a chance to embarrass Hervey and the Prince of Wales.

The nominal author of *The Modish Couple* was Captain Charles Boden (or Bodens), a military man who held a minor post at court as Gentleman-Usher Quarter-Waiter in Ordinary. He clearly knew how to get ahead, winning a succession of appointments and sinecures. Horace Walpole, who characterizes him as a 'man of some humour and [a] universal parasite', calls him author of the play. But Egmont states that Hervey and the Prince of Wales

---

* Fielding himself was writing for the stage. His comedy *The Modern Husband*, with a theme similar to *The Modish Couple*, was staged at Drury Lane only a month later.

were the authors, and that they arranged for Boden to claim it. Fielding's evidence, though equivocal, is more authoritative; Queen Ignorance (in his farce *Pasquin*) commends the play by name as being by a 'powerful hand'; and in his epilogue he wittily concludes:

> Soldiers, give Quarter to a valiant Brother,
> Courtiers are too wellbred to Damn each other.
> As the First Fault, ye Criticks, spare what's past,
> And spare him, Wits, in hopes 'twill be his last.

Certainly Hervey had a distinctive flair for dramatic writing, as can be seen in a long section of his *Memoirs* where he brilliantly portrays, by means of dialogue, the response of the court to news of his sudden death. If the play is scanned for signs of his wit and style only one speech qualifies: 'Yes, Madam,' says a fortune-hunting rake, 'to be virtuous, is to be wisely wicked and let no body know it. 'Tis to wench in the Dark and say one's Prayers in broad Daylight—to cheat in a Corner, and to be charitable at a Church Door—to get drunk over Night, and put up Prayers for your being cursed sick the next Morning—In short, Child, to be secret in Vice, is all the Virtue in Fashion.' As for the Prince of Wales, he piqued himself on being not only a patron of the arts, but upon his proficiency in both verse and prose. Most probably, *The Modish Couple* was written mainly by Boden with help from the other two men, who used their influence to have it produced at Drury Lane and tried to ensure its success—with dismal results. The play, when printed, bore a dedication to Lord Harrington, which was a neat touch since Hervey and the Prince of Wales were allied with him in another activity, intimate friendship with the Honourable Miss Vane.

8

'Rewards and Punishments'

1732–3

PARLIAMENT WAS CONVENED ON 13 JANUARY 1732, the very day that *The Modish Couple* was 'dismissed' from the stage, never to be played again. Hervey had not, in fact, looked forward to resuming his political activity. When Stephen Fox accused him of staying in town to talk sweet nonsense or to meddle in politics he protested: 'I am much too Old for a Coquet & too Lazy for a Politician: I look with more horror on the Meeting of the Parliament than my little Son does on Monday seneight [seven-night] when the Holydays determine & he is to go to school again.' He regarded his duties in the House of Commons as much more disagreeable than his attendance at court. A fortnight before the session opened he had dined with Walpole and his cohorts—Horatio Walpole, Dodington, Winnington, Lord Wilmington, Clayton (the future Lord Sundon), and Sir William Yonge; perhaps they met to plan their strategy. The conversation at table seemed to him silly and ridiculous, as he cynically reflected: 'these are the Men to whose care Nations are committed; who are to report Truth; to see, hear, & judg for others, to serve their Prince & their Country, to shine in our Senates, enact Laws, mend or preserve our Constitution & teach our Senators Wisdom!'

One of the first measures to be dealt with in the Commons was a motion by the Secretary at War for the maintenance of the standing army (about 17,000 men). This was perennially contested by the Opposition, who accused the Ministry of oppressing the country with a military and financial burden. The motion was opposed by Lord Morpeth (Lord Carlisle's son) as dangerous to the liberties of the nation; he proposed a reduction to 12,000 men, and was seconded by another Opposition speaker. Thereupon Hervey, in a brief speech, pointed out that the number asked for was modest enough, that a smaller one might encourage a Jacobite rebellion similar to that of 1715. For proof one only had to look at 'the many scandalous and seditious Libels' published against the government; he argued that the 'many Scribblers that are employ'd to vilify and asperse his Majesty and his Administration, and to sow Disaffection and Discontent among the People, is an evident Sign that we have as yet many Enemies, even within our Bosom, who would probably think of making use of other Weapons than the Pen, if we should be so unwise as to afford them the least Hopes of Success, by making a great Reduction in our Army.' The debate went on, with far longer and more detailed arguments on both sides, until the motion was finally passed by a substantial majority (241 to 171). On this measure Stephen Fox voted with the Government for the first time. He had been converted, probably through Hervey's influence, from a Tory in Opposition to a Whig in support of Walpole; and he continued to vote with the Government in all subsequent recorded divisions. Lord Bristol opposed the bill; and after it was passed in the Upper House, he was among those who signed a Protest. Perhaps he was punished for it later in the year, when he indignantly complained to Hervey that 'a company of soldiers with their concubines and bastards' had been quartered on his tenants at Sleaford (rather than at Newark) as a reprisal for his being a protesting peer. Although Hervey tried to persuade his father privately that a strong standing army was a necessary protection against a Jacobite insurrection, Bristol remained unconvinced of it.

As the Parliamentary session continued through the spring of 1732 Hervey served on various committees but apparently took no active part in the most important debates, on the salt tax and the Charitable Corporation scandal. But on a relatively unimportant bill (on 3 April) he followed Ministerial speakers in supporting payment of a debt to Denmark that the Opposition argued should be paid by France. Hervey made 'a very eloquent and cutting speech', in Egmont's opinion, 'to show that the disaffection of the people is not on account of the German dominions [whose defence England had undertaken], nor from the things themselves, but from bad insinuations within doors, and more bold speeches without'. In this instance his function among the Ministry's speakers was not to argue the specific issue but rather to criticize the Opposition's general tactics.

He may also have been the author of a Ministerial pamphlet, published in mid-February, which attacked the Opposition in general terms as hypocritical, self-proclaimed patriots. Issued by James Roberts, it bore the title *The Public Virtue of Former Times, and the Present Age Compared*. Its theme reverses the arguments generally advanced by the Opposition that England's liberties have been severely curtailed, and concludes that her truest patriots are not the vociferous minority but the King, Ministry, and Parliament.

ii

While he showed no sign of forgiving Hervey, the Prince of Wales's liaison with Miss Vane grew firmer. At the end of January 1732 Miss Vane asked the Queen for a leave of absence from her duties as Maid of Honour, and the Queen, knowing that she was being kept by the Prince, sent word that she might leave for good. The Prince then installed her in a house in Soho Square, furnished it with fine silver and furniture, and presented her with £1,600 a year. There was good reason for her to give up her court appointment (which in theory could be occupied only by a virgin) and for the Prince to subsidize her domestic life so generously: she was pregnant; and far from disguising her condition she flaunted it, to become the main topic of Court gossip. When she met the Dowager Lady Northampton on a visit, all she talked about was her expected child, her bed-linen, and her wet-nurse; nobody else, the Dowager thought, had ever strutted about 'so proud of a big belly'.

Once Miss Vane's position as the Prince of Wales's mistress was conspicuously secure, Hervey's emotions shifted from jealousy (for having been betrayed) to resentment, far more intense, that she had induced the Prince to discard him as intimate adviser in favour of Dodington. He determined in April 1732 to revive the Prince's friendship for him, and went about it in a foolhardy fashion. Since Miss Vane had ruined that friendship, he reasoned, then she could restore it. He composed a letter and asked his brother-in-law Bussy Mansel to take it to her, telling him that it merely recommended a midwife. Actually it castigated her for the ill service she had done him with the Prince, and threatened that if she did not repair the breach he would divulge what he knew of her, and use her as she deserved. Upon reading this scathing letter she fell into hysterics; and Mansel, when he read it, swore he would kill Hervey for deceiving him by making him the messenger of such an affront. To prevent murder Miss Vane then told the Prince of the letter, and he somehow placated Mansel but bitterly resented Hervey's ill treatment of his mistress. The King, Queen, and Walpole, when they heard of it, were also incensed with Hervey for his interference in a Royal pastime. Aware too late of his imprudence, Hervey tried to make amends. The King and Queen (and of course Walpole) were satisfied by his penitence but not the Prince, who (in Hervey's opinion) 'never forgot an injury or remembered an obligation'. Their friendship was never restored.

The shocking episode did not affect Miss Vane's pregnancy or her favour with her Royal protector, who soon bought her a house on Kew Green costing about £4,000. Then, to his great joy and satisfaction, she gave birth to a boy on 5 June at her London house, now in St. James's Street. One newspaper cautiously announced that a 'young Lady lately much talk'd on among the polite Part of the World' had been safely delivered of a son. He was christened by the Prince's chaplain as Cornwall Fitzfrederick; and his godfathers were Miss Vane's brother and Lord Baltimore, one of the Prince's Gentlemen of the Bedchamber.

Whether the Prince was indeed the father of the child—conceived, it must be remembered, in September 1731—was not regarded as a certainty. Although Miss Vane ascribed the child to him, Hervey and Harrington each assured Robert Walpole of his own paternity. The Prince's eldest sister had assured her husband that 'it was the child of a triumvirate, and that the Prince and Lord Harrington had full as good a title to it' as Hervey. At the time of the Prince's marriage a few years later the Queen begged Hervey to tell her whether her son was even capable of having a child. 'As for those of little Vane,* you know, my dear Lord,' she insisted, 'I have a thousand times told you that I was always sure they were yours; and if I wanted further proof of

---

* In April 1733 Miss Vane, still living with the Prince of Wales, gave birth to a daughter, who lived only two hours after having been baptised by the name of Amelia (*London Evening Post*, 21–24 April; *Weekly Journal or Gazetteer*, 28 April 1733).

their being so, your son William whom you so reluctantly brought to me this summer would have convinced me of it, because if he had been twin-brother to little Fitzfrederick, he could not have been more like him.' On another occasion the Queen insisted that the Prince was so solicitous of fathering a child by Miss Vane that he had asked Hervey to perform the necessary service for him; and although Hervey swore a thousand times that it was not true, the Queen refused to believe him. It is a question that can have no absolute answer, certainly not two centuries later; but the paternity may be awarded to the Prince for one decisive reason: he himself was convinced of it.

Hervey could claim uncontested paternity when, a month before Fitzfrederick's birth, his wife bore a son, the one who the Queen later thought resembled Miss Vane's. Lady Hervey was in their apartment in St. James's Palace for her lying-in, and the King considerately ordered the palace guards to mount without beating of drums in order to spare her the noise. The infant was baptised there by Benjamin Hoadly, the Bishop of Salisbury and given the name of William, with the Duke of Cumberland, his namesake, and Lord Chesterfield as godfathers, and the Princess Royal as godmother.

Miss Vane was as proud as she could be of her Royal bastard. She went about visiting in her sedan chair with her son on her lap and two nurses in their own chairs to attend her. For the summer (1732) Lord Baltimore lent her his manor at Epsom, in Surrey; and in the autumn she moved into a new house she had bought for £3,000 in Grosvenor Square, next door to the Bishop of Salisbury.

The peculiarity of her situation made her an easy target for scurrilous hacks of Grub Street as well as for scribbling wits at court. Lady Mary Wortley Montagu knew Miss Vane—in August a newspaper reported that Miss Vane and several other persons of distinction accompanied her to Tottenham Court Fair; and she could easily fashion satirical squibs or transcribe verse by others into her albums. One untitled poem she mysteriously labelled 'By——':

> When Vanella lay in & the Town had thought fit,
> To say that his Highness was cursedly Bit,
> Some Freinds of Vanella's acquainted the Dame
> How freely all People had treated her Fame:

Of a Hundred Amours, she (at least) was accus'd.
A Hundred! (she cries) Heavens, how I'm abus'd,
For I'll swear the dear Babe (or else may I starve) is
The Prince's, or Stanhope's, my Footman's, or Harvey's.

Both before and after Fitzfrederick's birth the episode was treated more elaborately in anonymous pamphlets. The most startling revelation that emerges in two of these is that before Miss Vane's liaison with the Prince she had been not only Hervey's mistress but the mother of a child by him. Although the author of *The Fair Concubine: or, The Secret History of the Beautiful Vanella* confessed his ignorance of this child's sex and ultimate fate he had no doubts as to the father. The author of *Vanella in the Straw*, a poem, merely mentioned that the heroine had borne a child by Almirus (Hervey) before he passed her on to the Prince.

The episode also enlarged Hervey's career as a satiric *persona*. *The Intriguing Courtiers*, the ballad-opera that ridicules Hervey as duellist, also deals with a Maid of Honour named Vanetta who is pregnant; and its sub-title, *The Modish Gallants*, glances at the literary collaboration of the Prince of Wales and Hervey. *The Humours of the Court*, another ballad opera in 1732, lists as one of its characters a rakish officer named Captain Modish and exposes the sexual triangle of Adonis (the Prince), Vanessa, and Aldemar, 'a gay young Rover of Quality, formerly Favourite with Vanessa'. James Miller's *Vanelia: or, The Amours of the Great*, a ballad opera published but never staged, shows Miss Vane as Lord Almirus's former mistress. In the flurry of lampoons generated by the scandal, 'The Court Garland', a ballad that circulated in manuscript, calls Hervey the pimp who first arranged for Miss Vane to become the Prince's mistress, and who then sends her a letter to vex her. When she tells her princely lover he reviles Hervey:

> Full hard I hold it right to tell,
>   Which Sex may justly claim thee,
> For those scarce know, who know thee well
>   What kind of thing to name thee.
>
> Thou powder-puff, thou painted toy,
>   Thou talking trifle, H——y;
> Thou doubtful he, she, je ne sçais quoy,
>   By G-d, the K-g shall starve ye.

Hervey rather than Miss Vane had now become the victim of scandalmongers. Each accretion of scandal and abuse was further preparation for his full-length satiric portrait by Pope that still lay ahead.

iii

At the beginning of June 1732 when the King left for a visit to Hanover, the Royal Family moved to Kensington Palace, from which they occasionally went to Richmond to hunt and dine. The Queen, relieved of her husband's demanding company, could spend more time with Hervey that summer, and their friendship grew closer. In August he could leave the court himself. After a visit to Walpole's seasonal house-party at Houghton, he went to Bury to look after his political interests there. At Ickworth, where he stayed, he found the park 'disagreably alter'd' because all the oak trees had been cut down. (Lord Bristol needed money for his 'multiplicity of children, continuation of heavy taxes, & other accidents').

While in Bury, with the Corporation sitting in the next room, Hervey could not restrain himself from writing to Stephen of his arrival at Ickworth: 'I live quite easy there, hear of no Court Intrigues, no Politicks &c.—every thing I say takes, & every thing I do is approved.' Busy as he was, he later tells Stephen (when he was back at Kensington), 'I thought of you often, at Ickworth, talk'd of you often & wish'd for you oftener . . . *by the Waters of Ickworth I sat down & wept when I remember'd thee O Redlynch*'. If his family home was a Babylon to him, Redlinch was his Zion— because of Stephen's presence there.

He could not arrange their reunion in September because the King was expected back from Hanover. When the Royal yacht was delayed by contrary winds, he asked Henry Fox, 'What manner of King is this, that the Winds & the Seas will not obey him? We talk of nothing here but the Wind & look at the Wether-Cock five hundred times a Day.' When the King finally arrived at Gravesend Hervey was a little late in meeting him, but the Royal coach graciously stopped and the King invited him to ride inside. They conversed for three hours before they reached Greenwich, where the official retinue took over. Hervey, who had travelled about sixty miles that day, had to wait until the evening to have his dinner. He was back in harness.

He consoled himself for being deprived of his favourite companions by writing to Henry as well as to Stephen. When Henry did not reply he testily wrote again, asking to be remembered to Stephen and the parson: 'My Service to Ste: tell Hill he's a Puppy, & for You, kiss my A——.' When he had a reply from Henry a few weeks later he rewarded him not only with a long letter but with a book, which, he explained, had been sent to him with this recommendation: '*There is so much Wit & so much Wickedness in this Paper that I conclude your Lordship will find it season'd to your Tast.*' Since these ingredients would make it fully as palatable to Henry, he continues, he is sending it without having read it himself: 'Adieu, I am in a great Hurry. If this Book is pretty, show it my Friend Mr. Sampson, for he does not like the Minute-Philosopher; & if you should guess who sent it to me I beg you would not say. I guess by the title it will not be a Sort of Book for Hill to understand or Ste: to be entertain'd with.' The book that he sent was a sixty-six-page pamphlet entitled *Some Remarks on the Minute Philosopher*, and the reason he was so evasive as to its authorship was that he himself had written this essay, not on politics (his usual concern) but on philosophy.

Alciphron; or, The Minute Philosopher, which Hervey had replied to, was a long treatise in the form of seven dialogues by George Berkeley, future Bishop of Cloyne. Published in March 1732 it was intended partially to refute the cynical thesis of Bernard Mandeville's *Fable of the Bees*, a notorious poem that, with its successive prose additions, had argued the paradoxical thesis that private vices are the cause of public benefits. Berkeley defines 'minute philosophers' (a phrase from Cicero) as 'a sort of pirates who plunder all that come in their way', free-thinkers who instead of following traditional Christian apologetics advocate a morality that is practical and utilitarian. His book had speedily become popular; and at court Queen Caroline, who dabbled in philosophy and theology herself, had discussed it with Berkeley. Hervey, because of his interest in the subject, was stimulated by Berkeley's treatise to compose a reply.

Its full title is *Some Remarks on the Minute Philosopher In a Letter from a Country Clergyman to his Friend in London*. Hervey thus assumes the role of a simple, ingenuous parson:

since the disagreeable Situation of a Country Clergyman with a small Living, not born a Fool, nor educated a Blockhead, is generally such, that his Taste and Understanding are as much above the Company he can keep, as his Fortune and his Circumstances are below the Company he would keep: And as Reading, in this Situation, is his only Resource, and Books his only Companions, he has no more Commerce with the Living, than with the Dead; and is no otherwise acquainted with any of the ingenious Men among his Contemporaries, than with those who lived two thousand Years ago.

He then, in his *Remarks*, tries to convict Berkeley of subverting the very Christian doctrine for which he has constructed his philosophical proof. He particularly objects to Berkeley's attack on free-thinkers, and chides him for advocating metaphysical proofs meaningless to ordinary men instead of the faith of traditional Christianity, its most solid support.

Since Henry rather than Stephen Fox shared his intellectual interests, Hervey sent him the pamphlet, knowing it would be appreciated. He later presented a copy to Voltaire, to whom it was delivered in Paris by Henry. Voltaire bestowed on it his greatest praise; it was, he said, as lucid and full of wit as Hervey himself.

iv

At the time of his marriage to Mary Lepell, Hervey enjoyed an easy friendship with Alexander Pope in the social circle of literary wits at court. But their relationship then changed, particularly because of their different political alliances. Pope's closest friends were Opposition Whigs or Tories, some of extreme persuasion— Bishop Atterbury before he went into exile, and Bolingbroke after he returned from it. Undoubtedly Pope and Hervey gossiped about each other, as they did about everyone. In the privacy of his correspondence with Stephen Fox, for example, Hervey allowed himself (in 1731) to call Pope the head of a sect of wits 'who think it incumbent upon them always to reflect & express themselves differently from the rest of the World . . . If he had never talk'd, one should have thought he had more Wit than any Man that ever lived.' A mild judgement, this, with its oblique praise of Pope's poetry. But Pope's *Epistle to Burlington* (in December 1731) had shocked the court circle with its portrait of the rich and ostentatious Timon, who, Pope's enemies insisted, was a lampoon of his friend the Duke of Chandos. Hervey detected some ridicule of Lord Burlington as well,

and expressed his surprise privately to Stephen as he may have
publicly to others: 'It is astonishing to me that he is not afray'd
this prophecy will be verify'd which was told him a Year or two
ago,

> In black & White whilst Satyr you pursue,
> Take Heed the Answer is not Black & Blue.

That kind of punishment had also been prophesied by Lady Mary,
Hervey's close friend, who had once been Pope's adored angel,
until, beginning with his 1728 *Dunciad*, she had become a target
of his satirical attacks.

When Hervey read the *Epistle to Bathurst* (in January 1733)
his opinion was more severe. Pope was 'so abusive in it,' he tells
Henry Fox, '& in so much plainer terms than in his Chandois-
Performance of impertinent Memory, that it is very probably
some of those to whom he pretends to teach the proper use of
Riches, may teach him the proper Use of Cudgels'. Perhaps
Hervey was again echoing Lady Mary's ruffian sentiments, for he
had not as yet any cause for personal complaint.

A few weeks later, however, the two friends were united as
fellow victims in Pope's first imitation of Horace's satires, a form
between translation and controlled improvisation, which allowed
him to create occasions to praise or damn whom ever he wished.
Compared to the poisonous couplet aimed at Lady Mary—
a Sappho who poxes by her love or libels by her hate—the
mention of Hervey seems mild:

> The Lines are weak, another's pleas'd to say,
> Lord *Fanny* spins a thousand such a Day.

Publishing his opinion of Hervey's flaccid couplets may be
justified, since it is true, but calling him Lord Fanny—a name
borrowed from Horace or Ben Jonson—was a gratuitous insult.
Hervey sent one copy of the poem to the Duke of Richmond and
another to Henry Fox, to whom he refrained from giving his
opinion 'because I am determined to indulge my Vanity so far
as to believe it would hinder my having your Opinion without
Prejudice; & that either from your Particular Partiality to me, or
your general Propensity to Contradiction you would certainly
be warp'd one way or the other'. Whether he was insulted by
having his verse called weak and prolix or himself Lord Fanny he
does not say; perhaps both.

In any case, he joined Lady Mary in revenge. Only three weeks after Pope's *Imitation*, A. Dodd published '*Verses Address'd to the Imitator of the First Satire of the Second Book of Horace*. By a Lady'; and on the next day Roberts issued the same satire, with one slight change, entitled this time *To the Imitator of the First Satire of the Second Book of Horace*, and with no mention of its authorship by a lady or anyone else. Of all the pamphlets that attacked Pope during his long career—at least one hundred and fifty-eight are known—this is one of the most effective in its bluntness, vigour, and cruelty:

> Whilst none thy crabbed Numbers can endure,
> Hard as thy Heart, and as thy Birth obscure.

And there is the repeated mention of physical punishment:

> And if thou draw'st thy Pen to aid the Law,
> Others a Cudgel, or a Rod may draw.

If Pope had once declared his love for Lady Mary only to be repulsed, as gossip reported, he was reminded of it by the couplet:

> But how should'st thou by Beauty's Force be mov'd,
> No more for loving made, than to be lov'd?

The final stroke of cruelty was to compare him to the Biblical Cain, predicting that with his crooked back he would 'Wander, like him, accursed through the Land'.

In any joint literary production the exact share of the collaborators is difficult to distinguish. The style of the *Verses to the Imitator* has a crude vitality and masculine robustness more characteristic of Lady Mary, who was remarkably versatile and could write verse of this sort, than it is of Hervey, most of whose verse is monotonously fluent and nerveless. The phrase on the title-page, 'By a Lady', is probably accurate; and Hervey's share must have been to assist in revising it and in seeing it through the press.

Although Lady Mary pretended, in a letter to Dr. Arbuthnot, that the verses were written without her knowledge by a 'Gentleman of great merit', Pope confided his opinion to Swift that the author was either Lady Mary or Hervey. 'They are certainly the Top wits of the Court,' Pope continues, 'and you may judge by that single piece what can be done against me; for it was labour'd, corrected, præcommended and post-disapprov'd, so far as to be

disown'd by themselves, after each had highly cry'd it up for
the other's.' Later, when Pope somehow found out more about
the poem's origin, he thought that 'both sexes had a share in it,
but which was uppermost, I know not. I pretend not to determine the exact method of this witty fornication'; and he concluded that whoever actually wrote it, Hervey had arranged for
its publication.*

Besides actively taking part in this pamphlet warfare, Hervey
was portrayed in a small role on the London stage when John
Gay's ballad opera *Achilles* opened at Covent Garden in February,
and played for twenty nights. One of its satiric scenes is a duel
between Ajax and Periphas, identified by a commentator as that
between Hervey and Pulteney. It was inevitable, in the warfare
of politics and poetry, that Hervey's activities in both should be
mingled. In *The State Dunces*, a satire inscribed to Pope by Paul
Whitehead, which scatters its shot on poets from St. James's to
Rag-Fair, Hervey is singled out as a prominent 'state dunce':

> To dance, dress, sing, and serenade the Fair,
> Conduct a Finger, or reclaim a Hair,
> O'er baleful Tea, with Females, taught to blame,
> And spread a Slander o'er each Virgin's Fame;
> Form'd for these softer Arts, shall *H—y* strain
> With stubborn Politicks his tender Brain!
> For Ministers laborious Pamphlets write,
> In *Senates* prattle, and with *Patriots* fight!

Hervey's position as Vice-Chamberlain was, after all, his main
profession; and his political activities as parliamentarian and
pamphleteer were closely associated with it. As a satiric *persona* he
had come into existence after his duel with Pulteney; and his
involvement with Miss Vane and the Prince of Wales had enlarged that aspect of his reputation. Now his altercation with
Pope emphasized his literary role, one that would become more
prominent, and eventually keep his image alive long after his
politics and pamphlets had been forgotten. He would have been
wise to take the advice the King offered: 'You ought not to write
verses; 'tis beneath your rank: leave such work to little Mr. Pope.'

* At a later date Hervey prepared a second edition (copy at Ickworth), which
was never published, and in its preface referred to the *Verses* as by himself, but this
must have been part of the obfuscation that surrounded the first two publications
of the poem.

V

In the Parliamentary session of 1733 Walpole's Ministry was confronted by its most perilous challenge. This was not the bill setting the size of the standing army, which as usual was debated by the Opposition in the vain hope of reducing its numbers; as in the previous session, Hervey spoke in its support, and it was passed. Far more inflammatory was Walpole's Excise Bill, which had been hotly argued in the press since the previous summer. In retrospect the measure seems simple and unexceptionable: wishing to reduce the land tax, Walpole saw that an effective way of raising additional revenue was to enforce the existing tax on tobacco and wine by an excise tax instead of the import duty so widely evaded through smuggling.

Early in February, a month before the debate on the bill opened, Hervey had sent a long, detailed analysis of it to Henry Fox, outlining its advantages and answering objections that might be raised. 'As for the Excises,' he tells him a fortnight later, 'I feel upon that Head as the Emperor in *Aureng-Zebe* does to his Wife: *If I but hear them named, I'm sick that Day*; from whence you must logically conclude I am in a constant State of very bad Health, for it is Physick I am forced to take from Morning to Night.' Exactly why he is taking such a great dosage of excises he does not say; he was actually writing a pamphlet on the subject as part of the Ministry's attempt to win public and Parliamentary support. His letter to Henry about the bill was, in effect, a sketch for his full explanation.

He headed his manuscript of the pamphlet 'A Letter to the Mayor of —— by a member of Parliament', and handed it over to Walpole. Dissatisfied with the title, Walpole struck it out and substituted in his own hand: 'The Reply of a Member of Parliament to the Mayor of his Corporation.' He kept the draft, with many alterations in Hervey's hand (perhaps dictated by him); and a fair copy was dispatched to the printer, who issued it through Roberts in March, in time to influence those inside as well as outside Parliament. Writing in a calm and reasonable tone, Hervey (as the anonymous M.P.) explains to the mayor why he is going to disobey his constituency's instructions, which he describes as the result of the torrent of malignant abuse poured on the bill by its opponents. He then patiently refutes the various objections raised, and explains the various benefits that will result if the bill is passed; tranquillity will be restored, and the public, seeing that they have been misled by malicious people, will recognize who their real benefactors are. Whether or not these arguments, and similar ones in other pamphlets or in newspapers, would persuade members of Parliament and calm the aroused London mob would soon be known.

The debate itself opened on 14 March with a masterly presentation by Walpole, more than two hours in duration, one of the best speeches of his entire career. Meanwhile, a great mob, encouraged by the bill's opponents in the City, milled about in the corridors and entrances of Westminster. As soon as the day's debate ended, at one o'clock in the morning, Hervey hurried to St. James's to tell the King all that had happened inside and outside the House. (He had already sent a written report at five in the afternoon.) The King then led him to the Queen's bedchamber, where they kept him until almost three o'clock pressing him for details of the debate, the words, actions, even facial expressions of the speakers. The King had been so firmly persuaded by Walpole of the excise scheme's importance that he could not have been more zealous in its favour had it been to settle his own succession.

When the bill was again debated, two days later, Hervey was among those who spoke in its favour. As its supporters steadily melted away the King grew more anxious. Before the bill's second reading (on 11 April) it was clear that even if Walpole could squeeze the bill through the Commons, it would not pass the Lords, where even members of the King's Cabinet-Council and several domestic officers planned to vote against it. On the eve of the fateful day Hervey sat among the dozen or so friends at supper with Walpole, who said to them, 'This dance it will no farther go, and to-morrow I intend to sound a retreat.' And so, before the bill was read, Walpole proposed that it be put off for two months (when it would be allowed to die quietly). The anti-excise mob outside, greater than before, hissed and insulted the departing M.P.s who had supported the Bill. Hervey and General Churchill, fearful that the mob might use stronger gestures against Walpole, returned to the House to warn him, but he refused to leave by a side door. Surrounded by an escort consisting of Hervey, Churchill, his eldest son, several friends, and two servants he braved the danger, and through a lane of forty to fifty constables made his way amidst the jostling and struggling mob. Although his son was hurt in the arm, and Hervey on the forehead, he escaped unharmed.

In the House the next day Walpole and his friends shrewdly profited by the dangerous riot. It was Hervey who made the speech in which he warned that if the opinion of the rabble was to be taken on every measure debated in the House, then their clamour and not the judgement of the Members would determine the decisions there;

and instead of the representatives of the people with decency and method considering what was proper and fit to be done, that he supposed he should see the Speaker at Charing-Cross or the stocks-market proposing laws to a tumultuous mob, who, like the Roman plebians, would enact, rescind, promulgate, and repeal, make, and break laws, just as the caprice of their present temper and the insinuations of their present leaders should instigate and direct.

So fierce was the indignation of most Members at the reports of the mob's action that the resolutions condemning it were passed unanimously, and the Opposition leaders joined in order to exculpate themselves. Walpole thus extracted some benefit from his defeat.

Although the Excise Bill was killed, the outpouring of lampoons about it did not cease. One of them, a ballad opera never staged, entitled *The Honest Electors, or The Courtiers Sent Back With Their Bribes*, lists one of its characters as Lord Challenge (a reminder of Hervey's duel two years before), who is a friend of the Prime Minister and a favourite of the ladies at Hampton Court.

Hervey, generally an undeviating supporter of Walpole, could differ with him on unimportant measures. When a bill 'to prevent the infamous practice of stock-jobbing' had its third reading in the House (at the end of April) Walpole spoke lukewarmly in its favour, while admitting that it could have been better drawn. It was in a sense a non-party piece of legislation. Hervey spoke and voted against it. (Passed by 55 to 49 it was eventually dropped.) On a Ministerial bill for a charitable lottery a few days later Hervey spoke in its favour, his loyalty untarnished.

In this session of Parliament the excise crisis had not only strengthened his loyalty to Walpole but had deepened his friendship with the King and Queen. To show their gratitude they chose a reward that would honour him and at the same time bring political profit to themselves as well. The excise affair had caused the defection from the Court party of prominent Lords—Montrose, Stair, Marchmont, Bolton, Cobham, and Chesterfield, who was one of their best speakers. The King and Queen suggested to Walpole that Hervey be brought into the House of Lords. Despite the strenuous opposition of the Duke of Newcastle (Hervey's bitter enemy), Walpole could not withhold this reward, even if he himself were so inclined, because it had not been solicited by Hervey. At this juncture of his fortunes Hervey says that as his 'pride and vanity were fed with the air of being called out of the whole House of Commons upon this occasion, and as he had a mind to strengthen the interest of his family in Parliament by bringing one of his brothers into his place, so he embraced this offer with too much readiness, and pushed the immediate execution of it with too much warmth, for the envy or ill-will of his adversaries to be able to stop it'. In June he 'kiss'd his Majesty's Hand' on the issuance of the writ that called him up to the House of Lords in his father's barony as Lord Hervey of Ickworth.

While he saw his elevation as a great benefit to his family's fortunes, his fond father, still stubbornly unsympathetic to Walpole, viewed it differently, fearful that his being 'kicked upstairs' (his father's phrase) would deprive him of his power yet keep him working for Walpole without any real or substantial reward. Still, at Hervey's request, he generously paid the necessary fees (£143) for the patent. On 12 June, escorted by Lord Delawarr and Lord Walpole (the Minister's eldest son) he was ceremoniously introduced into the House of Lords. Before going down to Westminster he had (in his own words) 'to run this kissing Gantlet throughout the whole Royal Family'. His elevation (along with that of others) to the Lords, it was generally assumed, was one of 'the Rewards and Punishments for their Merits and Demerits in the late Session'.

vi

If Hervey had chosen this moment, when he was so conspicuously honoured, to look back at his other rewards and his punishments, he would have seen an ample number of both. His post as Vice-Chamberlain, though not as exalted as his ambition would demand, was not contemptible as a lower rung on the ladder of court preferment; and he had held it only three years. That he often chafed under its duties and often complained because it deprived him of the freedom to be with his beloved Stephen were punishments inseparable from its rewards. He could occasionally seize a crumb of comfort. When forced to attend a dull opera with the King he was enraptured to hear a singer whom he and Stephen had heard in Naples, and he sighed a hundred times (he tells his 'caro & carissimo') at the recollection of that radiant interlude. If having a wife was punishment, then the fact that she patiently bore his children, accepted his neglect, and welcomed the friend he deeply loved could be counted an enormous reward. When Lady Hervey visited Goodwood, the Duke of Richmond's estate in Sussex, in the autumn of 1732 she arranged for Stephen to join them there. What more could a wife do!

His court appointment enabled him to enjoy the friendship of the Queen and Princess Caroline, of whom he was genuinely fond, but he also had to endure the frequently disagreeable company of the King and Princess Emily. His appointment had earlier enabled him to bask in the intimate friendship of the Prince of Wales, but that had ended unpleasantly. He expressed his view of life at court in some verse addressed to a friend:

> For *Courts* are only larger Familys,
> The Growth of each, few Truths, & many Lyes;
> Like you we lounge, & feast, & play, & chatter;
> In private Satirize, in Publick flatter.

(The final line is doubly witty, for he was satirizing in public as he no doubt flattered in private.)

In addition to his official duties he had an important political function, for he lent valuable assistance to Walpole by serving as his ally and his informal emissary to the Royal couple. Walpole had no reason to regret having retained his allegiance when Pulteney tried to win it away for the Opposition. Hervey also repaid that trust by supporting him in the House of Commons as he would in the future in the Lords. More useful, still, he wielded one of the ablest pens at the Ministry's command in the unceasing battle against the Opposition press. His loyalty to Walpole was unquestioned and unquestioning.

The combination of court and politics forced him into a life of hectic activity, particularly exhausting for one of his feeble constitution. Once (in January 1733) he sent Henry Fox a 'Journal of the Day' recording his attendance at several 'Theatres'. The first, that he attended with Stephen, was Walpole's levee, which he calls a farce: 'Kissing, whispering, bowing, squeezing Hands &c. were all acted there as usual by the political Pantomimes who officiate at those weekly Performances, where several Boons are asked, which are not so much as promised, & several promised which will never be granted.' He then went to the House of Commons, which he calls the Grand Theatre; then to 'the Theatre at St. James's, where the Tragedy of a Cabinet-Council was acted to the Sorrow of sixteen poor Malefactors, & a Comedy of a privy Council . . . [where the] Lord President perform'd his Part in this Scene with a great deal of dull Dignity & becoming Formality, his Hands full of Papers, his nose full of Snuff, & his Mouth full of Nonsense'. In the evening he attended the King to see the stage performance at the theatre in Drury Lane, after which he went to his fifth and last theatre of the day, at Lady Strafford's, to see a 'medly Farce call'd a modern Assembly', where 'every Body play'd something, & most People play'd the Fool'.

Considering the number of parts Hervey himself played in these various theatres one wonders what he regarded as his own genuine character. His most personal confidences, of course, he sent to Stephen Fox, but a man will often uncover deeper layers of self-awareness to a relative stranger than to his intimates (for whom he may be playing a carefully sustained part). The Revd. Robert Butts, who had been rector of Ickworth and had through Hervey's patronage become Dean of Norwich, somehow evoked from him in November 1732 a confessional statement that he called the description of his heart:

As I came very early into the World, [he writes] have lived long in what is call'd the top of it & had a satiating Swing in the showish Part of its Pleasures, my tast has taken a New turn, the Hey-Day of my Blood (as Shakespear calls it) is pretty well over. In the midst of crouded Court, I pass many, many Hours alone; I am disgusted of many People I used to love, undecieved in some I used to esteem, & have lower'd my Opinion of many more I used to admire. By these means I have contracted my Acquaintance into a narrow Compass, my Friendships into a narrower; & have exchanged the Amusement of many useless Companions for that of a few usefull Books. I am forced (alter'd I confess by Constitution rather than corrected by Reason) to take up with speculative Pleasures as my practical ones decay, & very prudently try if I can gain by experience one way as much as I have lost by it another.

Can he be serious—to describe such a retirement during his endlessly busy days and nights? It is a philosophic pose, in part, and a statement of his world-weary cynicism as well. These are only two strands in the fabric of his thought and feeling. He was not a simple man.

vii

Stimulated perhaps by his elevation to the House of Lords and by his growing intimacy with the Royal Family, Hervey decided to compile memoirs of the court. Since he knew that their contents would be varied and unsystematic—for he would be writing in the midst of the swirling life there—he used as his title 'Some Materials Towards Memoirs of the Reign of George II'. He begins by explaining why he is well qualified to undertake such a work: 'Boasting of intelligence and professing impartiality are such worn-out prefaces to writings of this kind, that I shall not trouble my readers nor myself with any very long exordium upon these topics.' Very briefly he then points out that his residence at court most of the year, observing its inhabitants in their public and private lives, has made accessible to him a rich source of information; and since the memoirs will not be published during his lifetime he can be frank and impartial. He is determined to report everything just as he sees it; and he warns the reader that 'those who have a curiosity to see courts and courtiers dissected must bear with the dirt they find in laying open such minds with as little nicety and as much patience as in a dissection of their bodies, if they wanted to see that operation, they must submit to the stench'.

Although he began to compile the memoirs in 1733 or 1734 he started logically with the accession of George II in 1727 and the state of the Whig and Tory parties at the time. He treated the early years of the reign in very broad outline compared to the detailed narrative and dialogue for the years after 1733, when he could depend on recorded notes, memoranda, journals, and (for the final weeks of the Queen's illness) a diary. Sometimes he set

down a conversation immediately after hearing it, or he tele-
scoped into one episode the conversations that were inter-
mittent over a long period. He seems to have had a Boswellian
sense of total recall: not short-hand (in the famous quip) but a long
head. When he needed them, he also relied on documents,
speeches, and letters, which he copied into the memoirs; he even
included a miniature three-act drama with which he had amused
the Queen, entitled 'The Death of Lord Hervey, or, A Morning at Court'. All these are the 'materials' that his title promises.

He was well aware of other memoirists, particularly the
Cardinal de Retz in France (whose memoirs were published in
1717) and Bishop Burnet in England. The first volume of Burnet's
History of His Own Time had been published in 1724; and
although neither Hervey nor his father subscribed to it he had
read it, and quotes from it in his own memoirs. The second
volume of Burnet appeared in February 1734; it may have stimulated him to begin his own, or spurred him on. He had a low
opinion of its contents. 'I think like you of Burnet's history,' he
told a friend, ''tis the Common Chit-chat of a talkative, credulous
old fellow that frequents coffee houses and reads newspapers.'
He condemns these two 'ecclesiastical heroes of their own
romances' who 'aim at that useless imaginary glory of being
thought to influence every considerable event they relate'. He
would steer clear of such 'disagreeable egotisms', he promises his
readers, by referring to himself in the third person; like the chorus
in Greek drama, he writes, he would comment only on the events
he observed.

This, at any rate, was his intention. But when he reached the
summer of 1734 (in the memoirs) he digresses to apologize for so
frequently mentioning himself, and expresses a more charitable
view of other memoirists. He now realized that since they generally
related events in which they were concerned they could not avoid
egotisms: what he had imputed to vanity he now finds from
experience was owing to necessity. He also apologizes for the
'loose, unmethodized, and often incoherent manner' in which his
memoirs are put together: he had too little leisure for writing
and revising. Instead he tells of 'things only just as they occur' in
his memory, he says (when he reached the year 1737), 'and as I
happen to have leisure to set them down' without the trouble or
time to go back and interweave them in their proper places. As

for his being too particular in 'relating little circumstances': since he has no guide to tell him what will please other people he has allowed himself to be guided by what pleases himself best. But it was more than self-indulgence that made him write with such particularity; he looked on these papers rather as fragments that might be wove into a history, than a history in themselves, and hence he put in the little details that few historians could discover for themselves.

The knowledge that what he heard and saw at court would find a place in his memoirs undoubtedly sharpened his ears and his eyes there; and during the next four years he was both involved actor and witty commentator, protagonist and Greek chorus, in the mixed human drama enacted on the various stages where his court duties placed him.

9

Pamphlets Political and Satirical

1733–4

THE PARLIAMENTARY SEAT FOR BURY that had been vacated by Hervey's elevation to the peerage was now to go to his next brother. Thomas Hervey, three years his junior, had also attended Westminster School but had then matriculated at Oxford. After a brief, idle spell as an undergraduate, with gambling as his main accomplishment, he left without taking a degree. Spurred on by his hopeful father he had been admitted to Lincoln's Inn in 1720 though he never practised the law. His appointment as equerry to the Queen in 1727 had indicated the route by which he hoped to gain further preferment.

In spite of Tom Hervey's poor health, which he tried to improve by visiting the spas, his father continued to advance him in the world. He had been elected 'chief Magistrate' of Bury in 1731, while he was away drinking the waters at Bristol; and his father promised that the duties were not burdensome and that he would pay the expenses. In the summer of the following year, although reported dangerously ill at Bristol, he had evidently been well enough to amass such a large gambling debt that his long-suffering father had to borrow £1,000 from Hervey to pay it. He was a man given to vice, Samuel Johnson said of him many years later, but he was 'one of the genteelest men that ever lived'.* He would now be M.P. for the seat traditionally occupied by a member of the family.

Hervey himself travelled to Bury to assist in his brother's election. He was accompanied by Stephen Fox, while Lady Hervey remained in London. His sole reason for making the journey, he wrote to the King, was 'to obey the Commands of Your

---

* It was of another brother, Henry Hervey, that Johnson said, 'He was a vicious man, but very kind to me. If you call a dog Hervey, I shall love him.'

Majesty's Speech to your Parliament, & as far as my Capacity will assist my Zeal to *undecieve the deluded* & point out *the force of Truth* with Regard to every misrepresented Measure of this last Winter, as well as the Arts & Designs of those Invidious Commentators who have endeavour'd to set all Persons & all things in a bad & false Light'. (He tactfully underlined the two phrases quoted from the King's speech in June.)

During the election festivities in Bury the new M.P. remained at Ickworth, ostensibly because of the prevalence of smallpox in the town. Hervey, who out of family duty and Ministerial loyalty had exchanged the *douceurs* of St. James's for the crude pleasures of the Bury election, did not feel much joy. 'I hear at present of nothing but Writs, Precepts, Sherifs, & Returns,' he complained to a newly acquired friend; 'I see nothing but Aldermen, smell nothing but Tobacco, & talk of nothing [but] Excises & South-Sea Directors. This delightful Rondeau, with all the etcætera Comforts of electioning (thank God) is to finish on Sunday, when I shall return to London, in as great haste & much more willingly than I left it.'

At the election itself (on 29 June) 'without one penny given or promisd', Lord Bristol boasted, the entire corporation of the borough had unanimously elected Thomas to the seat. Several thousand people then accompanied Bristol and his sons (except the victor) to the Guildhall with drums, music, ringing bells, and with many huzzas and repeated acclamations of 'Long live the honest Earl of Bristol and every branch of his noble family for ever'. Deeply moved, Bristol could not remember ever having witnessed a truer or more cordial affection. This demonstration occurred even before the crowd had drunk the ten hogshead of strong beer with which the evening concluded.

The election, however gratifying to Bristol, almost caused an estrangement between him and his wife. For she had apparently persuaded Thomas to shun the election, and remain at Ickworth, because of her dislike of Colonel Norton, her relation, who held the other Parliamentary seat for the borough. Bristol was so angry when he discovered this (he told Hervey) that he warned his wife 'if ever she offerd to meddle again with Corporation affairs, or mentioned Collonel Norton's name at my table but with the decency due to a relation & to one I had thought fitt to engage with, that I would neither eat nor coud live any longer with her, and that we must at last separate, after having reluctantly declind doing so before upon your and my familys account more than upon our own'. Her meddling also embarrassed Hervey, for he had been asked by the Queen and Walpole to instruct Tom to attend the election, and Tom himself had assured the Queen that he would. Now Hervey had the irksome duty of making excuses for his brother's disobedience, which he blamed on the 'vehemence of my Lady Bristol's Temper'. He firmly reprimanded Tom, and not for the first time insisted that he had done as much for the Hervey family as he could.

One of Tom's complaints was that the post of Vice-Chamberlain to the Queen's Household, vacant since February, had not been awarded to him (as a newspaper erroneously reported), and that Walpole had given it to another. Having patiently consoled him, Hervey then assured him: 'all your future good or ill in public Life depends on your Conduct here [at court] & in Parliament. My Advice I shall always be ready to give you, my Assistance too if you want it, & my good wishes will always attend you.' Hervey's five brothers were now grown, and their road to preferment, since Lord Bristol clung to his political martyrdom, lay to some extent through Lady Bristol's influence as Lady of the Bedchamber and mostly through Hervey's favour with the court and with Walpole. Political patronage has always been an essential element in the structure of government in England, and in the eighteenth century it was both pervasive and undisguised. Because of his increasing favour with Walpole and the Queen Hervey expected to wield more power through controlling and influencing patronage, and his family and friends knew this.

He had promised his brother Charles, ordained less than a year before, to appoint him one of his chaplains, but for some reason could not; and he had to bear his father's reproof for 'bestowing it on a stranger'. (The appointment went to the Revd. Jonathan Alleyne.) He was constantly harassed by his importunate family. Once, after having refreshed the Queen's memory about his brother Harry's ambitions, he told his father that 'Solicitations to the Ears of Princes are like Footsteps in the Sand; they drive one another out.' He had to keep stamping fresh footsteps.

The newly acquired friend to whom he had complained of the nuisance of the Bury election was one who became his most persistent claimant for patronage. A place-hunter in search of a patron, the Revd. Dr. Conyers Middleton was fifty years old at the time, the first Principal Librarian of Cambridge and Woodwardian professor, and as restless for advancement as an ambitious boy starting a career. He had been a Fellow of Trinity under the redoubtable Dr. Bentley, with whom he feuded in the College and the law courts. Bentley called him Fiddling Conyers or Fiddleton (a pun on his musical activity) and 'an arrant Pagan' (for his alleged deism). His book *A Letter from Rome*, the fruit of his travels in Italy, had exposed the pagan practices of the Roman Catholic Church; and he extended the same sceptical spirit of inquiry to his own Church. In his most celebrated controversy, with the theologian Daniel Waterland, he had cast doubt on the historical truth of Biblical miracles. Although he had been at Cambridge when Hervey was an undergraduate there, they had apparently been unacquainted.

His previous patron, Lord Oxford, had discouraged their friendship because of his growing reputation as a deist; and so he was glad to transfer his allegiance and expectations to one whose ideas were congenial to his own and, more important, whose appointment and friends at court promised greater potential rewards. That Hervey accepted his role as patron is clear, for on the day after he entered the House of Lords he assured Middleton: 'if it were in my Power, I would make it as much to your advantage to have known me, as I am sure it [will] always be to my Satisfaction to have known You.' Only a month later, when a University post was rumoured to be changed, Middleton applied to Hervey for his 'Protection', as he delicately phrased it. Hervey could not help him, but prepared the way for future favours by speaking to the Queen about Middleton, after having made her read the *Letter from Rome*; she then sent a message through Hervey that she liked it. To Middleton it must have seemed an auspicious beginning for the long road of preferment that stretched so temptingly before him.

But Middleton had prudently cast about for not one but two patrons. Hervey was his primary one, essentially because of his political influence; his other patron's connections were not negligible. The Honourable Thomas Townshend was, to begin with, Member of Parliament for Cambridge University, a constituency that put him in a favoured position for academic preferment. More important, he was nephew to both Newcastle and

Walpole. He possessed this unusual distinction because his mother, first wife of Lord Townshend, had been Newcastle's half-sister; and his step-mother had been Walpole's sister. Even after his father had been eased out of power and office in 1730 young Townshend remained loyal to Walpole and to his Administration. By 1735 Middleton was on very friendly terms with Townshend; and his obsequious verbal posture clearly displayed his role as a place-seeker before a patron.

ii

When Hervey returned to court after the Bury election and resumed his duties, the Royal Family were at Richmond for three weeks; and since he had no living quarters there he borrowed a room in the house at Kew owned by Charlotte Clayton (later Lady Sundon), the Queen's Woman of the Bedchamber. As a result he had to travel back and forth between the two villages, leading what he called a 'disagreable Stage-Coachman's Life'. When the Royal Family moved to Hampton Court (on 16 July) he settled into his own quarters and customary routine. Every Wednesday and Saturday, while the King hunted, the Queen followed in a chaise with Hervey on horseback at her side so that he could entertain her with his conversation while the others entertained themselves with hearing dogs bark and seeing crowds gallop. Every Tuesday, Thursday, and Friday morning he walked with the Queen and her daughters, conversing in greater comfort. As a respite from his constant duty he was permitted two days a week to himself, Sunday and Monday, and he always spent those nights in London. Although he told the King he went there only to gather news and observe people, his real business in London— he states in his *Memoirs*, somewhat ambiguously—was 'pleasure'.

While he was tied to the court, Lady Hervey had gone to Goodwood to join the Duchess of Richmond's house-party, which included Lady Tankerville and Stephen Fox. Their friends in London were shocked to read in the newspapers that two high-waymen had stopped their coach near Goodwood and held them up at pistol-point. Lady Hervey and Stephen had been robbed of their gold watches, Lady Tankerville of a gold snuff-box, and William Sherwin, a canon of Chichester, of his money. The ladies and Stephen already knew that the robbery was a plot aimed at Dr. Sherwin, and that the bandits were none other than the Duke of Richmond, a great practical joker, and his servant. Sherwin, who remained ignorant of the hoax for a long time, continued to tell about the adventure, adding touches of Falstaffian exaggeration. Hervey joined the house-party himself at the beginning of August for a short stay, and then he and Lady Hervey accompanied Stephen for a few days' visit to Redlinch. They all returned to Hampton Court so that Hervey could resume what he called his 'ordinary Gold-Key-Vocations'.

Stephen filled his 'private Hours as fully, & at least as agreably' as his public ones, Hervey confessed to his friend Benjamin Hoadly (Bishop of Salisbury). Yet his passion, so intense in their earlier friendship, was dwindling, as though it had begun to exhaust itself. Except for the few months when Parliament met, Stephen preferred to stay in the country; and living alone he feared that he was unfit for his brilliant friend's company in London, though Hervey gallantly assured him that he preferred Stephen 'rusty better than any other body polish'd'. One important drawback in their friendship, present since its beginning, was that Stephen lacked the varied intellectual interests that engaged Hervey on many fronts; and as their emotional attachment slackened no other common tastes took its place.

Hervey took a lively interest in the philosophical and literary currents of his day, and when possible cultivated the friendship of men who swam in those currents. He was familiar with Montesquieu's *Lettres persanes*, first published in 1721; and during the Frenchman's sojourn in England, from 1729 to 1731, both he and more particularly Lady Hervey, who was an ardent francophile, cultivated his friendship. Hervey read his *Considérations sur les causes de la grandeur des Romains et de leur décadence* when it was published in 1734, greatly admiring its learning, spirit, and enlightened view of religion.

His friendship with Voltaire was closer and of longer duration. Begun during Voltaire's visit to England, it had been strengthened when Hervey called on him in Paris in 1729. Remembering this, Voltaire had given his friend Thierot an introduction (in 1732) to Hervey as well as to Bolingbroke, Gay, Pope, and Pulteney; he instructed him to convey his respects 'to the great foes Mr. Pulteney, and mylord and lady Harvey'. When Henry Fox visited Paris, Hervey in turn had given him an introduction to

Voltaire, who enthusiastically thanked him (in September 1733) for sending a gentleman who had 'l'esprit doux et sage'. Voltaire concluded his letter in English: 'Adieu charming lord remember a frenchman who is devoted to your lordship for ever with the utmost respect, and loves you passionately.' (The extravagance of his language comes from his relative unfamiliarity with English.)

Hervey's friendship for Voltaire the man did not prevent him from criticizing Voltaire the writer. When he read the tragedy *Zaïre* (early in 1733) and sent a copy to Henry Fox, he was certain that like himself Fox would have 'some Compassion for a silly Christian [heroine] as well as the greatest regard, Esteem, & Affection for a noble, good, tender & charming Mahometan'— who through a tragic misunderstanding kills her. He was irritated, though, by Voltaire's dedication of the play to Edward Falkener, an English merchant. In France it was regarded as scandalous because it was addressed not only to a commoner but to a foreign one at that. Hervey told Henry Fox that he thought it 'bad, false, & impertinent . . . by a superficial Frenchman to an Englishman, & the Dedicator pretends to be better acquainted with our Country, our Manners, our Laws, & even our Language than the Dedicatee'. What could have aroused such a violent opinion? In the dedicatory epistle, after praising the high rank and regard the mercantile class enjoyed in England, Voltaire continues: 'I know very well that this profession is despised by our petits-maîtres; but you also know that our petits-maîtres and yours are the most ridiculous species that proudly crawl on the face of the earth'. This, rather than the general remarks about French and English theatre, could have been offensive to one who was certainly closer to being a petit-maître than a man of commerce.

In his letter of September 1733 Voltaire asked Hervey for an opinion of his *Lettres philosophiques* (first published as *Letters Concerning the English Nation*). Hervey had cause to be flattered, for in the twentieth letter of the book Voltaire pays a handsome compliment to 'the *English* Nobleman' who had come to see him in Paris after visiting Italy, and had shown him 'a poetical Description of that Country, which, for Delicacy and Politeness, may vie with any Thing we meet with in the Earl of Rochester'; and he begged the Englishman's pardon for his French translation (which he prints) 'so inexpressive of the Strength and delicate Humour of the Original'. Hervey's opinion of the book, whether or not he replied to Voltaire, was not sweetened by the compliment. He confided to Dr. Middleton that in its original language the *Lettres anglaises* was a lively, superficial book, but in translation flat and tiresome since it lacked the spirit and strength of the French diction. When he read Voltaire's *Temple du goût*, an evaluation of a wide range of French writers, he sent a copy to his father along with what his father called 'entertaining criticism' of the book and its author.

iii

As a writer Hervey practised two separate roles: a public one as a propagandist for the Administration, and a private one as a self-indulgent, amateur versifier. Although he could be unwise enough to engage so deadly an antagonist as Pope, he was more successful when he took on the Opposition's most formidable paper, the *Craftsman*. On 15 September 1733 that paper printed an essay entitled 'The Game of Chess', whose opening gambit promises an agreeable change from politics, but it then becomes a neat allegory of the English political scene. A week later Hervey played a return match with a brief pamphlet, *A Letter to the Craftsman on the Game of Chess*. Dating it from Slaughter's Coffee House, a centre for chess players, he cleverly corrects the *Craftsman*'s analysis, converting its allegory into a defence of his own party. Horatio Walpole recommended the pamphlet to Lord Carlisle as 'extremely ingenious, and very entertaining to those that have a notion of that game'. If he knew that Hervey had written it, he discreetly avoided mentioning it, probably for fear of post-office spies.

In his political journalism Hervey at least served a defensible cause; he could not, unfortunately, repress either his poetic itch or his hatred of Pope, which served no reasonable purpose. The climax of his altercation with Pope came about through his friendship with Dr. Sherwin, the victim of the bogus robbery near Goodwood. Just before that episode, while still at Hampton Court, Hervey had received from Sherwin a letter in Latin verse. Although he could read and write Latin fluently he preferred to reply in English. His verse epistle, almost two hundred lines in length, is mainly autobiographical but concludes with a long attack on Pope in which he trots out the familiar accusation that

Pope had been guilty of plagiarism in his satires and Homer translation. Unlike the *Verses to the Imitator of Horace*, written in collaboration with Lady Mary, Hervey's attack is aimed only at Pope's writings, without any reflections on his appearance or family; and unlike the *Verses to the Imitator* Hervey sent his epistle not to a publisher but to Dr. Sherwin and to Henry Fox. He had written it, he tells Henry, 'to entertain the Richmond-Caravan in their late Progress'—their journey from Goodwood to Hampton Court. It seems unlikely that he intended to publish his epistle; its autobiographical sections are such as one might send to thank a donnish friend for a flattering letter. He apologizes for replying in 'plain, native English' instead of the Greek or Latin he had learned from Dr. Freind at Westminster:

> I'm sure your courteous Rev'rence will forgive
> The homely Way in which you now recieve
> These hearty Thanks, from an illiterate Hand,
> For Favours which I barely understand.

Dr. Sherwin was so pleased to receive the verse that he indiscreetly showed it to others. It thus fell into the hands of a printer, as so much scandalous, privately circulated verse did, and was published (on 10 November 1733) under the title: *An Epistle from a Nobleman to a Doctor of Divinity*. Only one week earlier Pope had published *The Impertinent, or, A Visit to Court* (a reworking of one of John Donne's satires), in which he glances at Hervey's friendship with Queen Caroline:

> Not *Fannius* self more impudently near,
> When half his Nose is in his Patron's Ear.

For that reason the *Epistle from a Nobleman* could perhaps be regarded by its readers as Hervey's retaliation for this contemptuous mention of his friendship with the Queen.

After the *Epistle from a Nobleman* was published, when Hervey somehow heard of its effect on Pope, he did not hide his pleasure. 'Pope is in a most violent Fury,' he tells Stephen, '& J'en suis ravis.' When Dr. Arbuthnot called to ask why he had been so severe on Pope, he replied, 'Because he was a Rascal, had begun with me & deserv'd it, & that my only Reason for being sorry the Verses were printed, which I did not design they should be, was because I thought it below me to enter into a Paper-War with one that had made him-self by his late Works as contemptible as he was odious.'* This explanation would only exacerbate Pope further, he knew, since Arbuthnot had been sent by Pope and would probably repeat his unrepentant answer.

At about this time Hervey discovered that some other verse of his, a satire entitled 'Dr. Sherwin's Character, design'd for his Epitaph', had fallen into the hands of a printer who threatened to publish it. Either confused or intending confusion the printer advertised in the *Daily Courant* (of 20 November 1733) that 'Speedily will be Publish'd' the *Epistle from a Nobleman* and Sherwin's Latin epistle although these had actually been published a fortnight before. Since that newspaper was subsidized by the Ministry, Hervey asked the Duke of Newcastle to intercede; and so the newspaper, two days later, assured the public that 'there was no such Poem wrote by the Lord *Hervey*, nor *Latin* Epistle sent his Lordship by Dr. *Sherwin*'. This greatly embarrassed Hervey since he had generally admitted his authorship.

Taking advantage of the confusion, Pope inserted an advertisement of his own in the newspapers that unless Hervey 'shall this next week in a manner as public as the injury, deny the said poem to be. his, or contradict the aspersions therein contained, there will with all speed be published a most proper reply to the same'. (Perhaps Pope's joke here was to demand that even if Hervey should deny writing the poem he should contradict its aspersions.) Pope did not need much time to reply. He wrote and printed a long prose *Letter to a Noble Lord*, dated 30 November [1733], one of his most devastating pieces, a rebuttal not only of the *Epistle from a Nobleman* but of the *Verses to the Imitator*. Hervey knew that Pope had written the *Letter to a Noble Lord* and shown it to several friends, but even two months later he had not seen it himself though he had 'heard from those who did see it [that it] is very low & poor, ridiculing only my Person & my being vain of over-rated Parts, & the undeserv'd Favour of a Court'. But for some reason Pope withheld it from publication. One explanation is that he did so at the request of Horatio Walpole, who had procured an abbey from the French prime minister for a

---

* On his own printed copy of the verse (now at Ickworth) Hervey added four couplets to the top of page 8 justifying his attack on Pope: because 'the Spider first his venom shed'. He also put these couplets at the end of his manuscript of the *Epistle from a Nobleman*.

Catholic friend of Pope's. Or perhaps, as suggested elsewhere, Pope kept it back at the desire of the Queen, who was apprehensive that it might make her counsellor insignificant in the public esteem.

If Hervey was spared the publication of Pope's attack he faced embarrassment from another source—the printer holding his satirical 'Character' of Dr. Sherwin. Despite Middleton's reassurance that in Cambridge it was much applauded for being directed against 'an enemy to virtue & morality', Hervey was unwilling to lose Dr. Sherwin's friendship, and instructed Middleton to persuade those who read the verse that it had been meant not for Sherwin but for another clergyman. (The difficulty here was that the clergyman he named did not fit some parts of the portrait.)

Unwittingly Sherwin had his revenge when a literary prankster published *A Most Proper Reply to the Nobleman's Epistle to a Doctor of Divinity*, dated from Chichester on Childermas Day [28 December] 1733 and signed W. SH-W-N. 'My Lord,' it begins, 'I should long ago have answer'd your Lordship's *Epistle* to me; but comparing it with your Lordship's *Character* of me, which I have since received, I found *some Things hard to be understood*, 2 Pet. iii. 16.' The word *Character* was footnoted: 'The Character of Dr. Sh— which will be printed next Week.' The anonymous *Reply*, signed with Sherwin's name, castigated Hervey with a series of brief quotations from the Bible, including one from the Book of Ezekiel: '*Every* Cherubim *hath two Faces*.' The printer added, for good measure, a scene about Fannius from Jonson's *The Poetaster* and a parody of Hervey's epistle in the style of a bellman. Hervey was finally rescued from his embarrassment for having written the 'Character' through the intercession of the Duke of Richmond, Sherwin's patron, who persuaded the clergyman that the printer had made a mistake.

For other reasons Hervey came to regret the publication of his *Epistle from a Nobleman*; as he lamented to Henry Fox, the 'detestable Verses' he had imprudently sent to the imprudent Sherwin had made him 'the ⟨Load⟩ of ev'ry Press, & the Song of every Hawker for these last six Weeks'. Although Pope had kept back his own prose reply, versifying champions rushed to his defence. *Tit for Tat* (on 4 December) is a crude, coarse attack that parodies Hervey's epistle, and jeers at his effeminate manner, court favour, and duel. It was followed at the beginning of the

next year by *Flavia to Fanny*. Besides *A Most Proper Reply* (signed
by a bogus Sherwin), other lampoons appeared: *A Tryal of Skill
Between a Court Lord and a Twickenham 'Squire*, and an *Epistle
from a Gentleman at Twickenham To a Nobleman at St. James's*.
Not all the attacks were printed. Hervey himself owned one
in manuscript entitled 'An Apology for Printing "The Nobleman's
Epistle" ', a mercilessly abusive lampoon that ridiculed him for his
effeminate mannerisms and even questioned whether he had ever
'known' woman—as though his numerous children by a virtuous
wife was not proof enough. Once when a printer brought him
the manuscript of a new edition of *Tit for Tat* and offered to
suppress it, Hervey replied that he did not want to read it, and
that if it was very abusive the printer could make a great deal of
money and would have no trouble from him—since 'a rotten
Egg more or less after so many being thrown was of no Consequence' to him at all. In due course the new edition appeared.
Mrs. Mary Pendarves, a literary lady, sent a copy of it to a
friend, remarking that it was 'occasioned by an abusive poem of
Lord H—to a clergyman, where he mauls poor Pope unmercifully
and unskilfully'. At least the printer of *Tit for Tat* was impartial
enough to add Hervey's epistle to the pamphlet.

Not all of Hervey's published verse was so controversial; he
could write benignly too, as when he sent some couplets to
Stephen Poyntz, the retired diplomatist, who was tutor to the
Duke of Cumberland. Hervey greatly admired him as a man of
learning, sense, and reputation; and he paid tribute to him in
verse as the young Duke's teacher:

> You by Persuasion to Instruction join'd,
> Know without Force to cultivate the Mind. . . .
> At once you strengthen and adorn the Heart,
> With Spartan Virtue and Athenian Art.

His poem was printed in the *Daily Advertiser*, only a few days
after his ill-tempered *Epistle from a Nobleman* appeared, and helped
to neutralize the acid of his attack on Pope. His praise of the Duke
is as lavishly flattering as though he were Poet Laureate.

iv

At the opening of Parliament on 17 January 1734 Hervey made
his début as a Ministerial supporter in the House of Lords. He

was chosen, much against the Duke of Newcastle's will, to move the Address of Thanks; and with only two days' notice to prepare it, he was able to deliver an eloquent speech that lasted more than half an hour. The King, when he later saw it, told him it was the best he had ever read. Those who heard it and wished to depreciate it, Hervey complained to Henry Fox, did it the old way, 'by saying it was all study'd, wrote down, & got by Heart; the first is true, the two last false; & if I find I can speak off hand I am easy whether People think I do or no'. The fame of his eloquence extended to Cambridge, Dr. Middleton reported, adding his own compliment that Hervey now had a new opportunity of shining in a theatre worthy of his talents and abilities.

In quite a different fashion his speech was celebrated by a satiric squib that circulated in manuscript. Entitled 'The Lord H-r-y's First Speech in the House of Lords', it opens:

> Tho' when I stand upright,
>   You take me for a skein of silk;
> And think me with a face so white,
>   A perfect curd of ass's milk.

Its fourth stanza is most pointed:

> So I, the softest, prettiest thing,
>   This honourable House affords,
> Come here by order of the King
>   Created *Lady* of the *Lords*.

It is surprising, and revealing, that when Hervey obtained a copy he sent it to Henry Fox. Another Opposition pamphlet during that session describes him as 'DAPPER, a Youth smooth chin'd, and baby fac'd', who writes libels, epigrams, and songs, and out of cowardice keeps his sword in its scabbard. These lampoons contributed towards the satiric *persona* that was gradually taking shape. But Hervey the politician continued to work for the Ministry in the House of Lords.

One of the first measures there was the aftermath of the Excise Bill controversy. Among the peers punished by the King for their opposition to it were the Duke of Bolton and Lord Cobham, who had been deprived of their regimental commands. The Opposition (on 13 February) brought a bill into both houses to prevent army officers from being deprived of their commissions; in effect, it gave officers a lifetime tenure, even against the King's desire. As Hervey summarized the debate (to Henry Fox): 'Lord Chesterfield spoke much the best on that Side, & much the longest; he answer'd your humble Servant, who tho not best, spoke longest of any Body on our Side.' The burden of his speech was that the bill would weaken the prerogative of the Crown and threaten the monarchical system of government. On 6 and 18 March he again spoke, this time against an Opposition motion dealing with the Crown's attempt to control the Scottish peers.

In the previous session, when he had been in the Commons, he had opposed a mildly Ministerial bill to prevent stock-jobbing, and when a similar measure was introduced in the House of Lords (on 28 March) he again spoke against it. A far more important measure came up in the Lords the same day: a message from the King asking for power to raise additional troops during the Parliamentary recess. Here the Ministry was united and decisive. Hervey, the last speaker in the following day's debate, cleverly pointed out that the King's request was based on (among other reasons) a desire not to burden his people with the cost of an increased army until and unless it was needed. After a warm debate the bill was passed by a large majority (101 to 58). In telling Middleton about it Hervey called it 'one of the finest Debates of 6 Hours . . . that I ever heard'. He also asked Middleton for his opinion of a pamphlet he was sending along: 'I will not tell ⟨mor⟩e for fear you should think me partial to the Subject, or for fear I should really be so to the author, in whose Favour if I guess right I am apt to be prejudiced.'

What was the pamphlet so modestly described? His own, for although the Ministry had defeated the bill on army officers in February, the King and the Queen asked him to write a pamphlet on it, which he did; and Walpole then revised it. It was published on 3 April as *The Conduct of the Opposition*, with the subtitle 'and the Tendency of Modern Patriotism, (More particularly in a late Scheme to Establish a Military Government in this Country) Review'd and Examin'd'. It is an elaborately argued treatise of more than sixty pages, defending the Ministry on a wider front than the single issue of the army officers. In reply to the Opposition's self-proclaimed patriotism, and their accusation that the King was seeking arbitrary power, Hervey argues that the King has saved England from Jacobitism on the one side and from republicanism on the other. As in his other pamphlets he discusses general issues and principles, and with an air of calm candour and fair-minded reasonableness.

In his use of pamphlets as propaganda Walpole did not entirely depend on their public sale; he also dispersed large numbers of them through subsidies. By his order three thousand copies of *The Conduct of the Opposition* were sent to the Comptroller of the Post Office, and seventy-two hundred to the collectors of customs and excise, the clergy, peers, Members of Parliament, and other important persons in town and country. Thus, aside from the number sold, more than ten thousand copies of Hervey's pamphlet were distributed, at a cost of £510 to the Administration.

The publication of *The Conduct of the Opposition* a fortnight before the session ended was Ministerial preparation for the election of a new Parliament to take place that summer. During the session, which ended on 16 April, Hervey demonstrated unusual activity; he had been present at most of the sittings, had served on various committees, had spoken on the important measures, and had written a pamphlet. It was clear that he did not regard his elevation to the peerage as a form of retirement.

v

In the autumn of 1733 Hervey had faced his most complicated and arduous task as Vice-Chamberlain in the Royal Household— arranging for the marriage of Anne, the Princess Royal, to William, Prince of Orange. Like most dynastic marriages it had a political purpose: to bind Holland and England together in the uneasy balance of European alliances, when the throne of Poland needed to be filled and both France and the Austrian Emperor had put forward rival candidates. Princess Anne, two years older than William, and his superior in rank, fortune, and appearance— though she was grossly fat—had dutifully agreed to the marriage rather than remain a spinster who, after her father's death, would have to depend on her unsympathetic elder brother.

When the Prince arrived in London (on 7 November) he was lodged in Somerset House. The King, who considered him far inferior in rank until marriage would elevate him, reluctantly sent Hervey along with the Queen's Vice-Chamberlain to greet him. The young man whom Hervey met was so short as to seem a dwarf, and deformed by one shoulder being excessively rounded.

Horace Walpole, who also saw him that day, charitably remembered that he had seen many worse figures; his face was good, his back high but hidden by his very long curled hair; and while he was narrow waisted he had long and lean legs and hands. What Hervey found almost intolerably offensive was his bad breath. The next day, in an equipage supplied by the frugal King, the Prince drove in a miserable coach with only a pair of horses and a pair of footmen to St. James's Palace, where he was greeted at the head of the stairs by Hervey.

Beyond this simple protocol it was Hervey's responsibility to arrange the wedding, which was scheduled to take place five days after the Prince's arrival. On the fourth day the Prince suddenly fell ill of a fever, and the marriage had to be postponed. During his tedious and dangerous illness none of the Royal Family were permitted to visit him because the King considered it beneath their dignity to do so. As his health mended he moved to Kensington Palace, where Hervey had fixed an apartment for him; and after a few weeks he was well enough to go to Bath, in the hope of recovering his health entirely.

At the end of January 1734 when Lady Hervey bore a daughter, Hervey, always alert to opportunity, asked the Prince to stand as godfather, with the Princesses Caroline and Emily as godmothers. The Prince, who it was understood would be represented by a proxy, promptly accepted, and Hervey as promptly thanked him for his graciousness. In telling Henry Fox of his new child Hervey's tone was different: 'Lady Hervey is brought to bed of a nasty shabby Girl.' At her baptism, performed by Bishop Hoadly, the child was named Emily Caroline Nassau (the last name in honour of her godfather).

At the beginning of March, the Prince, completely recovered, returned to Somerset House to prepare for the wedding. In making his arrangements Hervey had not been able to solve one difficulty —the order of precedence for the Irish peers, who insisted on being treated as the equals of the English and Scottish in the procession. If he had acceded to their demands he would have antagonized the English peers, who threatened not to march if any Irish preceded them, and so he ruled that the Irish should walk behind the others. As a result they boycotted the ceremony.

It was a magnificent occasion, on the evening of 14 March, for although the King had been stingy in granting his daughter a marriage settlement he spared no expense in ordering a sumptuous ceremony. Four thousand spectators and three thousand guards on duty filled the covered gallery that had been built to connect the King's apartment with the chapel. At the ball that followed the wedding the Prince danced surprisingly well considering his shape. His grotesque figure was disguised by his long peruke, which hid his rounded back and made him look less shocking and ridiculous than after supper, when he had put on his night-gown and nightcap. His appearance was so astonishing that Hervey calls it indescribable—before describing it; for from 'the make of his brocaded gown, and the make of his back, he looked behind as if he had no head, and before as if he had no neck and no legs'. At one o'clock in the morning the newly married pair retired to their bedroom, where they received a procession of the nobility as they sat up in bed wearing their richly decorated night-clothes.

The next morning, in a private conversation, Hervey and the Queen discussed the ceremony and the Prince's appearance. 'Ah! mon Dieu!' exclaimed the Queen (who habitually spoke French to Hervey), 'when I saw that monster enter in order to sleep with my daughter, I thought I would swoon; I wavered before, but this blow has overwhelmed me. Tell me, Lord Hervey, did you carefully observe and examine that monster at that moment? and would you not have greatly pitied poor Anne? Good God! it's too stupid of me, but I still weep for it.' Unable to soften and unwilling to exaggerate what the Queen suffered, Hervey could only console her with a sympathetic cynicism, and replied, 'Lord! Madame, in half a year all persons are alike. The figure of the body one's married to, like the prospect of the place one lives at, grows so familiar to one's eye, that one looks at it mechanically, without regarding either the beauties or deformities that strike a stranger.'

Until the Prince and his bride sailed for Holland five weeks later Hervey saw them often, frequently in his own apartment, where they passed entire evenings. What seemed to him extra-ordinary was that the Princess behaved to her husband as though he were an Adonis; and while he hardly took notice of her, she lavished the most devoted attention on him in every way she could. When they embarked at Greenwich she seemed melan-choly in parting from her family who, except for the Prince of

10. Queen Caroline, 1736

Wales, came to see her off. (His excuse for not being there was
that he feared affecting her too much.) Her father, Hervey wryly
noted, 'gave her a thousand kisses and a shower of tears, but not
one guinea'.

On the day their daughter sailed, the King and Queen retired
to Richmond, and Hervey was free for his customary recess. He
left immediately for Redlinch, not only for the pleasure of visiting
Stephen Fox but for the political task of helping him retain his
Parliamentary seat, which was being contested. After a fortnight
he moved on to Bath to visit Princess Emily for two days, and
then—he pointedly informed Henry Fox—'I go to Richmond
not to attend *his* but her Majesty.'

vi

That summer (1734) Hervey was in greater favour with the Queen
than ever before. She would call him her 'child, her pupil, and
her charge'. She constantly told him that he was impertinent and
contradictory to her only because he knew she could not live
without him. 'It is well I am so old,' she often said (presumably
in his hearing), 'or I should be talked of for this creature.' Early
that year he had told Henry Fox, 'I cannot help bragging to you of
a Present the Queen made me . . . of the finest Gold Snuff-Box I
ever saw, with all the Arts & Sciences by her own bespeaking
carv'd upon it.'* She also presented him with a fine horse, which
he used on hunting days to ride by the side of her chaise—'the
prettyest & the agreablest new Horse you ever saw', he told
Stephen, 'he has infinite Spirit & never makes a false Step, two
qualities that rarely go together'.

At the same time, the King—who was not ordinarily of a
generous nature—added £1,000 a year to his salary. Only a few
months earlier, when Hervey had asked his father for a settlement
to augment his income, Lord Bristol had delivered a familiar
sermon on the ingratitude of his Royal master, and had ingeniously
turned down his request because (among other reasons) if Hervey's
financial burdens were eased then the King would say that he

---

* On 1 Feb. 1734 a jeweller's apprentice was committed to Newgate for
robbing his master of a gold snuff-box, the property of Lord Hervey (*Daily
Advertiser*). Can it have been this one, kept in the vault of the jeweller? Six months
later Hervey tells Henry Fox that the Queen has given him another fine snuff-box
(9 June 1734, BM MS.).

needed no additional reward. After the King proved to be so generous Hervey made no secret of it. To Mrs. Clayton he coyly refrained from passing on the King's compliments on that occasion: 'I should be as much ashamed to repeat as I was to hear, for Praises one is conscious one does not deserve, put one almost as much out of Countenance as Reproaches one does.' But since Stephen insisted on knowing exactly what was said, he repeated word for word the King's compliments and his own grateful appreciation.

In their conversations Hervey and the Queen frequently discussed political issues and principles. Once while she was at breakfast in her sitting-room at Richmond she complained of what a nuisance the disgruntled 'nasty' Whigs were, and praised the Tories for at least being more willing to give power to the monarch. Hervey then reminded her of the answer given to William III when he had threatened to take the Tories into the Government because they believed in supporting a King more than the Whigs did: 'This is very true, Sir, but you are not their King.' At this moment the King entered, and Hervey repeated the Queen's arguments and his own reply almost word for word but in softer terms and a lower voice. He held the King in more awe, and dared not presume the informality of his friendship with the Queen. For his part, he played up to her prodigiously, which he could do without strain since he genuinely loved and admired her, and gladly devoted all his time to her—in winter to her business and in summer to her amusement.

However personal his friendship with his Royal masters he never forgot that politics was its ground bass and that Walpole called the tune. At Richmond the King and Queen were awaiting the election results as anxiously as though their crown were at stake. Walpole was in Norfolk—where the Whigs had fared badly—staying at Houghton and 'solacing himself with his mistress' (in Hervey's words) while his enemies worked against him at Richmond by trying to persuade the King and Queen that the new Parliament would go against the Court. Observing that the King and Queen were being affected by this persuasion Hervey sent Walpole an anonymous note containing only a verse couplet about Antony and Cleopatra (adapted from Dryden's *All for Love*):

> Whilst in her arms at Capua he lay,
> The world fell mouldering from his hand each hour.

Walpole, recognizing both the hand and the cryptic message, came immediately to Richmond, where he easily set everything right with the King and Queen. His continuing ascendency owed something to Hervey's alertness and loyalty.

Among Hervey's rewards for his favour at court and allegiance to the Ministry was the patronage he could win for his family and friends. An army cornetcy for his brother Henry, a criminal's pardon at the request of the Foxes' brother-in-law, a Cambridge fellowship on behalf of a supporter in Bury—these were only a few of his endeavours. They encompassed a wide range, from the promotion of a bishop, to an appointment as Purveyor of Oysters to His Majesty, a post that went to the wife of his butler, no doubt through his influence.

The appointment and translation of bishops weighed heavy in the scale not only for their rich emoluments and patronage but for their political importance; the Ministry counted on their loyalty in the House of Lords. Benjamin Hoadly, Bishop of Salisbury since 1723, and a great friend of Hervey's, was disliked by the King, the Queen, and Walpole. Unjustly denied a promotion to Durham (in 1730) he had been promised Winchester by the Queen and Walpole as soon as that see should become vacant, though they hoped to avoid keeping their promise. As soon as Hervey was informed (in August 1734) that the Bishop of Winchester had been seized with an apoplectic fit, he immediately dispatched a letter by private messenger to Hoadly lest he, like Mahomet, 'sit still and fancy the mountain of preferment will walk to you to Salisbury'. Then, under the stress of his sharp anxiety, Hervey's tone was blunt and vigorous: Hoadly must not trust court promises, however solemn, but must apply to the King for the appointment, and must betake himself to Court. 'Write therefore now,' Hervey urged, 'come, speak, dun, and behave, not as your laziness inclines you, but as your interest directs, as common prudence dictates, as your friends advise, and as what you owe to yourself and your family requires.' The appreciative Hoadly took Hervey's advice; he sent letters at once and travelled up to London two days later to press his suit in person. While the appointment had been 'in *Dispute*', Hervey later told Henry Fox, 'I neither felt nor acted coolly'. His battle for Hoadly's translation to the rich bishopric was victorious; and it strengthened both his friend's gratitude and his own power at court.

As he won favours from the Ministry he generally repaid them in various way, including pamphleteering. Since Parliament was not in session in the autumn and specific legislation not under debate he could deal with general issues. In October 1734 he published a stout pamphlet entitled *Ancient and Modern Liberty Stated and Compared*, in which he attempts to demolish one of the Opposition's most persistent accusations against the Ministry— that it was destroying the liberty of Englishmen. After first refuting some arguments in two pamphlets by his old adversary Pulteney, he develops his theme: that the present Government has struck a reasonable balance between anarchy and tyranny. For proof, he compares the liberty of England in earlier times with the present, citing as the strongest proof of improvement, paradoxically, that the Government can be attacked so freely with impunity. He also, in the same witty vein, uses as the source for his historical survey the popular history of England by Rapin, whom he calls 'the Craftsman's own political evangelist'.

Hervey's purpose is to persuade readers not to be deceived by 'a few mercenary *Journalists* and testy *Pamphleteers*'. Far from being testy himself, he concludes his arguments with a rhetorical flourish, and asks '*the People* . . . whether it is to be imagined, that those who have shewn so little Regard to the Interest of the People when *out* of Power, would have much more Regard to it if they were *in*? Or having abused the People in order to acquire Power, whether it is reasonable to think they would abuse them less, when they would have the Means in their Hands of abusing them more?' Political pamphleteering was so much his forte that it is curious that the same cool, reasonable judgement that lay behind his pamphleteering could not restrain him from satiric versifying. Some quirk of personality, allied to his unashamed and flamboyant effeminate manner, impelled him to compete in a contest where, especially with Pope as an antagonist, he was so markedly inferior.

IO

The Achievement of Sporus

1735–6

WHILE HERVEY'S THOUGHTS WERE ENGROSSED by the political uncertainties of the Parliamentary session about to open in 1735, a surprise attack came from another quarter. Pope had flicked at him a few times during the previous year in his Horatian imitations—as the Lord Fanny who thinks a Song is better than the World's good word, and as a Lady or a Lord. But in the *Epistle to Dr. Arbuthnot*, published on 2 January, Pope reached the summit of his satiric achievement. Pitching it in the form of a Horatian dialogue with his peaceful physician-friend, the poet elaborates an eloquent apologia for his entire career, and pays off a score of enemies from Grub Street to St. James's. He brushes off Lady Mary with a couplet about her treacherous wit. With deceptive charity he mentions Hervey near the beginning of the poem as the 'gentle *Fanny*' who versifies flowery poetic themes; but then, after full portraits of Atticus and Bufo, he paints one that, in the whole range of English literature, is unsurpassed for satirical vividness and glittering malevolence.

Pope chose the names for his *satire-à-clef* very carefully. Atticus —his name for Joseph Addison—was a friend of Cicero; Bufo, the Latin word for toad, is a composite literary patron; Sappho (Lady Mary) is an ambiguously flattering label; and Paris, the name he first chose for Hervey, shares the same ironic ambiguity as Sappho. Then, because Paris could be applied only to a 'Noble and Beautiful Person', Pope changed the name to Sporus in the collected edition of his works issued three months later; and it remained Sporus thereafter. As the readers of Suetonius's *Lives of the Caesars* or of Dion Cassius's Roman history knew, Sporus was the boy whom Nero fell in love with, ordered to be castrated,

and then married and treated as a wife. Pope first introduces
Paris–Sporus as a 'Thing of silk' and a 'mere white Curd of Ass's
milk', and then announces his intention:

> Yet let me flap this Bug with gilded wings,
> This painted Child of Dirt that stinks and stings;
> Whose Buzz the Witty and the Fair annoys,
> Yet Wit ne'er tastes, and Beauty ne'er enjoys . . .*

Very cleverly Pope draws an analogy between Hervey's literary
style and effeminate mannerisms:

> His Wit all see-saw between *that* and *this*,
> Now high, now low, now Master up, now Miss,
> And he himself one vile Antithesis.
> Amphibious Thing! that acting either Part,
> The trifling Head, or the corrupted Heart!
> Fop at the Toilet, Flatt'rer at the Board,
> Now trips a Lady, and now struts a Lord.

Since Pope's political sympathies were strongly Tory—he has
been characterized as an 'opposition wit'—he did not overlook
Hervey's important function as Walpole's supporter in Parliament
and as the Queen's favoured companion:

> Whether in florid Impotence he speaks,
> And, as the Prompter breathes, the Puppet squeaks;
> Or at the Ear of *Eve*, familiar Toad,
> Half Froth, half Venom, spits himself abroad,
> In Puns, or Politicks, or Tales, or Lyes,
> Or Spite, or Smut, or Rymes, or Blasphemies.

If this is Pope's most brilliant satiric creation, it is also the
culmination of Hervey's career as a satiric object. That *persona*
had come into existence exactly four years before, in Pulteney's
pamphlet, from which the most telling strokes of Pope's portrait
were lifted. To accept that portrait as a realistic representation of
Hervey is to fail to appreciate Pope's rhetorical intention. Sporus
is a foil for the poet's own admirable qualities, which are immediately catalogued in the poem: not a worshipper of fortune or a fool
of fashion, not mad for lucre or a tool of ambition, not proud or
servile, the poet pleases by 'manly ways'. (At least one detail in

---

* In the anonymous *Tell-tale Cupids* (1735), tribute is paid to the sexual
prowess of 'pretty baby fac'd Lord *Dapper* . . . [whose] Talent lies in Writing'
and who has fought one cowardly duel (pp. 49–50).

the portrait, among the few concrete ones, is contradicted by what is known of Hervey: can he be a 'Child of Dirt that stinks' when he bathed daily?) The Sporus portrait looms large in the gallery of Pope's satires and in modern critical studies. A recent commentator very sensibly concludes that as 'the portrait of Sporus proceeds, the historical identity of Lord Hervey is submerged in the image of Satan, a proper object of intense and immoderate hatred'.

Setting aside the portrait of Sporus as literature, what—one may wonder—was its effect on Pope and on Hervey and the Court circle he frequented? Certainly Pope felt that he had scored, and was not reluctant to feel himself justified. 'The apology is a bold one, but True', he had told Arbuthnot while still writing it; 'and it is Truth and a clear Conscience that I think will set me above all my Enemies.' He had suppressed the prose *Letter to a Noble Lord*, an explicit self-defence and a counter-attack against Hervey; his Sporus has the same function, but was brilliant, memorable poetry published for all the world to read.

How did Hervey retaliate? His fellow victim, Lady Mary, had learnt her lesson since the *Verses to the Imitator*; and this time she sent a letter to Dr. Arbuthnot on the day following the *Epistle*'s publication, and while denying her identity as the Sappho she acknowledged that the 'Town . . . generally suppose Pope means me whenever he mentions that name'. Among Pope's other faults, she writes, 'he is now grown sensible that nobody will buy his verses except their curiosity is pique'd to it to see what is said of their Acquaintance'. She then asks Dr. Arbuthnot to show her letter to him; her retaliation was thus slight and private. Apparently Hervey neither retaliated nor even mentioned the attack in his correspondence. If so, then Pope's remark in the *Epistle* was justified: 'Satire or Sense alas! can *Sporus* feel?'

But Lord Bristol resented the insults aimed at his favourite son. When later in the year he read Hervey's learned letters (to Middleton) on the Roman senate, he wondered why his son's bright light should be hidden under a bushel. 'Let me beg your acquiescence,' he tells him, 'at least in the publication of these, were it only to mortify that little poysonous adder Pope, by shewing him yours is farr from being of that flimsy texture he endeavourd to represent it.' Less partial commentators had varying opinions of the controversy. To Sir Charles Wyndham, a Tory M.P. (and later Earl of Egremont) Hervey's portrait 'moves pity for him rather than mirth'. William Cole the antiquary, who was not acquainted with Hervey, later wrote that 'Pope for some Cause or other took a great Disgust at his Lordship & has been too severe in many of his Epistles & Satires upon him'; and he thought that the 'Poet's peevish & partial Spirit' had led him to abuse many other very worthy persons who very little deserved it.

To correct the distortions of Pope's satiric cartoon and achieve a more balanced view of Hervey's public 'image', one can read a long dedication to him that was published a short time before the *Epistle to Dr. Arbuthnot*. William Bond, a relation of the Hervey family, made a selection of essays from *The Plain Dealer* in two volumes; its dedication begins: 'My Lord, Famed for being a firm Friend to the Sciences and the Muses, as You indeed ought in Gratitude to be, since they have all, in their Turns, been so friendly to You . . .' Such fulsome flattery is an antidote to the corrosive acid of the Sporus caricature, and helps to restore a human dimension to Hervey's portrait.

ii

In the newly elected Parliament that met in January 1735 one of the most troublesome measures anticipated by the Ministry was the petition of the Scottish peers. The origin of the dispute lay in the Act of Union between England and Scotland in 1707 which provided that the Scottish peers, of whom there were one hundred and fifty-four, should elect sixteen among themselves to sit in the House of Lords. By this time the system of election had been manipulated by Walpole in order to be certain that the sixteen invariably supported the Ministry; and, joined to the bench of loyal bishops, they gave him a strong majority in the Lords. During the previous session, when the Opposition had brought to the floor of the Lords two motions on the Scottish election, Hervey had twice (6 and 18 March) spoken against them; but they were dismissed for lack of evidence. Now having gathered new evidence in the recent election, the Opposition were prepared to try again.

'They talk still of bringing in the Scotch-Petition', Hervey told Henry Fox. 'The English Oponents are heartyly sick of it, knowing there is nothing to be made of it; & yet they know not how to drop it.' On 13 February, finally, the Duke of Bedford presented the petition. The King and Queen, pretending to be indifferent—'with a sort of Falstaff bravery', Hervey calls it—were in a state of anxiety. The morning before the petition was to be read the Queen was so anxious to know what was said, thought, or expected that she sent for Hervey before she left her bed; and (he writes) 'because it was contrary to the queenly etiquette to admit a man to her bedside whilst she was in it, she kept him talking on one side of the door which opened just upon her bed whilst she conversed with him on the other for two hours together', and she then sent him to the King's room to repeat all that he had related to her.

In the debate that followed the petition Hervey spoke at length and with such eloquence that he proudly copied his speech into his *Memoirs*. In it he repudiated the protests that had been disseminated throughout the kingdom not only by the 'anonymous scandal of sixpenny books, or the yet cheaper calumny of weekly or daily journals; but pamphlets of far superior authority, with great and noble names affixed to them'. As to the sixteen Scottish peers sitting there, he tactfully remarks, they were so deserving of encomiums that it was unnecessary to state them. To Henry Fox he boasted (in a Latin letter), 'Your friend Hervey did well.' The Ministry was again victorious: the petition was dismissed, and the representative peers from Scotland continued to represent not only their fellow peers north of the border but the administration that could shower benefits on them.

The King's foreign policy was another of the Opposition's targets. Hervey and Newcastle spoke (on 6 March) to oppose the motion that the letters and instructions to the English ambassadors in Paris and Madrid should be laid before the House. The Ministry won by a large majority. This was only a skirmish compared to the attack a week later, when the annual question was raised of how large an army the King should be authorized to maintain. The Opposition wished the number to be reduced from 25,000 to 18,000, and their two main speakers, Carteret and Chesterfield, spoke superlatively well, Hervey concedes, while he himself closed the debate with a long speech defending the larger number. The Ministry squeezed through to win with a majority of only two.

Hervey's speech was his loyal, public performance. Privately, though, he thought it the most unreasonable victory ever won for the simple reason that the number of troops was too great if England was at peace and too small if she were to be engaged in war. Walpole, too, would have disapproved of the measure, in Hervey's opinion, but he needed 'to flatter the military genius of the King, who was always as insatiably covetous of troops as money'. It was necessary for Walpole to yield in small points in order to purchase great ones, Hervey realized; and he saw the necessity of following that policy himself.

Before long he was again confronted by a Parliamentary measure in which he had to vote contrary to his private judgement. It was a complex measure—putting him 'up to the Elbows in Acts of Parliament relating to the Sinking-Fund', he tells Middleton (in April). The debate in the House of Lords a week later would, he thought, deal with the 'Question that few Lords of our Side give themselves much trouble to sift to the Bottom, & one which fewer still of either Side understand'. He was so loaded down with work that he had to remain in the House every day until five or six o'clock. The bill, which permitted the King to use one million pounds from the Sinking Fund to pay the expenses of the current year, was passed—unwisely, in Hervey's opinion.

Much as he admired Walpole he observed what he thought one of his 'most impolitic unministerial acts'. A post in the Treasury having become vacant, he urged Walpole to appoint Winnington, which would open a vacancy in the Admiralty for another of his friends. But the Duke of Newcastle and his brother solicited the Treasury post for a candidate of their own, and Walpole, not wishing to decide between the two rival candidates, appointed his son-in-law Lord Cholmondeley. In this manoeuvre Hervey spoke out strongly to Walpole, though once the affair was settled he closed ranks by persuading the resentful Winnington to be thoroughly reconciled to Walpole. (The next year Winnington was promoted to a new vacancy in the Treasury.) There was no question of his own loyalty, however violently he had disagreed and expostulated with his chief.

Two days after Parliament rose the King impatiently departed for Hanover to visit his foreign dominions, where he had not been for three years. His Ministers had tried to dissuade him from going, for his distance from London made official business awkwardly slow; and at Hanover he would be surrounded by companions who favoured the Imperial interest and might influence him. But the Queen was content; in spite of some inconvenience she profited by his absence: she would not only serve as Regent, she would be manager of her own time and free of the fatigue and boredom of entertaining him, to be rewarded sometimes by his sallies of ill temper. Immediately after his departure she retired to Kew, attended only by the Lady and the Woman of the Bedchamber. Hervey had to be in attendance from eight in the morning until eleven at night, with only three hours in the middle of the day for himself. This stringent routine, sweetened as it was by the affectionate regard he and the Queen had for each other, lasted four weeks; and he could then depart for his holiday.

On his way to Somerset, where Stephen Fox awaited him, he stopped at Salisbury to visit Bishop Sherlock (Hoadly's successor). In former years he had been too impatient to be reunited with Stephen to pause *en route*. After staying only a week at Redlinch he visited Lord Poulett at nearby Hinton St. George. Poulett's son, Lord Hinton, had been raised to the House of Lords at the same time as Hervey, to whom he was so closely allied in his Parliamentary activity that the Bishop of Chichester called him Hervey's ape. He was a lively, high-spirited friend who could divert Hervey prodigiously. His gaiety was infectious, for Hervey sent an imaginatively amusing letter to the Queen in which he pretended that although he had died (by departing from her presence) and his body reposed in a mausoleum at Lord Poulett's, his spirit hovered over her, anxious for her welfare and doing any little service that lay in his power. (Perhaps he was thinking of Ariel in *The Rape of the Lock*.) He even, on this Sunday that he writes, does her the service of tearing six leaves out of the parson's sermon in St. James's Chapel, thus shortening it by six minutes. His resurrection, he concludes, will come as soon as the Queen pronounces that he may live again. He phrased the thought differently to Henry Fox: that after his Somerset visit he would return to Kensington for the rest of his life.

iii

As Hervey's friendship with the Queen deepened, the Prince of Wales, who was jealous of him, became more bitter and vindictive.

When he had heard of his mother's gift of the gold snuff-box he announced that it was less to favour Hervey than to insult and outrage him, and that it was shocking for his mother to favour a man who the whole world knew had been impertinent to him. For that reason, he told his sisters, he seldom visited the Queen. They replied that it was strange he should think of choosing his mother's companions as a condition of his paying his respects. Hervey's favour with the Queen thus widened the breach between himself and the Prince as well as between the Prince and his mother.

But Hervey's relationship with Miss Vane had undergone a radical change in the opposite direction. Following their quarrel, when they had met among company and he had tried to speak to her she refused—'with the haughtiness of an injured princess'— to bestow a glance or a word on him, though he addressed her in the most suppliant manner. After meeting in public places, however, they discovered that they wanted (in Hervey's words) 'to forget their past enmity, and renew their past endearments, till from ogling they came to messages, from messages to letters, from letters to appointments, and from appointments to all the familiarities in which they had formerly lived, both of them swearing that there never had been any interruption in the affection they bore to each other, though the effects of jealousy and rage had often made them act more like enemies than lovers'. This revival of their love affair had come about by the summer of 1734.

At first they met in an out of the way coffee-house, and then, after Miss Vane took a house at Wimbledon (for her son's health), she came to town secretly once a week and they met at her house there, often passing the whole night together. Although they realized it was very indiscreet their 'mutual inclination to meet' forced them to this dangerous course.

Their renewed friendship and liaison arose from other reasons as well. Through Miss Vane, Hervey discovered that Bubb Dodington, the Prince's chief adviser, was being displaced by others, particularly Lord Chesterfield—a clear sign that the Prince was drawing closer to the political Opposition. She would thus be able to transmit useful information to him. Her renewed taste for him could have been stimulated by the Prince's gradual distaste for herself; a year earlier, London gossip reported that he had fathered a child on her chambermaid, for whom he then bought a house, and that he had tried unsuccessfully to gain the favours of an Italian opera singer and the Duchess of Ancaster's daughter. The renewed alliance of Miss Vane and Hervey, then, was based on love, jealousy, and politics intriguingly mixed.

They continued to meet once or twice a week at her house in London, convenient because most of her servants stayed at Wimbledon, until because of the difficulty of getting tea, fruit, and supper there, in the summer of 1735 they moved their place of meeting to Hervey's apartment in St. James's Palace. (This was not too hazardous because the court was at Kensington, and Lady Hervey was in France, having accompanied the Duke and Duchess of Richmond at the beginning of June for a three-month visit to the Duke's estate of Aubigny.) Miss Vane generally walked from her house to the palace where Hervey himself let her in and out. They passed whole nights together without any fear of discovery. Once a frightful accident occurred when Miss Vane, who was subject to fits of colic, fell into a convulsion and became unconscious. In panic Hervey tried to revive her, cramming cordials and gold powder down her throat with no effect. He could not call for help since not a single servant was trusted with the secret of their meetings. His confusion and distress at the thought of her being dead were inexpressible. Fortunately she revived, and after he administered more cordial and gold powder and applied hot towels to her stomach he was able to dress her and lead her to a sedan chair in Pall Mall. Undeterred by fear of future accidents they continued to meet as frequently as before.

The Prince, who was now thoroughly tired of Miss Vane, saw a convenient way of ridding himself of her while advancing his own position. Twenty-eight years old and still unmarried, he was eager to acquire a consort if for no other reason than to be able to set up his own establishment and be independent of his parents. In Hanover that summer the King inspected, as though by accident, the Princess Augusta of Saxe-Gotha; and since he approved of her as a prospective daughter-in-law, negotiations for a treaty of marriage were begun. At his request the Queen informed the Prince of his future betrothal, suggesting that he ought to give up the mistress whom he kept so openly. This he was very willing to do, especially since (among other reasons) he had become firmly attached to a new mistress.

Lady Archibald Hamilton was the lady, neither young nor pretty, the mother of ten children by a husband old enough to

be her father; and she was cunning enough (Hervey thought)
to flatter her husband into a belief of her virtue and the Prince
'into an admiration of her beauty and understanding, which she
facilitated by the much easier task of making the Prince believe
she was entirely captivated by his'. To please her he sent Lord
Baltimore with a proposal to Miss Vane that if she would go
abroad for two or three years, leaving their son in England to be
educated, he would continue her pension for life. Miss Vane was
terribly shocked, or pretended to be, by the message as well as
the method of its delivery, for she had regarded Lord Baltimore
as her champion. (In Horace Walpole's opinion, he was 'a very
good-natured, weak, honest man'.) She therefore refused to send
a reply by one whom she did not regard as friendly.

Instead she immediately wrote to Hervey that she had to speak
to him the next day, although it was not their customary day for
meeting, and then related the entire interview to him, roundly
abusing both the Prince and his emissary. She would welcome
being rid of the Prince, she said, because she could then see Hervey
more freely; and that was why she would refuse to leave England.
Determined to reply to the Prince in writing she begged Hervey
to write a letter for her, and he was glad to comply since he could
thus vex the Prince and keep Miss Vane in England. What he
wrote was a masterly composition—which he copied into his
Memoirs—in which the forsaken mistress speaks in terms of injured innocence: 'I sacrificed my time, my youth, my character,
the world, my family, and everything that a woman can sacrifice
to a man she loves.' Because of her health, she refuses to leave
England; and because of her love for her child she refuses to give
him up, for he is her only consolation. At Hervey's insistence she
copied his draft then and there, and sent a copy to her brother for
his approval. (He guessed that Pulteney had written it for her.)

The Prince, enraged by the letter, then showed it to his
family and friends to justify the punishment he intended to inflict
on Miss Vane unless she told him who had advised her. She on
her part showed the letter to all her friends, telling them that the
Prince's verbal message brought by Lord Baltimore was that if she
would not live abroad she might starve in England. Condemned
for this brutality, the Prince denied sending the message, and
Baltimore denied delivering it. Since Miss Vane had no written
proof she was advised by her brother and Pulteney, among others,

View here three different States in real Life —
The Pimp the Miss forsaken and the Wife —
The Happy Pair with Mutual Transport Smile —
And by Fond Looks each others care beguile —
Backwards behold the Effects of Lawless Love —
Insolent Grief each heedless Maid reprove —
She feels the pangs of Scorn, her lovers hate —

Mourns her Undoing & grows wise too late —
The useful Pimp that necessary Tool —
A Blundering Sycophant a Polish'd Fool —
That True to Sacred Bands resigns his Post —
And Grieves to see his wonted Honours lost —
He's the Lady both in Secret pine —
And fret to see this *MODISH COUPLE Join.

Price 6.d

11. The Marriage of the Prince of Wales

to send a second letter to justify her first; and again Hervey held the pen that wrote it. As a consequence of these transactions she was allowed to keep the house in Grosvenor Street, awarded £1,600 a year for life and the custody of her son, and permitted to live where she pleased. The Prince had already seen to it that his son Fitzfrederick would be well off, having appointed him (aged two and a half) Lord Warden of the Stanneries and Steward of the Duchy of Cornwall.

In such comfortable circumstances, Miss Vane told Hervey, her life was likely to be the happiest she had ever enjoyed. Since her health was still poor she was advised to try the waters at Bath, and she went there with her son at the beginning of November (1735). As her health seemed to improve she remained, and sent her son back to London to stay with his aunt, Lady Grace Vane. He died there of convulsive fits, in February 1736, at the age of less than four years, and was buried in Westminster Abbey. The Prince seemed more afflicted by the loss of his son, the Queen and Princess Caroline observed, than they had ever seen him on any occasion. He could not have mourned as deeply for his son's mother; she died a month later, and was privately buried in the Cathedral Church at Bath. Although Hervey had been her lover, both before and after the Prince of Wales had taken her up, his love for her seems (on the evidence of his *Memoirs*) to have lacked the emotional intensity that infused his love for Stephen. A sexual object and a political pawn: these were her two functions in the intricate pattern of his life. Apparently her exit hardly affected him.

Death did not save Miss Vane from being memorialized by Grub Street. A month after her burial she was revived in a prose closet-tragedy entitled *Vanella*, in which she plays only a small role as the discarded mistress of Adonis, a prince who resolutely pursues other women. But her most enduring posthumous fame is not entirely ignominious. When Samuel Johnson sought exemplars for *The Vanity of Human Wishes* (published in 1749) he thought of her and of a mistress of James II:

> The teeming mother, anxious for her race,
> Begs for each birth the fortune of a face:
> Yet Vane could tell what ills from beauty spring;
> And Sedley curs'd the form that pleas'd a king.

At least she is endowed here with the excessive beauty that was not visible to her contemporaries.

iv

During the King's absence and Hervey's attendance at court this summer (1735) the Queen needed particular solace. For soon after his arrival in Hanover the King had met, courted, and won as his mistress a handsome young married woman, Amalie von Wallmoden. He then sent his wife long detailed letters about his new conquest—what the lady looked like, and every word and action that passed between them. The Queen had never objected to his amours as long as they did not interfere with her influence on his power and actions. Of his new amour she remarked to a courtier that 'she was sorry for the scandal it gave others, but for herself *she minded it no more than his going to the close stool'*. The previous autumn Lady Suffolk had suddenly resigned as the Queen's Mistress of the Robes (and as the King's mistress as well) and had left court, which displeased the Queen because no threat to her power over the King had ever come from that quarter. Instead of being jealous of the King's new mistress the Queen was fearful that people would think she was losing her power over him.

Among her diversions in his absence was picture-viewing, which Hervey was happy to share with her since he was something of a collector and connoisseur himself. The King, who was impervious to any art except music, disapproved of her going about visiting private houses. Now with Hervey to escort her she went one morning in July to breakfast at Sir Paul Methuen's, the retired diplomatist, to see his fine collection. She also took advantage of the King's absence to ask Hervey to remove several very bad pictures from the great drawing-room in Kensington Palace and to put good ones in their place.

During the summer Hervey also saw his mother more frequently as a new warmth infused their changeable friendship. He and his eldest son, George—fourteen years old and for three years in the Duke of Cumberland's grenadier guards—dined at Kensington with her (on 25 July) to celebrate the fortieth anniversary of her marriage; and he presented her with a little ring—'for a lucky entrance into the next forty years', she told Lord Bristol; 'I think Lord Hervey and I live as well together as any mother & son wish to do, for he has not missd seeing me any one morning since I came, & twice breakfasted & twice dind notwithstanding he has so many irons in the fire, some of which I wish were burnt out.' (Miss Vane may have been one of those irons.) And even as Lady Bristol was completing her long letter Hervey called at her window on his way through the garden to walk to Chelsea, and from thence to London. (At Chelsea he could call at Walpole's house to report on the Queen, with whom he customarily passed two hours every morning.)

He had less freedom after Lady Hervey returned (in September) from her long visit in France, and he came up to St. James's 'to meet the French Caravan' on their arrival. Lady Hervey by then showed signs of pregnancy, for a daughter was born to her in February of the following year.* Caroline was Hervey's eighth and last child, and he chose as her Royal sponsor the Princess Mary, thirteen years old at the time.

The King, who was reluctant to leave Hanover because of Madame von Wallmoden, finally returned only two days before his official birthday celebration on the last day of October. Irritated at having been forced to leave his mistress, he vented his ill humour on the patient Queen, his children, and all who crossed his path. And when he was in a good humour the Queen suffered in another way: he would describe the happy scenes of his Hanoverian idyll, including the details of his amorous amusements. He had even brought back paintings of the suppers, balls, shows, and masquerades, which he hung in the Queen's own dressing-room; and often while Hervey was there he would carefully relate the story shown in the pictures. During these lectures Hervey 'whilst he was peeping over His Majesty's shoulder at these pictures, was shrugging up his own, and now and then stealing a look to make faces at the Queen' in order to entertain her as she sat quietly in docile boredom and annoyance.

When the King noticed that some of the pictures in Kensington Palace had been replaced he ordered Hervey to put back the old ones. For the Queen's sake Hervey asked whether at least the two Van Dycks on either side of the fireplace could remain, but the King was inflexible. 'I suppose,' he snapped at Hervey, 'you assisted the Queen with your fine advice when she was pulling my house to pieces and spoiling all my furniture.' He again ordered Hervey to change the pictures. 'Would Your Majesty

* Lady Hervey had previously suffered a miscarriage—on 6 Oct. 1734 (Hervey to Henry Fox, 7 Oct. 1734, BM MS.).

have the gigantic fat Venus restored too?' he asked. 'Yes, my lord,' replied the King, 'I am not so nice as your Lordship. I like my fat Venus much better than anything you have given me instead of her.' The thought came to Hervey, though of course he dared not utter it, that if the King had liked his fat Venus of a wife as well as he used to, this disputation would not have taken place.

The implacable round of court duties now resumed for Hervey in full force. The visit of the Duke of Modena added some novelty, though unlike the Duke of Lorraine—who had so thoroughly won his admiration—the Italian seemed to be 'haughty & dull, & ignorant of every thing but forms and genealogys'. And to Horatio Walpole, who was now ambassador at The Hague, he fervently exclaimed, 'Thanks be to God the Duke of Modena is at Last departed. Sure that is the most impenetrable Piece of dignify'd dullness that ever any Princely family produced.'

For one whose health was precarious Hervey led a strenuous, bustling life, sustained by remarkable stamina and energy. But he also suffered bouts of illness; in December 1735 a very tedious and painful fever kept him confined to his room for ten days while he underwent every operation of physic and some of surgery. One cause of his ill health was his poor teeth—probably pyorrhoea, aggravated by dosing with mercury—but that cause had by now been removed. He was seen at court by a lady who noticed that he had 'the finest set of Egyptian pebble teeth' she had ever seen. He had taken advantage of this sophisticated kind of dentistry to be fitted, not with starkly white false teeth, but with brown mottled jasper that looked natural. It is all the more curious that one of the most frequently quoted descriptions of his appearance should be that made two years later by the vitriolic old Duchess of Marlborough: 'a painted face and not a tooth in his head.' The Duchess, who certainly had no wish to see him in a flattering light, must have recalled what he looked like before he improved his looks by means of dentistry.

v

Not far from the Fox seat of Redlinch stood the fine estate of Mells, the property of Thomas Horner, husband of Susannah

Strangways. Although she had added his name to her own they proved to be a thoroughly incompatible couple; she was a worldly, ambitious, and masterful woman, and he a bluff and stubborn Tory country gentleman. Their life together was so uncongenial that Mrs. Strangways Horner passed most of her time abroad with their only surviving child, Elizabeth, born in 1723, her excuse being the conventional one of poor health. Henry Fox had met Mrs. Horner in 1728, and soon progressed from admirer to lover. As Lord Chesterfield wittily put it, she was 'a very salacious English Woman, whose Liberality retrieved his Fortune, with several Circumstances, more to the Honour of his Vigour than his Morals'. During several periods of time Fox lived in France with her and her daughter, whose education he supervised. In the summer of 1735 Mrs. Horner returned to England, probably for the sake of her daughter's future.

When Mrs. Horner met Hervey (at Redlinch) she told their friend Lady Sundon of her impression: that she thought him 'extremely both good-natured and well-bred, and those two things, taking away all the terror and awe of his superior understanding, made me like him exceedingly'. Since she wished to present her daughter at court she asked Hervey if they could attend the Queen's Drawing-Room even though the girl did not have the formal attire required. Hervey, always the consummate courtier, brought her word that out of regard for her the Queen would be pleased to receive her daughter even without proper court dress.

Although the girl was now only thirteen years old her parents immediately began to seek a suitable husband. (A great heiress unmarried was a tempting catch for fortune-hunters.) One difficulty was Mr. Horner's odd requirement that whoever married his daughter would have to live in the house with him—though Mrs. Horner hoped that his resolution, like most of those he made, would not last. She had considered the Duke of Leeds as a prospective husband for the girl, but feared he would not be willing to wait. (He waited five years before marrying another heiress.) Another candidate was Lord Middlesex, but his father, the Duke of Dorset, decided that the girl was too young for his son. By this time (January 1736) Stephen Fox had entered the lists as a suitor. Encouraged by Mrs. Horner, he was stubbornly opposed by Horner because he was not only a Whig and in Walpole's circle but a renegade Tory. Mrs. Horner, however, enthusiastically championed Stephen's desire to be her son-in-law; and since she could not win over her husband she decided to take matters into her own hands.

On 15 March 1736 there gathered in the library of Stephen's house in Great Burlington Street a small conspiratorial group: Hervey, Mrs. Horner, Mrs. Digby (Stephen's sister), and the young couple. A parson, who owed his appointment to Stephen, performed the ceremony joining the child-bride to the thirty-two-year-old groom. Mrs. Fox then accompanied her mother home to Grosvenor Street. A few days later Mrs. Horner wrote to Stephen that her husband was still set against the match (which he did not know had been solemnized), and she outlined a scheme for him to elope with the girl and go through the marriage again. She was considerate enough to send the draft of a letter that Stephen was to write to her confessing that he had eloped with her daughter and begging her to intercede with Mr. Horner.

Exactly one week after the first wedding, the second took place—in the same house (though in a different room) with the same clergyman officiating. Hervey was again a witness, but the others there presumably did not know that they were witnessing a redundant marriage. It was duly reported in the newspapers (on 24 March) and gossiped about. 'The Town is at present very much entertain'd with little Ste: Fox's wedding', Lord Gower wrote to a friend, 'who on Monday night last run away with the great fortune Miss Horner, who is but just thirteen years old & very low & childish of her age.' A week later the young couple were presented at court, and although a peace of some sort was patched up with Horner it was not effective. Six months later he was more angry than ever with the girl, and threatened to discharge all her servants for helping to bring about the wedding. He arranged a legal separation from his wife, whom he granted £800 a year, and Stephen stood bound for her debts should she incur any.

The young couple, although they occasionally met at Redlinch or elsewhere through the connivance of Mrs. Horner, did not live together officially until three years later, when Mrs. Fox moved to her husband's house. The news of their marriage had greatly pleased Dr. Middleton; he pointedly congratulated Hervey as the one who, next to Stephen, would take the greatest pleasure in it, and he added the pious hope that the event would convince

Stephen that 'whatever else may be transacted there, matches, at least, are made in Heaven'. His prediction, with its characteristic flick at orthodox theology, was accurate; Stephen's marriage was a long and happy one.

How did it affect Hervey? He could hardly have been opposed to it since he assisted Mrs. Horner in its clandestine preliminaries and witnessed it twice. It is more than likely that he arranged for Stephen to marry Miss Horner, and that Henry Fox, with his considerable influence on the girl's mother, helped to bring it about. Ironically, Hervey, who believed that a man should marry an attractive woman for love or an heiress for wealth, had chosen the former for himself and the latter for Stephen. Just as his own marriage had not interfered with their intimate friendship, so there was no reason why Stephen's should. Yet the marriage did mark a decisive alteration. The earlier, passionate relationship between the two men had cooled and neither temperamental nor intellectual sympathies had developed in its place. Hervey's nervous and active career at court was antipathetic to Stephen's phlegmatic life as a country gentleman; and Hervey's literary and philosophical tastes found their resonance not in Stephen but in men like Henry Fox. Stephen's marriage, then, marked not the end of their friendship but only the end of its romantic phase.

II

Private Passions and Courtly Politics

1736–7

APART FROM HIS POLITICAL and court involvements, Hervey experienced an astonishing coincidence of events in his personal life at the end of March 1736: the birth of his last child, the marriage of Stephen Fox, the death of Miss Vane, and the beginning of a new love for one who aroused his emotional as well as intellectual passion. He had once (in 1730) assured 'dearest Ste:' that he alone possessed his 'Heart, which (if you were to abdicate your Empire there) yet from its own make & Bent could never venture to admit a Successor: when it ceases to open itself to You it will be shut for ever'. Stephen's marriage had confirmed the shutting of that door; and at that moment a new friend, handsome in face and figure, brilliant and cultivated in intellect, caused it to re-open.

Francesco Algarotti, newly arrived in London, was a strikingly good-looking young man of twenty-four, with large, dark eyes, full sensual lips, and high arched eyebrows. His slender nose, when seen in profile, hinted of an opportunistic side in his personality; he must always have looked at his admirers face to face, for he immediately charmed all he met. Bearing a letter of introduction from Voltaire he called on Hervey. He was truly charming, Hervey then assured Voltaire, because he combined the vivacity natural to his years with a good taste and precision of intellect that were rare at any age.

Algarotti was the younger son of a Paduan merchant settled in Venice. (Voltaire later dubbed him the Swan of Padua, a tribute to the grace with which he glided through the courts of Europe.) From an early age he had been remarkably precocious and versatile, and after completing his scientific and literary studies at the University of Bologna had moved to Rome, where

12. Francesco Algarotti

he met (among other cognoscenti) Martin Folkes, vice-president of the Royal Society, who encouraged his interest in England. In Paris, his next place of residence, he met Madame du Châtelet, Voltaire's mistress, and they both invited him to spend part of the winter at Cirey, her estate in Lorraine. 'We have here the marquis [Algarotti],' Voltaire informed a friend (bestowing an undeserved title on the Italian), 'a young man who knows the languages and manners of all countries, who writes verses like Ariosto, and who knows his [Locke] and his Newton.' It was reasonable for him to visit England since he was writing a series of dialogues on Newton's theory of optics, in frank imitation of the very popular *Plurality of Worlds*, dialogues on astronomy by the Abbé Fontenelle.

Not long after he arrived in London he attended a meeting of the Royal Society (on 1 April) at the invitation of Anders Celsius, the Swedish astronomer, whom he had met in Italy, and a week later he was nominated for membership. The following month he was elected an honorary member of the Society of Antiquaries in the category of 'Foreigners of Eminent Note & Learning', with his friend Folkes presiding in the chair. His ambition, however, extended beyond the world of learning, and his social aspirations higher than the circle of savants. Through Hervey he was graciously received by the Queen, with whom he conversed on scientific and learned subjects.

He also met Lady Mary. Battered by family disappointments and fretted by approaching old age—she was forty-seven—she found herself as captivated by the young Italian as Hervey was. At first she treated him with gay *esprit*, but her customary cynicism soon fell away, and she found herself the victim of a romantic passion such as she had never before suffered. She and Hervey could easily collaborate as allies in politics and poetry; whether they could in their love for Algarotti was a different matter.

ii

In Parliament that spring (1736) the most important measure was the Quakers Bill, introduced by the Ministry in the House of Commons (on 2 March) and very anxiously supported by Walpole. Its purpose was to relieve the Quakers from the very costly legal process used to sue them for the church tithes that for reasons of conscience they refused to pay. They were content to be forced to pay the tithes by the normal procedure used against delinquent Church of England clergymen. The established clergy, however, from the bishops down to the humblest curates, were stirred up to blazing opposition, and vociferous anti-Quaker pamphlets fed the flames. One of the most violent was *The Country Parson's Plea Against the Quakers Bill for Tythes* by Thomas Sherlock, Bishop of Salisbury. It needed to be answered, and Hervey once again served his party and his chief.

The Quaker's Reply to the Country Parson's Plea, which was written by Hervey and published 6 April, displays him at his best as a pamphleteer in the clarity of his arguments, the tone of reasonableness, and the touches of light humour. Since he assumes the *persona* of a Quaker his title-page quotes three excerpts from the New Testament instead of the customary tags of classical Latin. (Within the pamphlet appear a few Latin quotations; the 'Quaker' is evidently not devoid of learning.) He opens his argument on a humourous note:

For fear the Appellation of *Friend* should rather exasperate than soften the very *unfriendly* Mind that seems to have dictated the Paper before me; and lest the Simplicity of the Gospel-Terms *Thee* and *Thou*, should prove as offensive to your Ear, as the sight of a *broad Hat* and a *short Cravat* have been to your Eye; I shall in Compliance to your Weakness, tho' you seem so little inclined to shew the least Indulgence to mine, wave the ordinary Stile of our Fraternity in this Address, and occasionally, for once, conform to that more worldly Dialect, which, to act consistently with yourself, tho' not with your Profession, I know you must, merely for its being more worldly, prefer to any other.

He acknowledges that the 'country parson's plea' is witty and informed, though its tone lacks the true spirit of a parson and a Christian.

Hervey's own arguments are humanitarian: he defends the Quakers as worthy, virtuous men who benefit the nation by their trading and who look after their own poor. The Quakers Bill, he concludes, is 'so conformable to the Doctrine of Christ, the Principals of Toleration, the Nature of this Constitution, and the Genius of our Government; so consonant to Good-nature and good Sense, that in this Shape, and modell'd in the Manner I have mention'd, I can never believe it possible for a *Christian Clergy* to oppose it, or an *English* Parliament to reject it'. And he ends humourously with a paraphrase of the Lord's Prayer: 'From

Pride, Vain-Glory, and Hypocrisy, from Envy, Hatred, and Malice, and all Uncharitableness—GOOD PARLIAMENT deliver us.'

The Quaker's prayer was at least answered in the House of Commons, which passed the bill by a large majority. Although Walpole knew that the bill had a poor chance in the Lords because of the bishops' opposition he insisted on pressing it with un-diminished zeal. In the final debate (on 12 May) Hervey was among the speakers who supported it, stressing how much the Quakers were being oppressed and persecuted. His speech was applauded by foes as well as friends. But he had written and spoken in vain; the bill was defeated.

He also took an active part in the other important ecclesiastical legislation of the session—the Mortmain Bill, an Administration measure intended to prevent the clergy from bequeathing land or money to the church. It easily passed in the Commons. When it was debated in the Lords (in April) Hervey spoke for it, supporting his arguments with 'very judicious calculations', in the opinion of Sir Thomas Robinson, M.P. Hervey pointed out that 'one of the greatest intentions of the Bill before them was to prevent the erroneous judgments of dying cowardice, to prevent persons on their death-beds making their families miserable, from the mistaken notion of saving their souls, by donations to the Church. In short, [Robinson concluded his summary] I think there was a spirit of liberty against Church encroachments [which] must give a pleasure to every true lover of his country.' This time the bill passed. Hervey also spoke (in May) against the Opposition amend-ments intended to wreck a Ministerial bill to prevent smuggling; and it was finally passed. His summary of the entire session was that 'Parliament, like bull-dogs, sticking close to any hold on which they have once fastened, the poor Church this winter was as much worried as Sir Robert had been any other.'

iii

The sittings of Parliament had been interrupted by the marriage of the Prince of Wales, an event of great political consequence. When he had been asked in due form by the King whether he would marry the Princess Augusta of Saxe-Gotha, he had replied (Hervey writes) with 'great decency, duty, and propriety, that whoever His Majesty thought a proper match . . . would be agreeable to him.' At the Princess's arrival in April it was Hervey's duty to greet her with the King's compliments. He observed a seventeen-year-old girl, with a pleasantly modest and good-natured countenance (slightly pockmarked), and a tall, somewhat awkward figure. She could speak only a little French and not a single word of English. (Her mother had refused to have her taught English even after the match was first proposed because she was certain that with a Hanoverian on the throne most people in England spoke German.)

Two days later the marriage took place in St. James's Palace. Hervey dined with his mother that day, and both were so tired from the preliminary activities that they lay down on couches to rest until it was time to go to the chapel. During the service in the evening, it was Hervey's duty to conduct the bride and then the groom to their places and to stand next to the King until it was concluded. Like the other officiating noblemen he wore an expensive gold-brocade suit (costing between three and four hundred pounds). At supper he noticed that the Prince, while eating several glasses of jelly (reputed to nourish sexual potency), turned about to laugh and wink at several of his attendants. Afterwards the Princess changed into night-clothes, and was then seated in the nuptial bed next to the Prince, who looked comical in his tall nightcap (higher than any grenadier's cap in the army), while the procession of guests passed through their bedroom.

What happened afterwards was variously reported. Hervey and the Queen agreed that the bride looked so extremely fatigued before going to bed and so well refreshed in the morning that they concluded she had slept very soundly. Lady Bristol, however, gave a very different report of the wedding night: 'the Prince tasted all her Charms, & was in such Raptures in the morning that he squeez'd all his Servants by the hand, and told them he was the happiest Man alive, that his Princess was far beyond any other woman he had ever enjoy'd in all his Life.' On the evidence of Miss Vane's testimony, the Prince, though not impotent, had been ignorant in matters of sex to an inconceivable degree; but presumably he was now, thanks to her tutelage, highly educated.

His dutiful marriage, far from healing the antagonism between him and his parents, exacerbated it, for it raised once again the question of what his allowance should be. The King had increased it from £24,000 to £50,000 a year (instead of to £100,000 which he himself had been allowed as Prince of Wales). His excuse was that as the Prince did not yet maintain his own establishment he had no need of a larger allowance. To soften his firm decision, the King, who was impatient to be reunited with Madame von Wallmoden in Hanover as soon as he could, sent a message to the Prince that wherever the Queen resided, an apartment would always be provided for him and the Princess. The King irritated the Prince still further by refusing to appoint him Regent, instead of the Queen, during his absence.

Hervey spent almost the entire summer in attendance on the Queen at Kensington. As her confidant and adviser he found himself involved in her uneasy relationship with her son and daughter-in-law. The Princess, probably on the advice of her old governess, refused to receive the sacrament according to the Church of England, going instead to communion at the German Lutheran chapel. At Walpole's suggestion the Queen spoke to the Prince of the ill consequence this might have, not only with the clergy but the nation in general. He had spoken to the Princess, the Prince replied, but with no effect; she only wept and talked of her conscience. Hervey thereupon advised the Queen to tell the Prince that this might grow very serious indeed, for by the Act of Succession the heirs to the Crown had to conform to the Established Church; and it was possible that the law might be construed to extend to the Princess, in which case she could be sent back to Saxe-Gotha. 'All these arguments and conferences', Hervey writes, 'had their effect at last so well that the Princess dried her tears, lulled her conscience' and received the sacrament like the rest of the Royal Family.

The Royal chapel was the setting for another contest between the Queen and her recalcitrant son in which Hervey's judicious counsel averted an open breach. The Prince and Princess usually came to the chapel after the service had begun, which was a nuisance to the Queen because the Princess had to crowd by her, passing between her and her prayer book. To avoid this the Queen gave orders that the Princess should be admitted into the Royal pew by another door, but the Prince countermanded the orders. When the Queen complained to Hervey he advised her that although she was certainly in the right it was clear that the Prince was trying to force a quarrel in the King's absence, but she must avoid this at any cost; and even 'if the Prince was to sit down in her lap, that she would only say she hoped he found it easy'. She must not let him make the affair a matter of public dispute. The soundness of Hervey's counsel was proved when the Prince, on the advice of his own people, ordered the Princess either to enter chapel at the same time as the Queen or not at all; he thus avoided challenging or yielding.

Determined to maintain the peace with her son and daughter-in-law the Queen often invited them to dinner or entertained the Princess in the evening. She bore the young woman no ill will but only regretted that her lack of intelligence made her company so fatiguing. When Hervey came to the Queen in the afternoon after she had dined with the Prince and Princess she generally met him with yawns and complaints of the vapours brought on by the silly gaiety and tasteless jokes of her son and the silent stupidity of his boring wife.

In contrast, Hervey's clever and lively mind was all the more attractive to her, and their friendship deepened. During one of their conversations Hervey remarked, 'Supposing I had had the honour to be born Your Majesty's son—' when she impulsively interrupted him: 'I wish to God you had.' His company was so precious to her that she once speculated on the changes that would take place in the palace if he died, and said that many people would mourn and many rejoice. He replied that he could easily guess how it would be, and when she urged him to tell her he did so by writing a miniature drama in three acts entitled 'The Death of Lord Hervey, or, A Morning at Court'. It is so full of his sharp and cynical wit that the Queen must have been as amused by it as she was by Hervey himself.

iv

When Hervey could escape from his court duties he undoubtedly saw Algarotti, who remained in London during the summer. To Algarotti's friends in France it seemed that he was enchanted with England, and reluctant to leave. But since he had completed his Newtonian dialogues and needed to return to Italy to have them printed, he told his friends in England that he would soon be sailing from their shores. Lady Mary could not hide her agitated feelings, as she confessed that although she realized the folly of her enthusiasm for him she was unable to restrain it. The philosophical indifference that had made her life tranquil was gone; without him only mortal ennui awaited her.

Hervey also feared the ennui of being separated from Algarotti. Almost as soon as he escaped from Kensington to visit Redlinch (in mid-August) he was impelled to write to Algarotti (in French) to assure him 'in every way how dear' to him he was; and since Algarotti's departure was imminent Hervey was not certain of seeing him again. 'In any case,' he assures him, 'if you stay or if you go, do not forget me, my dear, for I will never forget you all my life ... you are too clear-sighted to have any need of instruction in things less obvious than the affection I feel for you, & I will not say more than you know, but much less than I feel, when I assure you simply that at present the thing in the world that I wish most for is to be able to keep you in England for the rest of your life, with the same advantage & pleasure to you that I would find here myself.' Lady Mary also wanted Algarotti to stay in England, but her 'false delicacy' (she later reproved herself) kept her from proposing it.

From Redlinch Hervey continued to send Algarotti 'fresh proof of the perpetual affection' he felt for him. Better still, when he returned to London (on 28 August) Algarotti had not yet departed; and so they could meet again. A week later he remarked to Henry Fox, 'Algarotti goes away on Monday, which I am extreamly sorry for, for he amuses me exceedingly'. He understated his true feelings. To celebrate Algarotti's last evening in London he invited him to supper, but Algarotti declined because (he said) he had promised to sup with Martin Folkes. But Algarotti lied, perhaps to spare his friend any pangs of jealousy. He spent his last evening in London with Lady Mary.

After Algarotti's departure Hervey suffered so keenly that his friends complained of his moodiness, and he frankly admitted the cause. He was annoyed besides that Algarotti had lied about the supper on the eve of his departure. For Lady Mary now boasted to everybody, Hervey reports to him, that she had been like Caesar in her conquest—which was, he adds, an insult to Algarotti's memory. Instead of resenting Algarotti's duplicity he resented Lady Mary's having benefited by it. Her physical charms were far inferior to her intellectual ones, he reminds him. 'How fortunate you are then to be gone! The absence that brings sadness to every other Lover will fulfill your Happiness, for she will speak to your Eyes & not appear before them; she will not destroy with her countenance the impression she will make by her mind . . .'

'But I am speaking too much of her,' he checks himself, 'now I must say a word about myself. I cannot say anything, however, on this Subject but what you already know, that is to say that I love you with all my Heart, & I beg you never to forget the affection I have for you, nor to let the affection you have expressed for me grow weaker.'

Yet how differently Lady Mary regarded herself!—not as conquering Caesar but as Dido abandoned by her wandering Aeneas. 'I am a thousand times more to be pitied than the sad Dido, and I have a thousand more reasons to kill myself', she tells Algarotti in her second letter soon after his departure. (She started her letter with an appropriate quotation from Virgil.) Like Dido she has thrown herself at the head of a stranger, but 'instead of crying perjurer and villain when my little Aeneas shows that he wants to leave me, I consent to it through a feeling of Generosity that Virgil did not think women capable of'. Gracefully and delicately, Algarotti had asked her permission to depart, she recalls, and she returns the compliment: 'I haven't the vanity to dare hope I please you; I have no purpose except to satisfy myself by telling you that I love you . . .' Like Hervey she defines her 'strong passion': 'My reason makes me see all its absurdity, and my Heart makes me feel all its importance. Feeble Reason! which battles with my passion and does not destroy it and which vainly makes me see all the folly of loving to the degree that I love without hope of return.'

What could have been Algarotti's thoughts upon receiving such effusions from his two English admirers? He did not have to send letters to keep the flames of their love ablaze. A fortnight after his departure Hervey still missed him so painfully that he mourned his great loss to Henry Fox, hardly disguising his emotions, while staying at Kensington 'in this House (triste Sejour) & generally seeing or thinking of the same thing. Adieu. I write like a Fool, think like a Fool, talk like a Fool, act like a Fool, & have every thing of a Fool but the Content of one.' His confessional letter was too naked and revealing for others to see. 'Pray burn it as soon as you have read it,' he tells Fox, '& pray allow it the only merit it pretends to, which is being a Piece of my silly Heart that I would trust to few Eyes & few Hands but your own.'

The passion that Hervey and Lady Mary felt for Algarotti aroused in them very different feelings towards each other—jealousy on his part, helplessness on hers. He boasted to her that Algarotti had written to him from France, while she had not heard from him two weeks later, although he had promised to write from Calais. 'How unhappy I am!' she exclaims to him (in her fourth letter), 'and what a stroke of Mercy a stroke of Lightning would be at this moment!' More calmly, she tells him that she will see Lord Hervey, who should have had news of him.

When she tried several times to arrange an appointment with Hervey he cruelly evaded her, until by accident he met her at Lady Stafford's, where she extracted from him a promise to meet her in two days' time. Although he again tried to put her off, on the appointed evening she appeared (with a little ugly singer as chaperone), and stayed until one in the morning. 'While she was with me,' Hervey tells Algarotti, 'she tried thousands of different ways to make me talk of you, & I would not even mention your name. At the same time she told me a thousand deliberate lies & a thousand accidental truths; & instead of finding out several things without saying anything, as she intended, she told me all without learning anything.' Nor does he forget to reassure Algarotti that however ridiculous and unstable Lady Mary is ('she was as drunk before as wine can make one, & you have added *Gin*'), he himself is unswerving in his devotion. 'Adieu. Preserve me in your esteem. I love you too much, my dear, not to strive all my life to deserve it . . . I wish you were here every day & almost every moment.'

How much more generous, in this instance, was Lady Mary in telling Algarotti of that same evening: when she had sent word to Lord Hervey that she wished to speak to him, 'You may beleive (with his politeness) I saw him soon after, and then I was in allmost as much difficulty to draw from him what I had a mind to know; that is, whither you were arriv'd safe at Paris?' Hervey told her 'that after so much neglect as I had shewn him he could not fancy I would honnour him with a message, except I had something to demand of him that I thought of importance to my selfe, and very generously made me all sort of offers of Services and assurances of obeying my commands, reasonable or unreasonable'.

Since she could not bring herself to ask him the direct question she postponed it to another time; but the very next day a letter from Algarotti in Paris came 'in very good time to save the small remains of my understanding', she tells him.

His two English admirers, though they unabashedly confessed their love to him, did not to each other. Hervey was far more controlled than Lady Mary; undoubtedly Algarotti loomed larger in her thoughts and fantasies than in his. When she left London to 'bury' herself in her country house in Twickenham for three months she had no regret in abandoning all the people she knew in town. 'You have taken from me not only the taste but the sufferance of those I see,' she tells him, 'but in recompence you have made me very entertaining to my selfe, and there are some moments when I am happy enough to think over the past till I totally forget the present.' She chose to see nothing but the trees, she tells him a month later, 'since I cannot see the only Object dear to my Heart and Lovely to my Eyes'.

Both Hervey and Lady Mary wanted to possess the irresistible young Italian. Hervey, in rather general terms, invited him to return to England: 'the only privilege I want is the power to be of service to you.' He expatiated on his devotion in his next letter: 'You cannot imagine how often I think of you, how often I take Occasion to speak of you, with how much regret I think of your Absence, & with how steady an affection & perpetual admiration I remember every mark of Partiality you express'd towards me. . . . If a Place in my Heart is what you think worth preserving, you need be in no Pain about losing it.' Along with these warm expressions of devotion he sent (as Algarotti had requested) a selection of the 'most shining Passages out of the most shining of our English Poets'. He offered him both heart and head, so to speak, though from a distance.

But Lady Mary was bolder: 'if your affairs do not permit your return to England,' she tells him a few months later, 'mine shall be arrang'd in such a manner as I may come to Italy.' As the aggressor in their romantic friendship perhaps she made this suggestion only to see how he would respond to it. But for the time being, while his English admirers pursued him with their anxious letters, he pursued his own plans and ambitions. On his way to Italy he paused in Paris, then made a brief visit to Cirey, where Voltaire and Madame du Châtelet entertained him. He was, in Voltaire's opinion, a young man beyond his years in everything, one who would be everything that he wished. By way of Lyons and Turin he reached Venice, and there settled down to the exacting task of preparing his Newtonian dialogues for publication.

v

Even had he wished, Hervey could not, like Lady Mary, retire to the country to brood over a distant lover. At Kensington he was too busily occupied in attendance on the Queen while the King, in Hanover since May, amused himself in the company of Madame von Wallmoden. The Queen awaited her spouse's return with tolerable patience and temper until she realized that he would remain in Hanover beyond his birthday, 30 October. Her injured pride made her reduce the length and moderate the warmth of her letters to him. When Hervey discovered this, fearful that her interest with the King would be weakened, he begged Walpole to prevent her from continuing in that course. Walpole candidly told her that she must submit to the King's desires, as she had always done successfully, and write to him that since she wished him to be happy he must bring his mistress to England. Accordingly she sent the King a submissive, kind, and tender letter, earnestly asking him to bring Madame von Wall-moden to England, and (as Hervey paraphrased it) 'giving him repeated assurances that his wife's conduct to his mistress should be everything he desired when he told his pleasure, and everything she imagined he wished when she was left to guess it'.

The King's reply was full of tenderness, friendship, and affection for his considerate wife; Hervey's strategy was sound. 'If you can but once get this favourite to St. James's,' he told Walpole (who repeated it to the Queen), 'she will in three months be everything Lady Suffolk was, but deaf.' (Lady Suffolk, now retired, had been cheerfully tolerated by Walpole and the Queen because she had no influence on the King.) The Queen then ordered Lady Suffolk's former lodgings in St. James's Palace to be enlarged and made ready, should the King's new mistress come to England.

His failure to return in time for his birthday celebration caused great discontent at court, as well as among shopkeepers, who lost trade by people's not coming to town; among citizens, who criticized him for favouring his German dominions; and among ordinary and godly people, who railed at him for treating his wife and children so shabbily. Although he asked the Queen to move to St. James's before his birthday, she thought it more seemly to remain at Kensington, declining any pomp in his absence and intending to return to London only to receive him on his arrival. On his birthday she drove to St. James's Palace only for the day and returned to Kensington after the ball that night. It was a thin occasion, with very little finery.

Hervey's duties that day, though arduous, left him time to write to Algarotti: 'I have been obliged all the Morning to hear the Bishops make Spiritual, & the Courtiers temporal Compliments to the Queen ... Sir Robert Walpole (who goes to morrow into Norfolk) dined with me, & ... I am obliged to go up at nine a Clock to take out a Parcel of bad Dancers to expose them-selves one after another at the Ball.' He had intended to leave for Suffolk the next day to visit his father for a fortnight but the Queen forbade him to leave Kensington.

In his daily attendance he often spent the entire day with her, conversing on many subjects. Some of his other duties were not so enjoyable or enlightening. 'I am just return'd with the Queen from a long dull Opera & a cold empty House', he tells Henry Fox, and then complains that he is being neglected by the brothers at Redlinch. He could be bored and lonely even with his beloved Queen when his intimate friends were so far from him. And his being so confined to the 'almost depopulated Palace' at Kensington had the further disadvantage of isolating him from London. The roads were so infamously bad that he might have been cast on a rock in the middle of the ocean, he complains to his mother, 'and all the Londoners tell us that there is between them & us a great Gulph of mud fix'd, so that those who would pass from them to us or from us to them can not. There are now two Roads through the Park, but the new one is so convex & the old one so concave that by these two different Extremes of Faults, they both agree in that Common one of being impassible.'

Although prevented from visiting his father at Ickworth Hervey asked him for a set of the classics to aid him in his studies. Lord Bristol, welcoming the request, ordered one hundred and forty-four volumes of a variorum edition of the classics that cost him the considerable sum of sixty guineas. It was only a small present, he told Hervey, 'to assist you in that study you are grown so fond of'; and then unwilling to let slip an opportunity for a pious reflection he continued: 'but as your mind is already compleatly stord with all the embellishments the belles lettres can give it, I hope your next pursuits in knowledge will be chiefly how to make your selfe more and more acceptable to the Deity, truely useful to your declining country, and at the same time enable your selfe to make all just and necessary provisions for our numerous family.' In order to shelve his new books suitably Hervey requested—and was provided by the Master of the Wardrobe with—a decorated bookcase for his apartment in St. James's Palace.

Shocking as it was for the King to miss his birthday it was inconceivable that he should be abroad when Parliament met in January. To everybody's relief, orders arrived in London near the end of November for the Royal squadron to sail for Holland, where the King would meet it. At the same time the Queen moved to St. James's to be ready to greet him on his arrival. It was assumed that he had set sail on Tuesday 14 December. That night the wind changed, and a violent storm arose that lasted four days, during which time there was no news at all of the King's safety. Every hour increased the apprehension that he had been lost at sea.

The Prince of Wales and his court did not remain idle. 'The Prince gives a dinner to morrow [Friday], at his House in Pall Mall to my Lord Mayor & a thousand Citizens who are to bring him his Freedom of the City to morrow morning in form,' Hervey tells Henry Fox, adding, 'I make no Comments.' In the privacy of his *Memoirs* it was safe for him to comment: that the Prince's alacrity 'on this occasion was not so ill-founded as it was indecent, nor so improperly felt as it was improperly shown'. When the Queen questioned him the next morning about the feast attended by the Prince he told her what he knew of it: that the Prince's speech was clearly pitched to win popularity, and that the after-dinner toasts were in the same vein.

My God, [she exclaimed,] popularity always makes me sick, but Fretz's popularity makes me vomit. I hear that yesterday, on his side of the house, they talked of the King's being cast away with the same sang-froid as you would talk of a coach being overturned, and that my good son strutted about as if he had been already King. Did you mind the air with which he came into my drawing-room in the

morning, though he does not think fit to honour me with his presence
or ennui me with his wife's of a night? I swear his behaviour shocked
me so prodigiously, that I could hardly bring myself to speak to him
when he was with me afterwards; I felt something here in my throat
that swelled and half-choked me.

The previous day Walpole had driven with Hervey to his house
to dine, and on the way had uttered many melancholy reflections on the sad fate of the Royal Family should the King be lost
and the throne occupied by the Prince, whom he characterized
as a 'poor, weak, irresolute, false, lying, dishonest, contemptible
wretch, that nobody loves, that nobody believes, that nobody will
trust'. As to the situation of the Queen, dependent on a son who
hated her, Hervey disagreed with Walpole; the Queen, in his
opinion, might manage to exert some influence on him. He
pointed this out to the Queen herself—that his opinion was very
different from hers in one matter. 'It is that Your Majesty in a
month, if he came to the crown, would have more weight with
him than anybody in England.' What was this opinion founded
on? she asked. 'Upon knowing, Madam, how susceptible he is of
impressions, and how capable Your Majesty is of giving them.
He is, Madam, a mere bank of sand, and anybody may write
upon one as easy as the other.' When she disagreed with his easy
reassurance he justified it with an elaborate analysis of her virtues,
which he was certain would persuade the Prince to depend on her
for guidance. The Queen sighed, then, and said she hoped it was
all empty speculation.

Still they could not help thinking of what the future would
hold if the King were now to be succeeded by his unloved heir.
Still holding to his belief that as Dowager the Queen would have
great influence on her son, Hervey said that he would absent
himself from her for some time to avoid irritating the new King
by his presence. 'No, my Lord,' she interrupted him, 'I should
never have suffered that; you are one of the greatest pleasures of
my life.' She would insist that he and his family live with her at
Somerset House at a salary not less than he now had; it was the
least she could do for her own honour and the best thing she
could do for her own pleasure. As for Walpole, who had said
he would retire, she would beg him on her knees not to desert
her son. Their uneasy conjectures ended, however, when a letter
arrived from the King reporting that he had not yet embarked.

'The King is still at Helvoetsluis,' Hervey tells Henry Fox, '& it is reported not alone, *ma non lo credo*.' His disbelief was justified, for the King had not brought Madame von Wallmoden with him. If he had, perhaps he might not have been so impatient to embark. For with a favourable wind two days later, it was correctly assumed in London that he had finally set sail. After two days, however, the wind changed, and a terrible storm swept over the Channel. Consternation again agitated the court. This time the King's danger was beyond doubt, and when Walpole brought the Queen a report that four men-of-war in the Royal convoy had been wrecked on the coast she could not restrain herself, and wept plentifully. It was Sunday morning, and in spite of her grief she went to chapel as usual—an unreasonable gesture, Hervey thought—to show the world that she would perform her duties as long as she could. A half hour later an express was brought to her that after one day of the frightful storm the King had cautiously returned to port, and so was safe after all.

It was almost an anticlimax, then, when he finally arrived on 15 January 1737, after having spent five weeks in the Dutch seaport. His cheerful temper to all and warm affection toward his wife reflected his pleasure in being home again in his English dominions.

vi

The most important Parliamentary business that the King faced during this session (1737) resulted from an odd mixture of family and constitutional policy growing out of his relations with his unfilial son. The Prince's friends had convinced him that at this time he should demand a rise in his allowance—from the £50,000 a year granted by the King from the Civil List to £100,000 granted by Parliament independently. When Hervey learned from Henry Fox, whose vote had been solicited by the Opposition leaders, that such a motion would be introduced in the House of Commons, he informed the King and then the Queen. At first she refused to believe him, but he convinced her that it was so, and the next morning told Walpole, who had also heard it from other sources. It was then talked of by everybody.

Many on the King's side, fearful that the Prince's friends might succeed with the motion in the Commons, hoped that he could be persuaded to desist. Hervey advised the Queen to speak to him herself, and provided her with the arguments, but she replied that her attempt would only stiffen his obstinacy. Walpole added his persuasion to Hervey's, with as little success. Instead, Lord Scarborough was chosen to speak to the Prince, but his advice had no effect. Several of the Opposition leaders in both Houses were against this rash measure because an attack on the King instead of their proper antagonist, Walpole and his Ministry, would be of disservice to the Whig party, traditionally the support of the Hanoverian family. As the day approached for the motion to be voted on, general opinion calculated that it would be passed, much to Walpole's alarm, who feared that his future as Prime Minister depended on the outcome.

The King preferred to regard the measure as a Parliamentary issue: that although the Civil List was granted to him by Parliament he alone should decide how to spend it; and if this was so, then he had the right to determine the amount of his grant to the Prince of Wales. If Parliament insisted that he must grant £100,000, then they were encroaching on his Royal prerogative. By thus shifting the issue to one of privilege he conveniently saved himself £50,000 a year. Publicly Hervey supported the King; privately he thought that both the King and the Prince were at fault, the former for not granting £100,000 as precedent would expect, and the latter for appealing to Parliament against his own father.

One day before the motion was to be introduced, Walpole told Hervey that he would advise the King to placate his son by promising to settle a jointure on the Princess of Wales immediately and his own allowance at £50,000 independently, but Hervey doubted that the proposal would be acceptable to the Prince or would change any votes. They then went together to St. James's Palace, and when first the Queen and then the King were convinced that the compromise should be presented to the Prince it was drawn up and delivered to him by the Cabinet-council. His reply to them was firm: 'Indeed, my Lords, it is in other hands; I am sorry for it.' As Hervey had foreseen, he was not to be deflected from the course he and his advisers had set.

As soon as the Queen was awake the next morning she sent for Hervey to ask what people in town were saying of the King's message. In the long conversation that ensued Hervey very acutely analysed the political impasse. As on previous occasions when the Queen had threatened to encourage Tory support, Hervey reminded her that the Hanoverians owed their establishment to the Whigs, and simply could not afford to entertain the idea of a Tory administration. While they were conversing they saw through the window the Prince walking across the courtyard. 'Look, there he goes—that wretch! that villain!' said the Queen, her face red with rage. 'I wish the ground would open this moment and sink the monster to the lowest hole in hell.' Then, seeing how astonished Hervey was at her outburst, she said, 'You stare at me; but I can assure you if my wishes and prayers had any effect, and that the maledictions of a mother signified anything, his days would not be very happy nor very many.' Thus began the day considered so crucial in St. James's Palace.

In the House of Commons Pulteney opened the debate (on 22 February) with great pomp because of the Royal rank of the persons concerned in the motion. He spoke for an hour and a half —'extraordinarily strong and learnedly', Egmont thought. In his reply Walpole, with very good effect, read out the King's compromise offer to the Prince and the Prince's rejection of it. The debate went on until after midnight; and on the division the motion was defeated by an unexpected majority of thirty, to the intense pleasure of the King and Queen. An M.P. there that day observed that Walpole 'made a long Pathetick Speech to move the Passions upon what might be the consequences of an entire Break between Father & Son . . . (He pretended almost to shed tears tho' as soon as He had carried his Question & the whole was over He turned the Affair into ridicule.)' Three days later Carteret introduced the measure in the Lords, where it was defeated by an even greater majority (103 to 40). Hervey attended the debate but apparently did not speak.

Although it had been so decisively defeated, Pulteney wished to keep the controversy alive, at least until the next session. In June, before Parliament rose, he reopened it with a long pamphlet entitled *A Letter from a Member of Parliament to his Friend in the Country upon the Motion.* . . . He was setting forth his thoughts on this matter, the anonymous M.P. explains, because it would probably be the subject of debate again in the next session; and so he rehearsed the whole affair once more. Probably at Walpole's suggestion Hervey drafted a reply several months after Pulteney's *Letter* was published, and entitled it 'An Examination of the Facts

& Reasonings contain'd in a Pamphlet intitled a Letter from a Member of Parliament to his Friend in the Country upon the Motion to address his Majesty to settle 100,000 p. pr. anm On his Royal Highness the Prince of Wales'. Three Latin tags follow, intended to adorn the title-page when published. Hervey gave his draft to Walpole, who revised it and added a few passages in his own rapid hand, taking advantage of his anonymity to comment with greater freedom than he could in Parliament. Walpole kept the draft of the 'Examination' with his papers. If the matter of the Prince's allowance were to be raised again in the next session of Parliament he would have ammunition ready for the battle.*

Hervey had already, during this session, wielded his pen in defence of the Ministry. The Opposition had launched (in February) a new paper called *Common-Sense*, to take the place of the *Craftsman*, which only appeared irregularly. Its essays, mostly by Chesterfield and Lyttleton, attacked Walpole and his policies on many fronts. The issue of 16 April dealt with taxes and tax collectors, a subject congenial to those who had defeated the Excise Bill several years before. Their theme this time was that 'where Custom-house or Excise officers are imployed, the Publick must either lose its Right, or the People their Liberties'. As a historical precedent they invoked the publicans used in the Roman empire to collect taxes, and then developed the idea that tax collectors and liberty are antithetical.

Soon after, Hervey replied to the paper with a slim pamphlet entitled *A Letter to the Author of Common-Sense; or The Englishman's Journal, of Saturday, April 16*. He is impartial enough to admit that some of the earlier essays in that paper had been written with 'so much Wit, Humour, and Vivacity' that he had looked forward to reading it with pleasure but now it had degenerated to retailing second-hand ideas from Mr. D'Anvers (*The Craftsman*) and Mr. Fog (*Fog's Journal*). The second half of his pamphlet is a lesson in Roman history and the Latin language; like a firm but good-natured schoolmaster he corrects the assertions made by *Common-Sense* about the Romans and their tax

---

* Evidently a few copies were printed with 1739 on the title-page: a copy is at Ickworth, and Horace Walpole lists it as Hervey's under the date in his *Catalogue*. But the measure was not raised again in Parliament; and in April 1742 (after Walpole's ministry was out of office) the King increased the Prince's allowance to £100,000.

collectors. It is a sprightly performance, lighter than Hervey's political pamphlets usually are; and he is even generous enough to quote a line from 'Mr *Pope*'s excellent Essay on Criticism'.

When the King opened Parliament on 1 February (late because of his delayed return from Holland) he had pointedly criticized 'Disturbers of the public Repose'. What he alluded to were the notorious riots incited by the Porteous case. In Scotland, where popular opposition to excise duties was particularly strong, two smugglers had been arrested in April of the previous year (1736) for robbing a customs collector. One of them escaped, the other was duly hanged. A crowd then gathered, and began to hurl stones at the town guard, who were commanded by a Captain Porteous. He ordered his men to fire into the crowd, killing six persons and wounding eleven. Tried for murder that summer, he was found guilty and ordered to be executed, but the Queen, then guardian of the realm in the King's absence, had granted him six weeks' reprieve because the jury's verdict had been doubtful. Two days later a mob of Edinburgh citizens stormed the prison, and after releasing the other prisoners hanged Porteous without any interference from the city magistrates. Such an outrage against the Government and Royal authority could not be ignored, yet the official inquiry in Edinburgh had made little headway against a conspiracy of silence and evasion.

Apprehensive Britons south of the Tweed regarded the Porteous incident as a frightening omen. 'I have had many terrors about an *insurection*,' Lady Hervey told Stephen Fox (in October 1736), 'which were not lessen'd by Captain Porteous's affair. I and my whole family have been hanged several times in imagination . . . I think we are all safe at least 'till the Parliament sits.'

Now that Parliament was sitting, the Porteous affair was the first important measure to come before the House of Lords. On that day (10 February) Carteret led the Opposition speakers; and at the end of the debate his motion was passed that in a month's time there should appear for questioning the provost and four bailiffs of Edinburgh, the commander of the city guards, and the commander of the King's forces; and that a transcript of the Porteous trial should be laid before the House. The Opposition's strategy was to force the Administration to deal harshly with the Scots in the hope that the representative peers would waver, and perhaps defect, in their support of Walpole.

During the month's postponement—while the Prince of Wales's grant occupied Parliament—witnesses and evidence had been brought from Scotland so that the Porteous case could be resumed in March. This time Hervey took an active part in the Scotch Bill, speaking three times in debate, and privately discussing it at length with the Queen and with Walpole. His general purpose, like Walpole's, was to prevent harsh penalties from being imposed on the Scots. But their colleague, Newcastle, supported Carteret in the Opposition because he nursed a grudge against the Duke of Argyll and his brother, Lord Ilay, who was Walpole's agent in Scotland. The bill, more severe than Hervey approved of, was passed in the House of Lords on 2 June much to his chagrin because he felt that Newcastle had got the better of him. It was now sent back to the Commons for approval.

Just then Hervey was informed that his father was seriously ill, and he hastened to Ickworth, where he arrived on 5 June, as his father recorded in his diary, 'notwithstanding the Parliament was still sitting, & staid with me till Thursday the 30th; for which I hope & pray that God will please to reward him for this fresh instance of his piety towards an aged father, as well as for his constant, dutiful behaviour towards me ever since he was born'.

In the meantime the House of Commons greatly softened the severity of the Scotch Bill's penalties, to the great indignation of the King and Queen, who felt that after such a long inquiry the atrocious crime and the impudent insult to the Government should be deservedly punished. The amended bill was then sent back to the House of Lords on 17 June; and although the King would have liked its harsh penalties restored it was, after the debate, passed. Far from satisfied, the King signed it into law on 21 June and prorogued Parliament. In retrospect Hervey wittily summed up the Scottish affair: 'the generality of mankind, who looked on these great transactions in cool blood, were not a little jocose on the two Houses of Parliament having been employed five months in declaring a man should never again be a magistrate who had never desired to be one, and in raising two thousand pounds on the city of Edinburgh to give the cook-maid widow of Captain Porteous, and make her, with most unconjugal joy, bless the hour in which her husband was hanged.'

Hervey's absence from the final debate had serious consequences, for the King was so angry at his defection that he refused to speak to him for several days after he returned to court. Perhaps Hervey, caught between the King's desire for harsh penalties in the Scotch Bill and his own for mild ones, preferred to solve the dilemma by avoiding it. For, aided by his welcome presence, his father's health had soon improved, so that on 11 June Bristol was well enough to write a long letter on a matter of business, and two days later Hervey himself could report to Henry Fox that his father was 'much better'. Had he wished, he could then have hastened back to London to resume his place in the House of Lords in time to debate and vote on the amended bill. Instead he remained at Ickworth until the end of the month.

A rumour of the King's displeasure reached his father, who then asked him whether political expediency rather than filial piety had sent him to Ickworth. In either case, Bristol hoped that Royal anger might cause Hervey to abandon Walpole's party: 'whenever you find your selfe made the least uneasy by any unworthy treatment from those who I know are incapable of setting a due value on your merit . . . you shall at all times be sure to find, not only my house & arms open to receive you & yours with the utmost joy & tenderness, but my purse so too.' The time had not yet come when Hervey would need to look to his father for protection.

12

A Royal Birth, a Royal Death

HERVEY'S ATTEMPT TO SECURE PATRONAGE for his friends—his 'almost quotidian application', as he called it—now took a new turn. During the Opposition's campaign in Parliament to increase the Prince of Wales's allowance, the Prince had promised Stephen Fox a peerage (in the future, of course) in exchange for his vote; and on Hervey's advice Stephen had refused. Such loyalty should be rewarded, Hervey told the King and Queen; and he suggested to Walpole that since a peerage was what Stephen wanted above all, why could he not be given one? When Walpole explained that the King was as reluctant to bestow honours as money Hervey had a reply ready: 'I will remove that difficulty on this occasion, with regard to Mr. Fox, by pawning my honour Mr. Fox shall never ask anything of you besides (if this is done) as long as you are a Minister; and further will engage, if the King is afraid of losing a vote in the House of Commons, that Mr. Fox shall for nothing bring in anybody you will name in his room at Shaftesbury.' Walpole promised to do what he could; and Hervey often spoke to the Queen on the same subject. He urged that if Stephen could not be favoured then at least Henry Fox should be; and that if nothing was done for these young men everybody would think that he had lost all his influence at court.

His persistence was partially successful. Just before Parliament rose (in June) the King distributed rewards and punishments for the session. Hervey, who had asked nothing for himself, only for Henry and Stephen Fox and his brother Thomas, saw Thomas awarded a sum of money and the promise of an appointment, and Stephen an absolute promise of a peerage when any new ones should be created. Henry Fox, however, was firmly rewarded with the post of Surveyor-General of His Majesty's Works, an office of dignity, paying more than £1,100 a year. An additional advantage was that as Vice-Chamberlain Hervey had to keep in touch with Henry. 'Which of all the Devils in Hell prompted you to tell the Queen that every thing in her Library was ready for the putting up of her Books?' he starts a letter to him, addressing the Surveyor-General as 'Neglector of his Majesty's Works'.

He could not treat all his dependents so light-heartedly, particularly Dr. Middleton, one of the most importunate, for whom he had not been able to win anything. Middleton had modestly remarked, the previous autumn, that his appetite for sacred and for temporal rewards was moderate, that he 'would be satisfied almost with any thing but mere emptiness. I have no pretensions to riot in the feast with the Elect, but with the sinner only in the gospel to gather up the crumbs that fall from the table.' To such modest and vague supplication Hervey replied with kind but necessarily vague promises.

When an opportunity arose for Middleton himself to remind Walpole of his hunger for crumbs, he seized it. A few old deeds of the Walpole family having fallen into his hands by accident, he sent them to Horace Walpole, the Prime Minister's youngest son, then a Cambridge undergraduate; and the boy sent him Sir Robert's assurance that even 'without a monitor, *He should remember his promise of serving*' him.

Since Thomas Townshend had already interceded, Middleton also thanked him for Sir Robert's kind message. 'You have done for me', he tells him, 'what your power & access to the Great enabled You to do, recommended me to those who can do more.' At the same time, he reminded Townshend of his other uncle, Newcastle, whom he had known at Cambridge and who might possibly have retained 'some prejudices not favourable' to his character: would Townshend do what he could to remove that obstruction? He kept each of his two patrons informed of the other's efforts in the hope that together they might be more successful. 'I commit my hopes therefore to Your culture & Lord Hervey's,' he tells Townshend, 'as most likely to thrive and ripen in that soil where they first sprung.'

Hervey tactfully reinforced Sir Robert's message by telling Middleton that it was sincere; and at the same time he shielded Walpole from Middleton's importunities by pointing out that as long as he possessed Walpole's good will any application for a specific favour might postpone his winning a different one. Hervey did, in fact, try his utmost with both the Queen and Walpole to win some preferment for Middleton, but the church powers prevented every attempt. Although Middleton was highly qualified by his intelligence, learning, and industry he shocked and repelled his brethren of the cloth (one of them wrote) by 'the Levity of his Writings, which have infused such a Degree of Scepticism & Contempt of the Fathers & Antiquity into not only the Layity but among the Clergy of this generation. . . . It is deplorable that a Man of Dr. Middleton's Sagacity should not see the Absurdity, Impropriety & Dishonesty of subscribing to Articles & taking Oaths at the same time that he disbelieved the one & disregarded the other.' The unorthodox cast of Middleton's religious thought was so similar to Hervey's that it made an intellectual bond between them, so that, ironically, what warmed Hervey's friendship cooled the sources from which church patronage flowed.

ii

Lord Bristol's generosity and hospitality toward Hervey and his family became the cause of friction between Lady Bristol and Hervey that (on her side, at least) was as intense as that between the Queen and Prince of Wales. Only the previous summer at Kensington they had lived as amicably as any mother and son could. Their main altercation began in the spring (1737) when she had asked him not to send his children to Ickworth during their school holidays since they had no need of country air, for if they did come, there would be no room in the house for her own children. Instead of treating her request as confidential Hervey told his father of it, whereupon—Lady Bristol confided in the Dowager Duchess of Marlborough—Lord Bristol 'fell into a Violent passion and said he wonderd how I come to dare to forbid any of my Lord Hervey's children the house'. She hoped that the Duchess would send Bristol her poor opinion of 'this Treacherous Villain', and thus assist her in the greatest distress she had known 'for many years from the Vile actions of the worst of men, and sons'. She put great store in the Duchess's influence on Bristol, who had obtained his first peerage through her efforts.

The Duchess on her part seems to have had no great admiration

for Lady Bristol, having characterized her a few years before as
'a mighty ridiculous woman, entirely wicked in all things'; and
though not a fool, a worthless person with a mixture of cunning
and sometimes a good deal of wit and sharpness in her conversation. But now she was happy to join Lady Bristol in loathing
Hervey, whose political alliance with Walpole was cause enough
for her hatred.

In May 1737, when Lady Bristol again begged the Duchess to
persuade Bristol that his darling heir was a villain, three of his
children were already at Ickworth and four more on their way;
and he himself was there during June to visit his sick father (and
perhaps to avoid the Scotch Bill). He had come there, Lady
Bristol later alleged, only in the hope that his father would die
and he could take possession of the title and estates. Her shrill complaints to the Duchess were intended to do more than relieve her
resentment; she begged her old friend to do justice to Lord Bristol
by being 'the happy instrement to oppen his eyes' to his son's
baseness, treachery, and ingratitude. The previous year she had
drawn up a will naming him one of her executors (along with her
husband and Sir Thomas Hanmer); she soon made a new one 'to
secure what few things I have of my own from the plunder of
a vile son'. Bristol, of course, was aware of their enmity, and tried
ineffectually to persuade them to live on better terms with each
other.

Hervey's visit to Ickworth was pleasant enough except for his
mother's company. Boring neighbours stayed away because of
his father's illness; and—he tells Stephen Fox—'if one mouth in
the House I could name was gag'd I should like this relaxation
very well, but that orifice is so like that of Mount Vesuvious, that
every thing that comes out of it that is not fire is rubbish . . .
Adieu. Mount Vesuvious is this moment roaring for my Letters
because the man that carrys them is to bring My Lord's Pills.'
From her own country retreat at Twickenham Lady Mary had
written to him extolling the pleasures of rural life, but he would
have none of it, as he scolded her: 'for God's sake, how can you
talk so like a canting Seneca of the Purity of Air & the Quiet
of Retirement raising one's Imagination?' In high spirits he
argues that the maxim of 'the Beauty of Nature being so much
superior to all Art' was the greatest nonsense. Yet he felt so content
and easy at Ickworth, he tells Stephen Fox, 'that I begin to think

I am fitter to live in the Country than I thought I was'—but not because of country sports or landscape, for his only pleasure lay in human creatures and in writing. Except for his mother he enjoyed his companions at Ickworth, especially his father. With so much leisure he let the couplets spin off his pen in verse letters to Lady Mary.

On his way back to London he planned to stop at Cambridge for a day and a night; and he wrote ahead to Middleton: 'I am extreamly glad Mr. Walpole is at Cambridge, & tho you seem to do the Honors for me of my respect to Alma Mater, if she knew the Shares Mr. Walpole & You have in my Visit to her, I fear her Portion would not be one which either She could boast of recieving or I of bestowing.' When they met, Horace presented him with a pamphlet written by a young, precocious friend, for he knew of his interest in literature. As Hervey continued on his journey he conversed with a fellow traveller (unidentified) on divinity and philosophy, topics which, he later told Middleton, are useless compared to politics; 'as long as Mankind are curious, envious, ambitious, & absurd, which I believe will be as long as they walk upon two Legs' politics would furnish 'perpetual Sources for lively & interesting Conversations'. He stayed at St. James's Palace a week before joining the Royal Family at Hampton Court; there he could experience politics in various manifestations. Even the pregnancy of a princess could give birth to troublesome political offspring.

iii

The Prince of Wales, still smarting from his recent defeat, had been persuaded that he could assert his independence from the King and prove to the world that he was his own master if he could have the Princess lie in where he wished, at St. James's Palace, without consulting his parents or asking their consent. They, however, had resolved that the birth should take place at Hampton Court, where the entire family were installed for the summer, because they feared that a false child might be brought into the family. With his usual scepticism Hervey warned the Queen that even if the King sent a positive order for the lying-in to take place at Hampton Court the Prince would find a way of circumventing it. 'Well, if it is to be so,' replied the Queen, 'I cannot help it; but at her labour I positively will be, let her lie-in where she will; for she cannot be brought to bed as quick as one can blow one's nose, and I will be sure it is her child.' She urged Walpole to send the order to the Prince, but he procrastinated, on the grounds that the Princess reckoned her time of childbirth to be the beginning of October, still more than a month away.

On Sunday 31 August, the Prince and Princess dined in public with the King and Queen, and then retired to their wing of the palace. That evening the Princess began to feel birth pangs. The Prince immediately ordered a coach, and although the Princess's 'water broke' he hurried her into the coach, assisted by his dancing master and an equerry. With others of his suite they drove full gallop to London, arriving there at ten o'clock. At St. James's Palace a midwife was hastily summoned, and necessary bedroom supplies for the accouchement were improvised. (No bedsheets being available, the Princess was put to bed between two table cloths.) Neither the Lord Chancellor, who was in the country, nor the Archbishop of Canterbury, who arrived too late, was present at the birth of a girl; two Lords of the Council, however, witnessed it.

The Royal Family at Hampton Court knew nothing of this frantic episode enacted in another wing of the palace and then at St. James's. After their customary card-playing in the evening—cribbage for Hervey and Princess Caroline—they all separated at ten, and went to bed at eleven. At half past one in the morning the Queen was awakened by Mrs. Tichborne, her Woman of the Bedchamber, with the news that the Princess was in labour. 'My God, my nightgown!' the Queen cried, 'I'll go to her this moment.' 'Your nightgown, Madam', replied Mrs. Tichborne, 'and your coaches too; the Princess is at St. James's.' The Queen could not believe it. 'Are you mad, or are you asleep, my good Titchborne! You dream.' She was soon convinced, dressed as quickly as she could, ordered her coaches, and sent for Hervey and the Duke of Grafton to accompany her. By four o'clock they reached St. James's, and as the Queen started upstairs to the Prince's quarters Hervey told her that he would order a fire and chocolate for her in his own apartment, since he did not think she would stay long with the Prince. 'To be sure,' she replied, 'I shall not stay long; I shall be mightily obliged to you'; and then she winked and in a lower voice added, 'nor you need not fear my tasting anything in this side of the house.'

The Queen was received in the Prince's rooms; and after she had congratulated the Princess, she greeted her first grandchild with the wry reflection (in French), 'God bless you, poor little thing! Here you've arrived in a nasty world.' The Prince then related the whole story of his wife's labour and the journey, indiscreetly revealing details that clearly proved his imprudence, while the Queen merely listened. She then walked across the courts to Hervey's apartment, and passed an hour talking to him. They were soon joined by Walpole, vexed and in bad humour. In the ensuing conversation the Queen remarked that her journey to St. James's was a gesture that would be greatly to the King's advantage (who had stayed at Hampton Court) if an open quarrel with their son should result. 'That is so true,' Hervey agreed (always alert for political consequences),

that upon the whole I think their behaviour is the luckiest affront any Court ever received, since everybody must condemn their behaviour in this particular, which will consequently put them, who were on the attack in the quarrel, now upon the defensive; and if they do bring their money question next year into Parliament, his asking for an augmentation of a father he has not only offended but affronted will not be thought quite so reasonable a request as when he could pretend to have never failed in his duty.

The Queen then sent for Lord Harrington, whom she teased about his gallantry, and left Hervey's apartment to return to Hampton Court, arriving there at eight in the morning.

The affair was far from over. It required first an explanation from the Prince for his disobedience to his parents. This was rejected by the King, who forbade him to come into his presence. The Prince then wrote a letter asking permission to be readmitted; and exactly how his letter should be delivered to the King caused some confusion because of the uncertain protocol. Hervey, in the midst of it all, complained to Henry Fox: 'I am tired to death of hearing nothing but this sort of Stuff over & over again. It *ennuis* me to a degree that is inconcievable.' As the controversy dragged on it soon became very clear that—in Hervey's phrase—'the whole war was to be made upon the Queen' on the grounds that she had stirred up the King's resentment and was keeping it aroused. When she asked Hervey whether he did not think this surprising he replied that 'if wise people had a mind to hurt effectually, they would certainly strike at one's head, and not at one's elbow or one's knuckles'. The Queen could easily be flattered by a reminder that even if her husband ruled the kingdom she ruled him.

After the infant had been baptized with due ceremony, the King decided that the Prince's imprudent actions, so disrespectful to him as King and as father, called for stronger measures than forbidding him his presence. He asked Hervey to compose a letter ordering the Prince and his family to leave St. James's Palace. In his memoirs, where he copied the draft, Hervey candidly admits being 'not a little pleased with a commission that put it in his power to make use of the King's character and authority to express and gratify his [own] resentment against the Prince'. The letter was first read and altered by Walpole; and after having been shown to the Lord Chancellor and Newcastle—who 'perused and cooked this message'—it was shown to the King. Then, in order to persuade the Cabinet Council to approve it, Walpole predicted to them that only a complete breach between King and Prince would insure an eventual, firm reconciliation.

'There was a Cabinet-Council here yesterday,' Hervey tells Stephen Fox, 'can you guess about what—when I tell you that one of the Cabinet-Counsellors was ask'd if a great many People had been condemn'd? & he answer'd no, there is nobody to be hang'd, & only one order'd for Transportation. I think it an excellent bon-mot: & you are very dull if it does not inform you as well as make you laugh.' His ennui with the affair had its refreshing moments.

On that day (10 September) the King's letter was formally read to the Prince by the Lord Chamberlain, and a copy left for him. In it, after stating the reasons for his disapprobation, the King ordered the Prince and his family to leave St. James's Palace. That the expulsion was more than a private family affair was made plain: 'until you return to your duty, you shall not reside in my palace, which I will not suffer to be made the resort of them who, under the appearance of an attachment to you, foment the division which you have made in my family, and thereby weaken the common interest of the whole.' On receiving the letter the Prince was visibly upset, but this did not soften his parents' hearts when reported to them.

The next morning at breakfast, while Hervey was present, the expulsion was discussed by the King and Queen, who made no attempt to conceal their satisfaction. 'I hope, in God, I shall never see him again,' the Queen said, and repeated that wish. 'Thank God,' was one of the King's valedictions, 'to-morrow night the puppy will be out of my house.' When the Queen remarked to Hervey that she thought the Prince was glad to be turned out—because, presumably, his self-proclaimed martyrdom would attract more followers—Hervey disagreed: 'There is a great deal of difference, Madam, between his being turned out on a parliamentary quarrel and for a personal family misbehaviour; and though he might wish it therefore in one case, he may be very sorry for it in the other.' But which of the Prince's advisers had enough sense to point out this distinction? asked the King; 'Who is there but boobies and fools, and madmen that he ever listens to?' Hervey laughed, whereupon the King, encouraged by such audible appreciation, continued with brief, verbal caricatures of the men in the Prince's circle.

As soon as the King left the room the Queen asked Hervey to send his father a copy of the King's letter. In spite of Lord Bristol's misguided belief in old Whig principles, she said, he was an honest, well-intentioned man; and 'with regard to this family quarrel, with all the fine messages your silly mother carries him from my silly son, I am sure he thinks that monster very good-natured, a little weak perhaps, but very ill-used'. In reply Hervey launched into a great and glowing eulogy of his father and of the love they had always felt for each other; and he assured her that Lord Bristol knew his wife and the Prince too well to be misled. 'He is', Hervey concluded, 'judicious, dispassionate, just, humane, and a thorough good and amiable man, and has lived long enough in the world to have this character of him (though given by his son) uncontroverted by anybody else.' While he was speaking he observed the Queen weeping, for a reason that she then revealed. 'He is a happy as well as a good man to have as well as to deserve such a son; and your mother is a brute that deserves just such a beast as my son. I hope *I* do not;'—she continued, before revealing the most astonishing part of her confession—'and [I] wish with all my soul we could change, that they who are so alike might go together, and that you and I might belong to one another.' This was not the first time that the Queen had confessed her deep, maternal love for Hervey.

iv

Neither the busy routine of Hampton Court nor the excitement that followed the Royal birth drove the memory of the enchanting Algarotti from Hervey's thoughts. 'Am I never to hear from you again?' he had anxiously asked (in July 1737). 'This is the third Letter I have written since I have recieved any from you.' He could never forget 'one of the most agreable Incidents of my Life . . . I really think of you very often, & in a manner I think of few People.' Apparently Lady Mary was paying Hervey back in his own coin; he continues: 'I enquire often of Lady Mary what she knows of You. Sometimes she says she hears from you, sometimes that she does not; which is true I know not, & wish it was less true that I can not help continuing to desire what I have so little Reason to expect, which is a Resurrection in your Remembrance & a Restoration to the little tenement I once flatter'd my-self I possess'd in your Heart.'

By then Algarotti was in Milan revising his Newtonian dialogues for the printer; and when Hervey received a reply (two months later) it said nothing of the book, but its other news was pleasing enough to him. He answered it the same day it came: 'As to all you say of the regard you retain for me, whether it be the effect of your Taste or your Partiallity I must either way be pleased with it', for he regards Algarotti as 'one whom of all the men I ever was acquainted with I should most wish to engage' and 'the best Companion I ever met with'. His long letter, full of strained wit, Latin quotations, and English verse, ends simply and personally with 'Adio Carissimo'.

His other friend whom he had once called Carissimo was not so distant as the Italian. Although Stephen Fox, who was not yet living with his child-wife, stayed in Somerset, Hervey kept their friendship alive with his letters—chatty or motherly or gossipy. Once he was stung to stronger expression when Stephen asked whether he felt neglected or forgotten. No, he insists, for he should certainly impute it to chance, inadvertence, or laziness. 'I have loved you ever since I knew you,' he continues, 'which is now many years, so much better than most People are capable of loving any thing, that for your own sake at least, you would not nor could not, I am sure—there is so great a Pleasure in being so well beloved—be insensible of it & consequently not desire to preserve it.' His declaration breathes an air of sincerity: 'I only wish it was in my Power to show you how well I love you, that all your Pleasures & Wishes depended on me only, & if they did you would find your-self never deprived of the one, or disappointed of the other.' Compared to Algarotti, Stephen was closer to the core of his emotional being; and although they had grown apart their love was firmly rooted. Hervey's nature and tastes were ample enough to encompass such intense friendships with two such disparate men.

v

On his expulsion from his father's palaces in September 1737 the Prince of Wales rented a house in St. James's Square and for his summer residence Cliveden in Buckinghamshire. His followers, as much as they could, tried to make political capital of his situation. At a performance of *Cato* that he attended at Drury Lane (on 4 October) he was loudly cheered; and that frigid tragedy was warmed by politics as it had been during its first run on the eve of the Hanoverian succession. The letters he had written to his parents were circulated in versions slightly distorted in order to set him in a more sympathetic light. To counteract this propaganda his parents determined to print all the letters and messages that had passed between them since the night of the Princess's accouchement; and at the Queen's request Hervey translated them from French into English, accomplishing his task in one day. He was particularly gratified to be able to prove, by authority of the Government, that the Prince was a liar.

When the letters were printed he sent an uncorrected copy to Middleton, who then reported to him that most people in Cambridge thought the King should have pardoned his son. 'Since we have no opinion of our own about an affair of such importance,' he continues, 'I beg your Lordship, who knows the bottom of it, to instruct us, what we are to think & say about it, for in all questions I shall be proud to be on Your Lordship's side, but in political ones especially always ambitious to follow You.' His loyalty was complete; by the time he received a corrected text of the letters he had come round to the opinion that 'the Prince's Letters seem calculated to move the people rather than His Majesty'. This was the officially approved interpretation.

At the King's birthday-celebration, which opened the court season, those who sympathized with the father attended. They were so numerous and so eager to display their loyalty that the Drawing-Room was much fuller than it had been since the King's accession ten years before. Many could not help being reminded of the rift between the King and his father, and of their rival courts.

The Queen seemed to be in such vigorous health and abundant spirits that it was all the more unexpected that, a month later, she should become ill. One morning (9 November), while in her new library in St. James's Park she suffered an attack of what she called the colic. At first she pretended that it was trivial, and attended the Drawing-Room that day. 'Is it not intolerable at my age to be plagued with a new distemper?' she told Hervey. 'Here is this nasty colic that I had at Hampton Court come again.' She looked so ill that Hervey asked her what medicine she had taken, and when she told him he raised his voice anxiously, 'For God's sake, Madam, go to your own room; what have you to do here?' But she continued to move about, talking to the company, until she soon returned to Hervey's side and said, 'I am not able to entertain people.' At last, after the King left, she was (by protocol) permitted to retire, and went immediately to bed.

That evening, when Hervey visited her she asked him what he used to take for the colic, and he, imagining it was a 'goutish humour', prescribed strong medicines, to which she replied, 'Pshaw! you think now like all the other fools, that this is the pain of an old nasty stinking gout.' But then her violent, painful retching made her so restless that she told him she would take what he recommended—snake-root and brandy. After asking the attending physicians for their approval she swallowed the mixture but could not keep it down. Other remedies and treatment were administered; she was blooded and blistered, given aperients, purges, and enemas, but nothing brought relief.

During the fortnight that followed, while she lay ill, Hervey was seldom absent from her apartment; it was the most melancholy period he had ever suffered in his life. He experienced every symptom of what he calls 'the two most turbulent sensations in a human mind, grief and fear'. He kept a record of these days and nights in a detailed diary of unusual clarity and vividness; putting into words what he saw and heard helped perhaps to make his grief and fear bearable. This section is one of the most dramatic and moving of his entire memoirs.

From the Prince of Wales came messages, which were relayed through Hervey, asking if he might see his mother. The King, when he found out, was indignant—a scoundrel's trick, he raged, the Prince wanted to insult his poor dying mother. 'No, no! he shall not come and act any of his silly plays here, false, lying, cowardly, nauseous, puppy.' Hervey, when instructed by the King not to plague him, cautiously advised against sending any verbal message lest it be distorted by the Prince and his advisers. Since the King refused to honour his son with another written message (after the proliferation of the recent one) Hervey thought of a prudent compromise: the King's command would be written down and read aloud to the Prince without being delivered in writing. 'Your Majesty', he explained, 'will at once show that you will neither honour them with a written message nor trust them with a verbal one.' The message was duly drafted by Hervey, and the King, after first demurring for its being too mild, grudgingly consented to it. Hervey then read it aloud to the Prince's emissary in the presence of Newcastle and another witness.

The Queen had no desire to see her hateful son, and even made the King promise that should she ever talk of seeing him the King must assume that she was not in her right mind and refuse her request. When she talked of dying, she sometimes exclaimed, 'At least I shall have one comfort in having my eyes eternally closed— I shall never see that monster again.' That, at least, is Hervey's version of this startling illustration of how imminent death did not dissolve the Queen's hatred. Or perhaps it did, for another account alters the picture without necessarily contradicting Hervey's: that the Queen sent her blessing and a message of forgiveness to her son, at the same time telling Walpole that she would have been pleased to see him but feared it might embarrass and irritate the King.

As the Queen grew steadily worse Hervey passed the nights on a couch in the room next to hers. He thus observed the unfolding drama. It pivoted on the Queen's secret, shared only by the King, that she had suffered from a rupture at her navel for the last fourteen years. Her secrecy came not from ill-timed coquetry but from the knowledge that her power over the King was based

rest, we will all go to bed, for ~~we~~ by staying here we do
the poor Q. no good, & our-selves hurt;
& so dismissing Ld. H. they all retired.
    I will ~~give~~ relate no farther Particulars
how the two following Days pass'd, as
such a narration would be only
recapitulating a Diary of the two
former, without any material Variation.
The Q. grew so ~~~~ perceptibly weaker
every Hour that every ~~~~ one she lived
was more than was expected; She
ask'd Fizier on Sunday in the Evening
with no seeming Impatience under
any article of her present Circumstances
but their Duration; how long he
thought it was possible for all this
to last? to wch he answer'd; je crois
que votre maj:té sera bien tôt soulagé
& she calmly reply'd — tant mieux.
about 10. a Clock on Sunday night
the K. being in bed & asleep on the
Floor at the Feet of the Q.s Bed,
& the Ps. Emely in a Couch-bed in
a Corner of yr Room, the Q. began
to rattle in yr Throat, & Mrs. Purcel
giving the allarm that she was
expiring, all in the Room started
up, Ps. Caroline was sent for & Ld
H. but before the last arrived the
Q. was just dead; all she say'd ~~~~
before she dy'd was — I have now
got an Asthma — open yr Window —
then she say'd — pray — upon wch
the Ps. Emely began to read some
prayers, which she never repeated

in part on her remaining physically attractive to him, and so she had persuaded him that it was an inconsequential thing, and had made him promise never to mention the subject again as long as she lived. Now, breaking his promise, he told her secret to the surgeons, but it was too late.

Clearly she could not survive much longer. She took leave in form of her son the Duke of Cumberland, her four daughters, and her husband, to whom she gave all her keys and the only ring she was wearing, a ruby he had given her at their coronation. She also urged him, as she often had in the past, to marry again after her death. He was so touched that he sobbed and wept profusely; and, then, wiping his eyes and sobbing between every word, he assured her, 'Non—j'aurai—des—maîtresses.' To this she only replied, 'Ah! mon Dieu! cela n'empêche pas.'

Her ordeal of pain continued on until Sunday evening, 20 November, at about ten o'clock she died. Hervey had been sent for but arrived too late. In spite of his own grief he had to console the others. As soon as the King went to bed he sent for him and talked about the manner of the Queen's death more calmly than one would have expected. Hervey then went to Princess Caroline's bedchamber, and stayed until five in the morning trying 'to lighten her grief by indulging it, and not by that silly way of trying to divert what cannot be removed, or to bring comfort to such affliction as time only can alleviate'.

He tried to lighten his own grief the same way. Two days later, when Henry Fox saw him, he seemed to be calm. It was the greatest misfortune that could happen to him, he said, and the loss of so much pleasure made the rest of his life not worth thinking of. A week later, still not recovered from the shock, he seemed calm and reasonable, took Ward's pills as usual, walked, looked after his health,

But [Fox tells his brother] 'tis a total Subversion of His Thoughts, Hopes, Pleasures. He lov'd Her, had Reason to love Her, and liv'd much & with much Delight in Her Conversation. He looks, I fear, thinner & worse than He did a Week ago, but He says His Health is in no Danger. I fear His sleep is little, & He wants much to repair the Fatigue of His waking Thoughts . . . His Life is spent in talking of Her, which I hope will [ease] His Mind to the Subject, & help time in weakening the sense, & preventing the Effects of this unexpected & sad Event.

He was so wrapped up in his grief that one day at dinner in the palace, as he sat among the courtiers and Maids of Honour, their indecent gaiety provoked him to say something very shocking to them, which he rarely did; and he left the table to sit by himself at the fireside.

In the Queen's funeral in Westminster Abbey (on 14 December) he had the honour of carrying the train of Princess Amelia, who was designated chief mourner. (Many spectators thought that she walked with too little gravity.) At the King's request he wrote an epitaph on the Queen in Latin and another in English. He sent a copy of the Latin one to Algarotti, to Middleton, to his father, and to Fox's sister, Mrs. Digby, modestly pretending that it had been written by someone else in order to hear their objective critical opinion. The Latin one cost him 'great Pains', he later confessed to Mrs. Digby; 'but the English none, for truth furnish'd the thoughts, & my Heart felt too much for Words not to flow from me on that Occasion as naturally and as plentifully as my Tears.'

His English epitaph was parodied in verse labelled as 'Written extempore by Lord H——, on the melancholy News of her Majesty's Death' and printed in the *Gentleman's Magazine*. In the worst mortuary taste, its final lines achieve bathos of remarkable profundity:

> Yet think not, mournful reader, aught amiss,
> She's gone to heav'nly joys and endless bliss;
> She's gone from care and pain to peace above,
> From GEORGE, that's first below, to him that's first above.

vi

For Hervey grief had to come to an end since life and politics would continue. He had to reassess his position now that he could no longer depend on his familiar and affectionate friendship with the Queen, which had made him so useful to the Ministry. He had been, in Walter Bagehot's words, Walpole's '*queen-watcher* . . . one of the cleverest men in England . . . induced, by very dextrous management, to remain at court during many years—to observe the queen, to hint to the queen, to remove wrong impressions from the queen, to confirm the Walpolese predilections of the queen, to report every incident to Sir Robert'. Even at the outset of the Queen's illness, when Walpole was at Houghton and Hervey feared that Newcastle was plotting with Princess Emily he urged him to return immediately to St. James's.

The Queen had been a force they could reckon with; and they might have echoed the squib that was pasted to the wall of the Royal Exchange:

> O Death, where is thy sting,
> To take the Queen and leave the King?

For as they had seen her sink toward death Walpole had confided his anxiety to Hervey, 'Who can tell into what hands the King will fall? Or who will have the management of him? I defy the ablest person in this kingdom to foresee what will be the consequence of this great event.' Hervey made a firm, optimistic prediction: 'He will cry for her for a fortnight, forget her in a month, have two or three women that he will pass his time with to lie with now and then, and to make people believe he lies with them day and night, but whilst they have most of his time, a little of his money, less of his confidence, and no power, you will have all the credit, more power than ever you had, and govern him more absolutely than ever you did.' For instead of having to deal with the King through the complicating intervention of the Queen, Hervey continues, Walpole would have direct access to him; and besides, the King would be easier to manage because he was easier to deceive, less suspicious, less penetrating, and less willing to converse with others. Walpole disagreed with this sanguine view, and gave his reasons. 'Notwithstanding all this,' Hervey insisted, 'I am convinced . . . that you will have him faster than ever.'

Few would have agreed with him. Lord Chesterfield, in Bath at the time, thought that Walpole must be in the utmost distress, and could never hope to govern the King. 'This truth is so obvious to everybody', he wrote, 'that many people in place will act very differently with respect to Sir Robert from what they used to do, while they knew that he governed her, who absolutely governed the King.' Instead, it was Hervey himself who was generally regarded as the King's first favourite. Walpole's enemies and his own injudicious friends tried to stir him up to use his perpetual access to the King to bring about Walpole's ruin; and he would besides have been supported by the Princesses, who were irritated by Walpole. Then, said Hervey's well-wishers, he could step into Walpole's place and unite the Whig party under his banner. However much his vanity might be flattered by his favour with the King, Hervey knew that fundamentally he could not depend on it, and that the influence of the Princesses on their father was negligible. He needed, instead, to fortify his position with Walpole.

Ten days after the Queen's death he sent Walpole a long, carefully composed examination of what their future might be. He first reassures Walpole that the King would continue to depend on him for his unmatched abilities. 'As to my own situation (it is the last time I will trouble you upon it, so bear with me),' he goes on, 'it is as well known to me as yours.' In brief, although he has served Walpole so faithfully for so many years he has not been deservedly rewarded; he has, in fact, been denied both honorary trifles and more essential favours—as though Walpole was convinced that he was 'fit for nothing but to carry candles and set chairs all my life, and that I am sufficiently raised, at forty years old, by being promoted to the employment of Tom Coke [Vice-Chamberlain for twenty-one years] and designed, like him, and on the same terms, to die in it'. Then, after dismissing the mistaken notion of some people that he was now the King's favourite, he sums up his position in stately Ciceronian cadences more suited to an epitaph:

all I mean to say is that I will be refused or disappointed no more, for I will ask and expect no more; that my enemies shall not conquer, for I will not struggle; that I could have made my peace with my greatest enemy [Pulteney] if I would have done it at your expense; that I scorned it, and do not repent the part I have acted; that I submit to be a nothing, and wish whoever you honour with your confidence, or benefit with your favour, may always serve you with as honest a mind, as warm a heart, and as unshakable an attachment, as you have been served by your neglected, etc.

What was his motive in sending this letter, and can it be taken at face value? His complaint about carrying candles and setting chairs has been cited as evidence that his court position was little better than menial, yet since he wished to complain of neglect he would naturally demean the post of Vice-Chamberlain. As to motive, speculation is superfluous since he tells it himself; to remind Walpole that he had not been well used would be, he thought, the likeliest way of preventing his being worse used.

Walpole was too wary a politician to answer such eloquence in writing. Instead he sent a verbal message for Hervey to meet him early the next morning. He was both surprised and afflicted by the letter, and he urged Hervey to trust him. 'Let us have no *éclaircissemens* on what is past,' he continued, 'commit your future interest to my care.' Their conversation ended with what Hervey calls 'an extorted promise' from himself that he would not alter his conduct, complain to anybody, or tell of their conversation unless he had any fresh reason to be displeased with Walpole's behaviour. Although he confesses to having little faith in Walpole's 'most lavish professions of kindness and esteem' he was satisfied that he would not have to break with Walpole when it 'was certainly his interest as well as his inclination to lie by and be quiet'. He could allow himself that inclination, at least until the next session of Parliament.

At this time Hervey abruptly ended his memoirs of the reign of George II, which he had begun to compile four years earlier. Perhaps the shock of the Queen's death dispirited him, and he no longer had the heart to describe the court whose principal ornament she had been. (Sometimes his memoirs seem to be materials for the reign of Queen Caroline.) Perhaps the uncertainty of his position at court also made him unwilling to chart its future course. As a legacy to his descendants the memoirs were appreciated by his grandson, the first Marquess of Bristol, to the extent that he destroyed a two-year segment. They were first published in 1848, edited by John Wilson Croker. Yet truncated as they are, the memoirs remain undimmed as a brilliant historical and literary legacy to posterity, and as Hervey's most enduring monument.

As a historical document they are unique. No other chronicler of his time can match Hervey's intimate and incisive depiction of the Royal family in their private and political life. Although several other prominent political figures of the time were reputed to be writing the history of George II's reign—Carteret, Bolingbroke, and Chesterfield—their memoirs (if written) have never come to light. Modern historians have attested to the accuracy of Hervey's; and those passages that cannot be verified by external sources—his private conversations with the King, the

Queen, and Walpole—ring true with a persuasive consistency and coherence.

In style the memoirs are easily in the same class as Horace Walpole's, his only other eighteenth-century rival as memoirist. His turn for wit, his love of antithesis—not so exaggerated and inept as in his verse couplets—and his sensitivity to the potential intricacy and nuance of prose make the memoirs a stylistic triumph. His love of paradox scatters throughout his pages a wry wisdom similar to La Rochefoucauld's; and his pen portraits, especially of those he despised, crackle with an *esprit* that is closer to La Bruyère than to any English model. The speeches and official papers he copied into the memoirs as well as the long disquisitions on foreign policy may strike the modern reader as dull compared to the passages in which people move and speak and come alive. His skill in building the dramatic confrontations of his characters glows, at its best, with genius. What memoirs can match the tragicomic deathbed scene of Queen Caroline, as she consoles her blubbering husband with the solace of mistresses and a new wife? His memoirs are so important a historical document and so accomplished a literary one that they alone justify the years he spent at the Court of George II.

vii

At the opening of Parliament on 24 January 1738, the King, visibly under strain, delivered a short, sombre speech. In the House of Commons it was Stephen Fox who had been chosen to move the Address of Thanks—which he did 'in the handsomest manner,' Horatio Walpole thought, 'as well as with the greatest decency and eloquence I ever heard; in short, it was a masterly performance.' As Fox's friend and mentor Hervey must have been proud of his performance; and it could not have done either of them any harm in the eyes of the King and of Walpole, who had presumably given Stephen the honour of moving the Address. When the speech was read by Dr. Wigan, a Latinist as well as physician, who had been tutor to the Fox boys, he sent Henry his opinion of it. 'Ste's Speech is a charmingly compleat Oration. What pleases me most in it is that I discover nothing of his Friend's stile in it. I wish him all assistance from the same noble Person in making him like or equal to himself in one Point [being

a peer]. I may say this to you tho I would not venture to say it to
Ste.' Yet in a satire published a few months later Pope accused
Hervey of having written the speech himself:

> The gracious Dew of Pulpit Eloquence;
> And all the well-whipt Cream of Courtly Sense,
> That first was H—vy's, F—'s next, and then
> The S[ena]te's, and then H—vy's once agen.

Stephen's conspicuous activity as a Ministerial supporter was
a portent of future rewards. Hervey could claim some credit
for it.

For other claimants to his patronage Hervey had contrived
ingenious and justifiable excuses. 'My misfortune,' he explained
to one applicant, 'like most other People's who have the Ear of
Princes, is to have my Credit & Interest so much over-rated that
I am envy'd by my Enemys for favours I am only thought to
possess & often reproach'd by my Friends for not exerting a
Power in their Service which I really have not.' His old physician
and friend Dr. Cheyne asked him to find some preferment for
a brother who was a clergyman. Gracefully and wittily Hervey
apologizes for the literary style of his reply, 'an Example that one
may write as ill in a vegetable Dyet as if one lived upon Pork,
Salmon & Duck all one's Life'. But his answer was firm and unequivocal: his own brother and Dr. Middleton were the two clergymen whose preferment he had at heart; after they were served
he would oblige Dr. Cheyne's brother.

Middleton was not one to sit by and wait with Christian meek-
ness and humility. From Cambridge he kept his friendship with
Hervey in constant repair that winter and spring with news of
his reading and writing, a disquisition on Latin style, and corrections to Hervey's epitaph on the late Queen. And Hervey recipro-
cated. When informed of Middleton's sore eyes he sent a medicinal
preparation that he had used with success and also sent a candle-
screen to protect the eyes. Unfortunately Middleton's eyesight
was not benefited, though he managed to read *The Divine Lega-
tion of Moses* by William Warburton, with whom he corresponded. At the beginning of May he found an opportunity for
Hervey to help him: 'Dr. Bentley, as I am well informed, was
seized on Sunday last with a dead palsy on one side of his body,
which to one of his years seems to threaten the approach of death.

This has induced me by the advice of my friends to beg Your Lordship's interest in case of a vacancy for the obtaining that desirable preferment'—the Mastership of Trinity College.

Hervey promptly went to Walpole only to discover that the appointment had already been promised by the late Queen, and her promise would have to be honoured. When informed of this Middleton applied directly to Walpole and to Newcastle, offering to let his application be judged by a poll of the Cambridge college heads. (But Bentley, a tough veteran of many battles, fought off death for almost four more years.) Plaintively Middleton tells Hervey, 'instead of advancing, I am really going backwards'; and then adds: 'I congratulate Your Lordship, however, on the advancement of Your friend to Ely, which the world looks upon as Your act.' It was a neatly aimed reproof, for Robert Butts, who had begun his ecclesiastic career as a humble curate at Ickworth, had climbed steadily; and after five years as Bishop of Norwich he had just been translated to Ely.

'I was surprized', Middleton continues, 'to find my name at its full length in Pope's last piece, for I had always receiv'd civilities from him; but he does me the greatest honour when he treats me as Your Lordship's friend.' In the same passage where Pope had named Hervey as the author of Stephen Fox's eloquence he had mourned the death of 'Distinction, Satire, Warmth, and Truth', and then after a few examples of their corruption he continues:

> O come, that easy *Ciceronian* stile,
> So *Latin*, yet so *English* all the while,
> As, tho' the Pride of *Middleton* and *Bland*,
> All Boys may read, and Girls may understand!

'I cannot guess the reason of his joining me with *Bland*,' Middleton goes on, 'he has certainly paired us very unequally: one who receives not a penny either from Church or State with the best beneficed Clergyman in the Kingdom.' (Henry Bland, a friend of Sir Robert Walpole, was Provost of Eton and Dean of Durham; his son and namesake was a prebendary of Durham and held two church livings.) Middleton then underlines the moral: 'it is a little discouraging, My Lord, to stand exposed to envy & Satire without so much as a trench or breast-work to defend me.' He had persuaded himself that there were 'secret motives' operating against him that he could not penetrate. What he overlooked was that unlike Bland he had offended the predominantly orthodox elders of his church by his free-thinking speech and writings. He now became so discouraged in Hervey's patronage that he stopped writing to him for several months; and when their correspondence resumed it was Hervey who graciously reopened it.

Hervey's father was never discouraged in his attempts to establish his numerous sons. Henry Hervey, an army captain since 1735, wanted to be promoted; and so Bristol sent Hervey his brother's English imitation of the Latin epitaph on the Queen because (Bristol thought) if it were given to Princess Caroline she might help obtain his promotion. That spring Thomas Hervey, M.P. for Bury, won the appointment of Surveyor of His Majesty's Gardens and Waters, evidently through Dr. Butts' intercession. Bristol then thanked him on Tom Hervey's behalf 'for having pitchd upon a place so well adapted to the indolence and in-activity of his temper, being, as you call it, a sort of sine cure. Had he been blessd with the same diligent, improving genius of his elder brother, what might not his excellent natural endowments have attaind to? But alass! what a vast inequality hath their different dispositions producd!'

Given such a diligent, improving genius, why did not Hervey himself win any greater appointment? As so often in the past, Bristol returned to that question: he feared that 'those very services, which ought alone to plead most powerfully for your advancement to stations much more significant and honourable than that they have kept you in for so many years, will at last be turnd into an argument for continuing you where you are.' For the time being, since it was a period of uncertainty, Hervey was content to stay where he was.

13

Exit the Vice-Chamberlain

URING THE 1738 SESSION OF PARLIAMENT Walpole's greatest challenge and threat arose from the Spanish question. For many years the Spanish coastguards patrolling their American possessions had been intercepting British ships to search for contraband; and although the Administration tried to ease the problem through diplomatic negotiations the Opposition was determined to press for stronger measures. A stream of petitions and papers flowed into the House of Commons, and a succession of witnesses as well, to dramatize the dastardly treatment inflicted on British ships and sailors by the Spaniards. The most inflammatory witness, a Captain Jenkins, testified that the Spaniards had pillaged his ship (in 1731), and before turning it adrift had tied him to the mast and torn off his ear. Taking advantage of the popular indignation aroused by this testimony Pulteney introduced three resolutions, the first asserting the right of freedom of the seas, the second specifying abuses committed by Spain, and the third stating that attempts to gain redress from the Spanish government had proved ineffectual. These were passed and sent (on 2 May) to the House of Lords, where the first two were accepted with only minor changes. Since the third in effect criticized the Government's diplomatic endeavours, the Ministry tried to block it.

Carteret was the most effective of the Opposition speakers; and after Newcastle tried to answer him, Chesterfield resumed the attack, his theme being that the English had not acted with the vigour and determination that their dignity required. It was then that Hervey stood up to reply, his strategy being to deflate the Opposition's patriotic wind. He promised that the Ministry, while recognizing the injuries suffered by English merchants, would try to gain redress; and he asked for parliamentary unanimity as the most effective way of promoting English interest. The Opposition succeeded, after all, and all three resolutions were passed and presented in an Address to the King.

From an unexpected quarter the Ministry found itself being defended by a new periodical. In his *Letter to the Author of Common-Sense* Hervey had wittily predicted: 'poor sickly *Common-Sense* after dwindling into *Common-Place*, is now sunk into such *Uncommon Nonsense*' and would finally expire. Six months later, on 16 December 1737, a weekly paper entitled *The Nonsense of Common-Sense* appeared, promising 'To be continued as long as the Author thinks fit, and the Publick likes it'. This anonymous author was Lady Mary Wortley Montagu. While pretending to be an impartial journalist, she clearly advocated the Ministry's policies by attacking *Common-Sense*, defending the excise scheme, denying that the press was persecuted, and ridiculing the Opposition's belligerent attitude toward Spain. She disagreed with Walpole on one issue only: a bill to lower the interest on the national sinking fund that had been defeated in the House of Commons (in March 1737) through Walpole's efforts. Since it had never reached the House of Lords, Hervey expressed no public opinion, but privately he believed it to be unwise, and took time in his *Memoirs* to explain why he was opposed to it. Lady Mary agreed with him.

The political bias of her essays was only slight and oblique; she dealt mainly with social problems—feminism, morality, the lower classes, the writing profession. Her ninth issue (in March 1738) was the last of *The Nonsense of Common-Sense*, its author thinking fit to discontinue it probably because the public did not like it. Its effectiveness in Walpole's journalistic campaign had been negligible, but it had at least enabled Lady Mary to exercise her literary versatility, and to demonstrate her sympathy with the political ideas of Walpole and Hervey.

As the Parliamentary session of 1738 drew to an end it was uncertain at court whether the King would return to Hanover to seek, in the arms of Madame von Wallmoden, consolation for his grief. Hervey discreetly told others he knew nothing of it, and believed the King would certainly not go. He must have known what the Bishop of Gloucester lamented: that the King intended to send to Hanover for his mistress as soon as Parliament rose.

Before she arrived the King chose lodgings for her at each of his palaces, and asked Lady Hervey to select her attendants. On 12 June she arrived accompanied by a large retinue including her husband, and the next day waited on the King, where she met 'with a gracious Reception' (newspapers reported). It was generally remarked that although not a great beauty, she had fair features and a good figure, and appeared to be at her ease in the Drawing-Room. Until her apartments were ready a house had been taken for her in Pall Mall; this would have been one of Hervey's chores as Vice-Chamberlain, and one of his last duties before he could leave London for the summer recess.

He paid his annual visit to Walpole at Houghton at the beginning of July, making the journey with the Duke of Marl-borough. (The Duke, who had been in Opposition, accepted a place from Walpole in this year, and henceforth supported the Ministry.) After a week Hervey had to return to court, by then at Kensington, because the Cabinet-council had been convened to deal with the Spanish question. 'Peace & War are at present the Topicks of all Conversation both publick & private, both of the high & the low, the rich & the poor,' he told Stephen Fox (in August); '& it is generally believed that Peace will at last be the result of all our Consultations, Armaments & Negociations, tho none but the Inhabitants of the Sanctum Sanctorum of Politicks, the Cabinet-Priests, who eat the Shew-Bread of Counsell are yet acquainted with the Particulars.' It was important for the Ministry to try to settle the problem before Parliament met again lest the Opposition press forward with their aggressive campaign.

Hervey also tried to amuse his father with a witty description of the Cabinet-council; but Bristol, while appreciating 'the comical characters', found the 'farce-like scene' too melancholy to be endured. He made it the occasion to try once again to persuade Hervey to abandon Walpole, whom he characterizes as one 'who instead of carefully considering & honestly directing what woud be best for the publick interest, calculates only what will most tend to secure the perpetuity of his own ill-purchasd power'. Hervey's loyalty was partly based on the expectation of securing some of that power for himself, and to use it to favour his family. Bristol somehow reconciled his high-minded morality with his pursuit (through Hervey) of the practical rewards of Walpole's ill-purchased power.

While Hervey had been at Houghton Lady Hervey had gone to Goodwood to visit the Duke and Duchess of Richmond; and their children, much to Lady Bristol's disgust, had been packed off to Ickworth. No grandmother could have been more unloving. In one of her hysterical complaints to the Duchess of Marlborough that spring she had excoriated her 'Villainus Son' and his 'fals, bold Wife' and had anticipated with dread the arrival of their children, whom she calls 'the Young Vermin'. As she had feared, that summer she was 'overwhelmed with Children and their Masters'. (One of the masters was Thomas Wright of Durham, mathematician and astronomer, who stayed for three weeks in order to instruct Hervey's eldest daughter in the principles of astonomy.) Ickworth became so crowded that Lady Bristol had to flee to her new house in Bury 'to take a little breath out of this kenell of vermin'. In her violent hatred she begs the Duchess of Marlborough, her confidante, 'to find something to lash my wicked pair with; for I don't doubt but that they are as infamous in publick life as I have felt them in private', but—fearful no doubt of Lord Bristol's wrath—she cautions the Duchess never to tell anyone that the request came from her.

On his own account Hervey had not endeared himself with the Duchess by his friendship with her grandson, the young Duke. When Walpole was ill, in September 1738, and staying at New Park, Hervey and the Duke went to see him, and stayed at his bedside for an hour. A week later both of them, accompanied by Hervey's indispensable valet Maran, rode to Stockbridge in Wiltshire, where Stephen Fox was to send a coach to meet them and bring them to Maddington. To memorialize this cheerful fellowship with the Fox brothers, Winnington, and the newly enrolled Marlborough, Hervey had commissioned William Hogarth to paint a conversation piece. It shows the men in an animated mood in the garden. Henry Fox is holding up an architectual drawing to show to Hervey; perhaps they were planning to build a house at Maddington to replace the simple shooting-box.

While Hervey was enjoying himself with his cronies Lady Hervey went her own way. After her visit to Goodwood she told Lord Bristol that since her health was poor she would have to go to Bath, while her children would remain at Ickworth. It was not poor health that sent Lady Hervey to Bath, some gossips said, but only a search for fresh pleasures; and others, who pretended to be more knowing, said her real purpose in going there was to spy on the Prince and Princess of Wales. Whatever the true reason, she remained among 'all the polite and gallant' for the full season, not returning to London until near the end of November. Hervey in the meantime occupied himself with court duties, advised Middleton on his life of Cicero, and prepared for the forthcoming Parliament.

ii

Before Parliament was to meet in January 1739 the Ministry had been frantically trying to settle the Spanish *détente*, which they knew would be the Opposition's main target of attack. The long-expected courier from Madrid, bringing the King of Spain's ratification of the Convention of the Pardo, did not arrive until the 16th; and so the opening of Parliament was delayed to enable the Ministry to prepare their defence. The King's Speech, on 1 February, announced his great satisfaction that a convention with Spain had been signed to settle their mutual demands and to appoint plenipotentiaries for regulating grievances. These terms were vigorously attacked in both Houses by the Opposition, who would not approve the Address of Thanks unless the specific provisions were taken out of it. Hervey, who had sat on the committee that drew up the Address, rose to defend it, pointing out that those who objected to it were speaking against matters either approved by Parliament or outside its province. 'If we object against a paper war,' he said succinctly, 'we may also object against a paper peace, and what other can there be?'

He was unusually active in supporting the Ministry on this measure, which Walpole regarded as of the highest importance; and he spoke again on 19 February. The great debate on the measure came on 1 March, when the final version of the Address was presented to the Lords for approval. Hervey stood as one of its main supporters while his father listened, admiring his abilities and detesting his politics. He opened his long speech with a promise not to rely on 'Turns of Wit' or 'Flowers of Rhetoric' to persuade his listeners. In one turn of wit that his own notes contain he said that the 'Debate on the Convention now [is] like trying Egyptian Kings after they were dead to see what sort of Burial they deserv'd'. He defended the Ministry's policy of accommodation and compromise by stressing the patent

14. Lord Hervey and his Friends

disadvantages of a war with Spain, which would deprive them of their American trade and perhaps expose them to a joint attack from Spain, France, and Sweden.

The debate, lasting nine hours, was enlivened in the late afternoon by the invasion of seventeen ladies, all of them supporting the Opposition, who flouted the rule that strangers should not be admitted, and by a ruse gained entry into the House of Lords. They stayed there until after eleven, reported Lady Mary (who was not among them), and during the debate applauded 'and showed marks of dislike, not only by smiles and winks . . . but by noisy laughs and apparent contempts; which is supposed the true reason why poor Lord Hervey spoke miserably'. Lady Mary may have received a biased report of Hervey's performance, for Lord Orrery, although strongly sympathetic to the Opposition, reported that Hervey 'spoke nicely, and was full of Peace, Plenty, and Sugar-Plumbs'. In the division, finally, the Ministry won. Bristol was among the Lords who signed the protest.

For almost two months following his speech Hervey did not attend any of the meetings of the Lords. He suffered from a persistent illness—caused, Lord Orrery quipped, by 'too violent a fitt of Eloquence'. He had actually been ill even before his speech, having gone the previous week to Kensington to benefit by the air, though his fever then returned and he had to be blooded. During his absence no important business came up in the Lords. After he resumed his attendance he spoke three times: in support of a bill empowering the King to augment his military forces, a bill providing annuities to the King's younger children, and a resolution regarding Spain's payment of her indemnity. In all of these he remained a firm Ministerial supporter. The leading Opposition speaker, Carteret, insisted that nothing short of a declaration of war against Spain would satisfy the British. On that bellicose note, echoing the mood of the country at large, Parliament rose.

iii

The previous summer (1738) when Hervey had resumed his correspondence with Middleton he had promised that although as a 'second-rate Courtier' he was mortified at his ill success he would never slacken his efforts to secure preferment for him 'let the Chace be ever so tedious'. Overcoming his disappointment,

Middleton graciously replied that he would be proud for the world to know he had chosen Hervey to be his patron. Instead of ecclesiastical or academic preferment, however, Hervey was able to help him in a far more profitable way—with his literary patronage.

As long ago as December 1734 Middleton had revealed that he was beginning work on a biography of Cicero, and Hervey had encouraged him enthusiastically. From the outset he pressed on him the idea that the book should not deal merely with the life but with the times of the Roman. His interest in it from the beginning was persistent, almost obsessive; in his own mind he was helping to recreate for his era the portrait of a great Roman in a golden age. For the next few years he continually prodded, cajoled, nagged, but Middleton's progress was snail-like. At last, in August 1738, he sent Hervey the pleasing news that the book was completed, and that a fair copy was being made, which he would send him in sections to read and correct.

Hervey read the first three packets of manuscript promptly, and praised them with his customary delicacy and tact, while suggesting various changes, from minor stylistic ones to the addition of 'an Exordium to the whole, giving a short Account of the State of Rome at that Period in which Cicero was born, & lived: with a little Deduction of the various transitions by which the Empire fell into that opulent, corrupt, factious, formidable, & powerfull Situation in which your Hero found it'. (Middleton included in his preface to the book as published an outline of the Roman government from its founding by Romulus to the birth of Cicero.) Hervey had persisted in advising not the mere biography of Cicero but the story of his times. Clearly he was involving himself as closely as he could with the book. The grateful author then divulged that he intended to dedicate the work to him—which, Hervey tells him, 'is what I shall be so proud of, that instead of thinking I do you a Favour, it is one I would have ask'd of you, if I had not been afray'd I might either have deprived you of making use of some Name which would do you more honor, or deprived my-self of the Pleasure by anticipating your Choice, of seeing you make that Determination voluntaryly'.

As the sections of manuscript arrived he read them aloud to Princess Caroline. 'She is charm'd with it,' he told Middleton, '& say'd whilst I was present before all her own Family, in her own apartment the other night (where the King constantly sups) that it was the prettyest & most entertaining thing she ever read in her Life.' The grateful author was no doubt dazzled to have a Royal audience. Even with his court duties and political chores during the next session of Parliament, Hervey found time to read and comment on his friend's work, continuing to offer suggestions, some of them substantial ones of content, others trivial, such as (Lady Hervey later recalled) blotting out 'many low words and collegiate phrases'.

One of Hervey's suggestions, far more important to Middleton's future, was that the book should be published by subscription. (Middleton later assured Thomas Townshend, his other patron, that 'agreeably to your advice, I am perswaded to publish by subscription'.) Such a plan, if a sufficiently large number of subscribers were enrolled, could be very profitable to a writer, who would thus keep all the profits, after paying the printer, without sharing them with booksellers. (Pope, after all, had established his fortune by publishing his Homer translations in this way.) By the winter of 1739 the book was so far advanced that Hervey could make specific suggestions for issuing the terms of subscription—two volumes to cost two guineas. Since Middleton, aware of a less affluent circle than Hervey's, feared that two guineas was too high, he planned to publish another issue as well, on small paper, for one and a half guineas. He also wrote a Proposal to be printed as an advertisement for the work, and even had it corrected by Hervey (who changed 'handsomely printed' to 'printed in the best manner'.) The arrangement devised was that subscribers to both printings should pay one guinea to start, and their Receipts would entitle them to the first volume of the large- or the small-paper issue, as they designated; and they would receive the second volume on payment of the balance.

When the Proposals were printed Middleton sent a number of them to Townshend and to Hervey. Both patrons immediately began to spread them, Hervey far more strenuously. For he soon asked Middleton to send him Receipts, which had also been printed. Only a week later he needed more Proposals and at least one hundred more Receipts. Since he was recovering from his illness and confined to the palace except for an airing he used emissaries; General Churchill was one of the most industrious. A few days later he begged for more Proposals and Receipts—he was writing to everybody he knew, even Chesterfield at Bath, seizing all he could lay hold of himself, and sending messages everywhere by his friends. One of them, Mrs. Horner, sold Lord Orrery a subscription. Another wrote to Horace Walpole, then in Paris on his Grand Tour; and Horace sold four and took three for himself. 'I pique my-self,' Hervey told Middleton, 'as I advised the Work & the manner of publishing it, upon making this Subscription the most universal one that was ever known in England . . . I look upon it as my affair as much as Yours.' More Proposals, more Receipts, was his constant cry.

When Hervey enrolled members of the Royal Family, Middleton was particularly grateful for 'what I may literally call a Royal list of Subscribers' and he confessed that he was no longer ashamed of having decided to issue the work by subscription. (Perhaps his shame was connected with his recollection that he had attacked Richard Bentley in 1720 for proposing to issue by subscription an edition of the *New Testament*; he had called it Bentley's Bubble, accusing him of basely selling scholarship and Holy Scripture.)

As the golden guineas rolled in, the result of Hervey's strenuous campaign, the exultant Middleton could not contain his gratitude. 'If I had ever entertained any doubt of Your Lordship's endeavours to serve me,' he assured him in April 1739, 'I now have fact & demonstration to confute all such scruples, but in truth, My Lord, I never did; I was deceived indeed a little in my notion of Your Lordship's power, which I measured by Your merit & my own wishes, & did not think it so difficult to procure somewhat for me, as I afterwards perceived it, tho' I could never penetrate the true reason.' Pleased with the success of his campaign, Hervey accepted the accolade modestly. But the book was still in manuscript, and he urged Middleton to deliver it to the printer so that the impatient subscribers who had laid out their guineas could have the volumes.

iv

The *Life of Cicero* was not the only book that engaged Hervey at this time. Algarotti's book had finally been published (in December 1737) as *Il Newtonianismo per le dame*, a set of six leisurely, elegant dialogues between the author and a lady named the Marchesa di E., outlining in non-technical language the Newtonian theories of light and colour. When Hervey received his copy of it a few months later, he thanked its author for the 'delightfull Book' and promised that he would lend it to all his friends who had sense and could read Italian. After carefully reading it himself he paid tribute to its author:

> When the gay Sun no more his Rays shall boast,
> And human Eyes their Faculty have lost;
> Then shall these Colours and these Opticks die,
> Thy Wit and Learning in oblivion lie;
> England no more record her *Newton*'s Fame,
> And *Algarotti* be an unknown name.

Flattery could hardly go further.

Algarotti's other ardent admirer had been as unrestrained in her enthusiasm, assuring him, 'I have read, I have re-read, and I shall re-read your book. I shall always find new beauties; none of its charms escapes me.' And since Lady Mary could dissolve into couplets as easily as Hervey she also sent Algarotti her tribute. After praising his 'dark Truths' and gay style, the one so mature and the other so youthful, she found her concluding metaphor in the *Old Testament*:

> So *Eden* rose, as we in *Moses* find,
> (The only Emblem of thy happy mind)
> Where ev'ry charm of ev'ry season meets,
> The Fruit of Autumn mix'd with vernal sweets.

Lady Mary, a full generation his senior, hopefully predicts the union of her autumnal charms with his vernal ones; Hervey, who looked so youthful, had no such need to rationalize. Algarotti proudly printed both poems, along with one from Voltaire and two other English admirers, in an enlarged edition of his dialogues published in Naples the following year.

But his book had not been well received by his countrymen— the first edition had been put on the Index—and he took stock of his future career. Through his brother he tried to win an appointment in the secret service of the Venetian state, but failed He then asked his brother to pay his way to England, with the assurance that there he would have the most promising opportunities with rich and important people (including Lady Mary and Lord Hervey). He then left Italy accompanied by a charming young man named Firmacon, who had beguiled his stay in Milan; and they began a leisurely tour of Provence.

His English friends, suffering from their abominable climate, thought of him in similar fashion. Lady Mary could not forget him, as she complains that a cursed toothache and factious politics —perhaps in *The Nonsense of Common-Sense*—make her dull 'when the Sun and you are both so distant from me; may the spring bring a return of both'. This may have encouraged him to promise Hervey in April 1738 that he would return to England before long. 'So shall the clouds be dispersed,' Hervey replies, 'that have hung over the sanguine wishes I have form'd for this last year of seeing you once more in England;' and he hoped that Algarotti was even half as eager to see him as his letter set forth. How neat that Hervey and Lady Mary should both see him as a celestial metaphor!—dispersing the clouds as he accompanies the sun.

Algarotti, in no hurry to brighten the English horizon, had remained in France; and during the winter of 1739 he stayed in Paris. His friends there did not regard his book very generously. Madame du Châtelet was particularly catty for two reasons: it was not, as she had hoped it would be, dedicated to her (Fontenelle had that honour); and it was a rival of Voltaire's own book on Newton. From Cirey, her house in Lorraine, she told Algarotti how much she envied him his imminent journey to England, where (she says) everybody is a *philosophe*; and she charged him to ask Hervey why he had not replied to a letter from Voltaire on that subject. Hervey was more attentive to Algarotti's letters and book. As with the subscriptions for Middleton's *Cicero* he had no compunction in recommending the Newtonian dialogues to political adversaries; he presented a copy to Lord Carteret, a man of formidable erudition, who (he then informed Algarotti) 'commended it for the matter, manner, and style so much, that he is not more profuse of his invectives against the administration, than he is lavish in your praises'.

Hervey also sent a copy to James Thomson, though only at the request of Algarotti, who admired him as 'ce nerveux poete, peintre de la nature'. But Hervey did not agree with his friend's admiration for the nature poet, and begged him not to quote from Thomson's poem on Newton, 'for he is an Author so little esteem'd, or rather so much decry'd, by all People of good Taste in this Country, that it will not do credit to any Body that cites him as an authority for any thing: he is an obscure, bombast,

LADY MARY WORTLEY MONTAGUE.

15. Lady Mary Wortley Montagu, 1739

laborious, *Diseur des riens*'. Hervey's harsh opinion was based less on the poet's verse than on his activity as a vociferous supporter of the Opposition and of the Prince of Wales, from whom he received a pension. Newtonianism and not politics was Algarotti's concern.

Lady Mary directed her attention and enthusiasm not so much on the book as on its author. She had already proposed to him that if he did not return to England she would not hesitate to retire to Venice, where they could live together. Now, while he stayed in Paris, so tantalizingly near, she confesses her fear that he is forgetting her 'before the eyes of some Parisienne Idol, painted and gilded, who receives (perhaps without appreciation) the homage that would make all my happiness'. Apparently the reason Algarotti did not cross the Channel to be reunited with her (and his other English friends) was that he needed financial assistance, and Lady Mary came to his rescue. 'You can believe,' she writes, 'that I am very much happier to facilitate your return than your departure.' She sent him a bill of exchange, and when it proved to be not easily negotiable she sent another. It was not long, then, before he reached London—in March 1739.

At first he visited Andrew Mitchell, a young man who had left Scotland to make his fortune in England, a member of the Royal Society, who had recently been called to the Bar. Algarotti stayed only a short time with him in his chambers in the Middle Temple, then moved to Hervey's apartment in St. James's Palace, and from there to Lord Burlington's villa at Chiswick. He was apparently seeking patronage of some sort, though it is difficult to guess what preferment could be found for an Italian in England. He and Hervey at least enjoyed each other's company. He probably read sections of Middleton's *Life of Cicero*, for he began to write a life of Caesar (which he never completed). In May he saw published an English version of his dialogues for ladies translated by a learned lady, Elizabeth Carter, under the title of *Sir Isaac Newton's Philosophy Explained*; it spread his fame among readers unfamiliar with Italian.

In London Algarotti had met Prince Antioch Cantemir, the Russian ambassador since 1733, a cultivated young man and accomplished poet, who greatly admired his book of Newtonian dialogues (which he later translated into Russian). Prince Cantemir encouraged the Italian to widen his horizons by travelling to Russia when an opportunity should arise. Then, unexpectedly, that spring Lord Baltimore invited Algarotti to accompany him to St. Petersburg for the marriage of the Czarina's niece, heiress to the throne, to a German prince. Baltimore, a seaman by training, a Fellow of the Royal Society, was still attached to the Prince of Wales. (His yacht was named the *Augusta*, after the Princess.) He may have lacked the intellectual interests that appealed to Algarotti—in Queen Caroline's opinion, he thought he understood everything but understood nothing, and was besides a little mad—but since Algarotti aspired to shine in a diplomatic post he hoped that Baltimore's quasi-diplomatic mission might lead to one, or perhaps to patronage from the Prince of Wales. His introduction to the Russian court would also be smoothed by a letter of introduction from Prince Cantemir to the foreign minister in St. Petersburg. On 21 May, after a sojourn of only about two months in England, he sailed from Gravesend.

Aboard the *Augusta* was a collection of machines for demonstrating experimental philosophy, owned by a man also on his way to St. Petersburg. 'What, however, undoubtedly excels them', Algarotti informs Hervey in his first letter, 'is our ample provisions of lemons and exquisite wines; and, above all, our French cook.' If Hervey, as a dedicated vegetarian and non-drinker, could not taste those pleasures, he could savour the conclusion of his friend's letter: 'Vouchsafe, my Lord, not to forget a poor traveller, who, sailing to the North-east, casts his eyes from time to time upon the rhumb of the compass that is to guide him back to you.'

v

During his voyage and visit in St. Petersburg Algarotti favoured Hervey with lengthy letters, mostly about Russia, though he remembered to add personal remarks as affectionate as Hervey could have wished. 'Adieu, my Lord, continue to love me, and sometimes think of me' concludes his first one from the Russian capital. In his next, after a long disquisition on the Russian army, he remembers Hervey's dietary regimen: 'I embrace you, my Lord. May the excellent milk which your fine park of St. James's furnishes you with in plenty, and the puddings which are your food, long preserve you in perfect health!'

Lady Mary would have been happy to receive such affectionate and solicitous messages; perhaps she did. Her response was far more intense than Hervey's, for she was now about to leave England, abandoning home, family, and friends to live with Algarotti in Venice. (Poor health was her declared reason for going abroad; only Hervey, of those she left behind, knew her real motive.) In July, on the day before her departure, she sent Algarotti a short fervent letter: 'At last I depart tomorrow with the Resolution of a man well persuaded of his Religion and happy in his conscience, filled with faith and hope . . . If I find you such as you have sworn to me, I find the Elysian Fields, and Happiness beyond imagining.' By then he had left Russia, and was sailing to Danzig; there he and Lord Baltimore disembarked to begin a brief tour of the German States.

When Hervey's love for Algarotti had been in its first flush he regarded Lady Mary as his rival; now that her passion had driven her into exile he became her sympathetic confidant. Her first letter to him was so festive, he tells her, that 'it was a sort of Insult to one who you knew was lamenting your Departure, to show you thought you had left nothing behind you worth lamenting . . . As to your proposing to me to follow you, unless you could give me the same motive that you have for jolting in Post-Chaises & lying in dirty Inns, I do not see I should get much by taking your Advice'; and he sends her a generous benediction in verse:

. . . . .

> May all the Transports jealous Minds suggest
> Are tasted in a happy Rival's Breast,
> And all the Envious fancy we enjoy,
> Gild ev'ry Scene, & ev'ry Sense employ;
> May ev'ry Hour in gay Succession move,
> Your Days all Luxury, your Nights all Love.

And he sent along a letter for her from the one who, he predicts, will be the partner of her days and nights.

He passed most of the summer at Kensington until early in September when he and Lady Hervey went to Bath to take the waters and enjoy the social life there. He did both moderately. His health was excellent, and instead of going to the Pump Room in the morning he preferred to stay in his lodgings to read for many hours. Several of his friends were there—the Duke and Duchess of Manchester, Dr. Cheyne, and his political rivals, Scarborough and Chesterfield, with whom social friendship continued.

The previous autumn he had quarrelled with Stephen Fox because of a letter that Stephen had resented as officious and impertinent; and he had replied sharply, promising to avoid offending him in the future 'by not only putting an end to this Letter, but troubling you with no more'. They had somehow become reconciled by 20 June 1739, when Hervey accompanied him, his child-bride, and her chaperon-mother for a visit to Redlinch. At the same time, through Hervey's efforts and certainly his own demonstrated fidelity to the Ministry, Stephen was appointed Joint-Secretary of the Treasury, a lucrative post of £3,000 a year.

The Fox brothers were at Maddington when they heard that Hervey and his wife were at Bath, and they immediately sent over some game and an invitation to Hervey to visit them. He declined, adding that 'if the Maddington Mahomets will come to the Bath Mountain' he would be 'unspeakably glad' to see them. On 3 October Henry left to visit Bath for a few days, after all, in the company of the Duke of Marlborough.

The stream of letters that Algarotti had been sending to Hervey was interrupted while he and Lord Baltimore visited Potsdam and Berlin, where King Frederick William of Prussia entertained them. Algarotti had heard so much from Voltaire about Crown Prince Frederick that he and Lord Baltimore went on to Rheinsberg, where they spent about a week at his court. Algarotti and Frederick, of equal ages and similar tastes, were immediately attracted to each other. The Prince was 'the lover and the favourite of the Muses', Algarotti boasted to Hervey, and 'the most intelligent and most amiable of men', who when he ascended the throne would prove to be one of the greatest of sovereigns. The two travellers then made their way to Hamburg to board the *Augusta* for their return to England. Algarotti had time for a last letter to Hervey: 'I fervently invoke that blustering East wind, so much an enemy to your countrymen, to blow soon, and waft me speedily to your Lordship at St. James's. I believe, my Lord, that I do not presume too much upon your friendship for me, in flattering myself, that, in your fine Park, "a votive heifer is fattening against [my] return". '

Personal in only brief passages, Algarotti's *Letters on Russia* were probably based on his copies of actual letters sent to Hervey, and then, for publication, expanded with ample guidebook information. He favoured other friends with more informal, intimate letters. From Hamburg he also advised Andrew Mitchell of his expected return to England. Instead of trying to relate everything he has heard and seen on his recent travels, he prefers to wait until they can sup together in London, he writes, 'where you will certainly be the tastiest dish for me [*le meilleur plat pour moi*] . . . If the wind continues as it is, I hope to embrace you in 4 or 5 days. Farewell, my dear friend; love me and believe until death, F.A.'

Only two days after receiving Algarotti's letter from Hamburg, Hervey (still at Bath) was agreeably surprised with another from London. The prodigal traveller had returned, though not to a fatted calf from St. James's Park. Hervey was 'infinitely rejoiced', he assured him, 'to find that a Russian Summer, which cools the Sun it-self, has not in so many months been able so far to cool the warmth' of his friend's affection. Perhaps his own warmth had cooled, for although Algarotti suggested joining him in Bath, he planned to stay there until the end of October and only cautiously extended an invitation: 'if you continue your Resolution of coming hither, I hope whenever you are not asleep, you will not think of being any where but at my Lodgings;' and after a flourish at the end of his letter, a simple 'Adieu'.

Apparently Algarotti, who occupied lodgings in Bond Street, was content to remain there; he had other friends nearby with whom he could spend his waking hours. Of his more distant acquaintance, Prince Frederick of Prussia still felt the power of his charm, and told Voltaire and Madame du Châtelet how enchanting he had found Algarotti; he assured 'the Swan of Padua' himself: 'Always remember the friends you have made here by simply showing yourself, and imagine what would be the result if we had the pleasure of possessing you forever.' Three persons of different rank and in different places wished to possess Algarotti —Hervey, Lady Mary, and the Crown Prince of Prussia. For the time being he cautiously waited to see where and to whom his destiny would lead him.

vi

While Hervey lingered on at Bath, taking the waters, gossiping, and reading, important political events were occurring in London, one of them directly concerned with him. The cabinet appointment of Lord Privy Seal was about to become vacant by the resignation of Lord Godolphin. Walpole persuaded him to postpone stepping down until a successor could be chosen, and that successor, he decided, would be Hervey. Perhaps, as some thought, instead of being Walpole's choice Hervey had 'the King's ear and favour'. Or, perhaps, Walpole was at last fulfilling the promises, made so often and so vaguely, of rewarding Hervey for the services he had (by now) been performing for ten years. Whatever the reason, he was Walpole's candidate at least as early as October 1739, against the most strenuous opposition from Newcastle.

At a meeting with Walpole at Claremont, Newcastle had made such angry remonstrances against Hervey's appointment that they had a 'violent altercation'. Determined to prevent the appointment, Newcastle appealed to his friend Hardwicke, the Lord Chancellor and also an enemy of Hervey's, pointing out how harmful it would be to both of them, to his brother Henry Pelham, and to the Duke of Grafton (the Lord Chamberlain). The world would assume that Hervey's advancement was intended to render him powerless. He therefore proposed that the four allies block the appointment by threatening to resign, thus forcing Walpole to choose between Hervey and them. They were evidently unwilling to go to such extremes; and when Newcastle was prepared to resign by himself he was persuaded by Hardwicke to submit and to make his peace with Walpole.

In his determination to block Hervey's appointment Newcastle even intrigued with the Opposition. After offering the Seal to Carteret, who consented to accept it, he moved that the Cabinet-council offer it to him. When Walpole said that he did not know whether Carteret would accept it, Newcastle replied that he could answer for him. Walpole then said, 'I always suspected you had been dabbling there, now I know it; but if you make such bargains, I don't think myself obliged to keep them.' Newcastle was defeated again.

Walpole resisted Newcastle's threats, according to one explanation, because he was being bullied from another quarter—by the cabal made up of Hervey, at the head, and Winnington, the two Fox brothers, and Charles Hanbury Williams; their 'violent and obstinate importunity and pressure' had forced him first to give

Stephen his appointment to the Treasury and then to designate Hervey for the post of Lord Privy Seal. Whether or not this is true, Newcastle's opposition to Hervey's appointment certainly succeeded in forcing Walpole to delay making any, while Godolphin obligingly remained in office.

Far more important than this squabble, in the autumn of 1739, was the worsened state of affairs with Spain. In spite of Walpole's attempt to maintain peace, the spirit of the country as well as the King's insistence forced him to declare war (on 19 October). The general frenzy of excitement throughout the nation did not send Hervey back to London; he waited out his two months' sojourn in Bath, returning to St. James's at the end of the month, in good time to prepare for the Parliamentary session called for mid-November.

The Address of Thanks for the King's opening Speech, attacked by Carteret, was conspicuously defended by Hervey, who pleaded for unity in time of war. The Address was then accepted as originally framed. Hervey probably helped write it, for he was able to send a draft to Middleton two days before it was spoken from the throne. The sittings that followed were remarkably peaceful, as Hervey tells Lady Mary: 'we have War abroad & Peace at home, for so quiet a Session was never known.' Both Houses almost unanimously voted the money requested by the Administration for land and sea forces. It seemed to him that the Opposition 'pretend to hate Spain, & really hate one another so heartyly that the ministerial objects of their former Resentment seem to be entirely forgot'. The month's session was so peaceful, in fact, that he hardly bothered to attend.

He had ample time now to enjoy the pleasure of being with Algarotti. They dined together, and occasionally walked in St. James's Park discussing such topics as Classical inscriptions. Algarotti seemed content to remain in England instead of joining Lady Mary in Venice, where she awaited him. Hervey, knowing of her dissatisfaction, wished to be helpful, but she gave him no instructions, and (as he told her) he generally preferred tacit to loquacious errors. Perhaps she needed no intermediary because she herself wrote frequently to Algarotti, and it would have been embarrassing to ask Hervey to extract replies from her neglectful friend. Algarotti finally wrote to her himself (in December) with the astonishing suggestion that they should live in Paris instead of Venice. She was roused to anger: 'You must remember that you agreed with me to live in the Venetian states . . . I have arranged all my affairs on this plan, and it is not possible for me to go to Paris, even if I had a Desire to, which I am very far from having.' She would be content with her life in Venice, she tells him, 'if it were not troubled by the remembrance of an ingrate who has forgotten me in an Exile that he caused'.

As her confidant Hervey knew of her frustration. One wonders whether Algarotti, when he received her angry letter, also confided in him. While writing a letter to her, Hervey paused to tell her: 'I had written thus far when our Friend came into the Room. I did not tell him to whom I was writing, and as you decline giving me any Directions for my Conduct, am at a Loss to know what sort of Conduct I should hold.' He then administers some good-natured teasing: 'what I really believe . . . is that as a Venetian when you was at London made you forget every Englishman, a Piedmonteze at Venice will make you forget every Venetian.' At least Hervey profited by her disappointed rendezvous, for he had more of Algarotti's company to himself.

The Parliamentary session that resumed in January 1740 remained relatively peaceful. Hervey did not attend until 21 February, and a week later spoke briefly on a procedural matter. A more important measure, passed by the Commons and debated in the House of Lords on 19 March, was the Opposition's perennial attempt to bedevil the Administration with a Pension Bill— that Members of Parliament should declare upon oath whether they held pensions from the crown, and that the House should decide whether these were 'just rewards'. Hervey attacked the bill with the arguments that it would embarrass the virtuous and be eluded by the vicious; the House of Commons would become an inquisition on the occasion of any gift, however trifling, from the Crown; and he concluded with a medical metaphor: an ineffectual remedy to a disease prevents the search for a truly effective one. The bill was defeated by a majority of twelve.

Hervey's appointment as Lord Privy Seal was still pending. As long ago as December he had cautioned Middleton to suspend printing the sheet of the dedication to the *Life of Cicero* in order to avoid the 'trouble of reprinting it upon an Alteration in the Title you must give me; what this Alteration will be I am obliged as yet to keep secret'. When Middleton read, in a newspaper a

month later, that Hervey was to be made Secretary of State—
could it have resulted from rumours of Newcastle's resignation?—
he immediately congratulated him. The report was wrong,
Hervey told him, though he could not yet divulge the truth.
Not until April could he reveal his definite appointment; and on
1 May 1740 he became Lord Privy Seal.

14

A Dedicatory Epistle

1740–1

As LORD PRIVY SEAL, Hervey could no longer occupy the Vice-Chamberlain's apartments at St. James's and the other palaces—which along with his gold key went to his successor, Lord Sidney Beauclerk, M.P. and son of the Duke of St. Albans. He rented instead a house in Grosvenor Street. He did not move there with his family for more than a month (on 9 June), and even then all was confusion, with workmen still engaged on alterations, and furniture scattered about helterskelter. Before moving from the palace, he had informed Lady Mary of his new appointment:

This is the last Letter, dear Madam, you will recieve from me dated from this Place, for this Morning I resign'd the Gold-Key that intitles me to reside here—nor do I flatter my-self that you are in great Pain till you hear whether Disgrace or Promotion is the Occasion of this Change; & as I hope that your long distance & absence, tho they leave you in a total Ignorance of what relates to me, have not reduced you to a total Indifference to what does so, I will keep you no longer in Suspense, but let you know the King has been so gracious as to reward my little Services with the great Dignity of Keeper of his Privy-Seal.

His great dignity made him a member of the Cabinet Council, the august body whose deliberations he had ridiculed as an outsider; and that mocking spirit did not desert him now that he found himself among them. Only a few days after his appointment he attended the first Council meeting at the Cockpit. He was one of fourteen; and without taking any part in its discussion he kept minutes of the topics discussed—mainly navy movements in Mediterranean and American waters and the King's speech to end the Parliamentary session. He noted how much time was wasted on fatuities and trivialities, mostly the fault of his *bête noire*

JOHN LORD HERVEY *Lord Privy Seal in the Reign of* KING George 2.

16. Lord Hervey as Lord Privy Seal

Newcastle. Perhaps for that reason he absented himself for the next few meetings. At last, at the third council meeting that he attended he spoke up. By the terms of a treaty with Sweden—whose King was the Landgrave of Hesse—England was to have 6,000 Hessian soldiers. Since a clause in the treaty forbade the troops from being used against Sweden, Hervey proposed to alter this so that it would stipulate that the troops could not be used to *attack* Sweden, a necessary distinction since without it England would be forbidden from defending her allies from Swedish aggression should any occur. Most of the council, he thought, stared and wondered at his speaking so plainly, but he insisted on the word *attack*, and when Walpole supported his point the others agreed at once, saying, 'To be sure, to be sure; these sort of things can never be made too plain.'

He interjected another comment at the meeting—that the Duke of Newcastle's long speculation (taking one and a half hours) about orders to be sent to an admiral at sea was pointless since they could not possibly reach the fleet in time to be acted upon. Perhaps, as a modern historian has remarked, Hervey was 'a lightweight in council'; his talent and usefulness lay rather in assisting such a formidable heavy-weight as Walpole.

Between the rising of Parliament (on 29 April) and the King's departure for Hanover a fortnight later, a Royal marriage was to be celebrated, that between Princess Mary and Prince Frederick of Hesse, heir to his uncle the King of Sweden. When the ceremonial procedures were detailed at the Cabinet Council, one difficulty arose from the fact that since the King would not be put to the expense of bringing the Prince to England for the marriage, nor would he demean his daughter by sending her to Germany unmarried, the ceremony would have to be performed in London with the Prince represented by proxy. This would cause complications in the marriage service to be read, as Walpole tried to explain to the King. The King's stubborn reply, imprudently repeated by Walpole to the Council, was: 'I will hear no more of your Church nonsense, nor of your law nonsense—I will have my daughter married here, and will have the marriage complete.' And thus it was—in the Chapel Royal of St. James's one evening, with the Duke of Cumberland acting as the bridegroom's proxy.

In the previous Royal marriage, that of the Princess Royal to the Prince of Orange, Hervey had aroused Lord Egmont's animosity by insisting that the Irish peers march behind the English in the procession, with the result that they had boycotted the ceremony. This time the Lord Chamberlain had assured Egmont that he might walk among the English peers—'So this day our claim of precedency received a confirmation', he complacently noted in his diary. Hervey had cause for complacency on his own account; as Lord Privy Seal he marched in the procession ahead of the dukes. The following day he had to dress in great haste (after writing a gossipy letter to Lady Mary) 'in order to pass the Day most agreeably in the Succession of a Levee, a Drawing-Room, a Feast, & a Ball'.

A week later the King, having announced: 'We have determined (by the Blessing of God) for divers weighty Reasons speedily to go in Person beyond the Seas' departed for Hanover. An unreasonable journey, some of the courtiers thought, since he could just as well stay in England with his mistress; and besides England was at war with Spain and on the brink of war with France. It was said that his only reason for going, with Madame von Wallmoden in tow, was to enable her to divorce her husband, a legality requiring her presence in Hanover. By virtue of Hervey's being Lord Privy Seal, the King appointed him one of the sixteen Lords Justices who were to rule in his absence abroad. It was the first time he served, and he took his new duties seriously enough to attend meetings at the end of May and throughout June.

ii

Algarotti had stayed in London through the spring of 1740, no doubt pleased to see his friend elevated to such a high government post. Perhaps he exercised the same finesse as Voltaire, who had congratulated Hervey by coupling his elevation with England's great victory in the West Indies the previous autumn: 'I compliment your nation, milord, on the capture of Porto-Belo, & on your appointment as lord privy seal.' From Italy, Algarotti had received a compliant plea from Lady Mary, whose anger had worn away, to choose another rendezvous if Venice did not suit him. But from Prussia he received more welcome letters from Crown Prince Frederick, mainly on literary subjects, which he eagerly answered. When he commended some of Frederick's poetical epistles (in May) Frederick effusively thanked him as one who was so lovable that to know him was to desire him. Perhaps Algarotti remained in England because he awaited a more emphatic compliment from Berlin. For Frederick's father had been seriously ill, and by February had prepared himself for death and spoken openly to his heir of the succession. On 20 May o.s. he died.

'My dear Algarotti,' wrote the new King of Prussia a few days later, 'my destiny has changed. I await you impatiently; don't let me languish for you.' The intimate, impatient summons made a deep impression on Algarotti. (He did not know, however, that Frederick had sent exactly the same note to his old tutor.) But the handsome Baron Keyserlingk, Frederick's prime favourite, added some verse to Algarotti's summons:

> Come, Algarotti, from the shores of the Thames,
> To share with us our fortunate destiny.
> Hasten your journey to these agreeable places;
> You will find here *Liberty* as the motto.

Algarotti departed for Berlin in such haste that he left some of his belongings at Hervey's house, clothes as well as furs (probably acquired during his visit to Russia); and since his funds were low, he borrowed money from Lady Hervey for his journey. Lady Mary apparently knew nothing of his summons and hasty departure.

He left London on Friday 6 June. For some reason Hervey could not bid him farewell in person, and so sent a note on the eve of his departure to tell him: 'I do not know whether I am sorry or glad not to have seen you . . . I wish you all sort of Good, & beg you not only not to forget me, but often to let me know you remember me; & to relate every Particular of your Reception, Continuation, & Occupation where you are going. Adieu.' In a postscript he implored Algarotti to write as soon as he landed in Holland.

Hervey's anxiety to hear from Algarotti after he reached Berlin had another motive besides personal affection, for the accession of Frederick to the Prussian throne introduced an unknown element into European politics. His father had been unfriendly to England, and his own attitude would soon be revealed. If Algarotti could send Hervey political gossip he would be able to make good use of it. Lady Mary had already offered to send political intelligence to Walpole from Venice, where she consorted with the Prince of Saxony and the diplomatic corps as well as the patricians; but Hervey, writing on Walpole's behalf, had declined her offer with an elaborately polite refusal. In that same letter to her he added a postscript with deliberate casualness: 'I am at present in great Affliction for the Loss of my Friend Algarotti, who left England last Friday for the Court of Berlin on a Summons he recieved from the new King of Prussia, and a very kind one, under his own Hand, before he had been five Days on the throne.'

Obedient to Hervey's request Algarotti sent word as soon as he reached land; and Hervey was more than ordinarily pleased (he tells him) 'with your early Punctuality in writing to me from Utrecht, as it gave me an agreable Ernest of your being no more likely to forget a very useless, tho a very faithfull Friend, than you are of being forgotten'. He did not doubt that Algarotti's merit would be rewarded by the King's ability to discern and distinguish it; and he was impatient to hear his sentiment confirmed. Lady Mary's expectation was very different. When she read Hervey's laconic news she sent a short note to be forwarded to Algarotti. 'I fear that your great visit is doomed to be a great folly,' she tells him. 'In that case I shall see you late. But I shall wait with so much patience and submission that they should deserve extraordinary rewards.' The difference between Hervey's and Lady Mary's attitudes towards their friend's glamorous mission to Berlin clearly highlights the difference between his courtier-like sense of reality and her fantasy of a romantic idyll with the elusive Italian.

iii

With the coming of summer Hervey went on his customary round of country visits. After attending a meeting of the Lords Justices on 26 June he travelled down to Goodwood, the Duke of Richmond's seat in Sussex, accompanied by his wife and by the Chevalier Osorio, the Sardinian ambassador. As a holiday it was pleasingly relaxed, for the Duke and Duchess did not oppress their guests with excessive civilities and attention, but left them free to do what they wished. The informality of this ducal hospitality

could not have pleased him more, he tells Algarotti. 'Our Manner
of living here is so thoroughly pastoral that we are seldom in the
House but when the Sun is in America; but the Magnificent is . . .
mix'd with the Rural . . . We dine every Day in the Garden, or
four Miles off under Tents in the Forest, where Jacquesmare [the
French chef], like a Circe or an Armida, seems to produce a Feast
which Patronius need not have been ashamed of providing,
merely by Enchantment.' Although Sir John Norris's squadron
of ships and the encampment on the Isle of Wight were less than
twenty miles away, he refused an invitation to see them because
(he quips) these were things he understood better upon paper
than upon earth and water. He spent ten days on this pleasant
visit.

In London again, he resumed his attendance at the meetings of
the Lords Justices but only for a few days. On 10 July he 'desired
leave to go out of town', and two days later accompanied Walpole, Hanbury Williams, and some others to Houghton. The
jovial house-party mixed poetry with politics when a ballad
written by Pulteney was answered at length by Hanbury Williams,
perhaps with the help of the others. Williams was a wealthy
young M.P. whose conspicuous loyalty to Walpole had already
earned for him the appointment of Paymaster of Marines (worth
£2,000 a year).

On his way to Norfolk, Hervey had stopped at Ickworth for
three days. His children were again there, but Lady Bristol was
to some extent reconciled to it because she had to see them only
at dinner. The eldest girl, Lepell, seventeen years old at the time,
sent word to her father in London (at the end of August) that
Lady Bristol continued to be civil. In reply he tells her that
whenever the 'variableness of her temper shall make her otherwise than civil, let me know, & I will send for you away.' He
was indifferent to the abuse his mother uttered against him, he
tells Lepell, since it was unbecoming for him to feud with her;
and 'considering her Age & the Infirmitys of her Mind & Body,
I assure you I often feel Compassion for her, & never any Resentment to her'.

That Hervey arranged for his daughter to be educated in
science was another source of irritation to Lady Bristol. Thomas
Wright of Durham, who had been at Ickworth previously, had
tutored Lepell in London (in January 1740). Lady Bristol now

complained to the Duchess of Marlborough that the 'most learned Ladys'—probably Lepell and her sister Mary—had been 'learning Algebra; and studying the Globes and all the stars in the Firmament, besides measureing my Lord's land. All these things occassiond so many hard words at dinner that I begd to have a Dictionary lye ypon the table to help my understanding in explaining of them.' Her ambition, she tells the Duchess, was only to enjoy peace and quiet in her old age, for she had neither health nor spirits to keep a boarding school for other people's children (her grandchildren) to the exclusion of her own.

In London Hervey again sat with the Lords Justices, but, as expected, no important business came before them, the King being in Hanover and Parliament recessed. On 13 October, finally, after delays of one sort or another, the King arrived home. He had failed to arrange a meeting with the King of Prussia to establish more friendly relations between their countries.

Hervey himself was not unknown to the Prussian King. For when young Lord Holdernesse, who had been in Berlin, returned to London he brought compliments to Hervey from the King. Hervey felt that an answer was 'absolutely necessary'; and how better to convey it than through Algarotti, to whom he explained,

I am not very diffident of the Propriety either of the Substance, Expression, or manner with which my thanks for the great Honor he has done me will be convey'd, when I beg the favor of you, with full Powers, to say whatever you think fit on that Occasion; & if his Majesty from his Ignorance of me can be induced to think your Words mine, I have no doubt of his approving extreamly what I say by Proxy, how incapable soever I might be of discharging that Duty agreably to his Expectation & my own Inclination if I were to do it without such an Embassador & auxiliary.

Perhaps his calling Algarotti an ambassador was meant to be literal as well as figurative. For Algarotti had asked his Royal master to send him on a diplomatic mission to England. With his customary tact Frederick replied that he was reserving him for more propitious opportunities (*bonnes occasions*). A more complicated reason why he could not make such an appointment was that Algarotti did not have a suitable rank. Frederick had informed King George (in Hanover) that the Prussian envoy to London would be a man of quality; but then, when a commoner was designated (Klingkraft by name), Lord Harrington, Secretary of

State, determined to send an English commoner in exchange. Thereupon the Prussians substituted a nobleman, Graf von Waldburg-Zeil, and the English matched him with the Earl of Hyndford. In spite of his rosy expectations, then, Algarotti remained simply a friend of the King and as yet unrewarded with any substantial or official favour.

iv

In the Parliamentary session that opened on 18 November 1740 the Opposition's strategy was to accuse Walpole of mismanaging the war against Spain and to harass him with demands that he reveal diplomatic and military letters, orders, and instructions. In the House of Lords, Hervey staunchly continued to defend his chief. It was proposed, to begin with, that the Address of Thanks be general rather than specific in listing the achievements of the previous session; the amendment was defeated. When the Opposition next demanded (on 1 and 8 December) that the Ministry's instructions to Admirals Vernon and Haddock be laid before the Lords, Hervey argued that this would be both a security risk and a foolhardy attempt to force a change of administration in time of war. Again the Ministry were successful. Hervey continued to defend them in important debates (on 9 December and 3 February 1741); and he spoke on such a trivial one (on 10 February) as that dealing with the seating arrangement of members of the House of Lords.

The most dramatic and crucial Parliamentary debate during that session was the Opposition's attempt (on 13 February) to remove Walpole from office. In the House of Commons the motion was introduced by Sandys, who blamed Walpole for England's misfortunes in foreign and domestic affairs and in the conduct of the war against Spain. He therefore proposed that an Address be presented to the King to remove Walpole 'from his majesty's presence and counsels for ever'. After the motion was seconded, Edward Wortley Montagu—a 'country Whig' since 1718— moved that Walpole leave the House while the charges against him were argued; but the motion was ordered withdrawn. (Lady Mary and her husband were as far apart in many ways as they now were geographically.) Stephen Fox was one of Walpole's most vigorous and distinguished defenders, and spoke extremely well. Walpole himself delivered a long speech in a most animated and dignified manner that made a deep impression on the House. The motion was defeated by an unusually large majority (290 to 106), the result of a schism between the Tories and dissident Whigs and of the secession of the independent Shippen and his followers, who usually voted with the Opposition.

In the House of Lords that day Carteret made the same motion. Hervey, one of the leading speakers against it, began by pointing out that the motion lay within the jurisdiction of the House of Commons, where the accused could be heard; and that the censure of the Lords was not harmless since it would convict a man without proof, and condemn him without a hearing: 'You would be worse than the Inquisition, if you would not hear the criminal. And if you did, you have no witness to confront him.' Other Ministerial speakers pursued the argument, and the motion was defeated there, again by a large majority (108 to 59). (Among those who signed the strong Protest was the implacable Lord Bristol.) The debate, lasting eleven hours, was considered by Hardwicke's son to be one of the finest ever heard there; and although he was fiercely inimical to Hervey he calls him one of the greatest speakers that day. And so Walpole remained, for the time being, as Prime Minister.

v

By the winter of 1740 the *Life of Cicero*, for which Hervey had exerted himself so strenuously, was finally ready to be published. Middleton planned an edition of 2,100 copies, and with the money so far received had been able to buy a farm near Cambridge, a 'little ragged house in a clean & sweet situation not far from the Newmarket road', where he hoped to entertain Hervey with the best milk and cheese from his dairy. When Hervey scolded him for delaying the publication of the book he had his excuses ready: the printing had been held up by the severe frost; then the paper from Italy had been delayed by the war at sea. As far back as May 1740, when Hervey had received the preface and final section of the book for his corrections he had merely praised them in general terms because he thought it more important to urge Middleton to have the book published as soon as possible; he did not try to conceal the impatience he and the many other subscribers felt.

In June 1740 Middleton had sent him a draft of the 'public Letter' or dedication, asking him to change what he thought unsuitable:

I have taken occasion, as you will observe, from the access which I have had to Your Lordship, & the opportunity of observing You in Your domestic life, to point out those particular passages of Your character which distinguish Your Lordship from the rest of the Nobility. If in any of them I have touched upon any point which it may be improper for me to meddle with, Your Lordship will be so good as to mark what you have scratched out, or give me some hint how I may reform it, which I shall readily execute as well as I am able.

Middleton's conception of his dedicatory epistle was clearly the same as that later expressed by Samuel Johnson, that 'the known style of a dedication is flattery. It professes to flatter.'

That Hervey read the dedication carefully is clear from his reply, sent a week later, in which after strenuously complimenting Middleton for his compliments, he continues: '& yet to let you know my thoughts on this Paper without any disguise, there are some few things in the first & second Page which I wish alter'd, as I think they may occasion some Sneers, which I dare say you would be as sorry to have your Words provoke, as you would to have them thought to import.' The dedication began with a eulogy of Cicero so elevated that no living man (Middleton states) can match his hero. 'You see, my Lord,' he continues, 'how much I trust to your good nature, as well as good sense, when in an *Epistle dedicatory*, the proper place of Panegyric, I am disparaging your abilities, instead of extolling them.' Hervey suggested that he change 'disparaging' to 'depreciating', and Middleton agreed.

Hervey also suggested omitting the phrase 'both in Prose & Verse'; it probably came in the passage where Middleton speaks of his patron's learned pastimes: 'for I have seen the solid effects of Your reading, in Your judicious reflections on the policy of those ancient Governments, and have felt Your weight even in controversy [*both in Prose and Verse*], on some of the most delicate parts of their History.' Why should Hervey have wanted that phrase deleted? Perhaps he feared that it would remind readers of the unsavoury attacks on him in Pulteney's pamphlet and Pope's satires. Yet while carefully expunging this reminder of his satiric past he let remain in it the material for a satiric future.

He had been far more concerned with Middleton's procrastination in putting the book through the press. A note of desperation had sounded in his complaint (in November 1740) of the importunity of the subscribers, 'who grow every day more impatient and more clamorous'. As the town filled up for the opening of Parliament, the subscribers would inquire and complain. Nearly two years had passed since he had begun to solicit subscriptions; and now, he tells Middleton, 'I know not what to say when ten times in a Day by different People I am ask'd—*Is Dr. Middleton's Cicero never to come out?* but that I expect every Day to see it advertised.' Busy as he was at the end of December with public and private business and with the 'tedious Forms and Ceremonys of a Wedding' in his family—his brother Felton's—he could at least congratulate Middleton on the absence of any further delays. February would be the best time for publication, he had suggested, since the business of Parliament would be pretty well over and the business of new elections not yet begun. Middleton then put an advertisement in the newspapers that his book would be published on 2 February 1741.

The subscribers' clamours were finally silenced when they received the handsome folio entitled *The History of the Life of Marcus Tullius Cicero*. They could take further pleasure in seeing their names printed in the twenty-three double-columned pages headed by the names of all five Royal princesses and the Duke of Cumberland, followed by a profusion of peers and peeresses including Hervey (twenty-five copies) and Lady Hervey (two); as well as Stephen Fox (five), Sir Robert Walpole (five), Mrs. Horner (five), Algarotti, Lady Mary Wortley Montagu—more than eighteen hundred names in all.

What is most remarkable in the flowery dedication, which was headed by a flamboyant print of Hervey's family crest and motto, is the amount of personal allusion to Hervey that it contains. Middleton obviously allowed himself such an expansive indulgence because he was very proud of his personal friendship with a peer in a high government post, for most dedications to well-known persons were written for a set fee by impecunious hacks who were generally not even acquainted with their patrons.

It was Hervey, writes Middleton, who advised him to undertake the life of Cicero, 'urged and exhorted' him to persist, and saw, corrected, and approved it before it went to press. Hervey, he continues, converses with the wits and scholars of the age, encourages literary conversation in his house; he rises early in the morning to engage with the Classical writers of Greece and Rome, a study made easier by greater leisure and health, resulting from his 'singular temperance in diet'. Thus, says Middleton in pursuit of a paradox, with all the accomplishments of a nobleman, Hervey leads the life of a philosopher, and while he shines as a principal ornament of the Court he practises the discipline of the College. The chief purpose of his dedicatory epistle, he concludes, is to thank Hervey for his friendship, and to tell the world of his share in encouraging and correcting the book and procuring its large subscription.

Although Middleton's *Life of Cicero* has a history of its own— half a century later he was posthumously accused of having plagiarized it from a seventeenth-century book—the dedication had an immediate and dramatic effect involving both the obsequious dedicator and the luckless dedicatee.

Elizabeth Robinson, soon to become Mrs. Montagu, and ultimately famous as a blue-stocking, had subscribed to the book. (She was related to Middleton by marriage, her grandmother having been his second wife.) As she tells a friend, she could not read beyond the dedication 'which I think a very good one & I wish for the sake of the Patron & Dedicator there was one word of it true. A Poetical licence is nothing in comparison of a dedica- tory Licence. Humility & prudence defend us from the Pride and folly of dedications; I had rather be hid in my obscurity than glare in the false light of panegyric.' This private comment was gentle and benign compared to what appeared in print a few months later.

The Death of M-L-N in the Life of Cicero was the title of an anonymous pamphlet issued in May 'By an Oxford Scholar'; and its ironic tone is set by the subtitle: 'Being a Proper Criticism on that Marvellous Performance' and by its dedication: 'To the Right Honourable, Right Reverend, Right Worshipful, Honour- able, Reverend, and Worshipful Subscribers to Dr. M—n's Life of Cicero. . . .' Although its main purpose is to attack the book, almost one quarter is a spirited ridicule of the dedication, in which Middleton (it says) has evaded responsibility for his blunders and misquotations: ''Tis plain enough, in troth, that he did not care what Censure he drew upon his Lordship, or he would never have blabb'd out this Secret: Nor would he have gone on to have boasted that *some Parts* of his Work had been *brighten'd by the Strokes of his Lordship's Pencil* . . .'

Obliquely Hervey was not spared his share of ridicule. 'For shame, for shame, Doctor. What talk to *my Lord Privy-Seal*, as if you was tattling to a *pretty Miss*? entertain a Peer of the Realm and a Privy-Counsellor with a *Lulla-by Baby-by*! Quite surfeiting! It has turned my Stomach to that Degree that I shall eat no more than his Patron to-day.' An anonymous scholar could have his fun in this way, but it was Hervey's misfortune that two of the greatest writers of the age were also provoked by the dedication.

Pope had subscribed to the *Cicero*, though certainly not at Hervey's request, and his name is duly enrolled in the list (for a small-paper copy). He met Middleton one afternoon at William Murray's house, and complimented the proud author on his book; but in the *New Dunciad*, published a year after the *Cicero*, he found place for a pungent comment on its dedication. As a procession passes before the Goddess of Dulness:

> There march'd the bard and blockhead, side by side,
> Who rhym'd for hire, and patroniz'd for pride.
> Narcissus, prais'd with all a Parson's pow'r,
> Look'd a white lilly sunk beneath a show'r.

By the time this relatively slight mention appeared, a long and robust commentary had amused a wide circle of readers at Hervey's expense.

Henry Fielding, whose political sympathies were firmly with the Opposition, had already directed some slight quips at Hervey as Walpole's understrapper. He now saw an opportunity to connect the Middleton dedication with Samuel Richardson's *Pamela*, which had been published the previous year and had become spectacularly popular. He called his parody-novel *Shamela*, and prefixed to it a brief dedication 'To Miss Fanny &c.' signed Conny Keyber, the combined names of Conyers Middleton and the actor-dramatist Colley Cibber, who had published his memoirs only the year before. Miss Fanny is identified as a 'young lady, whose wit and beauty might be the proper subject of a comparison with the heroine of my piece', an allusion to Hervey's effeminate manner, a feature of his satiric *persona* since the duel pamphlet. Miss Fanny is then extolled, in the mock-dedication, because she has 'tickled up and brightened many strokes' of the work, because she has conversed with the author himself, 'one of the greatest wits and scholars' of the age, because of her early morning studies, because of her 'forbearing to over-eat . . . in spite of all the luscious temptations of puddings and custards', because of her visiting the ballroom at Bath, and (finally) because of 'those pretty little sonnets, and sprightly compositions, which though they came from you with so much ease, might be mentioned to the praise of a great or grave character'. All these quips, directed at Hervey's private life, personality, and writings, grew out of Middleton's dedication.

It would have been odd if Fielding had disregarded Hervey's political character. Middleton had, in fact, devoted several paragraphs to a panegyric of Hervey as a high public official, 'a true friend to our constitution both in Church and State' who displayed his 'shining talents . . . in the defence of our excellent Establishment; in maintaining the rights of the people, yet asserting the prerogative of the Crown; measuring them both by the equal balance of the laws'. As political commentary it is mild enough, so general and so stilted that it could have been served up for almost any member of the Administration or even of the Opposition. At Bath, runs Fielding's mock-dedication to Miss Fanny, she 'was observed in dancing to balance your body exactly, and to weigh every motion with the exact and equal measure of time and tune; and though you sometimes made a false step, by leaning too much to one side, yet everybody said you would one time or other, dance perfectly well, and uprightly'. If this implies that Hervey had transferred his political loyalty from Pulteney to Walpole, it repeats an accusation (in Pulteney's duel pamphlet) that had no foundation in fact. Not since Hervey had been pilloried as Sporus had he been the butt of such a conspicuous and extensive satiric attack.

Why, one may wonder, had Middleton composed and Hervey accepted a dedication that even to disinterested contemporaries seemed so absurd? It is particularly puzzling because of Hervey's contempt for dedications in general. Some years before, when Stephen Fox had been offered a dedication and sent it to Hervey for correction, he had given his opinion that of all sorts of epistles he hated dedicatory epistles most, particularly if his name was at the top. And he had been aware, when he first read Middleton's dedication, that it might 'occasion some Sneers'. Perhaps the explanation is that during the profuse correspondence they had maintained for eight years, Middleton's abject obsequiousness and his own gracious condescension had come to seem ordinary and normal. They did not realize that what seemed natural in a private correspondence would be grotesquely inappropriate in a public dedication.

They could not have been unaware of it afterwards, too late. It may have caused a coolness between the two men, for they ceased corresponding until six months later, when Middleton wrote to Hervey to inquire after his health. He had another reason to revive their friendship, as can be judged by Hervey's reply to his letter: 'I am sorry you know a Want in your new habitation & wish from my Heart it may be in my Power to procure you that which will enable you to remove every Want you are acquainted [with].' (At about the same time, Middleton reminded Thomas Townshend that his 'Great relation', Newcastle, who had often given assurance of his favour had not yet given any real mark of it.) In spite of Middleton's enormous profit from his book and in spite of the dedication and its aftermath he easily resumed his familiar role of a place-hunter flattering a patron. It is strange, then, to find that some years later Middleton's widow said that he died ashamed of the dedication.

How much responsibility for the book itself is Hervey's can be seen in his candid appraisal of it. Middleton's style in general was excellent, he tells Algarotti, 'noble, simple, classical, and clear', but sometimes vulgar when he wished to be familiar, a fault due to his retired life in a college and his unfamiliarity with the elegant discourse of high life, which can be caught only by the ear and habit. His other grave fault, Hervey continues, is his partiality to Cicero. From the begining he had urged Middleton to treat Cicero as his subject and not his hero, and had altered the manuscript to conform to this principle, 'yet the naturall Obstinacy of an Author has still left this Work so liable to just Criticism & Censure upon this article, that he has since the Publication found him-self fallen upon for no Errors or Faults but such (vain as it may sound) as by recurring to the Letters which I wrote to him whilst this Work was in hand, he percieves, if he had follow'd my Advice & observed the Rules I gave him, he would have avoided'. He confided this opinion to Algarotti, to whom he had sent his subscribed copy of the book through the newly appointed English ambassador to Berlin, but he begged him not to repeat his comments, for Algarotti corresponded with other friends in England. Hervey wished to protect his friendship with Middleton now (in September) that they had resumed it.

The following year when Middleton was about to publish a translation of Cicero's epistles to Brutus, a by-product of his biography, he wished to dedicate it—not to Hervey, obviously, but to his other patron. 'My onely view in it', he assured Townshend, 'is to discharge my debt of gratitude to You.' But to his mortification Townshend was 'resolutely averse' to his request; and he accepted his patron's decision, for he had no desire (he told him) to expose his character to 'any hazard'. Hervey's misfortune had served as a lesson.

15

Fall from Power

1741–2

THE IMPATIENT ALGAROTTI had been reassured by King
Frederick of Prussia in October 1740 that instead of a diplomatic post in England more important favours lay in store
for him. He was not satisfied with vague promises. When Frederick
retired to Remusberg to recover from an illness he pointedly went
to Berlin instead, with the expectation that separation would
bring Frederick round. It did. Frederick promised to bestow a
title on him that winter and enough money to travel, but Algarotti
wanted more solid rewards than unfulfilled promises. He suffered
at this time from another discomfort. As Frederick teased him,
'Adieu, illustrious invalid of the empire of Love. Heal thyself of
the wounds of Cytherea, and at least let us at Berlin have the
advantage of your wit since the *p*[*utains*] cannot profit by your
body.' (The allusion to *p*[*rostitutes*] was probably a euphemism;
a month later Voltaire described in vivid detail the sexual activity
between the French ambassador's young male secretary and
Algarotti, who is depicted as a Venetian Socrates with large eyes
and aquiline nose.)★ Both of Algarotti's discomforts were cured
at the same time.

On 20 December 1740 Frederick enobled him as Count
Algarotti and sent him on a diplomatic mission to Turin. He
could not bestow the title in person, for he was leading his army
to invade Silesia, in violation of the Pragmatic Sanction by which
the late Emperor had hoped to keep his possessions intact for his

★ But when . . .
I see the tender Algarotti
Crush with passionate embrace
The handsome Lugeac, his young friend,
I imagine I see Socrates fastened
Onto the rump of Alcibiades.

daughter, Maria Theresa. Algarotti's mission to Turin, under the pretence of private business, was to discover the intention of that court and to persuade the King of Sardinia (Duke of Savoy) to form an alliance with Prussia. When he arrived in Turin, at the end of January 1741, he rented an apartment because (he told the French ambassador) the noise of an inn kept him from sleeping; and he busied himself with visiting the court and all the important families. The French ambassador, whom he called on several times, was impressed by him as a man of parts, very supple and extremely polite.

While he had waited impatiently at Frederick's court for more substantial rewards than mere friendship, Lady Mary waited in Italy for some sign of whether he would join her there. Since he had apparently not written to her from Berlin she had to send her letters to Hervey to forward to Algarotti. 'I send you inclosed another Letter from Sapho', Hervey had warned him in September 1740. 'They seem to me like Sancho's Geese & Banco's Kings, as if there was no End of them.' By then Lady Mary had left Venice for a succession of restless visits. From Florence, her first stop, she had sent Algarotti a brief, submissive note asking for his intentions: she was ready to go wherever he wished.

In Rome, where she led a quiet, contemplative life, she composed some verse that must have been autobiographical; one couplet is particularly poignant:

> Like a deer that is wounded I bleed and run on,
> And fain I my torment would hide.

After Rome, she travelled to Naples for six weeks, to Rome again, to Leghorn to collect the mountain of baggage and books sent from England by ship, and then to Turin, where she arrived in the middle of March 1741. Although she explained to her husband that she had left Rome because of Jacobite spies and the Pretender's court she could not tell him why she had made her way to Turin. It was a reason unsuited to a husband's ears.

Algarotti was well established in Turin by then, and when Lady Mary arrived she immediately informed Hervey of the meeting. Her letter (he told her) 'gave me the double Pleasure of finding you desire to contribute to mine, and are in a way of promoting your own'. As he knew, she was promoting her own pleasure more than a year and a half after having left

274 FALL FROM POWER 1741-

England for that purpose. What were Algarotti's feelings when he at last confronted this middle-aged, aristocratic Englishwoman? Their meeting was, he thought, one of the more curious episodes of a life that was otherwise singular enough. They spent some time together. Occasionally, when she wrote to Hervey, Algarotti added a paragraph or two to her letters. That was not enough for Hervey, who scolded him: 'I do not call Scraps in other People's Letters hearing *from* you, but *of* You.' At least he did not blame Lady Mary or try to denigrate her; instead, in this same letter he sent his best respects and wishes to Algarotti's 'delightfull Companion'.

Whether Algarotti found her a delightful companion is another matter. For it is certain that their meeting put an end to her romantic infatuation. In the cold clear light of reality she saw that while he could be full of charm and grace to others, he regarded her only with indifference and churlishness. This interlude in Turin was, in a phrase that Hervey used to repeat her description, a very disagreeable epoch of her life. Nor had Algarotti's diplomatic mission been a success. The political orientation of the court of Turin was so mysterious that he could discover nothing; and in mid-March he was recalled by Frederick and ordered to return to Berlin as soon as possible. He did not leave Turin until the middle of May, travelling north toward Prussia. A few days later Lady Mary also departed, in the opposite direction.

In Genoa she rented a house for the summer; she had to find her bearings now that the star she had pursued was out of sight. Since Hervey was her confidant she turned to him for advice, asking him whether she should give up her quest for happiness and return to England. He tried to answer her with wisdom and sympathy: her question was so difficult that Solomon and Socrates together could not give her as good advice as she could herself; and since she had only her own pleasure to consider, she must follow the dictates of her passions, affections, and inclinations, directed by her heart. The fact that she was faced with this problem late in life, as she had pointed out (she was fifty-two), made it even more important for her to improve the years that were left to her. He reinforced his diagnosis with a prescription, two lines from Ovid's *The Remedies of Love*:

By practice love comes into the mind, by practice love is unlearnt; All love is vanquished by a succeeding love.

Lady Mary could thus console herself with the wisdom of one of the Latin poets whom she always found sympathetic.

Algarotti apparently said nothing to Hervey afterwards of his rendezvous with Lady Mary; he needed no advice when his opportunism directed him back to Berlin. There he had a message from Frederick, who was at a military camp: 'My dear Algarotti, I await you with great impatience, happier to possess you as a friend than to receive your letters as an envoy.' Since he now knew that he would not return to England he asked Hervey to send his belongings left behind, and Hervey obliged—'not without many Sighs', he tells him, 'as I look'd upon the parting with the last Bitt that relates to you, as cutting up by the Root, the last, little Slender Hope I had of seeing you once more in this Country'. He would never be able to forget or replace Algarotti in his affections, he sighs; 'Adieu, busy your mind with ambition & you will never feel the Regret you give.' It was advice that Algarotti hardly needed.

ii

Lady Bristol's health had never been good, and the violent hatred she felt for her eldest son could not have benefited it. The previous summer she had been taken ill at Bath, so seriously that she had to be carried for part of the journey back to Ickworth. In that sad condition, one of her friends remarked, no one in her family attended her, and although the mother of many children she was left to the 'care or cruelty' of her servants. While in London (in May 1741) and taking the air in St. James's Park in her sedan chair she was seized by a fit. She was carried immediately to her house in St. James's Square, where nothing could be done for her, and she died. On 9 May she was buried in Ickworth Church, 'in the same vault', Lord Bristol wrote in his diary, 'with my most invaluable & ever to be lamented first wife'. In a will drawn up six months earlier, she had appointed her youngest son, Felton, as her heir. To Hervey she bequeathed 'my cabinet chest, large skreen and small skreen being white japan of my own work, in confidence that he will preserve them for my sake'. It is curious that she should expect such devotion from a son she regarded as a villain equal to Iago.

Although busy as one of the Lords Justices, appointed on 6 May, the day the King left London, Hervey visited Ickworth on the 11th (two days after his mother's burial), to console his father, and stayed five days. His father told him then that he was making him a present of £10,000, money perhaps released to him by Lady Bristol's death. His generosity may also have been connected with the career of Hervey's eldest son. For he, in spite of Bristol's objections, had been directed into an army career, and while on the Grand Tour had held an appointment as an ensign and then as a captain in Lord Cholmondeley's newly raised regiment. Hervey at this time promised his father to take his son out of the army immediately. The young man himself, when he returned from his travels a month later, visited his grandfather at Ickworth, at which time he and Hervey solemnly promised Lord Bristol that he would resign his commission as soon as the war ended. Satisfied by their assurance, Bristol revised his will, which had been altered, to restore to them the estate they in turn were expected to inherit.

However disappointed Bristol may have been in Hervey's political career he had brighter hopes for his grandson. The young man had, in his opinion, 'not only most extraordinary natural talents but a happy disposition to improve them'; and he urged Hervey to let him attend either house of Parliament, where he might learn 'the Ciceronian eloquence of his father & (may I say) the true Catonian patriotism of his grandfather'.

Hervey's eloquence in Parliament along with his loyalty to the Ministry continued to bring him rewards. For about four years he had been trying to secure a peerage for Stephen Fox; at last, in May 1741, Stephen was created Lord Ilchester, Baron of Woodford Strangways in Dorset. Stephen himself gave full credit for his peerage to Hervey, whom he later told: 'I am not only convinc'd I have that obligation to your Lordship, but I have industriously taken every opportunity of publishing it.'

But Stephen also earned his peerage in two other ways: by resigning his Treasury post, as he did in April, and by bribing the King's mistress. According to Newcastle's brother-in-law, Sir John Shelley, the King's mistress—who herself had been advanced into the peerage as the Countess of Yarmouth—had asked her master for £30,000; and when he refused to let her have it she fell into a passion of tears, saying that he did not love her, and that she would not go to Hanover with him. Frightened by her threat the King said that if she could find some way of raising the money he would agree to it. She suggested the creation of some peers as a simple method, and he agreed, with the stipulation that they be men whom Walpole would not find objectionable. Walpole then sent for Fox and another ambitious commoner (Bromley), told them of the situation, and bid them wait on Lady Yarmouth, which they did to settle the sum to be paid. Thus the King and Walpole fulfilled their promise to Hervey and at the same time placated the Royal mistress. The motto that Fox chose for his coat of arms is tantalizing on several counts: *Faire sans dire.*

Hervey's political eminence also involved him with Lady Mary, who while she enjoyed the summer at Genoa thrust herself into a political fracas there. In the naval campaign against Spain, England maintained a strict blockade of the Spanish possessions in Italy. Early in June an English captain, whose galley lay anchored in Genoa harbour, seized a bark flying the Genoese flag because she had no pass. Indignant at this breach of her neutrality the Genoese took action by imprisoning the captain's lieutenant and some of the crew who had gone ashore, but before they could seize the galley her captain sailed off to Leghorn taking with him the captured bark and its crew. The Doge and Senate protested to the English consul—who was 'as unlicked a poor cub' as Horace Walpole had ever seen—demanding that the bark be released. Lady Mary, convinced that the Genoese were in the right and the English captain and consul in the wrong, volunteered her services as mediator. To the annoyance of the consul she tried to have the captain broken, apparently writing to the Admiralty. She also appealed to Hervey.

During the King's absence abroad he was again one of the Lords Justices who made up the regency; he called himself the fifteenth part of a King. In reply to Lady Mary's repeated question as to what decision had been taken, he assured her: 'The Genoese Affair has been under our Consideration and very proper Directions in my Opinion have been given for the termination of it, which I make no doubt will be comply'd with, and prevent your being anyway inconvenienced by a farther dispute between our Court and that Republic.' (Exactly how Lady Mary was inconvenienced is not clear.) The Lords Justices were in no hurry to resolve the squabble, and in their decision later that summer, no doubt to Lady Mary's satisfaction, they firmly censured the English captain's conduct.

The meetings of the Lords Justices at the end of August were the last that Hervey attended; on 1 September he 'desired leave to go out of town', and the next day left for Bath. There he submitted to his customary cure. He rose at seven in the morning, and since he drank the waters in his lodgings (rather than in the Pump Room) he could write and read until he dined, alone, at four o'clock. His exercise was one hour's walking; and for the rest of the day he indulged himself in classical studies. He was quite content to be alone, he tells Algarotti, and 'whenever I put my Nose out of my own Lodgings (which blessed be God is never above three Hours in the 24) I meet with nothing but the full grown Harvest of all the seeds contain'd in Pandora's Box, & find a healthy Body here as great a Rarity as a healthy Mind any where else'. After he passed a month under this regimen the waters seemed to have lost their salubrious effect; probably for that reason he returned to London.

Instead of his house on Grosvenor Street he planned to return to the one in St. James's Square, which his father had given him along with all the pictures, medals, books, plate, and furniture, and which had been made ready for his occupancy by forty workmen. But on his arrival he stayed in Grosvenor Street, probably because his new house was not ready, and immediately fell violently ill of fever and vomiting. For three days nothing could give him relief. He was so ill that he was prepared to die, but then he slowly recovered. He was unable to leave his room for nine weeks as he gathered his strength to face the strenuous months ahead.

iii

In the autumn of 1741, with the King in Hanover and Parliament recessed, the political scene was deceptively quiet. 'Ill Health & Politics have hinder'd me writing to you lately,' Hervey had apologized to Lady Mary (still at Genoa); 'I am going to the Bath to mend the first, & what will mend the last God knows: it seems to labor under ⟨a⟩ very acute Complaint of a most malignant Fever &c. that a great deal of Blood will be let; but whether it will recieve any Benefit from it, is past my Skill to determine or con-jecture.' His medical metaphor describes the worsening state of Walpole's Ministry. For the summer elections had gone badly; Westminster, hitherto a secure bastion, was being contested; and the Prince of Wales and his friends had raised a rash of contested elections elsewhere. Walpole's own cabinet was divided, with Wilmington hoping to succeed him as First Lord of the Treasury and Newcastle itching to seize more power.

After Hervey's return to London from Bath, while illness confined him to his house, the ominous quiet continued. 'The politics of the age are entirely suspended,' Horace Walpole remarked in October, 'nothing is mentioned: but this bottling them up, will make them fly out with the greater violence the moment the Parliament meets.' His prediction was borne out in the first measure that came before the House of Commons, the Address of Thanks for the King's opening speech on 8 December. The Opposition speakers objected to thanking the King for the prosecution of the war with Spain. Walpole at first tried to defend the Address, and then for the sake of unanimity agreed to omit one paragraph. It was a sign of weakness; the Opposition pressed their advantage while his supporters began to fear for his declining power. Not long after, on 22 December, came the decisive sign: in the contest for Westminster, Walpole's candidates had won the election, but the two rejected ones petitioned the House of Commons to set the election aside, and they were supported by the majority. Two days later Parliament adjourned for a month, an interval during which political forces could realign themselves. Both sides spent the holiday trafficking for votes.

A few nights after his father's defeat in the contested election, Horace Walpole, knowing that Lady Hervey had company at home, called at her house. It seemed to him that Hervey, who had always favoured him, turned his back and retired for an hour to whisper to young James Hammond, Lord Chesterfield's protégé. At last he came up to Horace and begged him to arrange a concert at his house. This was duly done (on 6 January 1742) with two of the Italian singers from the opera performing. Horace then told his friend Horace Mann about it: 'I made the music for my Lord Hervey, who is too ill to go [to] operas; yet with a coffin face, is as full of his little dirty politics as ever. He *will not* be well enough to go to the House, till the majority is certain somewhere, but lives shut up with Lord Chesterfield and Mr Pultney—a triumvirate who hate one another more than anybody they could proscribe, had they the power.' (By 1737 Hervey had somehow become reconciled with Pulteney.)

Since Sir Robert was doomed to fall—his resignation was considered certain by both his friends and enemies—Horace had become suspicious of the actions and hypersensitive to the motives of those who he imagined were deserting his beleagured father. (Why, for example, should Hervey have asked him to arrange a concert at his house if he was snubbing him in his own house?) 'I forget to tell you', Horace tells Mann, 'that upon losing the first question [choosing the election-committee chairman on 16 December], Lord Hervey kept away for a week: on our carrying the next great one [laying the Austrian papers before the House on 18 December], he wrote to Sir Robert how much he desired to see him, "*not upon any business, but Lord Hervey longs to see Sir Robert Walpole*".' (Horace's sarcasm has expanded the interval of two days into a week.)

There can be no doubt as to what was uppermost in Hervey's thoughts during these weeks of the Ministry's dissolution: having risen to be Lord Privy Seal he was painfully reluctant to fall from office. Once it was clear to him that Walpole was doomed and that nothing he could do would delay or prevent it, he sought a way of retaining his own position. In Horace Walpole's opinion Newcastle, who feared to fall with Sir Robert and 'hoped to rise upon his ruins, dealt largely with the Opposition, to compass both'. Hervey also feared to fall, but as his later actions in the House of Lords and his pamphleteering demonstrated he tried to protect Sir Robert. He may have begun dealing with some of the Opposition in the early autumn, when Chesterfield, who was travelling in France, returned to Paris in October so that he might be within call of Hervey and George Lyttleton.

Another Hervey sat in Parliament—Thomas, who had been re-elected that summer to the family seat of Bury St. Edmunds. In the vote on 16 December—the division that caused Horace to remark: 'we are metamorphosed into the minority'—Tom Hervey voted against Walpole. He seems to have been mentally unbalanced. When asked why he had voted thus, he replied, 'Jesus knows my thoughts, one day I blaspheme, and pray the next.' By his own confession, he had long suffered from a disturbed mind in a distempered body. In the Ministry's defeat on the Westminster election the following week Tom Hervey was among those whose absence allowed the Opposition to win. Perhaps Hervey was blamed for his mad brother's actions.

After the Christmas recess, when Parliament met (in January 1742) the Opposition again took the offensive by asking for the papers and instructions of Admiral Haddock, who was in command of the Mediterranean fleet, hoping thus to condemn the Ministry's conduct of the war. When Chesterfield demanded to know whether the fleet had received orders to launch an attack, Hervey rose to speak. He pointed out that since it was impossible for anybody to doubt that such orders were given, the Administration should be believed in this matter. In spite of Horace's suspicions, then, and in spite of his dealings with Chesterfield, Hervey was still supporting Walpole's Ministry.

The Opposition's next tactic, on 28 January, centred on the fact that of the nineteen officers assigned to the island of Minorca only five were there—further evidence of how ineptly the war was being carried on. The motion of censure was defeated, by only 69 to 57. Hervey then moved an Address to the King to order some of the officers over. This would seem a conciliatory rather than anti-Administration motion. A far more important measure was being debated in the House of Commons—the disputed Chippenham election; and on this the Opposition mustered enough votes to defeat Walpole. It was crystal clear, then, that he would have to step down.

He should have resigned two years earlier, writes William Coxe, his sympathetic biographer, because he had really opposed the war with Spain; it would have been a noble and dignified move. Instead he endured mortification, insults, and a forced resignation. Why then did he not resign in 1739? 'The truth is', Coxe writes, 'that he had neither resolution or inclination to persevere in a sacrifice which circumstances seemed to require, and to quit a station which long possession had endeared to him. But ministers are but men; human nature does not reach to perfection; and who ever quitted power without a sigh, or looked back to it without regret?'*

Once the die was cast events moved quickly. On 2 February Walpole wrote to the Duke of Devonshire that he was determined to resign, that Wilmington was to succeed him, and that he wished the Whig party to remain united. A week later he was created Earl of Orford, and after two days resigned all his offices.

* The anonymous biographer of Coxe in the *D.N.B.* says that his 'writing is of the dullest and shows no higher qualities than those of the conscientious annalist'.

At his suggestion the King, overcoming his repugnance to Pulteney, allowed the Opposition leader to form a coalition ministry. He chose Newcastle and Hardwicke from Walpole's cabinet and added Carteret, Wilmington and Argyll. Several of Walpole's lesser supporters—Winnington, Pelham, and Yonge—retained their government posts. All that Pulteney wanted for himself, unexpectedly, was a place in the cabinet, and this evidently implied a peerage as well. He had once remarked to Queen Caroline that when he found he could no longer do any good in the House of Commons he might be willing to accept a seat in the House of Lords and end his days in that hospital of invalids.

But he refused to accept a title until he could obtain the Privy Seal for Lord Gower, and this was delayed for two reasons: Gower was obnoxious to the others in the Ministry, and the King insisted on keeping Hervey in the post. Aside from his own friendship the King persisted in supporting him for the sake of the late Queen.

False newspaper rumours in February and April reported that Hervey had been replaced first by Lord Carlisle and then by Henry Pelham. However precariously, he clung to his office, attending the House of Lords only infrequently—once out of every six sittings. In telling Lady Mary of his 'natural & political Health,' he writes (in May 1742)

I am still alive, & still Privy-Seal; it is all I can say for the Pleasure of one, or the Honor of the other; for since Lord Orford's Retireing, as I am too proud to offer my Service & Friendship where I am not sure they will be accepted of, & too inconsiderable to have those Advances made to me (tho I never forgot or fail'd to return any Obligation I ever receiv'd) so I remain as illustrious a Nothing in this Office, as ever fill'd it since it was first erected.

In spite of his enemies in and out of the new Ministry he remained Lord Privy Seal for only one reason: the King positively refused, in the most stubborn manner, to put him out, and did not intend to change his resolution.

That the King could be persuaded (or forced) to change his resolution was clear enough when he was reconciled with the Prince of Wales soon after Walpole's resignation. The event was celebrated with great rejoicing by the court and the populace though not by the two principals who created the occasion.

Bonfires blazed in several parts of Westminster, and a great ball was held (on 17 February) at Norfolk House attended by the 'greatest Number of Nobility and Persons of Distinction'. It is unlikely that Hervey was among them. The Prince of Wales did not have a forgiving nature; a few months later he was venting his princely resentment even upon the women, and refused to say a word to Lady Hervey when they met.

The day following the ball the Earl of Orford was introduced into the House of Lords. Hervey was not present that day, though his father and Lord Ilchester (Stephen Fox) were, to see how the fallen Prime Minister would be received. Not a single lord rose or took him by the hand, as was always done on such occasions by friends or any who were not enemies. (It was reported to Horace, however, that Chesterfield wished him joy.) After he took his oaths, looking very pale, he left immediately without taking his seat, and drove to his lodge at Richmond. On a visit to him there a few days later Lord Palmerston found him leaving to hunt. 'You see,' said Orford, 'I hunt whilst others hunt me.' It was no secret that his former Opposition intended to do what they had tried unsuccessfully the year before—call him to account for what they alleged was the dishonesty and corruption of his Administration.

If Hervey wished to demonstrate any disloyalty to Walpole in order to win favour with the new Administration, here would be a distinct opportunity. A Secret Committee was set up in the House of Commons in March to examine the last ten years of Walpole's Administration. Then, because witnesses refused to testify for fear of self-incrimination, a 'Bill to Indemnify Evidence' against him was brought into the Commons on 13 May, passed on the 19th, and sent to the Lords. To Horace Walpole it seemed too absurd a bill to have any chance of passing.

When it came up for debate (on 25 May) Carteret unexpectedly opposed it—on legal grounds. Then, after it was defended by another lord, Hervey rose to speak. There was no doubt of where he stood on the measure. He attacked the bill and defended Walpole with various reasons, among them that the former Prime Minister was presumed to be guilty without any kind of legal proof, and that the Civil List disbursements (which Walpole had been accused of using for bribery) were beyond scrutiny because that money was the King's private concern. Among the speakers who followed Hervey, Chesterfield supported the bill but to no avail; about seven in the evening it was defeated by almost two to one. For the moment, at least, Hervey's former chief was safe from the pursuing, vengeful pack; and Hervey himself could still shine as an illustrious Nothing.

iv

With the approach of summer, when Parliament would be prorogued, it became more urgent that the new cabinet be completed—and Hervey was still Lord Privy Seal. To Pulteney it seemed as though he stuck like a burr, and could not be brushed off; but once again driven by his bitter hatred Pulteney insisted that in spite of the King's protection he would have to go. The Prince of Wales had instructed him to find posts for several of his adherents, Lord Gower among them, and it was to him that the Privy Seal was assigned—when it could be vacated. The mixed composition of the new Ministry could not have been more blatantly announced than by including Gower, a Tory connected with the Jacobites. (So much for Walpole's wish for a united Whig party!)

In mid-June Horace Walpole reported that Gower was to have kissed hands on 11 June for the Privy Seal but that Hervey had carried the seal with him to Ickworth, and had been ordered to bring it back. Hervey may have visited Ickworth at the end of May, perhaps as a way of delaying his removal. Besides, Gower had gone to Berkshire for the last fortnight in June to recover from an attack of the gout. Even had it been available, then, he could not have taken possession of the Privy Seal.

The last days of Hervey's desperate attempt to keep his place at court are dramatized (in letters to his father) by his own masterly pen. The King met him (about 22 June) and offered him a pension of £3,000 in recompense for his resignation. Upon his refusing it, the King promised to ask Carteret to find some other way of pleasing him. Two weeks later (on 5 July) he had a long conversation with the King on the same subject. He did not mind so much being dismissed, he said, as he did having it done in this manner. The King assured him that he had been forced against his inclinations to appoint a new Lord Privy Seal. Why had he not been told sooner? Hervey asked; instead he had heard it 'from the

Prince and his people publicly singing their songs of triumph throughout the whole town for this victory being at last obtained over Your Majesty and me, and that your own Ministers should be whispering it about to every one in your antechambers that this thing was done'. The King replied that he had intended never to take this step, and that his son ('a vain puppy') and the Ministers were liars because they all knew that it should not be done until Hervey 'was made easy in the manner of doing it'.

Again Hervey refused the pension of £3,000—because it was so different from an equivalent compensation for what he was giving up, and he could regard it only as an additional disgrace since from the moment he consented 'to be rolled in the dirt of that pensionary gutter' he would lose his credit and reputation in Parliament. His rancour against the Prince of Wales flared up as he told the King that 'possibly the Prince might think his triumph over the ashes of a dead mother and the authority of a living father incomplete, unless he was gratified in the manner of my removal as well as the removal itself, and insisted on my being kicked out of His Majesty's Court as well as removed from my employment'. The King, Hervey continued, was really being manipulated by the Prince and Pulteney, who worked through Newcastle and Pelham. He then, for the King's benefit, analysed the members of the new Administration.

How could he object to these men, the King asked, when he had been the first to propose them? Only if the Whig party could not be united, he replied, and in order to keep out the Tories; and furthermore, if it was bad advice 'how comes it to be now adopted? and if it was good, can it be just in Your Majesty to make the first adviser the first sacrifice?' He summed up his argument by asserting that he wished his removal to be regarded as political and not personal, and he would accept anything that would show the world he had not forfeited the King's favour.

He followed up his conversation with a letter to the King the next day. To make his 'very mortifying removal in the least mortifying manner' he suggested that the King should appoint him a Vice-Treasurer of Ireland or a Lord of the Bedchamber with an added pension of £2,000 (which would still be less than his present income). He also offered the King some general advice on the new Ministry and on Newcastle's treachery; and the next day he advised him to force Pulteney to accept a peerage and thus to remove his power. This advice, he says, was taken by the King, who delivered the ultimatum to Pulteney. Yet according to Horace Walpole, Pulteney already had in his pocket a warrant for the earldom of Bath, and when he went to the King with the long list of new appointments (about 10 July) he was abruptly told that unless he took up his patent and quitted the House of Commons nothing should be done for him; whereupon he consented. Whether or not the King was following Hervey's advice cannot be determined with any finality.

Certainly the King could not offer him satisfaction on his own behalf. He appealed then to Carteret (on 7 July) because he was losing his time and hurting his health 'in dangling after an affair I am most heartily tired and sick of'. Carteret replied merely that he was quite ignorant of whether or not the Irish Vice-Treasurer's place would go to him.

The blow, so long anticipated, fell unexpectedly. Late on Saturday night (10 July) Hervey received a brief note from Carteret informing him that it was the King's pleasure that he should bring the Privy Seal to him on Monday morning. At their meeting the King again offered him a pension of £3,000 and again he refused it as a symbol of disgrace; again he asked for one of the three vacant appointments, and again was refused. He then delivered a little homily to instruct his Majesty that if assiduity and fidelity, which he had so demonstrably shown, were the two most dangerous qualities a man could bring into his Court, then the Court would be filled with bullies, knaves, and fools. The King should not permit a servant of his to be discarded and punished only for having served him well.

He then compared himself to a footman who protects the King's coach from an insolent mob. Could the King then turn away the footman at the instigation of that very mob? he asked. He could hardly believe his ears at the King's rejoinder: 'My Lord, there would not be so much striving for a footman's place.' But he had the last word—with a reference to the Scriptures: he 'hoped it would be thought no disrespect to say to His Majesty on this occasion what is said in the gospel of God himself, that I found with kings all things were possible'.

The entire episode of Hervey's struggle on surrendering the Privy Seal comes mainly from his own confidential letters to his father; and although he may have heightened a detail here and there the main outlines are credible and hang together. Should he have resigned at the same time as Walpole? Seen in retrospect, of course; since by refusing to relinquish his office he gained nothing but unpleasant confrontations. Yet one may echo Coxe's sentiment on Walpole's postponed and reluctant resignation: 'who ever quitted power without a sigh?' Sighing or not, Hervey did not quit his power without a fierce and tenacious struggle.

On the same day (13 July) that Pulteney was created Earl of Bath, Gower became Lord Privy Seal; and two days later Parliament was prorogued. For the first time in twelve years Hervey was out of office. From her lonely exile Lady Mary sent him cynical and sympathetic consolation:

> For what you have, return to Heav'n your thanks;
> Few share the prizes, many draw the blanks.
> Of breach of promise loudly you complain,
> Have you then known the world so long in vain?

v

Even in the political turmoil and anguish of these troubled months Hervey found time (on 9 March) to attend an auction of the Earl of Oxford's collection, which was sold at Christopher Cock's room in the Piazza of Covent Garden. Lord Oxford, who had died the previous year sodden with drink and loaded with debt, had gathered a vast accumulation of books, pictures, coins, and bronzes. Already the owner of a numerous collection of bronzes, Hervey wished to add some pieces to it. He bought the first two lots: a pair of 'Canopus's' (Egyptian vases) and seven marble inscriptions, and then another pair with six Egyptian lares (statuettes) and Roman lamps. For the third lot he outbid Horace Walpole, winning for ten guineas the sarcophagus of Gaius Vibius (a friend of Caesar's and governor of Gaul), described in the auction catalogue as 'of most curious Workmanship'. He afterwards begged Horace Walpole for its companion, but in vain. He also exercised his taste elsewhere as a connoisseur of painting by buying some pictures for Stephen; when hung in the house on Great Burlington Street they looked 'vastly well' to Lady Ilchester.

After his resignation he had the leisure for a long summer visit to Ickworth, to recover from the fatigue and strain of his ordeal. His father had built a new apartment for him, and without his mother there to bedevil him he felt completely at his ease. For most of August he had the instructive company of Thomas Wright, the astronomer; he had subscribed for two copies of Wright's book *Claris Cælestis* ('the Explication of a Diagram, entituled a Synopsis of the Universe: or, the Visible World Epitomized'). Besides these learned studies he resumed an activity as irresistible to him as politics—literary controversy, in which he joined Colley Cibber in combat with Pope.

The genial, good-natured Cibber had, in his long career, been actor, playwright, and since 1730 Poet Laureate. He did not take his art seriously, explaining, 'I wrote more to be Fed, than to be Famous.' As a frequent object of Pope's sneers he displayed considerable forbearance. In the *Epistle to Dr. Arbuthnot*, which contained the memorable portrait of Sporus, Pope had taunted him by name in the line: 'And has not *Colly* still his Lord, and Whore?' Cibber could have tried to revenge himself (in 1740) in his autobiography, *An Apology for the Life of Colley Cibber*, but he merely mentioned in passing that Pope was 'a little free' with him, and had been too severe in his portrait of Atticus (Addison).

When Cibber read Pope's *New Dunciad*, published in March 1742, which has only a line about his reclining on the lap of Dulness, he took up his pen to administer a scolding in a prose pamphlet. Published at the end of July, *A Letter from Mr. Cibber to Mr. Pope* bears an explanatory sub-title, 'Inquiring into the Motives that might induce him in his Satyrical Works, to be so frequently fond of Mr. Cibber's Name'. While acknowledging Pope's poetic genius Cibber deplores his malice, and as proof seizes on the line about Colley having a whore. His comment on this is to relate an incident that had occurred many years before: they had gone together to a house of prostitution, and after Pope had retired to a room with a whore, Cibber had interrupted 'this hasty Hero, like a terrible *Tom Tit*, pertly perching upon the Mount of Love!' This comical treatment of a scandalous, unknown incident in the celibate poet's biography aroused enormous interest and comment; and other pamphleteers took it up.

At Ickworth, where Hervey read the pamphlet soon after it was published, he was so delighted with it that he wished to thank Cibber publicly, though anonymously. His own grievance against Pope, aside from the scarifying portrait of Sporus repeated in each new edition of the *Epistle to Dr. Arbuthnot* (six since the first), was his being called, in the *New Dunciad*, the Narcissus of Middleton's dedication. Always facile with his pen, Hervey wrote his public letter to Cibber quickly, and on 19 August it was issued as a sixpenny pamphlet by his customary publisher, James Roberts. *A Letter to Mr. C-b-r, On his Letter to Mr. P* congratulates Cibber for his admirable piece; but, Hervey continues, he has missed his aim, 'for as you attack nothing but his Morals, which no body defends; and allow him several poetical Merits, which many People dispute' he will correct that deficiency. As a poet, he says, Pope lacks perspicuity and invention; as a satirist he relies on scurrility and name-calling; and as a philosopher he creates confusion (in his *Essay on Man*). Compared to Cibber, he concludes, Pope is demonstrably inferior and hypocritical—'a second-rate Poet, a bad Companion, a dangerous Acquaintance, an inveterate, implacable Enemy, no body's Friend, a noxious Member of Society, and a thorough bad Man'. Hervey proves that he himself is at least a reckless name-caller.

At the end of his *Letter to Mr. C-b-r* Hervey mentions his being at a distance from London, and after inviting Cibber to comment on Pope's works, he signs himself simply 'With the greatest Gratitude and Truth, most affectionately yours'. Undoubtedly he knew Cibber personally, both having been at court for more than a decade.* Pope knew that they were literary allies, for in his 1743 *Dunciad*, when he calls Hervey a 'Fool of Quality' he continues:

> Thou Cibber! thou his Laurel shall support,
> Folly, my son, has still a Friend at Court.

Not content with his prose attack on Pope, only a few days later Hervey published (again through Roberts) a short poem, *The Difference between Verbal and Practical Virtue*. Its burden is simple enough: that few authors follow the virtuous paths they recommend; and he cites as exemplars of his theory Horace, Seneca, Sallust, and finally Pope, whom he treats at great length.

---

* Hervey and Cibber had already (in 1739) been joined as fellow victims in *Manners*, a wretched satire by Paul Whitehead, which revived the Sporus caricature, and showed its political bias with praise of Chesterfield, Cobham, and the Prince of Wales.

Pope should not be satirized for his 'haggard Face' or 'Mountain Back', he writes, but for 'that worse Deformity, his Mind'. A puzzling part of this repellent verse pamphlet is its prefatory letter (in prose) from Mr. C-b-r to Mr. P. 'Have at you again, Sir,' it starts. 'I give you fair Warning that I would have the last Word; and by—(I will not swear in print) you shall find me no Lyar.' Pleased by his laurels in prose combat, Cibber's letter continues, 'I now resolve to fight you on your own Dunghill of Poetry, and with your own jingling Weapons of Rhyme and Metre. I confess I have had some Help; but what then?' Is this letter actually by Cibber? and had he joined Hervey, who had certainly written the verse? If Hervey intended confusion he has succeeded.

When it was published in London (in August) Hervey was still at Ickworth. At the beginning of September he sent his prose pamphlet as well as (probably) this verse one to the Revd. Dr. John Symonds, whom he had known since his boyhood. 'I send you inclosed the Poem I promised you on Mr. Pope,' he writes, 'together with a little Pamphlet I lately received from London intitled *a Letter to Mr. Cibber on his Letter to Pope*, in which I think there is as much Vivacity, true Wit & keen Satire as I ever saw in so small a Compas.' Then, having praised his own work so generously, he continues with a lie to hide both his immodesty and his authorship: 'it is certainly written by some very masterly Hand, & I hear Lord Chesterfield has the Honor of it. I have duplicates of both these things; if therefore you have any mind to keep them for a second Reading they are at your Service.'

When Charles Hanbury Williams received a copy of the poem from Henry Fox, he was willing to take an oath that Hervey had written it: ''tis too plain, both from the unpoetick thoughts and bad versification and the quaint antitheses, but above all from the many quotations out of Appian and Dion Cassius, books that he is very fond of and that hardly anybody else ever looks into'. Before long Hervey's authorship of the two pamphlets was known to Grub Street. The anonymous author of the *Scribleriad* clearly blames him for them, and warns his own cohorts that

> . . . if that Lord the *Pen* or *Press* invade,
> Rouse, rouse, ye Tribe! he'll undermine your Trade.

Hervey knew that Lady Mary, his collaborator in earlier satiric warfare, would enjoy reading the pamphlets; he sent her a large packet of them later in the year—political ones 'as well as the Ciberian Controversy with Pope', he writes, 'which during the Summer-Suspense of parliamentary Arms, made the Subject of the last Campain'. He knew that poetical warfare was merely a diversion; his political campaign still needed to be organized.

16

Various Conclusions

1742-3

AT THE TIME THAT HERVEY was dismissed as Lord Privy Seal (in July 1742) he assured Stephen that he would not go into opposition, and that he believed in a little time he would stop thinking of court, politics, or Parliament. He seemed void of resentment, and totally dispassionate. And from Ickworth later in that summer he assured Lady Mary that he had no need of her sage advice about checking the dictates of ambition since after seeing by whom the highest offices were held he could hardly be desirous of obtaining any for himself.

His pose of unconcern had persisted even after he went to Bath, where political intrigue was everywhere. He then assured Lady Mary that he paid no attention to 'the silly Actions of the silly Actors on our present Political-Stage'. Since he had left court, he tells her, he has enjoyed ease with cheerfulness, if not with dignity. Bath was filled with crowds of people, but he had no other commerce with them than playing whist two hours in the evening; and he conversed with only two people, his old schoolmaster Dr. Freind and his Aesculapius Dr. Cheyne: 'with the first talk of Books, with the last of health; & get instruction from both, at once improving my taste and Constitution.'

Another friend soon arrived in Bath, Charles Hanbury Williams, who had been staying with Henry Fox at Maddington, the shooting-box in Wiltshire where Hervey had been a welcome guest in previous years. By now his friendship with Henry Fox had ended, probably because of their political differences,* since

* Horace Walpole's explanation for their falling out is that Hervey had persuaded Fox to make love to the widowed Duchess of Manchester (in 1740) 'in order to betray this amour to rich Mrs Horner, who kept Mr Fox: she quarreled with Mr Fox, and flung herself and her presents into Lord Hervey's power, and the Duchess refused Mr Fox, who broke with Lord Hervey' (*Corr.*, 30. 313). The

Fox and Williams remained loyal to the King and refused to go into opposition. (By his refusal Williams was able to keep his post as Paymaster of the Marines, at £2,000 a year, while he poured out a stream of vitriolic anonymous lampoons against Pulteney.) Hervey called on Williams, stayed for two hours, apparently in a most gracious mood. But his distraction and absent-mindedness during these days can be judged by an embarrassing accident he suffered that Williams gleefully related to Fox a few days later. During a card-game with several other men he had gone into a neighbouring room to use a chamber-pot customarily kept there, and not noticing that the room had been unexpectedly taken over by some ladies for whist, he took up the pot, used it, and then, turning around as he buttoned his breeches, saw the ladies and fled, pursued by the sound of their laughter.

In the assembly rooms all whom Hervey met asked him whether the King would go abroad, but he answered them airily that he knew nothing of courts or politics. That did not prevent him from discussing political issues. He was all for carrying on the war vigorously though not for supporting it out of the Sinking Fund. He spoke openly and freely of his anti-Ministerial sentiments, and predicted that the next session of Parliament would see a sizeable Opposition. He was seen keeping the most unlikely company—Pulteney, now Earl of Bath, and Lord Gower, the new Privy Seal. If this gossip is true, it is difficult to think of what he could have been transacting with them. What is certain, however, is the intensity of his resentment towards the King.

He had expressed it privately to Lady Mary when he told her of refusing a pension on being turned out; and he had then spilled over into bitter couplets that ended with: 'Vice and Folly could be expelled from every throne except our own.' He spoke of his resentment openly, and when sent tickets for an entertainment to celebrate the King's birthday he returned them without any excuse. He flaunted his hatred of the King much more openly by writing a ballad that he called *The Patriots are Come; or, a Doctor for a Crazy Constitution*, which circulated in manuscript. Although Horace Walpole thought that he had disguised the 'niceness' of his style, Hardwicke's son—who of course found its attack on his

only part of this alleged intrigue that is verifiable is that the Duchess did not marry Fox. Once again Walpole refers to an affair between Hervey and Mrs. Horner (*Corr.*, 30. 27).

father offensive—thought that one might guess its authorship from the roughness of the numbers, hardness of the turns, and bitterness of the abuse. Hervey was versatile enough to write the ballad in the most effective style. It was soon published as a broadside.

It starts in a rollicking measure that is sustained for all of its twenty-seven stanzas:

> O England, attend, while thy fate I deplore,
> Rehearsing the schemes and the conduct of pow'r;
> And since only of those who have power I sing
> I am sure none can think that I hint at the King.

He then tells how the King, having been forced to depose 'old Robin', needs a doctor to restore his power, and calls on 'Doctor' Carteret to choose his cabinet. They are Newcastle, false, silly, and cowardly, who has betrayed Robin but will be kept because he spends his own money on elections; 'miser Hardwicke', who will be laughed into silence when he meddles with foreign policy; the 'Countess' of Wilmington, almost seventy and ineffectual, who will head the Treasury without having any power; and 'weathercock Pulteney', the new man, a fool of great parts, who will not stay in office. The Doctor then administers cordials to the King in the form of fleets, armies, wars; and the ballad ends with a lament for England:

> For though you have made that rogue Walpole retire,
> You are out of the frying-pan into the fire!
> But since to the Protestant line I'm a friend,
> I tremble to think where these changes may end!

Aside from paying off old enemies (not Walpole: it is Carteret who calls him a rogue), Hervey aims his main ridicule at his former Royal patron. What lay behind it was his disgust that the King, whom he had served so loyally for twelve years, should have abandoned him on the change of ministry. In this, Hervey may have regarded his situation in a rosier light because the new Ministry included others from Walpole's cabinet (Newcastle and Hardwicke). And when he took offence that the King would not compensate him with an equivalent post he was again obtuse: the King did not wish to make such an appointment without his Ministers' consent. It is difficult to explain Hervey's blindness in these respects. He had conceived of himself as the Queen's adoptive son (with her encouragement); perhaps he felt such irrational rage that he had been abandoned by his adoptive father.

His attack on the King struck others as shocking lese-majesty. William Murray (the future Lord Mansfield) did not conceal his surprise when he wrote to George Grenville: 'Lord H—y (would you believe it) is writing libels upon the King and his Ministers. It does not become him to be so employed.' His former political allies were even more disapproving. Walpole apparently condemned his ingratitude 'without the least Reserve'. It seemed shocking to him, as to other Whigs who remained loyal to the King in spite of Ministerial changes. 'Ld Hervey is talking anti-ministerially at Bath', Henry Fox warned his brother, 'and has put himself at court in a light that his greatest enemys could never have hoped to have seen him placed in.' Growing out of his pique, disappointment, and frustration, he planned—when Parliament next met—to exercise his fullest powers as a member of the opposition.

He was severely criticized for this by several of Walpole's Ministry who, while refusing to support the new Administration, still refused to go into opposition. Williams wrote some verse extolling Lord Lonsdale, who had resigned the Privy Seal (in 1735) without going into opposition; and he bitterly condemned Hervey for not following that example. His parting taunt is that

> . . . ev'n the dullest peer must see,
> The court had easily kept thee,
> Could'st thou have kept the seal.

Yet it is difficult to understand why Hervey was condemned for taking a step that seems normal in political life. If a man (along with his party leader) is turned out of office why should he not go into opposition? Carteret and Pulteney had done exactly that when, in an earlier era, they had left Walpole's Administration; and it had often been pointed out to Pulteney that while in office he supported many of the policies that he discovered to be bad after he was turned out of office in 1725. When Stephen Fox tried to dissuade Hervey from going into opposition he recognized its normality. 'I agree', he wrote, 'it has not been uncommon for those who have been ill usd at court to endeavour to distress the measures of that court, but how any one who does not quit the court from a dislike of Measures can reconcile such behaviour to themselves, or to a desire of preserving a character, I could never understand, unless all character is to be resolvd into resentment.'

As to 'Measures', Stephen asks Hervey to consider 'how unpleasant it must be, to vote & speak for place & pension bills, after having been the chief arguer for the rejecting of them. Consider how often you have refuted the arguments against Danes & Hessians, & remember how few questions except such as these are likely to come before the house of Lords.' The unpleasant situation that Stephen had foretold actually occurred a month later—but not to Hervey. The bill in Commons for defraying the cost of the Hanoverian troops was defended with some embarrassment by members of the new Administration who had so vehemently opposed such measures when brought in by Walpole. In that world of *realpolitik* absolute principles did not exist; party strategy ruled.

ii

Fearful that Hervey might try to persuade Stephen to join him politically in the House of Lords, Henry Fox urged his brother to attend Parliament lest his absence be interpreted as opposition. 'The King frequently and uneasily enquired about you,' he tells him in October 1742. 'And it must have arisen from himself, because I think (whether from Ld Orford's opinion or what I don't know) none of his ministers ever thought you would oppose.' He then advised Stephen to follow the dictates of his judgement and good sense, which are far superior to Hervey's, and to love his friend 'without letting him shew you to the world in a character most unsuitable to your heart and understanding'. Stephen replied that he preferred to stay in the country but would attend Parliament only if a measure relating to Walpole should come into the House of Lords. Henry was not wrong in foreseeing that Hervey would try to enlist Stephen.

While still at Bath, Hervey had written (on 6 November) that he was sorry to hear that Stephen did not plan to be in London for the Parliamentary session; '& to speak very freely to you, I had much rather release you from any Engagements your Partiality to me may have lay'd you under than have any Reluctance to show the Friendship you have been so good to profess for me, reduce you to such a State of Annihilation.' Even if others attempt to turn Stephen against him, he urges him not to remain 'in total Inaction, but without considering my Inclination, to come & act according to your own'. In a curiously parallel way both Hervey and Henry Fox urged Stephen to follow the dictates of his own conscience.

Stephen allowed himself four days to ruminate and then to compose a long, carefully reasoned, judicious reply to Hervey's request. While confessing his great obligation to Hervey he declares that only with the utmost reluctance could he bring himself to oppose the King's measures, for he would then be the only person placed in the House of Lords by the King to turn against him; and this at a time when the King's affairs were difficult and complicated, and faction ran high. 'What gives me a great & real concern', he tells Hervey, 'is that I think I perceive by the whole tenour of your letter that you are now come to a resolution of joining the opposition. This is what I heard would happen, what I did not expect & what I am sorry for.' In trying to persuade Hervey not to go into opposition he invoked the kind of wit that Hervey himself might use: 'Pensez y bien; remember that opposition is like matrimony, scarce any one ever embark'd in it without being heartily tir'd.' Only his respectful affection, he explains, makes him appeal so anxiously and uneasily.

Hervey himself was so anxious that he expected an immediate reply to his appeal. None came. And so on 13 November, by which time he had returned to London, he wrote again—on the very day that Stephen sent his reply from the country. This time his tone is more peremptory: disappointed not to have an answer, he can 'hope & conclude from thence that you will be soon in town, especially since you have not sent me your Proxy, which if you thought of staying longer in the Country you certainly would have done, as You must know not only how agreable it would be to me (tho otherwise quite useless I believe) to have the World see one Man at least can act rightly to me, but if you will give me leave to say so, because I think (considering all circumstances) it would be as right to your-self'. Then, as though to relax the intensity of his demand, he ended with casual gossip: 'Lord Orford comes to town to night. They talk of a very busy Session, but on what Points God knows, I neither know, inquire, or care.

Adieu.' Since he was not allied to any opposition group it may seem puzzling to understand why Hervey wanted Stephen's Parliamentary loyalty either by his presence or his proxy. Personally, he wanted proof that he was not being abandoned, as he had been by the King; and politically, he may have hoped to increase his weight in the House of Lords by controlling more than his own single vote.

As soon as he received Stephen's reply (to his first letter) he retaliated quickly and angrily, accusing him of one of the strongest instances of 'black ingratitude' he knew of, even in ancient history. Such a harsh accusation stung Stephen into replying almost immediately to protest against the accusation of ingratitude, for he had always acknowledged how much he owed to Hervey 'for solliciting, for pressing, & obtaining' his peerage. But that did not oblige him to turn against the person who had granted it—the King. Confident of his innocence, he had not arrived at such a pitch of villainy as to deserve such a letter as he had received, he wrote, before signing himself 'with great reguard [sic] & affection'. Thus ended, after fifteen years, the most profound friendship of Hervey's life.

Stephen resisted both the appeal from his brother and from Hervey; he remained at Redlinch, satisfying his own firm desire for the tranquillity of country life. Hervey had another potential supporter—his father; and there his task was easier because of Lord Bristol's detestation of the King and unwavering devotion to him. But Bristol loved the country, and as he grew older and his ailments multiplied, he increasingly disliked London and the arduous journey there. Still, he assured Hervey that if he could be 'of the least use to our sinking countrey or to your self' he would venture one more journey. Since important measures were generally not introduced into Parliament until after the Christmas recess he hoped in the meantime to gather his strength for a journey in the new year, when he would be at his son's disposal.

iii

At the opening of Parliament on 16 November 1742, Hervey heard the King's opening Speech. Its main points were the support of Maria Theresa (in the War of the Austrian Succession) and the hiring of Hanoverian and Hessian troops to augment the English army on the continent. Chesterfield led off with criticism of the Address, which was defended by Carteret, his former partner-in-Opposition. It was then accepted without a division, and sent to the Commons, which also passed it. Three important bills were introduced there, and the new Ministry succeeded in passing all. No important measure came before the Lords—a Land Tax bill on 7 December (when Hervey attended) and a Malt Bill. (Neither his father nor Stephen bothered to come up to London to attend.) Altogether the Lords sat on sixteen days before the Christmas recess; Hervey attended only three times and apparently took no part in the debates.

He preferred instead to set forth his political ideas in an anonymous pamphlet entitled *Miscellaneous Thoughts On the present Posture both of our Foreign and Domestic Affairs*, published on 1 December, in time to influence the debates in the House of Commons on Flanders and the Hanoverians. For wider sale it was issued in two printings, one at a shilling, the other at sixpence; and a second edition was advertised on 27 December. It is one of Hervey's most accomplished performances as a prose pamphleteer, for he allowed himself ample room (eighty pages) to set forth his carefully formulated 'miscellaneous thoughts'. His introductory section, a general disquisition on human nature, deflates the pretensions not only of the Administration but of men in general, with the Hobbesian notion that 'Selfishness is the fundamental Ingredient in the Composition of every Being throughout the whole animal Creation, and in human Kind, as well as the rest.' This leads him, in a neatly turned paradox, to reflect that the same human depravity that makes restrictive laws necessary makes them liable to be abused by the executive power that enforces them. The triumvirate who now control the Administration—Carteret, Pulteney, and Newcastle (though unnamed)—are like the famous Roman one of Octavius, Antony, and Lepidus. How effective they will be, he says, remains to be seen.

Then—what is most remarkable in his pamphlet—Hervey launches into a defence of Walpole that runs to ten pages, followed by an attack on the various policies of the new Ministry to show that they have not remedied what they had once charged were Walpole's faults, so that even this latter section is, in effect, a defence of Walpole and the previous Administration. England's relations with the Dutch, the army in Flanders, foreign subsidies, prosecution of the war against Spain, the national debt: in all these he defends Walpole's policies. To judge him by his own sceptical standards, his defence of Walpole and the previous Ministry was, in effect, a defence of himself. But in view of what lay in store for the fallen Prime Minister his defence was less for his own sake than for Walpole's.

He sent a copy of the *Miscellaneous Thoughts* to his father, who thought it so valuable that even if the postage had cost the pamphlet's weight in gold he would not have objected. Hervey had not needed to identify himself as its author, his father tells him, since he had not read twenty pages before he found it so marked by Hervey's style that he might as well have set his name to it. Its effectiveness was assessed by a less sympathetic critic, Hardwicke's son, who tells his brother that Hervey, having abused their father and Newcastle in a ballad, 'has just writ a Pamphlet wherein he attempts to show that if the Complaints against Sir Robert's Administration were groundless (as he insinuates very strongly they were) the New Comers have realized them; if those Complaints were just, they have greatly encreased them.'

With such outstanding pamphleteering to his credit Hervey could forego speaking his mind in that brief session of Parliament. He was in excellent spirits after the session ended, when he sent eight packets of pamphlets to Lady Mary—then living in Avignon —and only wished to talk to her of 'the different Scenes and Characters of our present tragical-comical political Drama' but like most other pleasures that was denied him [because of post-office spies]. 'My Health is mended to a miracle', he assures her, 'the Resurrection of Lazarus was hardly more surprising.' When Parliament reconvened, he may have wondered, would he achieve his political resurrection?

iv

Soon after Parliament met (on 14 January 1743), the newspapers advertised that in a few days would be published *The Question Stated, with Regard to Our Army in Flanders*. Written by Hervey and published on the 22nd, it was a preparation for an important measure still to be raised in the House of Lords; and as with the *Miscellaneous Thoughts* it was issued in two printings.

U   sing an elaborate sequence of arguments Hervey tries to prove that it is both inexpedient and unnecessary for England to maintain an army in Flanders. Being at war with Spain was bad enough, he argues; now, in a futile attempt to help Maria Theresa, England runs the risk of engaging France in a new war. He marshals every kind of reason to withdraw the army: it is contrary to common sense since England's interest rests on her being a maritime power, a trading nation, and an indebted nation. It is unconstitutional, and is contrary to the interest of the Royal Family—a paradoxical argument since it was the King who urged that policy. Compared to Hervey's other political pamphlets the *Question Stated* is poorly composed, and suffers from repetitiousness; he must have written it hastily. He was at the same time preparing to argue the question viva voce on the floor of Parliament.

The motion was introduced on 1 February beseeching the King to relieve the British of the burden of employing Hanoverian troops (to augment the army in Flanders). When Hervey spoke on it he did not confine himself to the issue of troops — hired by the King without Parliament's permission, as another speaker alleged—but attacked the larger one, that England should not risk new conflicts when she should be winning the war against Spain. War was ruinous to her economy, and peace the best road to prosperity. He was very aware of the fact that now, in his first speech since going into opposition, he might be accused of contradicting his Ministerial arguments; he therefore defies anyone to prove he had ever advocated that the English become entangled in disputes on the continent or use arms to regulate the affairs of warring nations. He had always believed—as indeed Walpole had—that peace with the ease of security was preferable to the honour of victory.

Horace Walpole, so unsympathetic to Hervey, had to confess that he spoke for an hour and a half 'with the greatest applause'. Among those who listened were his admiring father and his former friend, both of whom had left their country retreats to attend the debate and to vote. Again the Ministry won, defeating the motion 90 to 35; and although Hervey and his father were among the defeated they did not sign the Lords' Protest entered into the Journals of the House. (But the family was divided; in the Commons in December the eccentric Tom Hervey had voted for the Hanoverians.) As for the newly ennobled Earl of Orford, he and his son Lord Walpole stayed away because (in Lord

Oxford's opinion) 'they would not oppose so favorite a point as Hannover troops, nor would they Countenance a Scheme of Carteret's'.

Hervey's former association with Walpole was highlighted at this time by one of the replies to the *Miscellaneous Thoughts*, the pamphlet in which he had defended the fallen Minister. *Sapho to Phaon: an Epistle from a Lady of Quality to a Noble Lord*, published in February 1743, accuses him of having written Walpole's 'Apology for his own Life'. His pamphlet, the anonymous Lady of Quality charges, is an attempt to vindicate Walpole, to 'white-wash Him. . . . You know the MAN whom I mean, *Jacky*—your *Friend*, your *Patron*, for whom you have always been an Advocate, and for whom, in this your last Dying-Speech, you still remain a Champion'. This pamphlet was being read during the time Hervey was active in the Lords' debates.

He continued his activity a fortnight later on a bill, hastily passed in the House of Commons, for revising the duties levied on spirituous liquors and the licences to sell them—for the purpose of raising further revenue. His motion (on 21 February) that three physicians be invited to testify as to the pernicious effects of liquor was defeated. The next day in a highly emotional speech he painted a picture as graphic and horrifying as Hogarth's print of Gin Lane (published seven years later). He also dealt with the financial ramifications of the bill to link it with the burden of the Hanoverian troops. He spoke several times in that day's debate, and then again on the 24th and 25th, when the bill was put to a vote and passed. He had spoken in vain.

Until the session ended in April, more than two months later, he attended the House only a few times. (Stephen, however, was present at most of the sittings.) His inactivity and his lack of interest in politics are mirrored in his remark to Lady Mary (in April): 'The Public Affairs are in a strange Posture & I beleive You know as much of them where you are [in Avignon] & what we would be at, as any minister in the Cabinet. I am sure I know no more than if I had been born an Ideot.' Thus ended, less gloriously than he could have wished, the first (and last) session of Parliament that Hervey attended as a member of the Opposition.

Satisfaction of a different kind had come to him that winter when his eldest daughter, Lepell, had been married to Constantine

Phipps, grandson and heir of the proud, eccentric Duchess of Buckingham, illegitimate daughter of James II. (She was, Horace Walpole remarked, 'more mad with pride than any mercer's wife in Bedlam'.) When Hervey had once called on her at Buckingham House to discuss the match, that day was the anniversary of her grandfather Charles I's martyrdom; and she received him in the great drawing-room seated in a chair of state in deep mourning attended by her women also in mourning. She had arranged the marriage hastily—her grandson, twenty-one years old, was still at Oxford—probably because she was ill and had not long to live. The terms of the match were highly advantageous to Hervey, for he had to raise a dowry of only £3,000 while the bride received the very generous jointure of £1,200 a year and other settlements in proportion.

Only two weeks after she saw her grandson married the Duchess died. Her executors, appointed a month before, were Robert Walpole and Hervey, but Walpole declined and Lord Orrery took his place. The Duchess had left her great mansion in St. James's Park to Hervey for life, with all its furniture and silver, but he was too well lodged in St. James's Square to think of moving. Instead, he gave it to the young couple, who would eventually have it. At the funeral, on 8 April, the Hon. Mrs. Phipps was chief mourner when the Duchess made her stately exit in a procession that ended with her burial in the Henry VIII Chapel in Westminster Abbey.

Hervey's surge of good health at the beginning of the winter had not lasted, and soon after Parliament was prorogued (in April) he travelled down to Ickworth in the hope of recuperating. As one of his pastimes his wife read to him from the historical papers in the *Craftsman*, the political journal that had attacked Walpole's Ministry so violently in the 1730s; perhaps he was preparing for future political campaigns. He had to return to London in mid-May to deal with Lord Orrery, no doubt about the executorship of the Duchess's estate, and stayed at Buckingham House. Orrery, who observed that he was 'much be-diamonded', thought that he looked ill but spoke cheerfully.

On his way back to Ickworth he was delayed at Newmarket by his illness. His mood, after he arrived home, was philosophical, and stoical in the manner of his classical heroes. He expressed these sentiments to Lady Mary, still living in bored retirement in Avignon. 'The last stages of an infirm life are filthy roads,' he tells her (on 18 June), '& like all other roads, I find the farther one goes from the capital the more tedious the miles grow, & the more rough & disagreeable the ways. . . . May all your ways (as Solomon says of wisdom) be ways of pleasentness and all your paths peace. . . . Adieu.' His thoughts on human mortality were no mere verbal flourish.

A week later he decided to draw up his will. Not strong enough to write, he dictated it, and then read it over twice to correct the spelling. Most of its provisions were conventional enough: his eldest son to be sole heir and executor, annuities to all his children, dowries of £5,000 for his eldest unmarried daughter, Mary, and £4,000 each to the two other girls, annuities to his housekeeper and to his valet. But the bequest to his wife was astonishing: she could have only what he was obliged to leave her by the terms of their marriage contract, and nothing more; and while she could dispose of some things at her death, she must give security for all the money, silver, and jewels, and bequeath them to one of her children born during wedlock.

The same day that he dictated and corrected his will he wrote a brief letter (evidently in his own hand) addressed to Mrs. Strangways Horner. 'Dear Madam,' it runs, 'If you have a mind to shew any Regard to my Memory fullfill this my last Request & take my Daughter Miss Mary Hervey to live with You. She is very well disposed & will continue so living with one of your excellent Principles & real honest worth. I love and honour You. Adieu.' He gave the letter to his daughter with instructions that she deliver it to Mrs. Horner after his death. That event was not far off. By mid-July he was dangerously ill, and on 5 August he died. His father showed his love for him even at the burial a week later in the Ickworth church, for instead of a woollen shroud to clothe the corpse, as the law required, Lord Bristol chose another cloth (probably linen) and paid a fine of £5. The only other member of the Hervey family who enjoyed this posthumous luxury was Lord Bristol himself.

v

To Lord Bristol, Hervey's death was an 'irreparable loss'; he regarded it as a severe trial of his faith and trust in the wisdom of

God that he should have to submit to the loss of a son so remarkably distinguished by Providence with 'excelling genius and rare
talents'. With his sharp-eyed view of human nature Hervey had
once told his father that he could not bear to be talked about on
any occasion since most people were more inclined to censure
than to commend. Yet, surprisingly, Pope's sentiments seemed
benign; 'I just hear of the death of Lord Hervey,' he told Orrery.
'Requiescat in pace!' But in his final *Dunciad* that autumn he
expressed a more sincere sentiment by designating Hervey a 'Fool
of Quality'. Horace Walpole, however, after imparting the news
to Mann that Hervey was dead, added—'luckily I think for himself, for he had outlived his last inch of character'. Not quite; in
the aftermath of his death his character (in another sense) lived on.

His will was the chief topic of conversation in London, particularly its provisions for Lady Hervey. No one knew why he had
treated her in such a way; and it was said that he had refused to
see her for many weeks before he died. Because of her modest
jointure—only £300 a year—she would have to live with Lord
Bristol, no great hardship since they were devoted to each other.

Then, after the will had been read, early in September Mrs.
Horner was startled by a visit from Mary Hervey with a letter
from her late father. When Mrs. Horner overcame her surprise
she sent a copy of the letter to Lady Hervey, assuring her that she
was an 'utter Stranger to the Purport' before she was informed of
it by Miss Hervey, and that for many reasons she could not comply
with its request. Lady Hervey displayed impeccable tact in thanking
Mrs. Horner for her considerate letter: 'I am not surpriz'd at any
proof of Esteem given you by My Dear late Lord, knowing the
great Friendship he had for you, Madam; and I am as little so at
the very right Manner in which you have acted on this Occasion.'
Lady Hervey remained the most considerate of wives.

Even this, one of Hervey's last actions is—like so many others
in his life—puzzling. Molly Lepell, whom he had married for
love, had been (so far as is known) an exemplary wife: she had
borne his children, nursed and fussed over him in his illness, stood
by him loyally in his politics, solaced his father, shared his ill
relations with his mother, befriended most of his friends—
particularly Stephen Fox and Algarotti, whom she could justi-
fiably have spurned out of jealousy. (Her loyalty to another
friend, Lady Murray, kept her from sharing Hervey's friendship

with Lady Mary Wortley Montagu.) It seems impossible to defend Hervey's treatment of his wife, his humiliating her first through the provisions in his will and then through trying to remove their daughter from her care. Yet the question nags: why? Was he like Iago, a creature impelled by motiveless malignity? Or was there a motive whose history has not survived? In the absence of any clue at all, speculation must remain silent.★

It was a matter of conjecture how large an estate he had left. Some thought he had died much richer than expected, others that his possessions would have to be auctioned to raise the legacies for his children. Since his possessions remained intact and his widow and children continued to prosper he had apparently left a large, unencumbered estate. When Horace Walpole tried to buy the sarcophagus that Hervey had outbid him for at auction the new Lord Hervey told him that his father had ordered him never to part with anything (though he later sold it).

The grateful son and heir asked Dr. Middleton, who had so excessively appreciated Lord Hervey, to compose an epitaph for his monument. Middleton had learned his lesson; the Latin lines he sent are relatively restrained. They read (in translation): 'This brilliant man was equally versatile at everything, so that one said that whatever he did he was born to that alone.' Hervey himself had written an epitaph only the previous year while on a visit to Ickworth, and had given it to his father, who endorsed it: 'Long, o very long may it be before it will be engrav'd.' These six couplets, of a quality better than most of the other verse he wrote, sketch his character as he himself believed it to be:

> Few men he liked; and fewer still believ'd;
> Fewest of all he trusted, none deciev'd:
> But as from temper, principle or pride,
> To gain whom he dislik'd he never try'd,
> And this the pride of others disapprov'd,
> So lik'd by many, he by few was lov'd.
> To those he lov'd a real friend he brought,
> And in that character without a fault.

★ Lady Louisa Stuart, a granddaughter of Lady Mary Wortley Montagu, wrote that Lord and Lady Hervey 'lived together upon very amicable terms, "as well-bred as if not married at all" . . . but without any strong sympathies, and more like a French couple than an English one'. Her information must have come from her mother. But even if true—for Lady Hervey's letters tell a different story—this would still not account for the vindictive terms of Hervey's will.

What his opinions, Parts or conduct were,
This monument pretends not to declare;
He had a truly warm & honest breast,
Let his own writings speak the rest.

No man writes his own epitaph to depreciate his character (to paraphrase what Samuel Johnson says about letter-writing), and Hervey was no exception.

On another, less solemn occasion Hervey glanced at himself when he remarked that his coat of arms should be 'a *cat* scratchant, with this motto: "For my friends where they itch; for my enemies where they are sore." ' That would perhaps be a more suitable epitaph for him.

vi

Of those whom Hervey left behind, old Lord Bristol mourned most deeply, and fortunately could depend on his religious beliefs, shaken though they were, to sustain him. He lived until 1751, and was buried in the Ickworth church between his two wives. Lady Hervey had continued to live at Ickworth with her two younger daughters, who had a French governess to attend them. The eldest, who had been consigned to Mrs. Horner, refused to stay with her mother; perhaps Mrs. Horner took charge of her after all. A few years later Lady Hervey, who evidently had ample funds, left Ickworth for a house she ordered to be built in St. James's Place, where she lived in moderate elegance. The rank of earl's daughters was conferred on her girls to compensate them for the courtesy title of which they had been deprived by their father's death in his own father's lifetime. That did not prevent Lady Hervey from educating them to be 'rank Jacobites', her eldest son thought, and teaching them not only to reverence the Pretender but even to ridicule and censure the King. Hervey would have approved.

Lady Hervey, who had always been a francophile, paid several extended visits to France. In London, where she set up a modest salon, David Hume and Edward Gibbon were among those who frequented it; Gibbon thought it wonderful that instead of card-playing there was very good company and conversation. She became a warm friend of Horace Walpole's as one of the gentle old ladies with whom he liked to surround himself. He dedicated his *Anecdotes of Painting* to her (in 1762), praising her as one 'who has conversed familiarly with the most agreeable persons, dead and living, of the most polished ages and most polished nations'. At her family's request he composed an epitaph for her after her death in 1768. Even then she continued to observe the proprieties; in spite of her husband's humiliating legacy her remains were buried next to his in Ickworth church, and so they lie side by side forever.

Lady Hervey's friendship with Lord Ilchester (Stephen Fox) had survived the quarrel between the two men; and they continued for the rest of their lives to see each other and to correspond when they were not in the same vicinity. In August 1743, the very month when Hervey died, the uncertain Ministry was more firmly established with the appointment of Henry Pelham, Newcastle's brother, to the head of the Treasury (in place of Wilmington). 'There is scarce a man in England more thoroughly rejoic'd than I am', Ilchester congratulated Newcastle, adding the hope that Pelham would continue there 'with as much ease & honour to himself as I am sure it will be to the satisfaction of all your Grace's friends, among which number I shall think it the highest honour to be reckoned'. The appointment did Ilchester no harm. He received £400 a year from the secret service money dispensed by Pelham, although it is not clear what work he did for it. His brother Henry, the future Lord Holland, is called by Lewis Namier the most rapacious eighteenth-century statesman for his success in enriching his family at the expense of the King and the nation. Lord Ilchester was appointed joint-comptroller of army accounts in 1747, was raised to an earldom in 1756, became a member of George III's Privy Council in 1763, and died in 1776, leaving a splendid estate and mourned by a numerous family.

The other object of Hervey's homoerotic passion, Count Algarotti, also long outlived him. Dissatisfied with his rewards from Frederick of Prussia, he moved to Dresden in 1742 to enjoy the more generous patronage of the Elector of Saxony and King of Poland. He gathered a great collection of pictures for that art-loving monarch, some of them especially commissioned; and his duties allowed him to spend long periods of time in Italy and to increase the bulk and scope of his writings. After five years he returned to Frederick's court, remaining there until ill health drove him to Italy (in 1753), where he lived in retirement until his death in 1764, occupied with his writings and his learned friends there and abroad.

Lady Mary, after her four-year sojourn in Avignon, settled in the Venetian province of Brescia; and in 1756 she moved to Venice and resumed her correspondence with Algarotti, this time as a witty *bel esprit* instead of a lovesick matron. 'If we ever meet,' she wrote to him in 1758 (four years before her own death), 'the Memory of Lord Hervey shall be celebrated; his Gentle Shade will be pleas'd in Elysium with our Gratitude. I am insensible to every thing but the remembrance of those few Freinds that have been dear to me.' Perhaps, then, Hervey enjoys eternity in the company of the enchanting Algarotti and the witty Lady Mary.

Descent of Lord Hervey's Father[*]

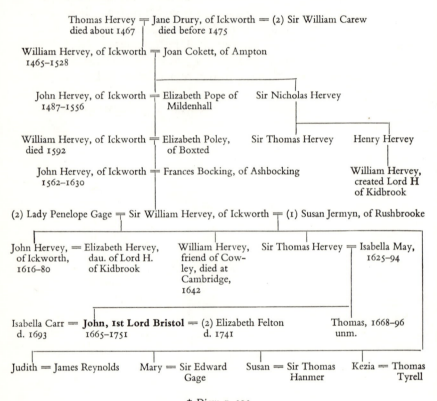

Thomas Hervey ╤ Jane Drury, of Ickworth ══ (2) Sir William Carew
died about 1467 │ died before 1475

William Hervey, of Ickworth ╤ Joan Cokett, of Ampton
1465–1528

John Hervey, of Ickworth ╤ Elizabeth Pope of   Sir Nicholas Hervey
1487–1556   Mildenhall

William Hervey, of Ickworth ╤ Elizabeth Poley,   Sir Thomas Hervey   Henry Hervey
died 1592   of Boxted

John Hervey, of Ickworth ╤ Frances Bocking, of Ashbocking   William Hervey,
1562–1630   created Lord H
                                                                   of Kidbrook

(2) Lady Penelope Gage ╤ Sir William Hervey, of Ickworth ╤ (1) Susan Jermyn, of Rushbrooke

John Hervey, ══ Elizabeth Hervey,   William Hervey,   Sir Thomas Hervey ╤ Isabella May,
of Ickworth,   dau. of Lord H.   friend of Cow-   1625–94
1616–80   of Kidbrook   ley, died at
                                    Cambridge,
                                    1642

Isabella Carr ══ **John, 1st Lord Bristol** ══ (2) Elizabeth Felton   Thomas, 1668–96
d. 1693   1665–1751   d. 1741   unm.

Judith ══ James Reynolds   Mary ══ Sir Edward   Susan ══ Sir Thomas   Kezia ══ Thomas
                                     Gage   Hanmer   Tyrell

★ *Diary*, p. 305.

[310]

Lord Hervey's Brothers and Sisters*

[father] John Hervey (1665–1751), Baron Hervey (1703), Earl of Bristol (1714)

m. (1688) Isabella Carr (d. 1693)
1. Isabella (1689–1711)
2. Carr (1691–1723), Lord Hervey (1714)

m. (1695) Elizabeth Felton (1676–1741)
1. **John (1696-1743)**, **Lord Hervey (1723)**, m. (1720) Mary Lepell (1700–1768)
2. Elizabeth (1697–1727), m. (1724) Bussy Mansel
3. Thomas (1699–1775)
4. William (1699–1776)
5. Henry (1701–48)
6. Charles (1703–83)
7. Ann (1707–71)
8. Barbara (1709–27)
9. Felton (1711–73)
10. Louisa (1715–70), m. (1731) Sir Robert Smyth
11. Henrietta (1716–32)

* Only those who survived to adulthood.

Lord Hervey's Children

1. George William (1721–75), 2nd Earl of Bristol (1751)
2. Lepell (1723–80), m. (1743) Constantine Phipps, later Lord Mulgrave
3. Augustus John (1724–79), 3rd Earl of Bristol (1775)
4. Mary (1725–1815), m. (1745) George Fitzgerald
5. Frederick (1730–1803), 4th Earl of Bristol (1779)
6. William (1732–1815)
7. Emily Caroline (1734–1814)
8. Caroline (1736–1819)

Acknowledgements

IN writing this book I have been generously treated by so many friends, strangers, owners of manuscripts and pictures, and staffs of libraries that I can only hope to mention my main benefactors.

Professor J. H. Plumb and the late Romney Sedgwick answered my frequent questions and checked the penultimate draft, and Professor James Sutherland read the final typescript. The Hon. David Hervey Erskine was irrepressibly helpful throughout; and others who helped in one way or another include J. M. Beattie, Patrick Doran, David Foxon, Isobel Grundy, Allen Hazen, W. S. Lewis, A. L. Rowse, Warren H. Smith, Lawrence Snow, James Thomson, David Woolley, and (with proofs) Aubrey Newman and Thomas F. Nally.

I also owe thanks to the John Simon Guggenheim Foundation for a fellowship in 1968–9, to St. John's College, Cambridge, for hospitality during the summer of 1971, and to the University of California, Riverside, for a grant toward secretarial assistance.

Private owners who allowed me to use their manuscripts are the late Theodora, Marchioness of Bristol, the Earl Cathcart, the Marquess of Cholmondeley, the Earl of Haddington, the Earl of Harrowby, the Earl of Ilchester, Mr. W. S. Lewis, the Duke of Marlborough, Mr. John Murray, the Marquess of Normanby, the trustees of the late Lord Sempill (Craigievar Castle MSS.), and the Earl Waldegrave.

The repositories for MSS. I have used are Archives des Affaires Étrangères (Paris), Archives of the Duchy of Cornwall, Bodleian Library, British Museum, Cambridge University Library, Goodwood Archives (West Sussex Record Office), Harvard University Library, Hoare and Company (London), Koninklijk Huisarchief (The Hague), Northwestern University Library, Public Record Office (London), Trinity College (Cambridge), Westminster Public Library (rate books), West Suffolk Record Office (Bury St. Edmunds), and Windsor Castle Archives. In the U.S.A. I have used the following libraries: Clark (U.C.L.A.),

Columbia, Huntington, Newberry, New York Public, Princeton, Yale; and in England: the Bodleian, British Museum, Cambridge University.

Of the portraits that are privately owned, plate 9 is reproduced by gracious permission of H.M. the Queen, plate 5 by permission of Lady Teresa Agnew, and plate 4 the Marquess of Normanby. Plates 1, 2, 3, 14, and 16 are here by permission of H.M. Treasury and the National Trust, Bristol Collection, Ickworth; plate 8 by permission of the Huntington Library; plates 7 and 11, the Trustees of the British Museum; plate 10, the National Portrait Gallery; plate 12, the Museo di Roma (deposito della Accademia dell'Arcadia); plate 13, the West Suffolk Record Office; and plate 15, by permission of Her Majesty's Stationery Office.

Notes

DOCUMENTATION FROM MANUSCRIPT SOURCES

In printing from manuscript this style has been used: exact spelling and numerals are retained; standard abbreviations are expanded except the ampersand (a sign of informality); raised letters are lowered; when required, punctuation is adjusted and capital letters are provided for persons, places, book-titles, and beginnings of sentences; apostrophes are added for possessives and deleted in plurals; square brackets [ ] are inserted for editorial additions, and angle brackets ⟨ ⟩ for doubtful readings. In the annotations, MS. will be used as the singular or plural of Manuscript.

FREQUENTLY CITED COLLECTIONS

Add MS.	Additional Manuscripts, British Museum.
Blenheim	Letters from the Countess of Bristol to Saráh, Duchess of Marlborough, Blenheim Palace Archives.
BM.	British Museum. Letters in the Holland House MS., which have not yet been given permanent catalogue numbers, will be cited by date followed by BM. MS.
Cholmondeley (Houghton)	Owned by the Marquess of Cholmondeley; on deposit at the Cambridge University Library.
Cocchi	Archives owned by Enrico Baldasseroni, Florence; microfilm on deposit at Northwestern University Library.
H	Hervey Manuscripts, West Suffolk Record Office, Bury St. Edmunds. Letters in this collection, which is thoroughly calendared, will be cited by date followed by H MS.
Mulgrave Castle MS.	Owned by the Marquess of Normanby.
Murray	Owned by Mr. John Murray, London.
PRO	Public Record Office, London.
Trinity College	Letters from Conyers Middleton to Thomas Townshend, M.P., on deposit at the Cambridge University Library.
WSL	Collection of Wilmarth S. Lewis, Farmington, Conn.

DOCUMENTATION FROM PRINTED SOURCES

Standard peerages, biographical dictionaries, and these Parliamentary reference works will not be cited: Richard Chandler, *History and Proceedings of the House of Commons* (1742–4); William Cobbett, *Parliamentary History of England* (1806–20); *Journals of the House of Commons*; *Journals of the House of Lords*; James E. T. Rogers, *Protests of the Lords* (1875); Romney Sedgwick, *The House of Commons 1715–1754* (1970); Ebenezer Timberland, *History and Proceedings of the House of Lords* (1742); John Torbuck, *Collection of Parliamentary Debates in England* (1739–42). Although the records of who spoke in Parliament are incomplete and sometimes inaccurate I have depended on what evidence survives, and have spared readers the cautionary 'evidently' and 'apparently'. I have not, however, quoted the exact words of speeches unless my source was a reliable one rather than the customary collections.

ABBREVIATED TITLES

Chesterfield *Letters*	Philip Dormer Stanhope, Earl of Chesterfield, *Letters*, ed. B. Dobrée (1932).
Coxe *Walpole*	William Coxe, *Memoirs of Sir Robert Walpole* (1798).
Delany *Corr.*	Mary Delany, *Autobiography and Correspondence*, ed. Lady Llanover, First Series (1861).
Diary	John Hervey, 1st Earl of Bristol, *Diary* [ed. S. H. A. Hervey] (1894).
Egmont	HMC 1st Earl of Egmont, *Diary* (1920–3).
Gray *Corr.*	Thomas Gray, *Correspondence*, ed. P. Toynbee and L. Whibley (1935).
HMC	Historical Manuscripts Commission Reports.
H *Mem.*	John, Lord Hervey, *Some Materials Towards Memoirs of the Reign of George II*, ed. R. Sedgwick (1931).
Ilchester *Fox*	Earl of Ilchester, *Henry Fox, First Lord Holland* (1920).
Letter-Books	John Hervey, 1st Earl of Bristol, *Letter-Books* [ed. S. H. A. Hervey] (1894).
LM *Letters*	Lady Mary Wortley Montagu, *Complete Letters*, ed. R. Halsband (1965–7).
Pope *Corr.*	Alexander Pope, *Correspondence*, ed. G. Sherburn (1956).
Pope *Poems*	Alexander Pope, *Poems*, Twickenham Edition, ed. J. Butt and others (1943 ff.).
Suffolk *Letters*	Henrietta, Countess of Suffolk, *Letters* [ed. J. W. Croker] (1824).
Voltaire *Corr.*	Voltaire, *Correspondence*, ed. Th. Besterman (1953–64).
Walpole *Catalogue*	Horace Walpole, *Catalogue of Royal and Noble Authors*, in *Works* (1798), 1. 450–3, 531.
Walpole *Corr.*	Horace Walpole, *Correspondence*, ed. W. S. Lewis and others (1937 ff.).

PREFACE

page vii, line 4   Lady Louisa Stuart, 'Biographical Anecdotes', in Lady Mary Wortley Montagu, *Letters and Works*, ed. Lord Wharncliffe (1837), 1. 64; Walpole *Corr.*, 17. 274 n.

        8   *Molly Lepell, Lady Hervey*, by Dorothy M. Stuart (1936); *The Earl Bishop: The Life of Frederick Hervey, Bishop of Derry, Earl of Bristol*, by W. S. Childe-Pemberton (2 vols., 1924).

      17   *Call a Dog Hervey*, by D. A. Ponsonby [1949]; *Lord Hervey and His Friends, 1726–38*, ed. the Earl of Ilchester (1950). Peter Quennell's perceptive review of the Ilchester selection is reprinted in *The Singular Preference: Portraits & Essays* (1952).

page viii, line 39   H *Mem.*, 1. 87.

PROLOGUE: 1740

page 1, line 12   Portrait by J. B. Vanloo (see Plate 16).

      17   PRO, P.C. 2/96.

      26   H. C. Maxwell-Lyte, *Historical Notes on the Use of the Great Seal of England* (1926), pp. 48–9.

      29   PRO, L.C. 5/73, f. 183; 5/75, p. 124 A.

page 2, line 5   PRO, Ind. 6762. Frederick obtained the clerkship in 1753, long after his father's resignation from office (and death).

      20   *Diary*, p. 86.

      28   *Letter-Books*, 3. 243.

      34   *Letter-Books*, 3. 251, 252.

CHAPTER I. 1696–1714

page 3, line 5   John Gage, *The History and Antiquities of Suffolk. Thingoe Hundred* (1838), pp. 285–6, 289.

      14   *Biographical List of Boys Educated at King Edward VI Free Grammar School, Bury St. Edmunds. From 1550 to 1900*, Suffolk Green Books No. XIII (1908), pp. 189, 191; Victoria County Histories, *Suffolk*, ed. W. Page (1907), 2. 321.

      16   *Letter-Books*, 1. 215.

      21   *Mæstissimæ ac Lætissimæ Academiæ Cantabrigiensis affectus* (1685), p. [sig. M 1].

page 4, line 12   *Diary*, p. 14; John Macky, *Memoirs of the Secret Services* [1704] (1733, repr. 1895), p. 80.

      20   *Diary*, p. 157.

      29   *Diary*, p. 88.

      31   *Diary*, p. 19.

      36   Augustus Hervey, *Journal 1746–59*, ed. D. H. Erskine (1953), p. 111.

      37   *Diary*, p. 21.

page 5, line 20   *Diary*, pp. 187–90.
        26   *Letter-Books*, I. 80.
        29   *Diary*, p. 23.
        32   *Letter-Books*, I. 95.
        36   *Diary*, p. 23.
        40   *Letter-Books*, I. 97.
page 6, line 12   *Letter-Books*, I. 103.
        20   *Diary*, pp. 25, 200.
        30   *Letter-Books*, I. 117.
        39   *Letter-Books*, I. 117, 125–7.
page 7, line 5   Documents printed in *Diary*, 204–12.
        7   LCC *Survey of London*, 29 (1960), 103–4; *Diary*, pp. 32, 46.
        14   *Diary*, pp. 210, 277.
        17   On the site of what is now called Ickworth Lodge.
        27   *Letter-Books*, I. 158, 159, 164–5.
        31   *Diary*, pp. 128–9.
        35   *Letter-Books*, I. 189.
page 8, line 16   Sarah, Duchess of Marlborough, *Memoirs* [*An Account of the Conduct of . . .*, 1742], ed. W. King (1930), pp. 90, 211–12.
        20   John Chamberlayne, *Magnae Britanniae Notitia* (1718), pp. 96–7.
        25   *Diary*, p. 39.
        32   John M. Beattie, *The English Court in the Reign of George I* (1967), pp. 69–70, 211.
        35   *Diary*, p. 48.
        39   PRO, Prerogative Court of Canterbury (wills), Lane, f. 55; *Diary*, p. 213.
page 9, line 4   *Wentworth Papers 1705–1739*, ed. J. J. Cartwright (1883), p. 78; HMC *Portland MSS.* 4 (1897), 590.
        9   *Diary*, p. 148.
        19   *Letter-Books*, I. 303.
        26   *Wentworth Papers*, p. 197.
        36   *Diary*, p. 55.
page 10, line 4   *Diary*, p. 43.
        14   *Diary*, pp. 44–5.
        22   *Letter-Books*, I. 241, 254–5.
        25   *Diary*, pp. 100, 183.
        31   *Letter-Books*, I. 247, 248.
page 11, line 1   *Diary*, pp. 57, 90, 167.
        3   Daniel Defoe, *A Tour of Great Britain* (3rd ed., 1742), I. 78.
        14   *Letter-Books*, I. 275.
        21   *Letter-Books*, I. 281, 288.
        25   *Letter-Books*, I. 297.
        36   *Diary*, p. 101.
page 12, line 9   *Gentleman's Magazine*, Mar. 1733, p. 152. (Pelham stands for the Duke of Newcastle.)

page 12, line 16 G. F. Russell Barker, *Memoir of Richard Busby* (1895), pp. 78–81; Frederick H. Forshall, *Westminster School Past and Present* (1884), pp. 409–13 *passim*.

19 H MS. 46/5.

27 Lord Hervey, *Epistle from a Nobleman* (1733), p. 4. In 1710 William King had published a *Historical Account of the Heathen Gods and Heroes*, which was widely used in schools.

36 John Sargeaunt, *Annals of Westminster School* (1898), p. 270.

page 13, line 1 Forshall in note to page 12 above.

4 Lawrence E. Tanner, *Westminster School Its Buildings and their Associations* [1923], pp. 52–3.

7 *Joseph Andrews*, ed. M. C. Battestin (1967), p. 230.

14 'Tirocinium', *Poetical Works*, ed. H. S. Milford (4th ed., 1950), pp. 246–7.

18 *Memoirs of My Life*, ed. G. A. Bonnard (1966), p. 38.

27 *Diary*, p. 56.

32 *Letter-Books*, 1. 325, 327.

page 14, line 4 *Letter-Books*, 1. 331–2.

14 *Diary*, p. 57.

33 *Letter-Books*, 1. 348, 350–1.

page 15, line 11 *Diary*, p. 58; *Letter-Books*, 1. 350, 354, 357.

32 *Letter-Books*, 1. 379–80.

37 *Diary*, pp. 59–60.

page 16, line 4 *Diary*, p. 60.

5 W. J. Harrison, *Life in Clare Hall, Cambridge 1658–1713* (1958), p. 38.

14 Edward Ward in *Cambridge Under Queen Anne*, ed. J. E. B. Mayor (1911), p. 410.

18 No. 78, ed. D. F. Bond (1965), 1. 335.

22 Z. C. von Uffenbach in J. E. B. Mayor, p. 124.

24 Gray *Corr.*, 1. 3.

27 Ralph Thoresby, *Diary 1677–1724* (1830), 2. 232.

30 von Uffenbach, p. 146.

34 Denys A. Winstanley, *Unreformed Cambridge* (1935), pp. 188, 193–4.

36 James H. Monk, *The Life of Richard Bentley* (1833), 1. 286–8.

page 17, line 6 *Letter-Books*, 1. 391.

16 *Letter-Books*, 1. 393.

19 *Diary*, pp. 102, 103.

23 William Whiston, *Memoirs of the Life and Writings* (1749), p. 26.

27 John R. Wardale, *Clare College* (1899), pp. 138–40.

37 Christopher Wordsworth, *Scholae Academicae: Some Account of the Studies at the English Universities in the Eighteenth Century* (1910), pp. 338–42.

page 18, line 10 1751, Chesterfield *Corr.*, 4. 1685, 1760.

16 Roger North, *Lives of the Norths* (New Edition, 1826), 3. 310.

page 18, line 22   *Cambridge Under Queen Anne*, ed. J. E. B. Mayor (1911), p. 419.

         25   *Verses at the Last Publick Commencement at Cambridge* (1714), pp. 2, 9.

         30   *The Modish Couple* (ed. Dublin, 1732), p. 16 (discussed on pp. 130–2 below).

page 19, line 2   1713, John Byrom, *Private Journal and Literary Remains* (Chetham Society), vol. 1, part I (1854), p. 22.

         4   Christopher Wordsworth, *Social Life at the English Universities in the Eighteenth Century* (1874), p. 40.

         8   Charles H. Cooper, *Annals of Cambridge* (1852), 4. 121.

       13   *Mœstissimæ ac Lætissimæ Academiæ Cantabrigiensis* . . . (1714), p. [sig. D 1].

CHAPTER 2. 1714–1719

page 20, line 9   *Diary*, pp. 61, 62.

       12   H MS. 46/2.

       24   *Letter-Books*, 1. 394.

       26   *Wentworth Papers*, p. 431.

       27   *Diary*, p. 62.

page 21, line 7   *Letter-Books*, 2. 5.

       17   She is called Cardelia in LM's town eclogue 'The Bassette-Table'.

       23   Mary, Countess Cowper, *Diary*, ed. S. Cowper (2nd ed., 1865), pp. 3, 6.

       32   Cowper, *Diary*, pp. 8, 14–15.

       36   Cowper, *Diary*, pp. 15–16.

page 22, line 1   *Diary*, p. 62.

        6   *Letter-Books*, 2. 2, 4.

       12   *Letter-Books*, 2. 8–9.

       23   Cowper, *Diary*, p. 102.

       26   *Diary*, p. 161.

page 23, line 7   *Letter-Books*, 2. 18–20.

       10   Cowper, *Diary*, p. 104.

       24   HMC *Stuart Papers*, 2 (1904), 140–1, 158. (The Princess is referred to as 'a certain lady'.)

page 24, line 4   Cooper, *Annals of Cambridge*, 4. 138, 142.

        8   Winstanley, *Unreformed Cambridge*, p. 80.

       20   *Diary*, pp. 63, 103.

       24   Chesterfield *Letters*, 2. 3, 7 n.

       28   Dudley Pope, *At Twelve Mr Byng Was Shot* (1962), pp. 30–1.

       39   John Carswell, *The Old Cause: Three Studies in Whiggism* (1954), p. 141.

page 25, line 11   LM *Letters*, 1. 442.

       12   Gray *Corr.*, 1. 104–5.

       17   Thomas Nugent, *The Grand Tour* (3rd ed., 1778), 4. 59–60; Martin Lister, *Account of Paris* (1698), ed. G. Henning [1823], pp. 185–6.

page 25, line 19 Philippe de Dangeau, *Journal*, ed. F. Conches (1860), 16. 400, 426.
    25 LM *Letters*, 1. 439.
    29 *Letter-Books*, 2. 24, 34.
    35 LM *Letters*, 1. 440.
    39 1725, *Orrery Papers*, ed. Countess of Cork and Orrery (1903), 1. 43 (corrected from MS.: Houghton Library, Harvard University, MS. Eng. 218.2F., vol. 1, p. 9).
page 26, line 13 Gray *Corr.*, 1. 105.
    22 Dangeau, 16. 409, 434; Jean Buvat, *Gazette de la Régence 1715–1719*, ed. E. de Barthélemy (1887), pp. 106–7.
    28 Dangeau, 16. 409; Buvat, p. 91.
    38 Louis, Duc de Saint-Simon, *Mémoires*, ed. A. de Boislisle, (1879–1930), 38. 74.
page 27, line 3 Buvat, p. 106.
    15 Gray *Corr.*, 1. 105.
    18 Tyrtée Tastet, *Histoire des quarante fauteuils de l'Académie française 1635–1855* (1855), p. 387.
page 28, line 24 *Letter-Books*, 2. 22–3.
    39 HMC *Polwarth MSS.*, 1 (1911), 47–95 *passim*.
page 29, line 16 *Letter-Books*, 2. 26.
    25 LM *Letters*, 1. 286–7.
    28 Cowper, *Diary*, p. 195.
    31 *Letter-Books*, 2. 42.
    36 LM *Letters and Works* (1861), 1. 126.
page 30, line 14 Cowper, *Diary*, p. 195.
    26 Charles-Lewis Pollnitz, *Memoirs* (trans., 1737), 1. 64.
    29 LM *Letters*, 1. 286; HMC *Laing MSS.*, 2 (1925), 196.
    34 *Letter-Books*, 2. 41.
page 31, line 1 *Verney Letters of the Eighteenth Century*, ed. Lady Verney [1930], 2. 33.
    27 *Letter-Books*, 2. 41–2.
    35 *Diary*, p. 64.
page 32, line 2 *Diary*, p. 65.
    6 *Diary*, pp. 103–4.
    8 H *Mem.*, 1. 104.
    10 *Diary*, p. 67.
    15 *Diary*, p. 66.
    20 *Diary*, p. 65.
    24 Joseph Spence, *Anecdotes*, ed. J. M. Osborn (1966), 1. 44.
    31 *Letter-Books*, 2. 47; *Diary*, p. 65.
    38 *Diary*, p. 65.
page 33, line 3 *Letter-Books*, 2. 86–8, 118.
page 34, line 5 Horace Walpole, 'Reminiscences', *Works* (1798), 4. 283.
    11 John M. Beattie, *The English Court in the Reign of George I* (1967), pp. 273–7.
    22 Wolfgang Michael, *England under George I: The Quadruple Alliance*, trans. A. and G. E. MacGregor (1939), pp. 27–8.

page 34, line 26   *Diary*, p. 67; John Chamberlayne, *Magnae Britanniae Notitia*
                   (1723).
page 35, line 3   *Letter-Books*, 2. 79, 85, 90.
          11   *Letter-Books*, 2. 56, 57, 59.
          16   *Diary*, p. 67.
          23   *Wentworth Papers 1705–1739*, ed. J. J. Cartwright (1883),
                   p. 526. A year later (1720) Vanbrugh again visited Ick-
                   worth, probably in connection with his architectural plans
                   (*Letter-Books*, 2. 95–6). Two pillars standing today in
                   Ickworth Park, and called the Chevington Gates, may be
                   from his design.
          29   Sir Thomas Robinson in HMC *Carlisle MSS.* (1897), p. 87.
          35   *Letter-Books*, 2. 53.
          37   *Letter-Books*, 2. 57, 62.
page 36, line 4   *Letter-Books*, 2. 64. Lady Bristol's mother was a Howard;
                   hence she was related by marriage to Mrs. Howard (later
                   Countess of Suffolk).
          12   *Diary*, pp. 67–8.
page 37, line 4   *Letter-Books*, 2. 73–4, 77, 78.
           7   *Letter-Books*, 2. 98.
          10   *Letter-Books*, 2. 76, 81.
          16   'An Account of My Own Constitution and Illness', H *Mem.*,
                   3. 964–5.
          20   *Diary*, p. 69.
          28   *Letter-Books*, 2. 78, 93.
page 38, line 1   *Letter-Books*, 2. 91–2, 94.
           4   *Letter-Books*, 2. 97.
          14   *Letter-Books*, 2. 98, 120.
          16   *Letter-Books*, 2. 100.
          26   *Letter-Books*, 2. 102.
          38   *Letter-Books*, 2. 106, 111–12.

CHAPTER 3. 1720–1725

page 39, line 14   *Letter-Books*, 2. 97, 100.
          26   Pope *Poems*, 6. 180–4.
page 40, line 10   Chesterfield *Letters*, 4. 1594.
          13   Windsor Castle Archives, citing PRO S.P. 35/69.
          14   Suffolk *Letters*, 1. 320. Croker takes the word to be a corrup-
                   tion of *chat* or *chatter*.
          26   Walpole *Corr.*, 33. 37.
          34   *Verney Letters of the Eighteenth Century*, ed. Lady Verney,
                   [1930], 1. 275–6.
page 41, line 4   *Letter-Books*, 2. 116; *The London Stage 1660–1800*, Part 2,
                   ed. E. L. Avery (1960), 2. 552.
          10   *Additions to the Works of Alexander Pope* [ed. G. Steevens]
                   (1776), 1. 97.
          20   Pope *Corr.*, 1. 427.

page 41, line 23   Ibid., 2. 41.
            28   Suffolk *Letters*, 1. 53.
            33   *Diary*, p. 69.
page 42, line 4   *Letter-Books*, 2. 122–3.
            12   *Letter-Books*, 3. 92, 244–5.
            14   *Original Weekly Journal*, 15–22 Mar. 1718.
            17   *Letter-Books*, 3. 244.
            22   H *Mem.*, 1. 194–5.
            26   Suffolk *Letters*, 1. 69.
            34   For a far-fetched, improbable explanation, see J. W. Croker's
                  edition of the H *Mem.* (1848), 1. xxiv–xxv.
            38   Rate Books in Westminster Public Library (Victoria).
page 43, line 8   *Letter-Books*, 2. 121–2, 123.
            18   *Letter-Books*, 2. 123, 129.
            26   *Letter-Books*, 2. 131–2, 135, 139.
            33   *Letter-Books*, 3. 244. He did not keep his word; by 1740 the
                  sum had shrunk to £8,000.
            38   *Letter-Books*, 2. 143.
            40   *Historical Register* (1720), p. 46. Newspapers announced the
                  marriage in connection with Miss Lepell's resignation as
                  Maid of Honour (*London Journal*, 29 Oct.–5 Nov.;
                  Weekly Journal, 5 Nov. 1720).
page 44, line 1   *Letter-Books*, 2. 296; H to Lady Bristol, 31 Aug. 1725 (H
                  MS.).
             3   *Diary*, p. 106. Later in the year, Bristol, who had custody
                  of Hervey's inheritance from Sir Thomas Felton, conveyed
                  £6,000 to him (*Diary*, p. 70).
             9   *New Foundling Hospital for Wit* (1784), 6. 224.
            17   LM *Letters*, 2. 8.
            28   *Diary*, p. 71.
            36   *Letter-Books*, 2. 153–5.
page 45, line 3   *Diary*, pp. 118–20.
             7   *Letter-Books*, 2. 161, 180.
            11   *Letter-Books*, 2. 189; Victoria County Histories, *Surrey*, ed.
                  H. E. Malden (1902–12), 3. 468–9, 473.
            25   H *Mem.*, 1. 7.
            30   *Letter-Books*, 2. 195–6.
            32   *Letter-Books*, 2. 195, 201.
page 46, line 4   Thomas Hearne, *Remarks and Collections*, 7 (1906), 321–2.
            16   27 Jan. 1721/2 (H MS.). This is Hervey's earliest surviving
                  manuscript letter.
            19   LM *Letters*, 2. 24.
            24   *Letter-Books*, 2. 213.
            34   LM *Letters*, 2. 17.
            36   Ibid.
page 47, line 8   Letter to Lady Bristol, 3 July 1722 (H MS.).
            11   *Diary*, p. 72.
            15   *Letter-Books*, 2. 220.

page 47, line 24   *Letter-Books*, 2. 226, 229, 233–4.
          28   *Letter-Books*, 2. 243.
          37   *Letter-Books*, 2. 233, 234.
page 48, line 7   *Letter-Books*, 2. 235, 236.
          16   *Letter-Books*, 2. 237.
          28   *Letter-Books*, 2. 243, 251, 258.
          38   *Letter-Books*, 2. 228, 231, 250.
page 49, line 2   *Diary*, p. 73.
          11   *Letter-Books*, 2. 261, 266.
          15   *Letter-Books*, 2. 275, 282.
          22   *Letter-Books*, 2. 292–3.
          30   *Letter-Books*, 2. 262, 264, 274.
page 50, line 6   *Letter-Books*, 2. 268–9, 285–6, 296; *Diary*, p. 73.
          13   *Letter-Books*, 2. 293, 298.
          23   *Diary*, pp. 73, 107; *Letter-Books*, 2. 294, 300, 301, 320, 322–3.
          28   *Letter-Books*, 2. 315.
          30   Suffolk *Letters*, 1. 107.
          37   H MS. 53/1.
page 51, line 7   *Letter-Books*, 2. 319, 321, 330.
          10   *Letter-Books*, 2. 336.
          16   *Letter-Books*, 2. 249.
          37   *Letter-Books*, 2. 287, 339.
page 52, line 5   LM *Letters*, 2. 41.
          12   *Diary*, p. 74.
          21   *Letter-Books*, 2. 341–2.
          23   *Letter-Books*, 2. 345.
          25   *Diary*, p. 74.
page 53, line 7   A. Barbeau, *Life and Letters at Bath in the XVIII Century* (1904), chap. 3.
          22   *Letter-Books*, 2. 357–8, 363.
          35   *Letter-Books*, 2. 362, 365–6.
          39   *Letter-Books*, 2. 368.
page 54, line 2   *Letter-Books*, 2. 374.
          12   *Letter-Books*, 2. 377.
          15   *Diary*, p. 74.
          21   LM *Letters*, 2. 45.
          24   Suffolk *Letters*, 1. 194.
          31   *Letter-Books*, 2. 381. For the borough seat only £300 a year was necessary; the county seat required £600. Reynolds, who was related to the Hervey family, held the appointment of Justice of the King's Bench until 1730, when he was advanced to Lord Chief Baron of the Exchequer.
          40   *Letter-Books*, 2. 379–80.
page 55, line 5   *Diary*, p. 75.
          8   LM *Letters*, 2. 48.
          21   *Letter-Books*, 2. 390.

CHAPTER 4. 1725–1727

page 56, line 4   *Letter-Books*, 2. 392; *Diary*, p. 75.

            19   HMC *Portland MSS.*, 6 (1901), 6; Coxe *Walpole*, 1. 208.

page 57, line 5   'Account of Illness', H *Mem.*, 3. 968–9, 971.

            18   Suffolk *Letters*, 1. 126–74, 182–3.

            23   Ibid., 191.

            24   *Diary*, p. 75.

            26   H to Lady Bristol, 12 Aug. 1725 (H MS.).

            34   Henry B. Wheatley, *London Past and Present* (1891), 1. 111–12.

            40   31 Aug. 1725 (H MS.).

page 58, line 8   12 Aug. 1725 (H MS.).

            14   H to Lady Bristol, 31 Aug. 1725 (H MS.).

            20   LCC Survey of London, 32 (1963), 508.

            29   Quoted in Dorothy M. Stuart, *Molly Lepell, Lady Hervey* (1936), pp. 56–7.

            33   See p. 104 below.

            37   LM *Letters*, 2. 56.

page 59, line 8   16 Oct. 1725 (H MS.).

            19   LM *Letters*, 2. 58–9.

            21   Walpole *Corr.*, 34. 259.

            40   *New Foundling Hospital for Wit* (1784), 6. 225, 227.

page 60, line 2   Jonathan Swift, *Corr.*, ed. H. Williams (1963–5), 3. 179.

            8   *Universal Passion*, 3rd satire (1725, ed. 1763), p. 51.

            11   H *Mem.*, 1. xvii.

            18   *Letter-Books*, 3. 5.

            28   *Letter-Books*, 3. 2–3; *Diary*, pp. 76–7.

            30   H *Mem.*, 1. 78. He was pilloried in Pope's 1743 *Dunciad* (IV. 105–14) as the pompous Montalto, editor of Shakespeare.

            33   This bizarre episode, which caused Lord Bristol to cast him off, is exposed in *A Letter from the Hon. Thomas Hervey, to Sir Thomas Hanmer, Bart.* [1742].

page 61, line 5   *Diary*, p. 109.

            19   Horace Walpole, *Letters*, ed. Mrs. P. Toynbee (1903), 4. 375–6; Walpole *Corr.*, 34. 256; Delany *Corr.*, 6. 163; Lewis Melville, *Maids of Honour* (1927), pp. 210–11.

            31   *A Collection of Poems by Several Hands* [ed. Robert Dodsley] (1766), 4. 85.

            35   Harrowby MS., vol. 255.

            38   Information from David Foxon. The publication (1726) may have been arranged by James Arbuckle, Irish essayist, who reprinted it in 1728 along with his own topographical poem *Glotta*. A unique copy of the 1726 pamphlet is in the Royal Irish Academy. Another ambitious poem composed by Hervey during the 1720s is *A Satire in the Manner of Persius: in a Dialogue between Atticus and Eugenio*, published as a pamphlet in 1730 and again in 1739. Its Christian stoic point of view is not characteristic of his thinking.

page 62, line 14   Lord Chesterfield, 'Characters', BM. Stowe MS. 308, f. 13.

31   23 Nov. 1726 (H MS.).

page 63, line 15   3 Dec. 1726 (H MS.).

28   15, 27 Dec. 1726 (H MS.).

page 64, line 18   3 Dec. 1726 (H MS.).

21   S. A. Seligman, 'Mary Toft—The Rabbit Breeder', *Medical History*, 5 (1961), 349–60; Marjorie Nicolson and G. S. Rousseau, '*This Long Disease, My Life*', *Alexander Pope and the Sciences* (1968), pp. 109–15.

30   10, 19 Jan. 1727 (H MS.).

37   *Diary*, p. 75. Her birth was celebrated in some anonymous satiric verse published as a broadside (Pope *Poems*, 6. 441–2).

page 65, line 8   H *Mem.*, 1. 6.

10   Lord Chesterfield, 'Characters', BM. Stowe MS. 308, f. 8.

15   Earl of Ilchester and Mrs. Langford-Brooke, *Life of Sir Charles Hanbury-Williams* (1928), p. 63.

22   Charles B. Realey, *Early Opposition to Sir Robert Walpole 1720–1727* (1931), pp. 158–9.

27   H *Mem.*, 1. 263.

31   It is undated, but in David Mallet's 1809 edition of Bolingbroke's works it ends: 'From my Garret, Jan. 1726–7.' The copy in the Yale University Library is accompanied by a wrapper postmarked 28 December.

page 66, line 35   Lady Hervey's copy of the pamphlet is still at Ickworth, and on its title-page, probably in the hand of General William Hervey (Hervey's son), is 'L.H.'. The pamphlet is also attributed to Hervey in Walpole *Catalogue*.

page 67, line 7   Sir Edward Knatchbull, *Parliamentary Diary 1722–1730* (1963), p. 67. In his will Bolingbroke acknowledged his authorship of the *Occasional Writer*, Nos. *I*, *II*, and *III* (*Works*, 1809, 1. ccxix).

15   Realey, p. 200.

30   Knatchbull, p. 68.

33   Attributed to Hervey in Walpole *Catalogue* and on the title page of Lady Hervey's copy at Ickworth (probably in the hand of Gen. William Hervey).

page 68, line 4   H *Mem.*, 1. 104.

13   *Lord Hervey and His Friends 1726–38*, ed. Earl of Ilchester (1950), plate facing p. 128. Stephen weighed only 126 lb. (9 stone), his brother 168 (12 stone)—as recorded in 1736 (Ilchester, p. 86 n.).

17   *Memoirs of the Life of Sir Stephen Fox* (1717), pp. 101–2.

20   Memorandum by Henry Fox, dated 1718 (BM. Holland House MS.).

25   To Henry Fox, 28 Sept. 1753 (BM. MS.).

page 69, line 5   1 June 1727 (H MS.).

31   13 June 1727 (H MS.).

page 69, line 38   30 May 1727 (H MS.).
page 70, line 3   H to Stephen Fox, 13 June 1727 (H MS.).
            7   H *Mem.*, 1. 37.

CHAPTER 5. 1727–1729

page 71, line 15   H *Mem.*, 1. 22–7; J. H. Plumb, *Walpole: The King's Minister*
                   (1960), pp. 164–6.
page 72, line 1   *Diary*, pp. 77–8.
            3   *Letter-Books*, 3. 26.
           10   H *Mem.*, 1. 28.
           32   H *Mem.*, 1. 32–4.
           38   H to Stephen Fox, 27 June 1727 (H MS.).
page 73, line 7   H *Mem.*, 1. 35.
            9   Plumb (1960), pp. 168–9.
           14   *Diary*, p. 78.
           17   *Letter-Books*, 3. 17.
           25   H to Stephen Fox, 14 Aug. 1727 (BM. MS.).
           35   Suffolk *Letters*, 1. 267–8.
           38   *Letter-Books*, 3. 18; Chamberlayne, *Magnae Britanniae Notitia*
                   (1728).
page 74, line 7   'Account of Illness', H *Mem.*, 3. 967.
           14   *Letter-Books*, 3. 24–5.
           19   'Account of Illness', H *Mem.*, 3. 973.
           21   H to Mrs. Griselda (later Lady) Murray, 25 Sept. 1727
                   (Mellerstain MS., owned by the Earl of Haddington).
           23   H to LM, 7 Nov. [1727] (H MS.).
           38   LM *Letters*, 2. 85–7. In his *Memoirs* Hervey devotes only one
                   brief paragraph to it, mainly about the Queen's borrowed
                   jewels (1. 66).
page 75, line 2   H *Mem.*, 3. 972.
           10   *Letter-Books*, 3. 25–6.
           17   30 Dec. 1727 (H MS.). Since Hervey lived in Great Burling-
                   ton Street, Stephen probably rented lodgings in Jermyn
                   Street.
           22   28 Dec. 1727 (H MS.).
           29   30 Dec. 1727 (H MS.); 9 Jan. 1728 (BM. MS.).
           38   H to Lady Bristol, 26 Dec. 1727; to Stephen, 28 Dec. 1727
                   (H MS.).
           40   H to Stephen Fox, 11 Jan. 1728 (H MS.).
page 76, line 5   9 Jan. 1728 (BM. MS.).
           13   H *Mem.*, 1. 75.
           18   P. D. G. Thomas, *The House of Commons in the Eighteenth
                   Century* (1971), pp. 39, 41.
           20   Coxe *Walpole*, 2. 546–7.
           23   Nicholas Tindal, *History of England*, 20 (1759), 83–4.
           28   *Letter-Books*, 3. 27.
           34   'Account of Illness', H *Mem.*, 3. 973.

page 76, line 37   Delany *Corr.*, 1. 160, 168, 171.
           40   H *Mem.*, 3. 973.
page 77, line   7   18 June 1728 (H MS.).
           13   22 June 1728 (BM. MS.).
           20   25 June 1728 (H MS.).
           24   *Diary*, p. 79.
page 78, line   2   H *Mem.*, 3. 974.
           11   'To Mr. Fox, written at Florence', *A Collection of Poems*, [ed. Robert Dodsley] (1748), 3. 240. This is a very free imitation of an ode by Horace (II. vi).
           19   Wigan's letters to Henry Fox (BM. Holland House MS.).
page 79, line   2   H *Mem.*, 1. 252; 3. 828.
           14   Thomas Nugent, *The Grand Tour* (3rd ed., 1778), 1. 262.
           17   'Account of Illness', H *Mem.*, 3. 974–5.
           28   30 Sept. 1728 (H MS.).
           33   E. J. F. Barbier, *Chronique de la Régence et du règne de Louis XV (1718–1763)* (1857), 2. 47, 49.
           40   30 Sept. 1728 (H MS.).
page 80, line   2   Suffolk *Letters*, 1. 326.
           6   20 Sept. 1728 (BM. MS.).
           10   Winnington to Henry Fox, 29 Sept. 1728 (BM. MS.).
           14   H to Lady Bristol, 30 Sept. 1728 (H MS.).
           16   Stephen to Henry Fox, 4 Nov. [1728] (BM. MS.).
           26   Winnington to Henry Fox, 18 Jan. [1729] (BM. MS.).
           32   *Letter-Books*, 3. 31; H to Lady Bristol, 30 Dec. 1728 (H MS.).
           36   Lady H to Stephen Fox, 20 Sept., 9 Dec. 1728 (BM. MS.).
page 81, line   2   Winnington to Henry Fox, 10 Jan. [1729] (BM. MS.).
           12   *Letter-Books*, 3. 30.
           17   PRO S.P. 85/16, ff. 480, 482, 484, 494–5.
           28   'Account of Illness', H *Mem.*, 3. 978.
           32   Ibid., 976–7.
page 82, line   3   Ibid., 976.
           6   Stephen to Henry Fox, 21 May 1729 (BM. MS.).
           20   12 May, 2 June 1729, PRO S.P. 85/16, ff. 537, 543.
           23   Suffolk *Letters*, 1. 336.
           26   Ibid.; *Letter-Books*, 3. 47.
           34   24 June 1729 (BM. MS.).
page 83, line   1   Suffolk *Letters*, 1. 336.
           4   *Diary*, p. 111.
           13   A. H. Scott-Elliot, 'The Statues by Francavilla in The Royal Collection', *Burlington Magazine*, 98 (1956), 77–84; Walpole *Corr.*, 21. 481; H to Antonio Cocchi, 16 Nov. 1730 (Cocchi MS.).
           23   'Account of Illness', H *Mem.*, 3. 978–9.
           32   23 July 1729 (H MS.).
page 84, line   2   H to LM, 16 July 1729 (H MS.).
           5   Stephen Fox to Cocchi, 25 Oct. 1729 (Cocchi MS.).

page 84, line 7 Walpole *Corr.*, 20. 389; H to Henry Fox, 13 Sept. 1731
                 (BM. MS.).
          11   Egmont 2. 207.
          29   Walpole *Corr.*, 17. 186, 430.
page 85, line 4 H to Lady H, long verse-letter [Oct. 1729] (BM. MS.);
                 H to LM, 12 Oct. [1729] (H MS.).
          11   *A Collection of Poems* [ed. Robert Dodsley] (1766), 4. 223;
                 Voltaire, 'Parallèle d'Horace, de Boileau, et de Pope'
                 (1760), *Œuvres complètes*, ed. L. Moland (1883–5), 24.
                 225.
          15   *Diary*, p. 94.
          22   Voltaire, Letter 20.
          28   Stephen Fox to Cocchi, 25 Oct. 1729 [N.S.] (Cocchi MS.).
          32   *Diary*, p. 79.

CHAPTER 6. 1729–1731

page 86, line 13 Dodsley, *Collection* (1748), 3. 240–1.
          19   LM, *Letters and Works*, ed. Lord Wharncliffe and W. M.
                  Thomas (1861), 2. 462.
page 87, line 31 Pulteney with his wife dined at his house in November
                  (H to Stephen Fox, 18 Nov. 1729, H MS.).
page 88, line 11 H *Mem.*, 1. 103–10.
          22   15 Nov. 1729 (H MS.).
          27   H *Mem.*, 1. 110.
          35   15 Nov. 1729 (H MS.).
page 89, line 8   18 Nov. (H MS.); 19 Nov. 1729 (BM. MS.).
          12   Delany *Corr.*, 1. 218–19.
          22   18 Nov. 1729 (H MS.).
          35   29 Dec. [1729] (H MS.).
page 90, line 19 Sylvester Douglas (Lord Glenbervie), *Diaries*, ed. F. Bickley
                  (1928), 1. 4.
          36   1 June 1727 (H MS.).
page 91, line 12 [?23] Aug. 1743 (BM. MS.).
          16   Charles Hanbury Williams, *Poems* (1822), 2. 33–5; Walpole
                  Corr., 30. xxvii, 35–6, 74, 307–10.
          20   Walpole *Corr.*, 30. 49–50.
page 92, line 16 15 Jan. 1730 (BM. MS.).
          17   Egmont, 1. 2–4.
          20   H *Mem.*, 1. 111.
page 93, line 24 H *Mem.*, 1. 296.
page 94, line 1   Cholmondeley (Houghton) MS., P 73 (13). Since Lords'
                  Protests were printed at the end of the session (H *Mem.*,
                  1. 260) this Protest and Hervey's reply can be dated the
                  early summer of 1730.
          8   [29 Jan. 1730] (BM. MS.).
          12   H *Mem.*, 1. 114.
          16   [5 Feb. 1730] (BM. MS.).

page 94, line 23   Egmont, 1. 27, 31. (As Viscount Perceval; he became Earl of Egmont three years later.)

26   H to Henry Fox [5 Feb. 1730] (BM. MS.).

28   J. H. Plumb, 'Sir Robert Walpole's Wine', *Men and Places* (1963), p. 150.

page 95, line 1   Cholmondeley (Houghton) MS., Foreign Papers 25.

5   H *Mem.*, 1. 116.

17   17 Feb. 1730 (BM. MS.).

38   Egmont, 1. 55.

page 96, line 6   J. H. Plumb, *Walpole: The King's Minister* (1960), pp. 211, 216–17; Coxe *Walpole*, 1. 323–4.

14   3 Mar. 1730 (BM. MS.).

24   H *Mem.*, 1. 117.

29   15 and 24 Jan. 1730 (BM. MS.).

37   H *Mem.*, 1. 118–19.

page 97, line 3   *London Evening Post*, 28–30 Apr. 1730; PRO L.C. 3/64, p. 206.

18   *British Journal*, 30 May 1730.

20   *Suffolk Notes From the Year 1729. Compiled from the Files of the Ipswich Journal* (1883), p. 137.

35   John M. Beattie, *The English Court in the Reign of George I* (1967), pp. 24–6; Edgar Sheppard, *Memorials of St. James' Palace* (1894), 1. 136.

39   PRO L.C. 3/12; cf. *Calendar of Treasury Books and Papers 1731–1734*, ed. W. A. Shaw (1898), pp. 45, 167; and Beattie, pp. 184, 209.

40   See p. 171 below.

page 98, line 6   Croker exaggerates Hervey's discontent: 'a long, rankling, and by no means unreasonable mortification' that he got no better post than the 'almost menial services' and that he was dissatisfied with it from the outset (H *Mem.*, 1848 ed., 1. xxvii, 1).

18   H *Mem.*, 1. 227.

34   *Letter-Books*, 3. 29.

36   HMC *Carlisle MSS.* (1897), p. 55.

page 99, line 10   H *Mem.*, 1. 97–8. The Prince is favourably described by two modern historians: Betty Kemp in *Silver Renaissance: Essays in Eighteenth Century English History*, ed. A. Natan (1961), and John Brooke, *King George III* (1972), chaps. 1, 2.

13   *London Evening Post*, 14–17 Mar. 1730.

16   *Daily Post*, 11 June 1730.

20   PRO L.S. 13/116.

22   H to Stephen Fox, 13 June 1730 (H MS.).

31   19 June 1730 (H MS.).

34   *Daily Courant*, 22 June 1730.

37   Suffolk *Letters*, 1. 376.

page 100, line 5   H to Lady Murray, 8 Aug. [1730] (Mellerstain MS.). He had related this anecdote to his mother on 8 July (H MS.). Both these letters may be 1732.

page 100, line 11   'Twitenham, Monday' (H MS.).

13   *Weekly Journal or British Gazetteer*, 4 July 1730.

19   July [1730] (H MS.).

26   13 June 1730 (H MS.).

30   H to Stephen Fox, 29 July 1730 (H MS.).

page 101, line 2   14 Aug. 1730 (H MS.).

7   17 Aug. 1730 (H MS.).

20   21 Aug. [1730] (H MS.).

24   26 Aug. 1730 (H MS.).

30   Mellerstain MS.

37   *Daily Journal* and *Daily Post*, 4 Sept. 1730; *Diary*, p. 80.

page 102, line 1   H to Dr. Butts, 3 Sept. 1730 (H MS.); H to Stephen Fox, 4 Sept. 1730 (H MS.).

7   4 Sept. 1730 (H MS.).

16   9 Sept. 1730 (H MS.).

19   9 Sept. 1730 (H MS.). The Duchess's favourite house was Windsor Lodge, which she held on a Crown lease (David Green, *Sarah Duchess of Marlborough*, 1967, pp. 192, 297).

33   27 Sept. 1730 (H MS.).

38   14 Sept. 1730 (H MS.).

page 103, line 5   16 Sept. 1730 (H MS.).

14   24 Sept. 1730 (H MS.).

19   25 Sept. 1730 (H MS.).

24   PRO L.S. 13/116.

29   Dodsley's *Collection* (1766), 4. 103–4.

30   H to Henry Fox, 3 Mar. 1730 (BM. MS.).

35   *Daily Journal*, 27, 28 Oct.; *British Journal*, 31 Oct. 1730.

page 104, line 1   *Faithful Memoirs of Mrs. Anne Oldfield* (1731), Appendix II.

13   14 Nov. 1730, Greater London Council Archives, 1730/3/261; 18 Nov. 1730, Hoare & Co. Archives.

26   16 Nov. 1730 (Cocchi MS., trans. from French).

page 105, line 2   Punctuation adjusted.

37   The first two of these three pamphlets are attributed to Hervey in the Ickworth copies by his son Gen. William Hervey, by Horace Walpole in his *Catalogue*, and by Pulteney in *A Proper Reply* (see p. 110); the third is so similar that it has been accepted as his by G. F. Russell Barker in the *D.N.B.* All three are attributed to him in Laurence Hanson, *Government and the Press 1695–1763* (1936), pp. 27, 126.

page 106, line 8   8, 10 Dec. 1730 (H MS.).

10   Two 'duplicate' letters, 15 Dec. 1730 (H MS.).

29   Copies of both letters [n.d.] (H MS. 47/1). Egmont noticed that the Prince was sometimes more childish than became his age (*Diary*, 1. 208).

page 107, line 4   H to Stephen Fox, 5 Jan. 1731 (H MS.).

17   7 Jan. 1731 (H MS.).

page 107, line 19   Coxe *Walpole*, 1. 363 n. On the Ickworth copy the dedica-
                    tion is attributed to Hervey probably in the hand of Gen.
                    William Hervey. Horace Walpole's copy of the pamph-
                    let (now WSL) bears his note on the title-page 'by Lord
                    Hervey;' but he did not list it as Hervey's in his *Catalogue*.

page 108, line 24   H *Mem.*, 1. 36.

           30   H to Stephen Fox, 5 Jan. 1731 (H MS.).

           37   H to Stephen Fox, 11 Jan. 1731 (H MS.).

           38   Cathcart Diary, 8 Jan. 1731 (Cathcart MS.); diagnosed
                    today as an 'epileptiform attack' ('Account of Illness',
                    H *Mem.*, 3. 987).

page 109, line 11   Thomas Pelham to Waldegrave, 22 Jan. 1731, Coxe
                    Walpole, 3. 80.

page 110, line 8   H to Stephen Fox, 10, 12 Dec. 1730 (H MS.).

page 111, line 1   H *Mem.*, 1. 103; see above, p. 87.

            6   Philip C. Yorke, *Life and Corr. of Philip Yorke, Earl of
                    Hardwicke, Lord High Chancellor of Great Britain* (1913),
                    1. 159 n., for example; also in the *D.N.B.* article on
                    Hervey (by G. F. Russell Barker) and the GEC standard
                    peerage entry for Lord Bristol. Even J. W. Croker, first
                    editor of the *Memoirs*, held this belief: he speculates that
                    the missing pages from Hervey's autograph 'evidently
                    contained the elements of his first secession from Pulteney
                    & his connexion with Walpole' (to Lord Arthur Hervey,
                    8 May 1847, H MS. 63/5). This is argument *ab silentio*
                    with a vengeance.

           37   Chesterfield *Letters*, 2. 174.

page 112, line 6   Lady H to Lady Murray, 2 Feb. 1731 (Mellerstain MS.,
                    vol. X).

                         CHAPTER 7. 1731–1732

page 113, line 12   Probably the rhetorical questions on p. 23 of Pulteney's
                    pamphlet.

page 114, line 17   These details from Lady Irwin in HMC *Carlisle MSS.*
                    (1897), p. 80.

           30   Thomas Pelham to Waldegrave, 28 Jan. 1731, Coxe *Wal-
                    pole*, 3. 89.

           36   Lady H to Lady Murray, 2 Feb. 1731.

           40   Lady Irwin; Thomas Pelham; newspapers (*Daily Post*,
                    28 Jan.; *Daily Journal*, 29 Jan. 1731); and the French
                    Ambassador (Angleterre, vol. 373, ff. 64, 113, Archives
                    des Affaires Étrangères, Paris).

page 115, line 11   *The London Medley* [1731].

           12   *Daily Post*, 30 Jan. 1731.

           15   *Daily Post*, 29 Jan., *London Journal*, 30 Jan. 1731.

           21   HMC *Carlisle MSS.* (1897), p. 80.

           26   *Diary*, p. 81; *Letter-Books*, 3. 68.

page 115, line 35   *A Review of the Whole Political Conduct of a Late Eminent Patriot* . . . (1743), p. 56. The author erroneously identifies Stephen Fox (though not by name) as Hervey's second in the duel.

page 116, line 3   Chesterfield *Letters*, 2. 172.

         5   It is attributed to Hervey only in the *D.N.B.*

       26   p. 44.

       32   Archibald S. Foord, *His Majesty's Opposition 1714–1830* (1964), pp. 198–9.

page 117, line 17   BM. Prints Nos. 1867, 1868.

page 118, line 11   *Iago Display'd* (1731).

       20   p. 48. See p. 138 below.

       25   [Alexander] Burnet, *Achilles Dissected: Being a Compleat Key of the Political Characters in that New Ballad Opera, Written by the late Mr. Gay* (1733), p. 13. Burnet's interpretation is far-fetched, for Ajax challenges Periphas because of their rivalry for a woman (Act III, Scene iii). Hervey, who saw the opera, thought it a puzzling disappointment, and only praised the comical acting of Ajax (to Duke of Richmond, 17 Feb. 1733, Goodwood Archives, West Sussex Record Office).

       27   *The Honest Electors* (1733). The fame of the duel led the editor of Hanbury Williams's ballad about a duel between a peer and a lawyer mistakenly to identify the peer [Lord Micklethwaite] as Hervey (Charles Hanbury Williams, *Poems*, 1822, 3. 43).

       36   *Political Ballads of the Seventeenth and Eighteenth Centuries/ Annotated*, ed. W. W. Wilkins (1860), p. 47.

page 119, line 13   Ibid., p. 49.

page 120, line 1   14 June 1731 (BM. MS.).

        5   Copy of pamphlet at Ickworth with 'Arnold' in H's hand.

        8   Laurence Hanson, *Government and the Press 1695–1763* (1936), pp. 112–13.

       13   *Posthumous Letters Addressed to Francis Colman* . . ., ed. George Colman the younger (1820), p. 33.

       30   14 June, 3 July 1731 (BM. MS.).

       34   Lady H to Stephen Fox, 14 June 1731 (BM. MS.); *Daily Post*, 10 July 1731.

       36   J. H. Plumb, *Men and Places* (1963), p. 147.

page 121, line 2   H to Prince of Wales, 16 July 1731 (H MS.).

       12   H to Prince of Wales, 21 July 1731 (H MS.). Hervey expressed his unflattering opinion of Burlington's famous little villa at Chiswick with the witticism that 'it was too small to live in, and too large to hang to one's watch' (Croker (ed.), *Mem.*, 2. 145 n.). He also wrote two poems on the same subject, published in the *New Foundling Hospital for Wit* (1786), 1. 244–5.

page 121, line 16 Lady H to Stephen Fox, 26 July 1731 (BM. MS.).
20 12 Aug. 1731 (H MS.).
24 PRO L.S. 13/116.
28 H to Stephen Fox, 14, 17 Aug. 1731 (H MS.).
36 H to Stephen Fox, 17 Aug. 1731 (H MS.); *Wentworth Papers 1705–1739*, ed. J. J. Cartwright (1883), pp. 473–4.
page 122, line 8 *Diary*, p. 95.
13 *Letter-Books*, 3. 68–9.
19 16 July 1731 (H MS.).
27 21 July 1731 (H MS.).
32 H to Stephen Fox, 23 Aug. 1731 (H MS.).
34 H to Prince of Wales, 8 Nov. 1731 (H MS.).
page 123, line 1 17 Aug. 1731 (H MS.).
6 26 Aug. 1731 (H MS.).
22 31 Aug. 1731 (H MS.).
31 2 Sept. 1731 (H MS.).
35 Dodsley's *Collection* (1748), 3. 242.
page 124, line 1 H *Mem.*, 2. 490.
8 4, 18 Sept. 1731 (H MS.).
13 H to Stephen Fox, 9, 11 Sept. 1731 (H MS.).
16 2 Oct. 1731 (H MS.).
24 H to Stephen Fox, 12 Oct. 1731 (H MS.).
32 H to Stephen Fox, 14 Oct. 1731 (H MS.).
page 125, line 7 Robert Pick, *Empress Maria Theresa—The Earlier Years* (1966), pp. 25–6.
8 Chesterfield *Letters*, 2. 233.
15 Coxe *Walpole*, 3. 122.
22 15 Oct. 1731 (H MS.).
37 H to Stephen Fox, 19, 23 Oct. 1731 (H MS.).
page 126, line 9 23 Oct. 1731 (H MS.).
14 H to Stephen Fox, 23 Oct. 1731 (H MS.).
17 *Daily Post*, 2 Nov. 1731; H to Stephen Fox, 28 Oct. 1731 (H MS.).
21 H to Prince of Wales, 10 Nov. 1731 (H MS.).
23 *Daily Advertiser*, 12 Nov. 1731.
31 18 Nov. 1731 (H MS.).
39 H to Stephen Fox, 25 Nov. 1731 (H MS.).
page 127, line 8 H to Stephen Fox, 2, 4 Dec. 1731 (H MS.).
13 H to Stephen Fox, 7 Dec. 1731 (H MS.).
18 H to Henry Fox, 8 Dec. 1731 (H MS.).
20 11 Dec. 1731 (H MS.).
25 25 Dec. 1731, HMC *Hastings MSS.*, 3 (1934), 8.
page 128, line 1 6, 10 Nov. 1731 (H MS.).
5 Dowager Lady Waldegrave to Waldegrave, 10 June 1729 (Waldegrave MS.). For her tragic history, see LM *Letters*, 2. 295 and n.
8 Egmont, 1. 92, 93, 208.

page 128, line 11   C. H. Collins-Baker and Muriel I. Baker, *The Life and Circumstances of James Brydges First Duke of Chandos* (1949), pp. 255–6 (date 8 Nov. 1731 from Huntington Library MS. ST 57, vol. 38, p. 267).

    19   Miss Vane to Lady Oxford, 24 Nov. 1730, Portland MS., BM. Loan 29/117.

    20   Lady H to Lepell, 20 June 1738 (Mulgrave Castle MS.).

    25   Suffolk *Letters*, 1. 409.

    27   *British Journal*, 7 Feb. 1730; Egmont, 1. 236.

    36   Egmont, 1. 235–6.

    37   *Daily Courant*, 1 Apr. 1730.

page 129, line 4   Horace Walpole, *Memoirs of the Reign of King George the Second*, ed. Lord Holland (2nd ed., rev., 1847), 1. 75.

    7   Egmont, 1. 235.

    18   14 Dec. 1731 (one of two letters: H MS.).

    22   *Letter-Books*, 3. 81–2.

    39   25 Dec. 1731 (H MS.).

page 130, line 8   H *Mem.*, 1. 176, 386; Walpole *Catalogue*. Walpole often said that Hervey and Dodington were the only two he ever knew who were always aiming at wit and generally finding it (*Corr.*, 25. 503).

    37   *Daily Post*, 6 Dec. 1731.

page 131, line 13   Henry Fielding, *Joseph Andrews*, ed. M. C. Battestin (1967), p. 240.

    17   *Daily Journal*, 14 Jan. 1732.

    28   Egmont, 1. 216.

    30   Charles B. Woods, 'Captain B—'s Play', *Harvard Studies and Notes in Philology and Literature*, 15 (1933), 243–55. A similar episode occurred a few years later when William Popple withdrew his comedy after four performances because he claimed that a report had spread all over town that 'the Play was a Party Play, and supported by the Court, and therefore to be opposed' (Preface to *The Lady's Revenge*, 1734).

    35   *Weekly Journal or British Gazetteer*, 6 Oct. 1739.

    36   Quoted in Chesterfield *Letters*, 5. 2027 n.

page 132, line 1   Egmont, 1. 205.

    4   *Works*, ed. L. Stephen, 10. 181.

    13   H *Mem.*, 2. 585–96. He also wrote a rhymed tragedy entitled *Agripinna* (to Henry Fox, 16 Sept. 1736, BM. MS.; Walpole *Catalogue*). A fair copy (not in H's hand), formerly in Lord Ilchester's library, was acquired by the BM. in 1973 (Eg. 3787).

    20   p. 44.

    22   H *Mem.*, 1. 309; 3. 866.

CHAPTER 8. 1732–1733

page 133, line 10 H to Stephen Fox, 28 Dec. 1731 (H MS.).

           20 H to Stephen Fox, 30 Dec. 1731 (H MS.).

page 134, line 11 These words from Chandler are only a paraphrase of Hervey's speech.

           24 8 Dec. 1732, *Letter-Books*, 3. 87–8. Bristol had inherited this Lincolnshire property from his first wife (*Letter-Books*, 3. 322–3).

           26 18 Aug. 1733, *Letter-Books*, 3. 99–100.

           38 Egmont, 1. 253.

page 135, line 5 Attributed to Hervey only by G. F. Russell Barker in the *D.N.B.*

           17 Egmont, 1. 218, 225 (who gives her pension as £3,000); Hervey's figure of £1,600 is more reasonable (*Mem.*, 2. 476). Her last quarterly payment as Maid of Honour is recorded Christmas 1731 (Windsor Castle Archives), and her replacement announced in the *Daily Journal* of 7 Feb. 1732.

           25 HMC *Hastings MSS.*, 3 (1934), 11–12.

page 136, line 9 Egmont, 1. 264–5.

           12 H *Mem.*, 1. 274–5.

           16 HMC *Portland MSS.*, 6 (1901), 43.

           21 Egmont, 1. 280; *London Evening Post*, 3–6 June 1732.

           24 *Marriage, Baptismal, and Burial Registers of Westminster Abbey*, ed. J. L. Chester, Harleian Society Publications (1876), p. 345.

           29 Horace Walpole, *Reminiscences*, ed. P. Toynbee (1924), p. 81 n.

           31 H *Mem.*, 1. 290.

page 137, line 8 H *Mem.*, 2. 614, 616.

           21 *Diary*, p. 82; *Daily Courant*, 15 May, 3 June 1732.

           24 Sarah, Duchess of Marlborough, *Letters of a Grandmother 1732–1735*, ed. G. S. Thomson [1943], p. 59.

           28 *London Evening Post*, 5–8 Aug. 1732; *Daily Post*, 26 Aug., 30 Nov. 1732; Victoria County Histories *Surrey*, ed. H. E. Malden (1902–12), 3. 275–6. Since Baltimore served as governor of Maryland in person in 1732–3 he evidently did not share the house with Miss Vane.

           33 *Daily Advertiser*, 11 Aug. 1732.

page 138, line 4 Harrowby MS., vol. 255 (owned by the Earl of Harrowby). Stanhope was Lord Harrington's family name.

           12 (1732), pp. 23–31.

           40 BM. Stowe MS. 180, f. 197.

page 139, line 14 H to Stephen Fox, 31 Aug. 1732 (BM. MS.).

           16 *Letter-Books*, 3. 92.

           21 26 Aug. 1732 (BM. MS.).

           24 31 Aug. 1732 (BM. MS.).

page 139, line 32   19 Sept. 1732 (BM. MS.).

           38   H to Stephen Fox, 26 Sept. 1732 (BM. MS.).

page 140, line 5   19 Sept. 1732 (BM. MS.). The Revd. Samuel Hill (1693–
                    1753) was rector of Eisey, Wilts., an appointment of
                    Stephen Fox's, from 1731 to 1733, and then (1733–53)
                    Kilmington.

           13   Henry Sampson (1696–1773) was rector of Croscombe,
                    Somerset (1723–50).

           16   10 Oct. 1732 (BM. MS.).

           20   Horace Walpole's copy (now WSL) has on its title-page
                    'By Lord Hervey', and he listed it as Hervey's in his
                    Catalogue.

           27   Bernard Mandeville, *The Fable of the Bees; or, Private Vices,*
                    Publick Benefits, ed. F. B. Kaye (1924), 2. 412–14.

           33   Mrs. [K.] Thomson, *Memoirs of Viscountess* [*sic*] *Sundon . . .*
                    Including Letters from the Most Celebrated Persons of Her
                    Time (1847), p. 171.

page 141, line 19   'Voltaire's Correspondence with Lord Hervey: Three New
                    Letters', ed. T. J. Barling, *Studies on Voltaire and the*
                    Eighteenth Century, 62 (1968), 22.

           33   4 Sept. 1731 (H MS.).

           38   George Sherburn, ' "Timon's Villa" and Cannons', *Hunt-*
                    ington Library Bulletin, No. 8 (Oct. 1935); Pope *Poems,* 3,
                    ii. 170–4.

page 142, line 6   21 Dec. 1731 (H MS.).

           10   Robert Halsband, *The Life of Lady Mary Wortley Montagu*
                    (1956), pp. 135–6.

           16   Tuesday night [16 Jan. 1733] (BM. MS.).

           27   Pope *Poems,* 4. 5.

           30   Fannius is a vain poet in Horace's satires and in Jonson's
                    The Poetaster.

           37   17 Feb. 1733 (BM. MS.).

page 143, line 9   J. V. Guerinot, *Pamphlet Attacks on Alexander Pope 1711–1744*
                    (1969).

           36   LM *Letters,* 2. 100.

page 144, line 2   Pope *Corr.,* 3. 366.

            7   'Letter to a Noble Lord' (1733), Alexander Pope, *Works,*
                  ed. W. Elwin and W. J. Courthope (1871–89), 5. 430.

           13   See above, p. 118.

           25   [Paul Whitehead], *The State Dunces* (1733), pp. 7, 17.

           36   Thomson, *Memoirs of Viscountess Sundon* (1847), 2. 224;
                  quoted, with the addition of the phrase 'it is his trade',
                  by A. S. Collins, *Authorship in the Days of Johnson* (1927),
                  p. 171.

page 145, line 20   6, 17 Feb. 1733 (BM. MS.). The quotation is adapted from
                    Act II of Dryden's heroic tragedy *Aureng-Zebe* (1675).

           31   Cholmondeley (Houghton) MS. 73 (23). Neither the
                  D.N.B. nor Horace Walpole attributes this pamphlet to

Hervey, as the Ickworth copy does, probably in the hand of his son Gen. William Hervey.

page 146, line 10 Coxe *Walpole*, 3. 129.

          21 H *Mem.*, 1. 148–9.

page 147, line 3 H *Mem.*, 1. 162, 163–5; Egmont, 1. 361–2.

          20 H *Mem.*, 1. 167–8.

          27 Edmond McA. Gagey, *Ballad Opera* (1937), p. 181.

page 148, line 16 H *Mem.*, 1. 204.

          18 *Daily Post*, 12 June 1733.

          25 *Letter-Books*, 3. 92; *Diary*, p. 112.

          29 H to Middleton, 12 June 1733 (Dyce-Forster Coll., Victoria and Albert Museum).

          32 Earl of March, *A Duke and His Friends* (1911), 1. 243.

page 149, line 9 4 Nov. 1732 (BM. MS.).

          14 Lady H to Stephen Fox, 20 Nov. 1732 (BM. MS.).

          25 Dated 20 Sept. 1733, not in H's autograph, and sent with his letter to Henry Fox on 20 Oct. (BM. MS.); later printed as *Epistle from a Nobleman* (see above pp. 161–2).

page 150, line 20 25 June 1733 (BM. MS.).

page 151, line 4 14 Nov. 1732 (H MS.).

          30 H *Mem.*, 2. 347.

page 152, line 3 H *Mem.*, 2. 621; 3. 719.

           9 H *Mem.*, 2. 585–96. Lady Hervey regarded it as 'the best thing he ever wrote' (Walpole *Corr.*, 33. 253).

          15 H *Mem.*, 1. 72.

          16 *Gentleman's Magazine.*

          20 H to Middleton [10 Apr. 1734] (H MS.).

          37 H *Mem.*, 2. 362–3.

          40 H *Mem.*, 3. 683. He even repeats unknowingly a long passage on the Prince of Wales: 1. 311–12; 3. 875–7.

page 153, line 3 H *Mem.*, 1. 87.

           8 H *Mem.*, 2. 621.

CHAPTER 9. 1733–1734

page 154, line 16 *Letter-Books*, 3. 70–1.

          17 *Daily Advertiser*, 17 July 1732.

          20 *Diary*, p. 82.

          26 (Miss) Lepell Hervey to Lady H, 20, 27 June 1733 (Mulgrave Castle MS.).

          29 Boswell, *Life of Johnson*, ed. G. B. Hill and L. F. Powell (1934), 1. 106; 2. 341.

page 155, line 6 18 June 1733 (H MS.); H *Mem.*, 1. 204.

          19 H to Conyers Middleton, 20 June 1733 (H MS.).

          30 *Letter-Books*, 3. 94.

page 156, line 3 *Letter-Books*, 3. 100–1.

          10 Nov. 1733 (H MS.).

          13 *Daily Post*, 10 Mar. 1733.

page 156, line 18   Nov. 1733 (H MS.).

          25   J. H. Plumb, *The Growth of Political Stability in England 1675–1725* (1967), pp. 188–9; John Carswell, *The Old Cause: Three Studies in Whiggism* (1954), p. 159.

          33   *Weekly Journal or British Gazetteer*, 7 July 1733; *Letter-Books*, 3. 101. Charles already held a Lincolnshire living; and when Ickworth became vacant in 1736—on the promotion of Robert Butts—Lord Bristol appointed him to it.

          37   31 July 1733 (H MS.).

page 157, line 8   R. J. White, *Dr. Bentley A Study in Academic Scarlet* (1968), p. 175.

          21   Middleton to H, 24 June 1733 (H MS.).

          25   12 June 1733 (Dyce-Forster Coll., Victoria and Albert Museum).

          31   25 July, 6 Sept. 1733 (H MS.).

page 158, line 8   Fifty-two letters from Middleton to Townshend (1735–45) (Trinity Coll. MS.).

          15   H to Mrs. Clayton, 14 July 1733, Add MS. 20, 104, f. 4. For his admiration of Mrs. Clayton, see H *Mem.*, 1. 67.

          28   H *Mem.*, 1. 221.

          36   *London Journal*, 21 July 1733.

page 159, line 5   Earl of March, *A Duke and His Friends* (1911), 1. 264–73.

           7   Lady H to Lepell H, 5, 7 Sept. 1733 (Mulgrave Castle MS.); H to Benjamin Hoadly, 14 Aug. 1733 (H MS.).

          12   14 Aug. 1733 (H MS.).

          18   29 Nov. 1733 (BM. MS.).

          26   H to Stephen Fox, 13 June 1727 (H MS.).

          29   Robert Shackleton, *Montesquieu* (1961), pp. 126, 142.

          32   H to Middleton, 1 June 1734 (H MS.).

          39   Voltaire *Corr.*, 2. 299, 321.

page 160, line 5   'Voltaire's Correspondence with Lord Hervey: Three New Letters', ed. T. J. Barling, *Studies on Voltaire and the Eighteenth Century*, 62 (1968), 22–3.

          18   Theodore Besterman, *Voltaire* (1969), p. 166. The Englishman is more properly Everard Fawkener.

          21   8 Feb. 1733 (BM. MS.).

          33   'Voltaire's Correspondence with Lord Hervey', ed. Barling, *Studies on Voltaire*, p. 23. The translation was published on 10 Aug. 1733 (*Daily Advertiser*).

page 161, line 6   15 Nov. 1733 (H MS.).

           9   *Letter-Books*, 3. 97.

          20   Attributed to H on the Ickworth copy (by Gen. William Hervey) and in Walpole *Catalogue*.

          25   HMC *Carlisle MSS.* (1897), p. 123.

page 162, line 17   Verse dated 20 Sept. (not in Hervey's autograph), and sent to Henry Fox with his letter of 20 Oct. 1733 (BM. MS.).

          27   Pope *Poems*, 4. 41.

          34   6 Dec. 1733 (BM. MS.).

page 163, line 2   H to Henry Fox, 31 Jan. 1734 (BM. MS.).

22   Alexander Pope, *Works*, ed. W. Elwin and W. J. Courthope (1871–89), 5. 263.

26   It was first published in Warburton's 1751 edition of Pope's *Works*.

33   H to Henry Fox, 31 Jan. 1734 (BM. MS.).

page 164, line 1   Walpole *Corr.*, 9. 116.

4   William Warburton in the 1752 edition of Pope's *Works*; Thomas Tyers, *An Historical Rhapsody on Mr. Pope* (1782), p. 45.

9   Middleton to H, 8 Nov. 1733 (H MS.).

13   Middleton to H, 21 Nov. 1733 (H MS.).

31   H to Henry Fox, 31 Jan. 1734 (BM. MS.). A copy of the verse in Stephen Fox's hand accompanied this letter.

36   31 Jan. 1734 (BM. MS.).

page 165, line 4   *The Grub Street Journal* sporadically noticed or attacked Hervey: 22, 29 Nov., 6, 8, 13, and 27 Dec. 1733; 14 Feb., 4 Apr. 1734; 26 June, 23, 30 Sept. 1736; see also James T. Hillhouse, *The Grub Street Journal* (1928), pp. 75 ff.

9   *Lord Hervey and His Friends, 1726–1738*, ed. Earl of Ilchester (1950), pp. 298–9.

16   H to Henry Fox, 14 Feb. 1734 (BM. MS.).

20   Delany *Corr.*, 1. 431. The new edition was published 26 Jan. 1734 (*Daily Journal*).

26   H *Mem.*, 2. 345.

32   15 Nov. 1733; reprinted in *New Foundling Hospital for Wit* (1786), 1. 242–3.

page 166, line 9   21, 31 Jan. 1734 (BM. MS.).

12   31 Jan. 1734 (H MS.).

26   Ilchester, *Lord Hervey and His Friends*, p. 296.

29   *The State Weathercocks* ([Mar.] 1734).

page 167, line 4   14 Feb. 1734 (BM. MS.).

20   H *Mem.*, 1. 258–60.

26   Saturday [30 Mar. 1734] (H MS.); acknowledged and praised by Middleton in his reply on 2 Apr. (H MS.).

30   H *Mem.*, 1. 245; also attributed to him in Ickworth copy (by his son Gen. William Hervey) and in Walpole *Catalogue*.

31   *Daily Advertiser*.

page 168, line 11   Cholmondeley (Houghton) MS., P 75 (6).

page 169, line 5   H *Mem.*, 1. 194–5; Horace Walpole, *Reminiscences*, ed. P. Toynbee (1924), p. 110.

9   H *Mem.*, 1. 230–1.

19   H to Stephen Fox, 6 Dec.; H to Duke of Richmond, 27 Dec. 1733 (H MS.).

23   H to Prince of Orange, 29 Jan. 1734 (H MS.).

25   6 Feb. 1734, H MS. 47/1; H to Prince of Orange, 9 Feb. 1634, Koninklijk Huisarchief, The Hague.

page 169, line 27   31 Jan. 1734 (BM. MS.).

                29   *London Journal*, 9 March 1734; *Diary*, p. 83.

                38   Egmont, 2. 59–60. The previous autumn (2 Nov. 1733) Egmont had presented a memorial to the King from the Irish peers in protest against their exclusion from the ceremonies connected with the approaching marriage.

page 170, line 6   Delany *Corr.*, 1. 437.

page 171, line 4   H *Mem.*, 1. 263–72 *passim* (trans. in part), 289–90.

                12   11 May 1734 (BM. MS.).

                18   H *Mem.*, 2. 349.

                22   20 Jan. 1734 (BM. MS.).

                26   10 Aug. 1734 (BM. MS.).

                28   H *Mem.*, 2. 348–9.

page 172, line 1   *Letter-Books*, 3. 116–18.

                 6   10 Aug. 1734, Add MS. 20, 104, ff. 12–13.

                 9   16 Aug. 1734 (BM. MS.).

                19   H *Mem.*, 1. 292–3.

                26   H *Mem.*, 2. 348–9.

                31   H *Mem.*, 1. 291.

page 173, line 3   H *Mem.*, 1. 294.

                10   *Letter-Books*, 3. 72; H to Lord Bristol, 21 Dec. 1731; H to Stephen Fox, 25 Dec. 1731; H to Bromley, 27 Dec. 1733 (all in H MS.).

                13   *Weekly Journal or British Gazetteer*, 22 Dec. 1733.

                37   H *Mem.*, 2. 395–9.

                38   7 Oct. 1734 (BM. MS.).

page 174, line 6   Attributed to Hervey on Ickworth copy (by Gen. William Hervey) and by Walpole in his *Catalogue* as well as on his own copy (now WSL).

                10   *Politics on Both Sides* ([Jan.] 1734, 2nd ed. [Apr.] 1734), *An Inquiry into the Conduct of Our Domestic Affairs from the Year 1721 to the Present Time* ([Apr.] 1734).

                17   p. 51.

                19   p. 61.

CHAPTER 10. 1735–1736

page 175, line 7   Pope *Poems*, 4. 61, 75, 83.

page 176, line 18   Archibald S. Foord, *His Majesty's Opposition 1714–1830* (1964), p. 120.

                36   For an appreciation of the *Epistle to Dr. Arbuthnot* see Elder Olson, 'Rhetoric and the Appreciation of Pope', *Modern Philology*, 37 (1939), 13–35, and Maynard Mack, 'The Muse of Satire', *Yale Review*, 41 (Autumn 1951), 80–92.

page 177, line 3   'Account of Illness', H *Mem.*, 3. 985.

                 8   Peter Dixon, *The World of Pope's Satires* (1968), p. 202.

                15   Pope *Corr.*, 3. 431.

page 177, line 27   LM *Letters*, 2. 99–101.
            39   *Letter-Books*, 3. 138.
page 178, line 2   H to Charles Hanbury Williams, 22 Jan. [1735] (MS. owned
                    by WSL).
             8   1757, Add MS. 5829, f. 136.
            26   A. S. Turberville, *The House of Lords in the XVIII Century*
                    (1927), pp. 137–8.
page 179, line 2   10 Feb. 1735 (BM. MS.).
            13   H *Mem.*, 2. 434–5.
            22   H *Mem.*, 2. 426–7.
            24   20 Feb. [1735] (BM. MS.).
page 180, line 10   H *Mem.*, 2. 435–46.
            18   H to Middleton, 10 Apr. 1735 (H MS.).
            20   H to Middleton, 24 Apr. 1735 (H MS.).
            22   H *Mem.*, 2. 446–9.
            33   H *Mem.*, 2. 451–5.
page 181, line 22   H *Mem.*, 2. 542.
            23   H to Henry Fox, 11 May 1734 (BM. MS.).
            33   H to the Queen, [22 June 1735] (H MS.).
            35   19 May 1735 (BM. MS.).
page 182, line 7   H *Mem.*, 1. 274–5.
            15   Jan. 1733, HMC *Carlisle MSS.* (1897), p. 96.
            30   H *Mem.*, 2. 388–9.
page 183, line 2   Egmont, 1. 390.
            25   H *Mem.*, 2. 477–8.
            36   See Plate 11 (BM. Print 2270). This anonymous engraving is
                    adapted from Hogarth's 'Henry the Eighth and Anne
                    Boleyn' [*c.* 1728]; it is mentioned in Ronald Paulson,
                    Hogarth's Graphic Works (1965), 1. 139. Miss Vane is also
                    satirized (in prose and verse) as the discarded mistress in
                    Tell-tale Cupids (1735).
page 184, line 12   H *Mem.*, 2. 475–7; *Walpole Corr.*, 20. 30.
page 185, line 5   H *Mem.*, 2. 476–83. Egmont's gossip (2. 198) of the final
                    settlement differs in details.
             8   Warrant dated 22 Nov. 1734 (Archives of the Duchy of
                    Cornwall, London). Its emoluments amounted to £453
                    a year (warrant dated 16 Apr. 1736).
            13   H *Mem.*, 2. 483; *London Evening Post*, 13–16 Dec. 1735.
            16   *Daily Advertiser*, 2 Jan., 24, 26 Feb. 1736.
            19   H *Mem.*, 2. 483.
            21   *Daily Advertiser*, 29 Mar., 7 Apr. 1736.
            38   *Poems*, ed. E. L. McAdam, Jr. with G. Milne (1964), p. 106.
page 186, line 9   Peter King, *The Life of John Locke* (1830), 2. 111; HMC
                    Carlisle MSS. (1897), p. 167.
            11   Egmont, 2. 299.
            18   H *Mem.*, 2. 457–8.
            25   H to Middleton, 10 July 1735 (H MS.).
            28   H *Mem.*, 2. 488.

page 187, line 5 *Letter-Books*, 3. 131–3.

7 *Letter-Books*, 3. 140.

10 H to Lady Bristol, 18 Sept. 1735 (H MS.); *Daily Advertiser*, 20 Sept. 1735.

14 *Diary*, p. 84.

20 H *Mem.*, 2. 492–8.

30 H *Mem.*, 2. 528.

page 188, line 7 H *Mem.*, 2. 488–9.

13 H to Horace Walpole, 21 Oct. 1735, *Supplement to the Letters of Walpole*, ed. P. Toynbee (1925), 3. 97.

17 18 Nov. 1735, Coxe *Walpole*, 3. 303.

23 H to Horatio Walpole, 23 Dec., Coxe *Walpole*, 3. 311; H to Middleton, [27 Dec.] 1735 (H MS.).

24 'Account of Illness', H *Mem.*, 3. 987.

27 1 Dec. 1735, Delany *Corr.*, 1. 544.

33 *Opinions*, pub. 1788, in Sarah, Duchess of Marlborough, *Memoirs* [*An Account of the Conduct of* . . . , 1742], ed. W. King (1930), p. 296.

page 189, line 12 'Characters', BM. Stowe MS. 308, f. 13.

14 Ilchester *Fox*, 1. 32–5.

15 *Daily Advertiser*, 15 July 1735.

37 Mrs. [K.] Thomson, *Memoirs of Viscountess* [*sic*] *Sundon* (1847), 2. 344, 350–1, 355, 360.

page 190, line 27 *Daily Advertiser*; Add MS. 27, 735, f. 123.

28 *Daily Advertiser*, 29 Mar. 1736.

31 Mrs. Horner to Lady Sundon, Add MS. 20, 104, ff. 18–19. In his will Horner cut off his daughter with a bequest of ten guineas (copy of will dated 6 Dec. 1740, BM. Holland House MS.).

33 Mrs. Horner to Lady Sundon, 29 Mar. [1737], Add MS. 30,516, ff. 21–2.

37 Ilchester *Fox*, 1. 44–7 for account of marriage. The parson was Peter Lewis Willemin (or Villemin), a Frenchman educated at the University of Paris. He was presented to the vicarage of Eisey a year later (26 Oct. 1737) by its patron, Stephen Fox (Archives of Diocesan Record Office, Salisbury). He is the parson depicted in the Hogarth conversation piece (Plate 14).

page 191, line 2 30 Mar. 1736, Add MS. 32, 458.

CHAPTER II. 1736–1737

page 192, line 10 8 Dec. 1730 (H MS.).

18 Two ink sketches drawn by Jonathan Richardson, sen., in 1736 (LM *Letters*, 2. facing 104).

23 'Voltaire's Correspondence with Lord Hervey', ed. Barling, *Studies on Voltaire* (1968), p. 24.

page 192, line 27   *Œuvres complètes*, ed. L. Moland (1883–5), 10. 296.
page 193, line 9   Voltaire *Corr.*, 4. 168–9 (spelling of names corrected).
           19   Archives of the R.S. and the Society of Antiquaries.
           23   Ida Treat, *Francesco Algarotti* (1913), pp. 24–71 *passim*.
           29   For a full discussion of LM's friendship with Algarotti, see Halsband, *Life of LM* (1956), chaps. 10–12, 15.
page 194, line 10   H *Mem.*, 2. 531; also attributed to H in Ickworth copy (by Gen. William Hervey) and in Walpole *Catalogue*. Date of publication from *Daily Advertiser*.
page 195, line 11   *Letter-Books*, 3. 155.
           16   Egmont, 2. 242.
           26   HMC *Carlisle MSS.* (1897), p. 169.
           32   H *Mem.*, 2. 530.
page 196, line 7   *Verney Letters of the Eighteenth Century*, ed. Lady Verney [1930], 2. 139; HMC *Carlisle MSS.* (1897), p. 170.
           14   *Letter-Books*, 3. 150.
           26   H *Mem.*, 2. 548–53; *Weekly Journal or British Gazetteer*, 1 May 1736; *Daily Advertiser*, 29 Apr. 1736.
           30   H *Mem.*, 2. 553.
           35   29 Apr. 1736, H MS. 46/11, pp. 695–6 (omitted from *Letter-Books*, 3. 150).
           37   H *Mem.*, 2. 615.
page 197, line 9   H *Mem.*, 2. 553–5.
           30   H *Mem.*, 2. 560–1.
page 198, line 8   H *Mem.*, 2. 561–2.
           17   H *Mem.*, 2. 564.
           22   H *Mem.*, 2. 618.
           28   H *Mem.*, 2. 574–5, 585–96.
           34   Voltaire *Corr.*, 5. 203.
page 199, line 4   LM *Letters*, 2. 103.
           18   14 Aug. 1736 (Murray MS.).
           20   LM *Letters*, 2. 106.
           22   22 Aug. 1736 (Murray MS.).
           26   4 Sept. 1736 (BM. MS.).
page 200, line 10   9 Sept. 1736, trans. (Murray MS.).
           29   LM *Letters*, 2. 104–6, trans.
page 201, line 2   16 Sept. 1736 (BM. MS.).
           11   LM *Letters*, 2. 107, trans.
           29   28 Sept. 1736, trans. (Murray MS.).
page 202, line 4   LM *Letters*, 2. 108.
           17   LM *Letters*, 2. 108–9.
           30   28 Sept. trans.; 30 Oct. 1736 (Murray MS.).
           34   LM *Letters*, 2. 110–11.
page 203, line 2   Voltaire *Corr.*, 5. 269.
           25   H *Mem.*, 2. 597–600; also in Egmont, 2. 307.
           34   H *Mem.*, 2. 604.
page 204, line 8   H *Mem.*, 2. 621.
           15   30 Oct. 1736 (Murray MS.).

page 204, line 19   H *Mem.*, 2. 621.

           23   13 Nov. 1736 (BM. MS.).

           34   H to Henry Fox, 25 Nov. (BM. MS.); H to Lady Bristol, 27 Nov. 1736 (H MS.).

page 205, line 8   *Diary*, p. 96; *Letter-Books*, 3. 164.

           11   24 Dec. 1736, PRO L.C. 5/75, p. 109.

           17   H to Henry Fox, 25 Nov., H to Stephen Fox, 4 Dec. 1736 (BM. MS.).

           30   16 Dec. 1736 (BM. MS.); H *Mem.*, 2. 624.

page 206, line 5   H *Mem.*, 2. 628.

           14   H *Mem.*, 2. 625–6.

           26   H *Mem.*, 2. 628–31.

           39   H *Mem.*, 2. 640–1.

page 207, line 2   21 Dec. 1736 (BM. MS.).

           17   H *Mem.*, 2. 635–6.

           29   This was supplemented by about £9,000 a year from the Duchy of Cornwall (A. N. Newman in *The Historical Journal*, I, 1958, 70–1).

page 208, line 24   H *Mem.*, 3. 661–7 *passim*.

           30   H *Mem.*, 3. 672.

           36   H *Mem.*, 3. 673–5.

page 209, line 13   H *Mem.*, 3. 677–81.

           17   Egmont, 2. 355.

           27   Diary of Edward Harley, Tory M.P. (MS. Add 6851, f. 77, Cambridge Univ. Library).

           32   Dodington's long, circumstantial account, dated 5 Mar. 1737, is printed as an appendix to his *Diary*, ed. H. P. Wyndham (1784).

page 210, line 5   Cholmondeley (Houghton) MS. 73 (37).

           8   Coxe *Walpole*, 1. 532–3.

           28   Attributed to Hervey on Ickworth copy (by Gen. William Hervey) and in Walpole *Catalogue*.

page 211, line 7   Hervey's full account in *Mem.*, 3. 707–26, 734–8.

           29   9 Oct. 1736 (BM. MS.).

page 212, line 13   H *Mem.*, 3. 716.

           21   *Diary*, pp. 84–5.

           26   H *Mem.*, 3. 734.

           27   Date from *Journal of House of Lords*; Cobbett gives 13 June.

           38   H *Mem.*, 3. 735.

page 213, line 1   *Letter-Books*, 3. 170.

           8   13 June 1737 (BM. MS.).

           20   *Letter-Books*, 3. 170.

CHAPTER 12. 1737–1738

page 214, line 3   H *Mem.*, 3. 669.

           22   H *Mem.*, 3. 667–9. In 1735 Walpole had promised Stephen the post of secretary (worth £2,000 p.a.) to Lord

Scarborough, whom he intended to appoint Lord
Lieutenant of Ireland, but Scarborough declined (H *Mem.*,
2. 454–5).

page 215, line 2   H *Mem.*, 3. 740–1; *Daily Advertiser*, 18 June 1737.

7   Thursday night [Aug. 1737] (BM. MS.).

17   13 Sept. 1736 (Add MS. 32, 458).

24   Middleton to H, 4 Jan. 1737 (H MS.).

37   23 Dec. 1736, 4, 16 Jan. 1737 (Trinity Coll. MS.).

page 216, line 2   8 Jan. 1737 (H MS).

5   Walpole *Corr.*, 15. 292.

14   William Cole, Add MS. 5846, p. 21.

24   See above, pp. 186–7.

36   14 Apr. 1737 (Blenheim MS.).

page 217, line 5   Sarah Marlborough, *Letters of a Grandmother 1732–1735*, ed.
G. S. Thomson [1943], p. 93.

10   Lady Bristol to Duchess of Marlborough, 7 May 1737
(Blenheim MS.).

20   *Letter-Books*, 3. 155–6.

22   Lady Bristol to Duchess of Marlborough, 13 Aug. 1737.

24   *Letter-Books*, 3. 178–9.

32   11 June 1737 (BM. MS.).

39   18 June 1737 (H MS.).

page 218, line 3   H to Stephen Fox, 25 June 1737.

13   27 June 1737 (H MS.).

14   Middleton to H, 7 July 1737 (H MS.).

21   12 July 1737.

30   H *Mem.*, 3. 776.

page 219, line 19   H *Mem.*, 3. 757–9.

40   H *Mem.*, 3. 759–60.

page 220, line 25   H *Mem.*, 3. 761–8. Much of this account is confirmed in the
Queen's letter to the Princess Royal (R. L. Arkell,
Caroline of Anspach George the Second's Queen, 1939, pp.
297–9).

34   Friday [5 Aug. 1737] (BM. MS.).

page 221, line 1   H *Mem.*, 3. 785.

12   H *Mem.*, 3. 807.

18   H *Mem.*, 3. 808–10.

25   10 Sept. 1737 (BM. MS.).

page 222, line 16   H *Mem.*, 3. 815, 816–17.

38   H *Mem.*, 3. 817–20.

39   See above, p. 198.

page 223, line 15   29/18 July 1737 (Murray MS.).

26   17 Sept. 1737 (H MS.).

30   11, 25 June, 10 Sept. 1737 (BM. MS.).

page 224, line 5   15 Oct. 1737 (BM. MS.).

15   H *Mem.*, 3. 839; *The London Stage 1660–1800, Part III:
1729–1747*, ed. A. H. Scouten (1961), 2. 685.

25   H *Mem.*, 3. 841–2.

page 224, line 37 25 Oct., 3 Nov. 1737 (Add MS. 32, 458).

page 225, line 5 H *Mem.*, 3. 854.

            10 From Queen's illness to death, H *Mem.*, 3. 877–915.

page 226, line 21 Newcastle's copy: Add MS. 33, 045, f. 31.

            34 Coxe *Walpole*, 1. 550. That she forgave her son though she refused to see him is corroborated elsewhere (Egmont, 2. 446; Swift, *Corr.*, ed. H. Williams, 1963–5, 5. 75).

page 227, line 29 Ilchester *Fox*, 1. 71.

            39 29 Nov. 1737 (BM. MS.).

page 228, line 5 *Letter-Books*, 3. 188.

             9 Egmont, 2. 456.

            14 26/15 Jan. 1738 (Murray MS.), 4 Feb. 1738 (H MS.); *Letter-Books*, 3. 196.

            18 4 Mar. 1738 (H MS.). A translation of 'a celebrated Latin Epitaph', probably his, was published in the *Daily Advertiser* of 2 Mar. 1738.

            27 Dec. 1737, p. 759.

            37 Norman St. John-Stevas, *Walter Bagehot* (1959), pp. 122–3.

page 229, line 8 Egmont, 2. 458.

            28 H *Mem.*, 3. 904–5.

            35 Chesterfield *Letters*, 2. 311.

page 230, line 2 H *Mem.*, 3. 924.

            33 H *Mem.*, 3. 921–3.

            37 See above, p. 98.

page 231, line 17 H *Mem.*, 3. 923–4.

            37 H *Mem.*, 3. 755.

            38 Basil Williams, *The Whig Supremacy* (2nd ed., 1962), p. 440; Sedgwick in H *Mem.*, 1. lx–lxi; Hans Gerig, *Die Memoiren des Lord Hervey als historische Quelle* (1936).

page 232, line 23 Egmont, 2. 461.

            28 HMC *14th Report*, Part 9 (1895), p. 10.

page 233, line 2 11 Feb. [1738] (BM. Holland House MS.). A draft of the speech in Fox's autograph and a copy are also in the Holland House MS.

             7 Pope *Poems*, 4. 303, 323. (Fox is mistakenly identified as Henry instead of Stephen.)

            17 H to Mrs. —, 4 Feb. 1738 (H MS.).

            25 31 Jan. 1738 (H MS.).

            33 18 Feb. 1738 (H MS.).

            36 9 Mar., 23 Apr. 1738 (Add MS. 32, 458).

page 234, line 6 H to Middleton, 2 May (Add MS. 32, 458); 4 May 1738 (H MS.).

            37 30 May 1738 (Add MS. 32, 458).

            39 25 Oct. 1737 (Add MS. 32, 458).

page 235, line 11 *Letter-Books*, 3. 209.

            20 *Letter-Books*, 3. 204–5.

            27 *Letter-Books*, 3. 203.

CHAPTER 13. 1738–1740

page 237, line 9   p. 10.
13   Ed. R. Halsband (1947).
23   H *Mem.*, 3. 727–32.
38   H to Algarotti, 22/11 Apr. 1738 (Murray MS.).
page 238, line 2   Egmont, 2. 482, 489.
5   *Weekly Journal*, 17 June 1738.
8   HMC *Townshend MSS.*, 4 (1887), 356; *Wentworth Papers*, ed. J. J. Cartwright (1883), p. 541.
14   *Daily Advertiser*, 13 July 1738.
25   10 Aug. 1738 (BM. MS.).
35   *Letter-Books*, 3. 217–18.
page 239, line 2   *Letter-Books*, 3. 215.
8   22 Apr. 1738 (Blenheim MS.).
13   Thomas Wright of Durham, 'Early Journal', ed. E. Hughes, *Annals of Science*, 7 (1951), 14.
20   10 Oct. 1738 (Blenheim MS.).
28   H to Henry Fox, 12 Sept. 1738 (BM. MS.); Ilchester *Fox*, 1. 51.
31   Plate 14; Ronald Paulson, *Hogarth: His Life, Art, and Times* (1971), 1. 458.
34   The persons depicted in the conversation piece are (from left to right) the Revd. P. L. Willemin, Stephen and Henry Fox, Hervey, the Duke of Marlborough, and Thomas Winnington.
page 240, line 2   Lady Bristol to Duchess of Marlborough, 10 Oct. 1738 (Blenheim MS.).
4   LM *Letters*, 2. 124; *Daily Advertiser*, 21 Nov. 1738.
14   H to Middleton, 16 Jan. 1739 (Add MS. 32, 458).
37   H MS. 47/10.
page 241, line 3   Egmont, 3. 29.
12   LM *Letters*, 2. 137; also in Delany *Corr.*, 2. 44–5; A. S. Turberville, *The House of Lords in the XVIII Century* (1927), pp. 14–15, 238.
16   *Orrery Papers*, 1. 257 (corrected from MS.: Houghton Library, Harvard University, MS. Eng. 218. 2, vol. 4, pp. 34–5).
23   H to Middleton, 24 Feb. 1739 (H MS.).
38   24 Aug. 1738 (H MS.).
page 242, line 2   27 Aug. 1738 (Add MS. 32, 458).
8   3 Dec. 1734 (H MS.).
10   22 Mar. 1735 (H MS.). As a by-product of Hervey's interest in the book he and Middleton corresponded on the subject of how the Roman Senate was constituted; Middleton published his own letters in 1747 as *A Treatise on the Roman Senate. In Two Parts.*
17   27 Aug. 1738 (Add MS. 32, 458).

page 242, line 37   11, 18 Nov. 1738 (H MS.). Edward Young 'was informed by a good hand' that Middleton had wanted to dedicate his book to Philip Yorke, the Lord Chancellor's son, and had been repulsed (Young to Yorke [?18 Mar. 1742/3], Young, *Corr.*, ed. H. Pettit, 1971, p. 153). But this rumour seems implausible.

page 243, line 3   9 Dec. 1738 (H MS.).

             9   Lady H, *Letters* [ed. J. W. Croker] (1821), p. 124.

           11   Middleton to H, 27 Aug. (Add MS. 32, 458); H to Middleton, 29 Aug. 1738 (H MS.).

          14   13 Mar. 1739 (Trinity Coll. MS.).

          21   24 Feb. 1739 (H MS.).

          27   3 Mar. 1739 (H MS.).

          33   Middleton to Townshend, 13, 18 Mar. 1739 (Trinity Coll. MS.).

          36   H to Middleton, 15 Mar. 1739 (H MS.).

          39   22 March 1739 (Dyce-Forster Coll., Victoria and Albert Museum).

page 244, line 4   *The Orrery Papers*, ed. Countess of Cork and Orrery (1903), 1. 254–5.

             6   Walpole *Corr.*, 15. 6–8.

             9   27 Mar. 1739 (H MS.).

          14   Middleton to H, 25 Mar. 1739 (Add MS. 32, 458).

          18   R. J. White, *Dr. Bentley A Study in Academic Scarlet* (1968), p. 184; James Henry Monk, *The Life of Richard Bentley, D.D.* (1830), pp. 434–9.

          28   10 Apr. 1739 (Add MS. 32, 458).

          32   14 Apr. 1739 (H MS.).

page 245, line 3   17/6 Mar. 1738 (Murray MS.).

          15   LM *Letters*, 2. 117, trans.

          39   Treat, *Algarotti* (1913), pp. 63–7.

page 246, line 6   LM *Letters*, 2. 115.

          11   22/11 Apr. 1738 (Murray MS.).

          21   Voltaire *Corr.*, 7. 356; 8. 3, 74.

          25   Voltaire *Corr.*, 9. 47.

          32   8 Mar. 1739 (Murray MS.). Hervey also lent a copy to Lord Cobham, another prominent member of the Opposition (H to Algarotti, 22/11 Apr. 1738, Murray MS.).

          35   Algarotti to Mitchell, 28 June 1738 (Craigievar Castle MS.).

page 247, line 1   28 Dec. 1738 (Murray MS.).

             4   Douglas Grant, *James Thomson Poet of 'The Seasons'* (1951), pp. 169–70, 175–6.

            8   LM *Letters*, 2. 116.

          12   LM *Letters*, 2. 132, trans.

          18   LM *Letters*, 2. 134–5, 137–8.

          30   Treat, *Algarotti*, pp. 74–6.

page 247, line 40   Marcelle Ehrhard, *Le Prince Cantemir à Paris (1738–1744)* (1938), p. 31; H. Grasshoff, *Kantemir und Westeuropa* (1966), pp. 121–3.

page 248, line 9   H *Mem.*, 3. 817.

            12   Treat, *Algarotti*, p. 79.

            26   Francesco Algarotti, *Letters on Russia* (trans., 1769), I. 3, 18.

            36   Ibid., I. 96, 121.

page 249, line 10   LM *Letters*, 2. 140, trans.

            30   17 Aug. 1739 (H MS.).

            39   H to Henry Fox, 11 Sept. (BM. MS.); H to Algarotti, 29 Sept. 1739 (Murray MS.).

page 250, line 5   7 Dec. 1738 (BM. MS.).

             8   *Daily Advertiser*, 22 June 1739.

            11   *Gentleman's Magazine*, June 1739, p. 328.

            16   H to Henry Fox, 11 Sept. 1739 (BM. MS.).

            18   H to Algarotti, 29 Sept. 1739 (Murray MS.); Ilchester *Fox*, I. 52.

            37   Algarotti, *Letters on Russia*, 2. 33–4, 36 (Latin quotation from Horace; Loeb trans.).

page 251, line 9   29 Sept. 1739 [N.S.], trans. (Craigievar Castle MS.).

            22   29 Sept. 1739 (Murray MS.).

            31   Frederick the Great, *Œuvres* (1851), 18. 4, 6, trans.

page 252, line 7   Egmont, 3. 140.

            15   Coxe *Walpole*, 1. 622–3; Philip C. Yorke, *Life and Corr. of Philip Yorke, Earl of Hardwicke, Lord High Chancellor of Great Britain* (1913), 1. 231.

            23   Yorke, *Hardwicke*, pp. 229–33 (Add MS. 35, 406, ff. 164–9).

            26   William Coxe, *Memoirs of the Administration of Henry Pelham* (1829), 1. 14.

            34   Horace Walpole's MS. 'Commonplace Book of Verses, Stories . . &c,' p. 67 (owned by WSL); also in Walpole's *Memoirs of George II*, 1. xx, n.

page 253, line 2   Etough Papers, Add MS. 9200, f. 211. Horace Walpole writes that the appointment was made 'against the inclination of the Minister' and forced by Hervey, Hanbury Williams, Winnington, and the Fox brothers (Horace Walpole, *Memoirs of the Reign of George the Second*, ed. Lord Holland, 2nd ed., rev., 1847, 1. 205).

            20   H to Middleton, Tuesday night [13 Nov. 1739] (Add MS. 32, 458).

            27   H to LM, 31 Dec. 1739 (H MS.).

            31   LM *Letters*, 2. 160; Algarotti to H, Algarotti, *Opere* (1765), 7. 217.

            36   H to LM, LM *Letters*, 2. 160.

page 254, line 7   LM *Letters*, 2. 164, trans.

            18   LM *Letters*, 2. 167.

            34   Egmont, 3. 123.

            40   18 Dec. 1739 (H MS.).

page 255, line 4   20 Jan. (Add MS. 32, 458); 24 Jan. 1740 (H MS.).

CHAPTER 14. 1740–1741

page 256, line 9   Lady H to Lepell H, 10 June [1740] (Mulgrave Castle MS.).
19   21 Apr. 1740 (H MS.).
page 257, line 2   H *Mem.*, 3. 927–9.
18   H *Mem.*, 3. 932–5.
20   Basil Williams, *The Whig Supremacy* (2nd ed., 1962), p. 231.
Williams also calls Hervey 'formidable in satire'; this is
true for his political pamphlets but not his poetical ones.
38   H *Mem.*, 3. 930–1.
page 258, line 6   3. 138.
8   H. C. Maxwell-Lyte, *Historical Notes on the Use of the Great
Seal of England* (1926), p. 25.
11   9 May 1740 (H MS.).
14   PRO, P.C. 2/96, p. 61.
20   Egmont, 3. 141, 163–4.
32   Voltaire *Corr.*, 10. 127, trans.
35   LM *Letters*, 2. 175–6.
page 259, line 2   Frederick the Great, *Œuvres*, 18. 11–12.
6   Norwood Young, *The Life of Frederick the Great* (1919), p. 70.
18   Frederick the Great, *Œuvres*, 17. 283; 18. 15.
25   Moses Mendes to Algarotti, 23 June 1741; H to Algarotti,
7 Oct. 1740 (Murray MS.).
33   [5 June 1740] (Murray MS.).
page 260, line 11   LM *Letters*, 2. 195.
19   17 June 1740 (Murray MS.).
25   LM *Letters*, 2. 198–9, trans.
32   PRO S.P. 44/299.
34   *Daily Advertiser*, 25 June 1740.
page 261, line 12   H to Algarotti, 2/13 July 1740 (Murray MS.).
16   PRO S.P. 44/300.
17   *London Evening Post*, 12–15 July 1740.
20   Lady Bristol to Duchess of Marlborough, 25 Aug. 1740
(Blenheim MS.).
36   26 Aug. 1740 (Mulgrave Castle Archives).
40   Thomas Wright of Durham, 'Early Journal', ed. E. Hughes,
Annals of Science, 7 (1951), 15.
page 262, line 10   25 Oct. 1740 (Blenheim MS.).
30   22 Sept. 1740 (Murray MS.).
35   Frederick the Great, *Œuvres*, 18. 18–19.
page 263, line 4   Harrington to Dickens, 11 Nov., 12 Dec. 1740, PRO S.P.
90/48.
10   Coxe *Walpole*, 1. 643.
34   P. D. G. Thomas, *The House of Commons in the Eighteenth
Century* (1971), pp. 37–8.
page 264, line 1   Elizabeth Montagu, *Corr., 1720–1761*, ed. E. J. Climenson
(1906), 1. 105.
6   Coxe *Walpole*, 1. 644–69.

page 264, line 21   Philip C. Yorke, *Life and Correspondence of Philip Yorke, Earl of Hardwicke, Lord High Chancellor of Great Britain* (1913), 1. 199, 202.

29   21 Oct., 9 Dec. 1739 (Add MS. 32, 458).

32   26 Feb., 6 Apr. 1740 (ibid.).

37   27 May 1740 (H MS.).

page 265, line 11   17 June 1740 (Add MS. 32, 458).

14   James Boswell, *Journal of a Tour to the Hebrides . . . 1773*, ed. F. A. Pottle and C. H. Bennett (1961), p. 254.

30   24 June 1740 (H MS.).

page 266, line 11   13 Nov. 1740 (H MS.).

17   27 Dec. 1740 (Add MS. 32, 458).

19   Middleton to Townshend, 7 Dec. 1740 (Trinity Coll. MS.).

page 267, line 27   21 Feb. 1741 (Huntington Library MS. MO 1013).

page 268, line 16   Middleton to Warburton, 5 Apr. 1741, Middleton, *Miscellaneous Works* (1752), 1. 408.

22   Pope *Poems*, 5. 351.

page 269, line 27   *Shamela*, ed. M. C. Battestin (1961).

30   Fielding's *Joseph Andrews*, published in Feb. 1742, contains a slight reference to Middleton's *Cicero* and an extended caricature of Hervey under the name of Beau Didapper, who is an effeminate fop in pursuit of the virtuous Fanny, and is also the minion of a 'Great-Man' [Walpole] (ed. M. C. Battestin, 1967, pp. 239, 303-33 *passim*; Sean Shesgreen, *Literary Portraits in the Novels of Henry Fielding*, 1972, pp. 83-4).

35   T[homas] Dampier thought that Hervey had been 'very justly and prettily ridiculed' in the *Shamela* dedication (HMC *12th Report*, vol. ix, 1891, p. 204).

40   Sunday [Jan. 1733] (H MS.).

page 270, line 1   24 June 1740 (H MS.).

16   12 Sept. 1741 (H MS.).

19   29 Oct. 1741 (Trinity Coll. MS.). Newcastle had subscribed for 5 copies of *Cicero* through Lord Lincoln, his nephew (19 Apr. 1739, ibid.).

23   Walpole *Corr.*, 15. 304.

39   14 Sept. 1741 (Murray MS.).

page 271, line 2   LM *Letters*, 2. 232.

13   30 Sept., 7 Oct. 1742 (Trinity Coll. MS.).

CHAPTER 15. 1741–1742

page 272, line 14   Frederick the Great, *Œuvres* (1851), 18. 25-6, trans.

30   Voltaire *Corr.*, 10. 341, trans.

page 273, line 4   Frederick the Great, *Politische Correspondenz*, 1 (1879), 146; Treat, *Algarotti*, pp. 109-12.

10   Archives des Affaires Étrangères, Sardaigne, vol. 202, 4 Feb.–13 May 1741 *passim*.

page 278, line 18   22 Sept. 1740 (Murray MS.).
            21   LM *Letters*, 2. 206.
            26   LM *Letters*, 2. 210.
            38   LM *Letters*, 2. 232.
page 274, line 4   LM *Letters*, 2. 232 n.
            11   29/18 May 1741 (Murray MS.).
            16   LM *Letters*, 2. 237.
            18   LM *Letters*, 2. 240.
            22   Frederick the Great, *Politische Correspondenz*, 1. 198, 206.
            40   LM *Letters*, 2. 240–1.
page 275, line 8   Frederick the Great, *Œuvres* (1851), 18. 28.
            16   21 June 1741 (Murray MS.).
            24   Frances, Countess of Hertford, and Henrietta Louisa, Countess of Pomfret, *Correspondence 1738–1741* (1805), 2. 20; *Letter-Books*, 3. 251.
            30   *Diary*, p. 87.
            34   *Diary*, p. 235.
            36   Lady Bristol to Duchess of Marlborough, 25 Oct. 1740 (Blenheim MS.).
page 276, line 2   *Diary*, p. 87.
             3   H to LM, 16 May 1741 (H MS.).
             9   *Daily Advertiser*, 20 Feb. 1740.
            10   *Letter-Books*, 3. 272.
            16   *Daily Advertiser*, 19 June 1741; *Letter-Books*, 3. 275. He did not resign until March 1744.
            23   *Letter-Books*, 3. 278.
            28   PRO, Ind. 6762.
            31   Stephen Fox to [Hervey], 20 Nov. 1742 (BM. MS.).
page 277, line 6   Egmont, 3. 259–60.
            12   Halsband, *Life of LM*, pp. 216–17.
            25   Walpole *Corr.*, 17. 92.
            30   H to Algarotti, 18 May 1741 (Murray MS.).
            36   LM *Letters*, 2. 245.
            40   *Daily Advertiser*, 31 Aug. 1741.
page 278, line 8   H to Middleton, 12 Sept. 1741 (H MS.).
            13   14 Sept. 1741 (Murray MS.).
            15   H to LM, 30 Sept. 1741 (H MS.).
            21   H to LM, 12 Sept. 1741 (H MS.).
            23   H to LM, 5 Nov. 1741 (H MS.); *Daily Advertiser*, 11 Nov. 1741.
            36   1 Sept. 1741 (H MS.).
page 279, line 4   Coxe *Walpole*, 1. 683–5.
            10   Walpole *Corr.*, 17. 171.
            24   Egmont, 3. 233; Coxe *Walpole*, 1. 691–2.
            39   Walpole *Corr.*, 17. 275.
            40   H *Mem.*, 3. 684–5, 790–1.
page 280, line 2   Coxe *Walpole*, 1. 693.
            13   Walpole *Corr.*, 17. 276.

page 280, line 23   *Memoirs of George II* (1847), 1. 164.
               28   Chesterfield *Letters*, 2. 476.
               36   Walpole *Corr.*, 17. 242, 244; 30. 22–3.
               37   Thomas Hervey, *A Letter from the Hon. Thomas Hervey, to Sir Thomas Hanmer, Bart.* [1742], pp. 43–4.
               39   Walpole *Corr.*, 17. 272 n.
page 281, line 17   Coxe *Walpole*, 3. 591.
               33   Coxe *Walpole*, 1. 625.
               37   Coxe *Walpole*, 3. 592.
page 282, line 12   [John Newton], *The Lives of Dr. Edward Pocock . . . and of Dr. Thomas Newton* (1816), 2. 66–7.
               16   Coxe *Walpole*, 1. 716.
               18   Horace Walpole, *Reminiscences*, ed. P. Toynbee (1924), p. 81.
               21   *Daily Advertiser*, 13 Feb., 8 Apr. 1742.
               31   20 May 1742 (H MS.).
               35   H *Mem.*, 3. 943.
page 283, line 3   *Daily Post*, 18 Feb. 1742.
               7   Walpole *Corr.*, 17. 391.
               16   Egmont, 3. 255; Walpole *Corr.*, 17. 338.
               19   Egmont, 3. 256.
               31   Walpole *Corr.*, 17. 425.
page 284, line 3   Walpole *Corr.*, 17. 436.
               10   [Newton], *Lives*, 2. 63.
               11   Etough Papers, Add 9200, f. 211.
               14   Egmont, 3. 264.
               22   Walpole *Corr.*, 17. 457.
               23   H to Middleton, 22 May 1742 (H MS.).
               26   John, 4th Duke of Bedford, *Corr.*, ed. Lord John Russell (1842), 1. 3; Walpole *Corr.*, 17. 478.
               32   *Letter-Books*, 3. 281.
page 285, line 33   H *Mem.*, 3. 942–8.
page 286, line 2   H *Mem.*, 3. 951–4.
               9   Walpole *Corr.*, 17. 494.
               16   H *Mem.*, 3. 957–8.
               38   H *Mem.*, 3. 954, 956.
page 287, line 17   LM, *Letters and Works* (1861), 2. 455.
               32   Catalogue of Harleian Collection, p. 6 (Walpole's copy now WSL); Walpole *Corr.*, 15. 12; 17. 357–8.
               35   To Lord Ilchester, 12 Aug. [1742] (BM. MS.).
page 288, line 1   *Letter-Books*, 3. 279.
               4   Thomas Wright of Durham, 'Early Journal', ed. E. Hughes, *Annals of Science*, 7 (1951), 17.
               13   *A Letter from Mr. Cibber to Mr. Pope* (1742), p. 9.
               37   Norman Ault, *New Light on Pope* (1949), p. 302.
page 289, line 7   Attributed to Hervey by Horace Walpole in his *Catalogue* and on his own copy (now WSL). The copy at Ickworth has on its title-page 'By my dear Father J. Lord Hervey' in the hand, probably, of Gen. William Hervey.

page 289, line 29   Pope *Poems*, 5. 291. Although Pope quotes a sentence from
                     Hervey's pamphlet in his 'Testimonies from Authors' he
                     does not name any author (*Poems*, 5. 41).

          32   It was advertised as early as 11 Aug. in the *Daily Advertiser*;
                     reprinted by the Augustan Reprint Society in 1967.

page 290, line 16   Symonds, born in Bury St. Edmunds the same year as
                     Hervey, attended the grammar school there, matriculated
                     at Cambridge the same year as Hervey, and was rector
                     of Horringer, the village next to Ickworth.

          26   Dyce-Forster Coll., Victoria and Albert Museum.

          32   Lord Ilchester and Mrs. Langford-Brooke, *Life of Sir
                     Charles Hanbury-Williams* (1928), p. 62.

page 291, line 4   20 Dec. 1742 (H MS.).

CHAPTER 16. 1742–1743

page 292, line 5   13 Nov. 1742 (BM. MS.).

           9   8 Sept. 1742 (H MS.).

          20   1 Oct. 1742 (in secretary's hand) (H MS.).

page 293, line 6   Ilchester and Langford-Brooke, *Life of Hanbury-Williams*,
                     p. 62.

          14   Williams to Henry Fox, 25 Oct. 1742 (BM. MS.). Horace
                     Walpole, then at Houghton, briefly mentions the
                     chamber-pot episode (Walpole *Corr.*, 18. 96); he prob-
                     ably heard it from the same source.

          17   Ilchester and Langford-Brooke, *Life of Hanbury-Williams*,
                     p. 62.

          22   Williams to Fox, 25 Oct. 1742 (BM. MS.).

          24   Walpole *Corr.*, 18. 89.

          30   8 Sept. 1742 (H MS.).

          33   Ilchester and Langford-Brooke, *Life of Hanbury-Williams*,
                     p. 62.

page 294, line 3   Walpole *Corr.*, 18. 80; Charles Yorke to brother [Joseph],
                     25 Oct. 1742 (Add MS. 35, 360, f. 97).

          26   Walpole *Corr.*, 18. 80–4 (from MS.); printed as *The New
                     Ministry* (1742), and in *Political Ballads of the Seventeenth and
                     Eighteenth Centuries*, ed. W. W. Wilkins (1860), 2. 273–9.

page 295, line 7   *Grenville Papers*, ed. W. J. Smith (1852–3), 1. 16–17.

           9   Etough Papers, Add MS. 9200, f. 211.

          14   Ilchester *Fox*, 1. 85–6.

          27   Charles Hanbury Williams, *Poems* (1822), 2. 47–54. The
                     modern biographer of Henry Pelham points out that
                     there were only three cases of political retaliation by
                     victims displaced by the new administration: Hervey,
                     Lord Sidney Beauclerk (who returned to the fold in 1744),
                     and Sir Thomas Frankland (who was very erratic):
                     John B. Owen, *The Rise of the Pelhams* (1957), pp.
                     119–20.

page 295, line 35 Charles B. Realey, *Early Opposition to Sir Robert Walpole 1720–1727* (1931), p. 166.

page 296, line 10 13 Nov. 1742 (BM. MS.).

16 William Coxe, *Memoirs of Horatio, Lord Walpole* (1802), p. 246.

28 Ilchester *Fox*, 1. 85–6.

31 Stephen Fox to H, 13 Nov. 1742 (BM. MS.).

page 297, line 5 6 Nov. 1742 (BM. MS.).

24 Stephen Fox to H, 13 Nov. 1742 (BM. MS.).

page 298, line 1 H to Stephen Fox, 13 Nov. 1742 (BM. MS.).

7 Absent peers could assign their proxy, but no peer could receive more than two proxies (Maurice F. Bond, *Guide to the Records of Parliament*, 1971, p. 174). Proxy votes were not infrequent: 27 out of 166 on 25 May 1742, and 39 out of 136 on 22 Feb. 1743 (House of Lords MS., Register of Protesting Peers, vol. 1).

19 20 Nov. 1742 (BM. MS.).

33 *Letter-Books*, 3. 282–3.

page 299, line 14 Ascribed to Hervey by Horace Walpole in his *Catalogue*; his copy 'By John Lord Hervey' is now WSL.

18 *Daily Advertiser*.

30 pp. 7, 12.

31 Identifications by Horace Walpole in his copy.

page 300, line 12 *Letter-Books*, 3. 283.

19 Joseph Yorke [to Charles], 3 Dec. 1742 (Add MS. 35, 363, f. 16).

28 20 Dec. 1742 (H MS.).

33 *Daily Advertiser*, 17 June 1743. Ascribed to Hervey by Horace Walpole in his *Catalogue*; his copy 'by Lord Hervey' is now WSL.

page 301, line 31 Walpole *Corr.*, 18. 159.

page 302, line 3 Diary of Edward Harley (MS. Add 6851, f. 63, Cambridge Univ. Library). Formerly an M.P., he now sat in the Lords.

13 pp. 4, 8, 17–18.

27 Charles Hanbury Williams wrote some satiric verse on Hervey's opposition to the bill (*Poems*, 1822, 2. 129–35).

35 4 Apr. 1743 (H MS.).

page 303, line 4 Walpole *Corr.*, 17. 253–4.

8 Horace Walpole, *Reminiscences*, ed. P. Toynbee (1924), p. 96.

10 Walpole *Corr.*, 18. 185.

14 H to LM, 4 Apr. 1743 (H MS.).

18 *General Evening Post*, 17–19 March 1743; Pope *Corr.*, 4. 446.

21 H to LM, 4 Apr. 1743 (H MS.).

22 *Daily Advertiser*, 17 June 1743.

25 *General Evening Post*, 2–5 Apr., *Daily Advertiser*, 26 Apr. 1743.

page 303, line 30 Lady H, *Letters* [ed. J. W. Croker] (1821), p. 11.

          36 *The Orrery Papers*, ed. Countess of Cork and Orrery (1903), 2. 193.

          38 *Daily Advertiser*, 13 June 1743.

page 304, line 6 29/18 June 1743 (H MS.).

          19 PRO P.C.C. Boycott, f. 264.

          27 23 June 1743 (copy in Henry Fox's hand) (BM. MS.).

          30 *Daily Advertiser*, 22 July 1743; epitaph in Ickworth church. Newspapers give the date as 6 Aug.

          35 *Ickworth Parish Registers. Baptisms, Marriages & Burials 1566 to 1890* [ed. S. H. A. H.] (1894), pp. 54–5; W. E. Tate, *The Parish Chest* (3rd ed., 1969), pp. 68–9.

page 305, line 3 *Letter-Books*, 3. 288, 289.

          6 *Letter-Books*, 3. 291.

          10 Pope *Corr.*, 4. 466; Pope *Poems*, 5. 291.

          12 Walpole *Corr.*, 18. 294.

          17 Lady Oxford to LM, 17 Sept., 22 Oct. 1743 (Harley MS. on deposit in BM.).

          19 HMC *Denbigh MSS.*, Part V (1911), p. 173; HMC *Astley MSS.* (1900), p. 285.

          26 Mrs. Horner to Lady H [n.d.] (BM. MS.).

          30 10 Sept. 1743 (BM. MS.).

page 306, line 11 Philip C. Yorke, *Life and Correspondence of Philip Yorke, Earl of Hardwicke, Lord High Chancellor of Great Britain* (1913), 1. 281 n.; HMC *Denbigh MSS.*, p. 174.

          16 Walpole *Corr.*, 15. 12 n.

          19 Add MS. 32, 458, ff. 182, 183.

          22 *Ickworth Parish Registers*, p. 75.

          41 LM, *Letters and Works*, ed. Lord Wharncliffe (1837), 1. 66.

page 307, line 4 H MS. 53/1 (Commonplace book of Gen. William Hervey).

          11 Horace Walpole, *Letters*, ed. Mrs. P. Toynbee (1903), 4. 239.

          19 *Diary*, p. 246.

          20 HMC *Astley MSS.* (1900), p. 286.

          24 Walpole *Corr.*, 9. 150.

          29 Augustus Hervey, *Journal 1746–1759*, ed. D. H. Erskine (1953), p. 105.

          35 Ernest C. Mossner, *The Life of David Hume* (1954, rept. 1970), pp. 395, 440; Edward Gibbon, *Letters*, ed. J. E. Norton (1956), 1. 117.

page 308, line 4 Dorothy M. Stuart, *Molly Lepell, Lady Hervey* (1936), p. 346. Lady Hervey's own will was peculiar enough to arouse comment (*Grenville Papers*, ed. W. J. Smith (1852–3), 4. 357–8).

          20 29 Aug. 1743 (Add MS. 32, 701, f. 60).

          26 Lewis Namier, *The Structure of Politics at the Accession of George III* (2nd ed., 1957), p. 228.

page 309, line 11 LM *Letters*, 3. 150.

Index

at Bury election, 154; assisted by H
in election, 171; marriage, 189–90;
later relationship with H, 191, 223–4;
H asks for peerage for, 214; delivers
Address of Thanks, 232–3; satirized
by Pope, 233; in Hogarth conversation piece (plate 14), 239; quarrel
with H, 250; appointed a secretary
of the Treasury, 250, 252–3, (resigns) 276; defends Walpole in Parliament, 263–4; secures peerage,
276–7; H buys pictures for, 287;
opinion of H's attack on King,
295–6; warned by brother against
H, 296; resists H's persuasion, 296–8;
end of their friendship, 298; later
career and death, 308.

Francheville, Pierre de, sculptor: 83.

Francklin, Richard: printer of Opposition papers, 109, 112.

Frederick, King of Prussia: 263; friendship with Algarotti, 250–1, 258–60,
272–4, 275, 308; compliments H,
262.

Frederick, Prince of Hesse: marriage to
Princess Mary, 257–8.

Frederick Christian, Prince of Saxony:
260.

Frederick Louis, H.R.H., Prince of
Wales: 35, 83, 100, 111, 170–1;
as Prince Frederick in Hanover,
30–1; brought to England, 98–9;
godfather to H's son, 101; friendship
with H, 106, 122–3, 124, 125–6,
127–8, 132; amatory pursuits, 127–8,
182–3; and Miss Vane, 128–9,
135–8, 182–5; enmity toward H,
130, 135, 181–2; and *The Modish
Couple*, 130–2; father of Fitzfrederick, 136–7, 185; relations with
mother, 181–2, 183, 197–8, 205–6,
207–8, 208–9, 218–20, 221–2, 226;
and the political Opposition, 182,
205, 224, 278–9; marriage, 195–6;
allowance from father, 197, 207–10;
and the Princess's lying-in, 218–20;
punished by father, 220–2, 224;
reconciled, 282–3.

Frederick William, King of Prussia:
250; death, 259.

Freind, Dr. Robert: headmaster at
Westminster School, 11–12, 13,
162, 292.

French ambassador in London (Fran-
çois Marie, Comte de Broglie): 75.

French ambassador in Turin (Jean
Charles, Marquis de Saint-Nectaire):
273.

Garth, Sir Samuel, physician and poet:
visits Lord Bristol, 32.

Gay, John: 159; verse quoted, 41;
Achilles, 118, 144.

Gentleman's Magazine: epitaph on
Queen, 228.

George I (as Elector of Hanover): 9,
15, 19; (as King of England):
arrival in England, 20; godfather to
Bristol's daughter, 21; reproaches
Lady Bristol, 23; at Hanover, 28–31;
quarrel with son, 33–4, 36, 44;
death, 71.

George II, H.R.H., Prince of Wales
and (after 1727) King of England:
1, 22, 25, 30, 39, 50, 57, 69, 81, 86,
92, 98, 99, 102, 105, 125, 136, 149,
154–5, 158, 214, 225, 232, 240, 253,
278, 279, 281, 296, 298, 301; appoints
Carr H, 20; quarrel with father, 33–4;
sent gift by H's father, 35; and
Peerage Bill, 36; suggests H be M.P.,
37, 38; godfather to H's son, 52;
becomes George II, 71; H's father
solicits, 71–2; Civil List grant to, 73;
appoints H Vice-Chamberlain, 96–7;
visits to Hanover, 139, 180 and
187, 197 and 203–7 *passim*, 258
and 262, 275 and 278–9; on H's
writing verse, 144; and Excise Bill,
146; rewards H with a seat in the
Lords, 147–8; with a pension, 171;
with the Privy Seal, 254–5; H's
memoirs of reign of, 151–3, 231–2;
praises H's speech, 166; daughter's
marriage to Prince of Orange, 168–
71; political wavering, 172–3; anxiety over 'Scotch-Petition', 178–9;
chooses wife for son, 183; mistress
in Hanover, 186, 187, 203–4, 207,
237–8, 258; and son's allowance,
197, 207–10; and Scotch Bill (Porteous case), 211–13; angered by H's
absence, 212–13; punishes son, 220–
2, 224, 226; at wife's deathbed,
226–7; his future predicted by H,
229; H's supposed favour with,

George II (*cont.*):
229–30; daughter's marriage to Prince of Hesse, 257–8; allows mistress to sell peerages, 276–7; and H's resignation as Privy Seal, 282, 284–7; attacked in ballad by H, 293–5.
George III: 130, 308.
Gibbon, Edward: on public schools, 13; visits Lady H, 307.
Gloucester, Martin Benson, Bishop of: 237.
Godolphin, Francis, 2nd Earl of: godfather to H's son, 52; as Lord Privy Seal, 2, 252–3.
Godolphin, Sidney, 1st Earl of, Lord Treasurer: 8.
Gower, John Leveson-Gower, Lord: 190; H's successor as Lord Privy Seal, 282, 284, 287; friendly with H, 293.
Grafton, Charles Fitzroy, 2nd Duke of, Lord Chamberlain: 54, 97, 219, 221, 252.
Grand Tour: 68; Carr H on, 9, 15, 20; H on, 24–9, 31; Wharton on, 24–5; H continues, 77–85.
Gray, Thomas, poet: 90, opinion of Cambridge, 16.
Grenville, George, statesman: 295.
Griffin, Edwin, Lord: 60.

H: *see* Hervey, John, Lord.
Haddock, Admiral Nicholas: 263, 281.
Halifax, George Montagu, 1st Earl of: 60.
Hamilton, Jane (Hamilton), Lady Archibald: mistress of Prince of Wales, 183–4.
Hamilton, Hon. Charles, youngest son of the 6th Earl of Abercorn: 101.
Hammond, James: 279.
Handel, George Frederick: 77.
Hanmer, Sir Thomas, M.P.: 37, 38, 60, 217.
Hanover, Germany: 71; seat of the Elector, 15, 29–30; H visits, 29–31; George I visits, 28, 36; George II visits, 139, 180–1, 186, 187, 197, 203, 258, 262, 278.
Hardwicke, Philip, 1st Earl of Hardwicke, Lord Chancellor: 219, 221, 300; placates Newcastle, 252; joins

coalition ministry, 282; attacked by H in ballad, 293–4.
Harrington, William Stanhope, Lord: 132, 220; as Secretary of State, 97, 262–3; as Miss Vane's lover, 128; as father of Fitzfrederick, 136, 138.
Hearne, Thomas: 46.
Hephestion, friend of Alexander the Great: H calls himself, 122, 127.
Herring, William: at Cambridge, 17.
Hervey, Ann, H's sister: 54, 60.
Hervey, Augustus John, H's 2nd son: birth and christening, 52.
Hervey, Barbara, H's sister: 54; death, 74.
Hervey, Caroline, H's 4th daughter: birth, 187.
Hervey, Carr, later Lord Hervey, H's half-brother: 8, 10, 16, 22, 33, 34, 35; birth, 4; on Grand Tour, 9, 15, 20; elected M.P., 20; court appointment, 20; refuses to marry, 42–3; sells Aswarby to invest in South Sea, 43, 51; illness, 45–6, 51; loses Parliamentary seat, 47–8; death, 51.
Hervey, Revd. Charles, H's brother: promised chaplaincy by H, 156.
Hervey, Elizabeth, *see* Mansel, Elizabeth.
Hervey, Elizabeth (Hervey), Lord Bristol's aunt: death, 7.
Hervey, Emily Caroline Nassau, H's 3rd daughter: birth and christening, 169.
Hervey, Felton, H's brother: page to Princess of Wales, 50; marriage, 266; heir to Lady Bristol, 275.
Hervey, Frederick, H's 3rd son: 2, 3; birth and christening, 101–2.
Hervey, George William, H's 1st son: birth, 44; health, 45; sent to Ickworth, 45; military career, 186, 276; and H's epitaph, 306.
Hervey, Henry, H's brother: 156; at Westminster School, 11; at Oxford, 32–3; Samuel Johnson's opinion of, 154 fn.; appointment to army, 173; solicits promotion, 235.
Hervey, Isabella (Carr), Lord Bristol's first wife: 4, 10, 307.
Hervey, Isabella, H's half-sister: birth, 4.